Cross-Cultural Approaches to the Study of Alcohol

World Anthropology

General Editor

SOL TAX

Patrons

CLAUDE LÉVI-STRAUSS
MARGARET MEAD
LAILA SHUKRY EL HAMAMSY
M. N. SRINIVAS

MOUTON PUBLISHERS · THE HAGUE · PARIS
DISTRIBUTED IN THE USA AND CANADA BY ALDINE, CHICAGO

Cross-Cultural Approaches to the Study of Alcohol

An Interdisciplinary Perspective

Editors

MICHAEL W. EVERETT
JACK O. WADDELL
DWIGHT B. HEATH

MOUTON PUBLISHERS · THE HAGUE · PARIS

DISTRIBUTED IN THE USA AND CANADA BY ALDINE, CHICAGO

General Editor's Preface

Anthropology looks at species-wide variations in human behavior. The first lesson the student of anthropology learns is that geographically-related differences in physical type do not correlate with behavioral differences. Rather, the differences we find among populations are environmental and cultural. Alcohol use is so widespread in the species that even if it were not considered by some to be a "problem," it would be an excellent test case of the interrelationships between cultural and physiological/psychological factors in human behavior. Precisely because in many societies alcohol use is an important social problem with emotional overtones, it is in the interests of policy as well as science to get the species-wide, cross-cultural perspective that anthropology provides. That is the purpose of this book which grew out of — and had the advantage of discussion in — an international conference related to a worldwide Congress.

Like most contemporary sciences, anthropology is a product of the European tradition. Some argue that it is a product of colonialism, with one small and self-interested part of the species dominating the study of the whole. If we are to understand the species, our science needs substantial input from scholars who represent a variety of the world's cultures. It was a deliberate purpose of the IXth International Congress of Anthropological and Ethnological Sciences to provide impetus in this direction. The *World Anthropology* volumes, therefore, offer a first glimpse of a human science in which members from all societies have played an active role. Each of the books is designed to be self-contained; each is an attempt to update its particular sector of scientific knowledge and is written by specialists from all parts of the world.

Each volume should be read and reviewed individually as a separate volume on its own given subject. The set as a whole will indicate what changes are in store for anthropology as scholars from the developing countries join in studying the species of which we are all a part.

The IXth Congress was planned from the beginning not only to include as many of the scholars from every part of the world as possible, but also with a view toward the eventual publication of the papers in high-quality volumes. At previous Congresses scholars were invited to bring papers which were then read out loud. They were necessarily limited in length; many were only summarized; there was little time for discussion; and the sparse discussion could only be in one language. The IXth Congress was an experiment aimed at changing this. Papers were written with the intention of exchanging them before the Congress, particularly in extensive pre-Congress sessions; they were not intended to be read aloud at the Congress, that time being devoted to discussions — discussions which were simultaneously and professionally translated into five languages. The method for eliciting the papers was structured to make as representative a sample as was allowable when scholarly creativity — hence self-selection — was critically important. Scholars were asked both to propose papers of their own and to suggest topics for sessions of the Congress which they might edit into volumes. All were then informed of the suggestions and encouraged to re-think their own papers and the topics. The process, therefore, was a continuous one of feedback and exchange and it has continued to be so even after the Congress. The some two thousand papers comprising *World Anthropology* certainly then offer a substantial sample of world anthropology. It has been said that anthropology is at a turning point; if this is so, these volumes will be the historical direction-markers.

As might have been foreseen in the first post-colonial generation, the large majority of the Congress papers (82 percent) are the work of scholars identified with the industrialized world which fathered our traditional discipline and the institution of the Congress itself: Eastern Europe (15 percent); Western Europe (16 percent); North America (47 percent); Japan, South Africa, Australia, and New Zealand (4 percent). Only 18 percent of the papers are from developing areas: Africa (4 percent); Asia-Oceania (9 percent); Latin America (5 percent). Aside from the substantial representation from the U.S.S.R. and the nations of Eastern Europe, a significant difference between this corpus of written material and that of other Congresses is the addition of the large proportion of contributions from Africa, Asia, and Latin America. "Only 18 percent" is two to four times as great a proportion as that of other Congresses;

moreover, 18 percent of 2,000 papers is 360 papers, 10 times the number of "Third World" papers presented at previous Congresses. In fact, these 360 papers are more than the total of ALL papers published after the last International Congress of Anthropological and Ethnological Sciences which was held in the United States (Philadelphia, 1956).

The significance of the increase is not simply quantitative. The input of scholars from areas which have until recently been no more than subject matter for anthropology represents both feedback and also long-awaited theoretical contributions from the perspectives of very different cultural, social, and historical traditions. Many who attended the IXth Congress were convinced that anthropology would not be the same in the future. The fact that the next Congress (India, 1978) will be our first in the "Third World" may be symbolic of the change. Meanwhile, sober consideration of the present set of books will show how much, and just where and how, our discipline is being revolutionized.

The conference on alcohol was held in conjunction with one on the use of another common drug which resulted in a companion volume, *Cannabis and culture*, edited by Vera Rubin. In this series are many other volumes related to these topics, on mental health, religion, and medical and psychological anthropology; on food; on youth, urbanization, ethnicity and identity problems; and on the variety of cultures of the world as seen traditionally in a process of change.

Chicago, Illinois   SOL TAX
April 1, 1976

Foreword

Man is an animal who creates pleasure and suppresses pain for the mind that is inseparable from his body. As Gustav Eckstein reminds us in his book *The body has a head* (Harper and Row, 1970), we have been carried away with our rhetoric of psychopathology and have created an insoluble dichotomy. To which we would add, the mind and body exist in a culture, unique and peculiarly its own by virtue of its history, language, customs, and institutions. We customarily carve up the study of man into disciplines which ignore the fundamental interrelations of all his parts, external and internal, his habitats, and his ornaments. Therein we falter, like the blind wise men looking at the elephant, each from his own peculiar vantage point, and each mistaking the leg or a trunk for the whole being.

The Conference on Alcohol Studies and Anthropology was an attempt to bring this whole man/woman back together again. With our support, Drs. Everett, Waddell, Heath, et al. drew together scholars from a number of areas, some of whom talk to each other only peripherally through uncomfortable distance in journal articles far removed from their usual fields. Their express purpose, which I am sure you will agree has been achieved when you have had an opportunity to peruse the papers that grew out of the Conference, was to apprise people who were often laboring in relative physical isolation from one another, though not necessarily distant in the community of their ideas or conceptual frameworks, of what progress had been made in the anthropological studies of alcohol-related behavior during the past decade.

It gives me great pleasure to read the work of old friends and colleagues — for that work has influenced much of my own thinking — and to see it brought up to date. At the risk of singling out a few of these, and I should say that the quality of all these papers is quite impressive, I would like to point out briefly where I think the cultural study of alcohol has been heading.

Although anthropology has always taken relativistic positions on the value systems expressed by various cultures, its "value-free" posture has never gone undebated. When Horton's paper first appeared, psychoanalysis was in full bloom, and many of its tenets seemed to offer great promise for giving structure to what were often chaotic results from transcultural comparisons. The emphasis in this approach was largely, although not wholly, upon the limitations of human beings as people, looking systematically at what had been viewed heretofore as quirks of personality. Although Field later pointed to some severe limitations in Horton's work, the general perspective of emphasis on personality has persisted in both psychiatry and anthropology, and has only lately shifted towards examining what aspects of behavior are functional (promotive) or dysfunctional (harmful) in a given situation for a particular person of peculiar ethnolinguistic background.

It interests me, though I do not necessarily agree with his premises, that in his article Barry speaks of the "Cultural benefits of alcohol," those positive uses of the beverage which go a long way towards explaining why man has been a drinker for so many thousands of years and will undoubtedly continue to be so. In our concern for the ill effects of drinking alcohol, we are generally quite overbalanced in the direction of condemnation and judgment of the drinker who violates the social norms. The fact of the matter is that people drink for perfectly valid reasons, social and personal (and no construction of drinking practices in a particular locale could be complete); and these reasons have no reference to the uses which these practices serve.

We have recently been adapting many of the principles of the work that has been carried out in cross-cultural comparative studies into a national philosophy for the prevention of alcoholism in America. We are not so immodest as to say that drawing attention to the norms for drinking-related behavior will, or should necessarily, modify these practices. What we have in mind is to stimulate open discussion of current codes of behavior. For, unlike a number of other cultures, ours is profoundly ambivalent about the use of alcohol. There is no consistency or consensus about what is functional behavior, although we have many unwritten agreements by which we ignore the difficulties engendered from the dysfunctional behavior surrounding alcohol usage. What we have in mind is not a drinking code of Hammurabi. It is not to be imposed either from above or by any one faction upon another. Rather, I envision a measure of mutuality including frank interchange among people of different descent about the respects in which they can agree, and agree to disagree, about the customs which stem from their cultural heritages. We used to speak of a "melting pot," but, as Glazer and Moynihan pointed out, we have come to recognize that customs retain a tenacious persistence into the second and third generations and beyond, and we need to come to some better understandings about our differences.

It is clear that, in order to spread abroad information about alcohol, its physiological effects, and the consequences of its use, a greater effort in education for all ages is necessary. This is, I think, a direct consequence of my presumption that there must be open interchange about the issues of alcohol-related behaviors. The presence of Jan de Lint's excellent paper in this collection reminds me, as de Lint is wont to do, that an educational campaign, however necessary, is hardly sufficient basis by itself for a national governmental prevention policy on alcoholism. The urgency of examining the economics of the market for alcoholic beverages; the regulation of their sale, usage, and effects of various strategies of regulation; and the resultant drinking practices has become increasingly compelling. Epidemiology, sociology, anthropology, and economics all have important contributions to make to the understanding of these phenomena.

Throughout this volume there are frequent and warranted calls for a better theoretical underpinning for such studies, both at the broadest philosophical and at the microenvironmental levels. I am reminded of the famous French writer who remarked of a fellow artist, *"Chose merveilleuse — un homme qui pense avant décrire!"* Wonderful to behold, the scholar who sets his task into an explicit design. To which I would add that there is an important place for such thoughtful, purposive work in understanding our national postures towards helping people, how our social interventions succeed or fail, and what lessons we can abstract and adapt from other societies and our own subcultures to a more general application.

Morris E. Chafetz, M. D.
Director, National Institute on Alcohol Abuse and Alcoholism

Preface

Since its inception, the Smithsonian Institution's Center for the Study of Man has had a strong interest in getting anthropologists and other human scientists to look at worldwide social problems. It has felt that such research ought to be undertaken by human scientists from every country on earth. The results should then be exchanged and become a part of the wisdom and knowledge available to guide the efforts of policy-makers in every nation.

In 1972 a conference on human scientists and worldwide social problems was held in Cairo, Egypt. Anthropologists and others from twenty countries were present. They strongly supported the Center's position and urged that it begin organizing a series of conferences to assess some of the contributions which have been made in understanding pressing social problems.

As a result the Center began to talk with funding agencies concerned with specific problems to see if they were interested in getting an international anthropological/human-science point of view. The National Institute on Alcohol Abuse and Alcoholism was one of the organizations which expressed an interest. With this encouragement, the Center began to consult with a number of human scientists doing research on alcohol to get the names of individuals who might help in organizing a conference. As a result three anthropologists, Michael Everett, Dwight Heath and Jack Waddell, were selected to organize the conference and edit the papers.

Labor was divided as follows: the editors, in conjunction with the Center, selected the participants and planned the program; the Center undertook all of the administrative work, with the exception of some typing and reproduction done on a subcontract with the University of Kentucky after the conference.

The conference itself lasted from August 28-30, 1973, and was held at the Center for Continuing Education in Chicago, Illinois. Immediately following the conference, the organizers made a presentation to the International Congress of Anthropological and Ethnological Sciences, also meeting in Chicago.

The volume that has resulted from the conference owes much to many people: to Sol Tax and Sam Stanley for their role in bringing the agency and the human scientists together, to Bill Douglass for seeing that preparations for the meeting were coordinated and run on schedule, and finally to Valerie Ashenfelter for her masterful articulation (with able assistance from Judy Crawley Wojcik) of all the needs and demands that are inevitable in any successful scientific meeting.

MICHAEL W. EVERETT   JACK O. WADDELL   DWIGHT B. HEATH
Tribal Health Director,   *Purdue University*   *Brown University*
White Mountain   *West Lafayette,*   *Providence,*
Apache Tribe,   *Indiana*   *Rhode Island*
Arizona

Table of Contents

INTRODUCTION

Alcohol Studies and Anthropology

This volume is an outgrowth of the Conference on Alcohol Studies and Anthropology, jointly organized by the editors, that was held at the University of Chicago, August 28-30, 1973. Part of the IXth International Congress of Anthropological and Ethnological Sciences, the conference was sponsored by the Smithsonian Institution's Center for the Study of Man, with funds provided by the National Institute on Alcohol Abuse and Alcoholism, National Institute of Mental Health.

There has been one specific goal for both the conference and this volume, namely, to assess interdisciplinary contributions toward the cross-cultural study of alcohol use, in both behavioral and physiological terms. Our central purpose is not that of adding to the already voluminous literature on alcohol studies, nor is it that of merely adding further descriptive and substantive material to the existing body of knowledge in this area. A cursory review of alcohol literature reveals that a component of major significance is conspicuously absent — a perspective on cross-cultural variation. Anthropological contributions in this regard have been unsystematic and sporadic, while those of other disciplines have not utilized an appropriate cross-cultural framework.

The selections included in this volume are the combined works of anthropologists, psychologists, sociologists, physicians, psychiatrists, and pharmacologists. Hence, the volume preserves the character of the conference by addressing itself to the interface between the cross-cultural perspective of anthropology and other disciplines interested in alcohol studies. The selections of the book largely follow the sequence of topics as they were discussed at the conference and, like the conference, the articles seek to assess and evaluate the past and current role of cross-cultural perspectives in alcohol research as well as to suggest new research orientations.

Alcohol is probably the most ancient and widespread psychoactive substance in the world. It is a naturally occurring substance wherever free-floating carbohydrates are available and thus is widely known and used. Clearly, there are alcohol uses related to health, nutrition, entertainment, religion, law, and a variety of other social activities. Since the uses of alcohol vary so widely while the occurrence of alcohol is virtually universal, it is essential that an assessment and evaluation of the relationship between alcohol studies *per se* and the cross-cultural perspective of anthropology be undertaken. In this volume we hope to contribute to this assessment and evaluation.

Anthropologists interested in alcohol research are the beneficiaries, over many years, of a very large and diverse collecion of studies on alcohol from a variety of perspectives. But this literature includes very few contributions by anthropologists, and these contributions have been only sporadic and highly individual in both character and quality. The result is that a number of people who utilize and have an interest in the literature on alcohol are not familiar with the contributions of anthropology. Similarly, a number of anthropologists who occasionally contribute to our understanding of aspects of alcohol and drinking are not familiar in depth with the enormous range of relevant work that has been done on these subjects by scholars of other disciplines. It is this awareness of a need for a greater amount of interdependence between anthropologists and those of other disciplines that makes the issues proposed in this volume so essential to pursue.

The volume differs from the conference in that the conference, rather than emphasizing the presentation of formal papers, stressed round-table discussion by a limited number of invited participants. The volume brings together a few of the keynote papers that were presented at the conference to stimulate discussion. To these are added a number of selections submitted subsequently by some of the participants in the Chicago conference. We have incorporated the individual selections for their evaluative merit as well as for their descriptive content. The main emphasis is not intended to be on ethnographic data. The emphasis instead is on (1) the variety of ways that drinking behavior can be observed, described, analyzed, and interpreted; (2) what the cross-cultural perspective of anthropology has contributed to alcohol studies; and (3) what alcohol studies conducted in other disciplines have contributed to this cross-cultural perspective.

Part 1, "Pioneering Works and Their Reassessment," provides an opportunity to share in the retrospective evaluations of two scholars who look at their earlier works and critically reassess them from the vantage point of the present. Ruth Bunzel, whose work in two Middle American communities, Chamula in Mexico and Chichicastenango in Guatemala, was one of the first anthropologists to give us a detailed and somewhat comprehensive ethnographic report on drinking. Her paper, published in 1940 in the journal *Psychiatry* (a significant location itself), was also a fairly rigorous example of the method of controlled comparison with special attention to social organization, child training, and psychoanalytic interpretations of culture.

Professor Bunzel reflects on this early but significant piece of research. She characerizes her research in terms of what she had set out to do, what she felt had been accomplished, and the feedback which she has had in the decades since her work. Her experience was like that of most anthropologists who have written about alcohol (with very few exceptions), in that research on alcohol was an unforeseen by-product or spin-off of work which had not been done with drinking as a focus of study. Rather, as Bunzel reflects, she was looking at human behavior in the holistic sense of the traditional ethnographer and found, quite adventitiously, that alcohol was important to the people in those two communities and that it provided a convenient handle for understanding some aspects of what was going on in each community. It is noteworthy that most of what has been done by anthropologists on alcohol up until the past few years has had the same kind of secondary character.

Margaret Bacon was part of another pioneering work, a large-scale cross-cultural study in which she collaborated with two other psychologists, Herbert Barry and Irvin Child. This is the Bacon, Barry, and Child cross-cultural study best known for the theory of dependency conflict to explain drunkenness. In that project a series of hypotheses about drinking and drunkenness were tested by statistical correlation of forty-nine specific variables within a worldwide sample of 139 societies. In the second selection in Part 1, Bacon not only reviews the strengths and shortcomings of that research project but, more importantly, emphasizes a number of statistically significant correlations that were revealed in that study and that have not been subjected to subsequent investigation.

Three cardinal points seem to stand out in the reassessment of Bunzel's and Bacon's pioneering studies. First, most of the anthropological literature on the subject of alcohol to date has been of an almost incidental or coincidental nature. In those institutions where alcohol is the focus of both intensive and extensive research, anthropologists have played a relatively minor role. This is true not only in the United States but in other countries where such institutions exist. Second, with very few notable exceptions, most of them recent, those anthropologists who have written about alcohol have usually done so as only a small part of research which was focused on other topics. Finally, anthropological studies of alcohol are concerned not only with the problem aspects of drinking, which tend to be focused on by a great number of sociologists, physiologists, and psychologists, but also with the more normal customary range of alcohol use. Thus, much of the alcohol literature written by anthropologists is phrased in terms of ideal patterns. This leads to the not too surprising conclusion that more data are needed. But, as both Bunzel's and Bacon's reviews reveal, we particularly need more data on the range of variation among individuals in any given population, in terms of groups by age, sex, and a number of other variables that may very well be significant, but which have been virtually ignored until now. This seems important whether studies are of the controlled comparison type (Bunzel) or of the more global type (Bacon, Barry, and Child).

Part 2, "The Ethnographic Data Base," is concerned with the data pool generated by cross-cultural alcohol studies. It is not intended to focus on anecdotal comparisons of drinking practices in first one culture and then another. Clearly, such a strategy would be counterproductive in evaluative terms. Instead, the intent of the selections is to provide a semiglobal survey and review of the kinds of data extant, a discussion of some of the trends that the data suggest still need pursuing, and recommendations as to how to go about getting these data, a topic which is dealt with in greater depth in Part 6.

Several salient points are raised in the selections found in Part 2. First, the existing ethnographic literature on alcohol use is rather rich but not altogether complete. Moreover, the history of anthropological interest in drinking indicates that it is only recently that investigators have made any effort to integrate this wealth of disparate data. Thus, the selections provide a combination of anthropological perspective, ethnographic overview, and specific ethnographic reporting. Our main concern here is the manner in which these rich yet fragmentary sources of ethnographic data on human alcohol use can be integrated.

A second point underscored by the selections is that there is a need to relate a general, common interest in alcohol to the field research of those specifically concerned with drinking behavior. The real question of course is: can ethnographers make their data more relevant to others who might have a particular interest in using such information? This is critical because, as Dwight Heath points out in the first selection in Part 2, in the past only a portion of the ethnographer's field research has focused on collecting data on drinking, and the data were usually only parts of a larger ethnographic report dealing with the total cultural or social unit.

The third point derived from this selection of articles is that the kinds of information to be found in the cross-cultural literature on alcohol use are quite varied. The literature reveals a substantial amount on ceremonial drinking, the manufacture of various kinds of intoxicating beverages, the social rules and the regulation of drinking behavior, and the cultural norms and meanings of alcohol use that are operative in particular societies. In addition, much of the ethnographic literature emphasizes the integrative functions of alcohol, which makes it of special interest in relation to notions of problem drinking. Heath's summary provides a perspective on the kinds of interests that have captivated ethnographers and cross-cultural researchers in the area of alcohol studies. Clearly, this kind of historical perspective is indispensable for an assessment of the kinds of information yet needed in particular problem areas of alcohol research.

Trends in the history of the development of anthropological interest in alcohol studies clearly indicate that only recently has there been any kind of collective concern by ethnographers and anthropologists, theoreticians and those interested in applied problems, about pressing research problems and how these can be most strategically attacked. Mac Marshall, in the second selection in Part 2, provides a valuable review of *kava* and alcohol research in Oceania, suggesting future research possible in that area. Salme Ahlström-Laakso makes it quite clear in her selection that we need to do much better in (1) recording and documenting variations in drinking habits and the meanings associated with them within a population, social unit, or national boundary, and (2) in not assigning a false sense of homogeneity to groups and to populations in either culture-specific or survey-oriented research. Joan Ablon and Frances Ferguson, in the two remaining selections in Part 2, provide examples of how ethnographic researchers interested in alcohol studies can relate to culture-specific research. Both studies emphasize the significance of dealing with variations within a specific cultural context.

In Part 3, "Historical Approaches," Larissa Lomnitz notes in her documentary and ethnographic study of 400 years of Mapuche drinking that longitudinal studies of changing patterns of drinking and alcohol usage are also needed. Further, in addition to holistic and diachronic studies of cultures and societies, life histories of single individuals are urgently needed to underscore the necessity of accurately representing the ranges of variation in drinking styles. The selections by Ade Obayemi and Alfredo Velapatiño Ortega are similarly ethnohistorical although they do not deal with as great a time depth as Lomnitz.

For a long time, it was thought that beverage alcohol, ethanol, had the same effect on people all over the world, regardless of its particular form and despite variation in cultural context. This provided for anthropologists an illusionary security in the notion that alcohol is a fairly uniform substance that produces fairly uniform physical effects, a position which clearly supports a focus on cultural and psychological drinking variables rather than physiological ones. Increasingly, this comfortable view is being challenged by metabolic research on alcohol use.

Part 4, "Physiological and Biomedical Aspects of Alcohol Consumption," is important to this volume for two reasons. First, alcohol is a substance which bridges both biological and social life, and this necessitates a biomedical perspective. Second, a number of recent studies purport to show that there are ethnic differences in the ability to metabolize alcohol. Clearly, these issues are relevant to a cross-cultural evaluation of alcohol studies.

The initial selection in Part 4 by William Madsen focuses largely on the false dichotomy perpetuated in the nature/nurture controversy and reminds us of the significance of considering biological and cultural factors simultaneously. The same perspective was shared at the conference by physiologist Leonard Goldberg of the Karolinska Institute of Stockholm, who viewed alcohol in an epidemiological context. Such a view considers that man, as a biological organism, consumes alcohol, an agent of action, in a social and physical environment. Thus, in order to adequately understand the physiology of alcohol consumption, it is necessary to refer not only to alcohol as a substance which can produce physiological responses but also to the environment in which it is consumed. For example, the peak of blood alcohol concentration, the maximum effect that an individual drinker can expect to get from a drink of alcohol, will be dependent upon the specific type of beverage imbibed, the drinker's emotional state, and the pattern of intake. Quite obviously, all of these are going to be dependent upon cultural background. Thus, in order to analyze the effects that a given single dose, even a uniform dose, of alcohol has on an individual, his culture as well as the amount of alcohol consumed must be considered.

Goldberg also stressed that anthropologists should be aware of the effects which alcohol has on the central nervous system. There are a number of these, but from an anthropological perspective the most important one is probably its ability to affect the processing of cognitive data. The human cortex is bombarded by an extraordinarily large amount of sensory input each minute. Some sort of selective mechanism must operate in order to insure that all the data are not processed at once and that certain selections can be utilized for making decisions and taking action. One of the effects of alcohol is to blur this decision-making process.

Obviously, alcohol also affects behavior itself. Goldberg's own studies show that people who regularly drink alcohol do so to achieve a specific level of blood alcohol content; that is, over a period of time, anyone who continuously drinks alcohol will attempt to achieve a certain maintenance level of intoxication, which, of course, differs from person to person. Moreover, there is a quantitative difference in the amount of alcohol and the effect of alcohol that one can expect from different beverages. Distilled beverages produce a higher blood alcohol content than many beverages, EVEN when the absolute amount of alcohol ingested may be the same.

The second selection in Part 4 is a reprint (the only one in the entire volume) of a controversial but important study by a Canadian team of researchers dealing with differential alcohol metabolism among Anglos, Indians, and Eskimos. It is significant both from its implication that there are racial differences in alcohol physiology and from the standpoint of methodology employed. The paper, presented at the conference by J. A. L. Gilbert, a physician at the Royal Alexandria Hospital, provoked a spirited discussion led by Dr. Eugene LeBlanc of Addiction Research Foundation of Ontario, in which some of Gilbert's findings were challenged. First, it was noted that medical students were hardly a random sample and probably not representative of the white population. Moreover, it is hard to imagine that hospital patients constitute a random sample of Eskimo or Indian populations. Second, Goldberg noted that the very high rate of alcohol metabolism in the Anglo sample was much more akin to alcoholics which he had tested rather than to average Anglo individuals which he had also tested. Third, it was noted that a genetic difference need not be invoked since there was no attempt to estimate the variation within each of the samples. Despite these difficulties, the study by Gilbert and his colleagues is a seminal effort in the investigation of alcohol metabolism, an opinion also expressed in the final selection in Part 4 by Joel Hanna, who provides a physical anthropological perspective of the same issues raised by Fenna, Mix, Schaefer, and Gilbert.

These selections in Part 4 focus on three major problems in alcohol studies. The first is that biological variability within populations has not been studied. It is known from a number of studies that we can expect metabolic variability due to age, habitual consumption, self concepts of alcoholism, and sex. Surprisingly enough, there are no studies which compare men and women in alcohol tolerance. Second, there are a number of recent alcohol studies now being published which have not been adequately evaluated, especially in political terms. Some concern should be expressed about the use of these studies for political action. It is suggested that when such studies are completed, the ethics of their publication, in the absence of adequate controls or adequate review, be looked over more carefully. Finally and perhaps most important, even if there are demonstrable metabolic differences in alcohol tolerance between populations, the cultural significance of these differences and intrapopulation metabolic variation is yet to be established.

Part 5, "The Current Status of Cross-Cultural Theories," deals with cross-cultural theoretical approaches to drinking. The selection by Herbert Barry, III, reviews the dependency theory of Bacon, Barry, and Child, a theoretical strategy that relates both drinking and drunkenness to feelings of inadequacy and strivings for dependency. According to this theory, drunkenness is, thus, a behavioral way of achieving dependency. An alternative approach provided by Richard Boyatzis represents the theoretical position of David McClelland's work on alcohol and power. This perspective stresses that through drinking the drinker, whether social drinker or alcoholic, alleviates feelings of powerlessness by becoming intoxicated, by assuming a psychological state where he or she deludes himself into feeling godlike or omnipotent. These two psychological theories are similar in kind to other culture stress and social deprivation theories such as Horton's anxiety thesis, where alcohol is defined as a mechanism of stress reduction.

In the third selection of Part 5, James Schaefer critically subjects psychological stress theories to cross-cultural testing. The selections by Barry, Boyatzis, and Schaefer are examples of the predominant role that psychologists have played in the field of theory building in relation to drinking behavior, virtually to the exclusion of other behavioral scientists. The various theories evolved by psychologists from cross-cultural data deserve critical examination, but alternative or complementary theories seem to be lacking. Several key points can be made in this regard. The first is that theories of drinking have been overly unitary or monotypic. In other words, there has been an attempt to explain complex and diverse kinds of behaviors in rather simplistic terms. However, those who developed these theoretical constructs point out that their theories have really received more attention than they originally intended, perhaps because of the paucity of other theory building in this field.

A second point is that present psychologizing theories are of such a nature that the behavioral phenomenon in question can be explained equally well by resort to any of the various alternative theories. The theories do not appear to be very strongly distinguished from one another since both behavior A as well as the opposite behavior, non-A, can be explained adequately by each of the approaches. By attempting to explain virtually anything and everything in abstract motivational terms, these theories are reduced to explaining very little. Because of this difficulty, these theoretical notions are not especially useful in guiding social planners, clinicians, and legislators in their work within social institutions and agencies and with individuals who encounter problems with their drinking behavior.

As a third point it can also be stressed that these theories, in addition to having been developed by psychologists, have been developed by American psychologists, which may account for the ethnocentric, perhaps American, trap of thinking in dichotomizing, "either-or" terms. Instead of forcing one theory to the detriment of another, collaborative and complementary theoretical strategies should be explored to explain the phenomena in question. The selections by Jan de Lint and Margaret Sargent call for a broader, more pragmatic theoretical base upon which this collaboration in building complementary theories might take place.

By way of a critical summary, there may be a need for more micro-theory at this point. A stage of macro theory does not yet seem possible, and perhaps case-specific intracultural theory building might be more appropriate, as both de Lint and Sargent imply. There is clearly a link between theory building and method, but theory and method are frequently separated as though they are not related, when in fact the crucial theoretical question is: what kinds of methods should be employed to test specific kinds of theories? Moreover, the ethnocentric, Western approach to theory building for explaining drinking behavior may be inadequate. It can also be argued that there is the tendency to use theories whose terminologies derive from physics, hydrology, and sometimes abstract psychodynamics rather than theories which might focus on social as well as cultural phenomena where direct behavioral observations would be brought more into play.

Part 6, "Methodological Considerations and Data Collection," is concerned with the various kinds of methodological and data acquisition strategies that have been developed by investigators and utilized within a cross-cultural context or which have had some kind of potential for cross-cultural application.

The first selection is a critical review and evaluation of clinical approaches to the study of alcohol by Joseph Westermeyer. He discusses a variety of methodological tools which have been utilized in medical and clinical settings, including questionnaires, psychometric devices, genetic techniques, blood alcohol levels, cirrhosis measures, monitored alcohol ingestion, and a number of others. It should be noted that clinical approaches tend to exhibit two major kinds of weaknesses: they tend to focus on alcoholism rather than drinking *per se*; in addition, it is sometimes quite difficult to control for sampling problems within clinical environments.

Martin Topper, in the second selection in Part 6, discusses techniques developed from cognitive and linguistic methodology that provide a means of getting at culture-specific data on drinking behavior. Topper, along with a number of other anthropologists, is working in the area of computer-modeled decision-making processes, one context of which is the "ethnography of the day." A key tool in this approach is the "verbal action plan," a set of sequential-action protocols with decision criteria specified at decision nodes. The focus of this particular kind of methodology is the character of cultural knowledge and how this relates to bio-environmental aspects of human existence.

Since the tendency has been for anthropologists to apply their research skills to non-Western or exotic "primitive" tribal or peasant societies, it seems appropriate that students of our own society should ask what anthropologists might contribute to a study of current concerns about drinking behavior in modern contemporary society. Donald Cahalan, in the third selection, points out a number of specific areas of data, derived largely from quantitative survey research, to which anthropological methods of data gathering and analysis might fruitfully be applied.

The last selection in Part 6, by Mark Keller, is a brief report about the documentation and information services available at the Center of Alcohol Studies, Rutgers University, which would be valuable for cross-cultural research on alcohol and behavior.

The various selections in Part 6 demonstrate that interdisciplinary research is necessary and desirable in the area of alcohol studies.

Several ways of expediting cooperative research are possible. One way would be to produce research proposals and projects as joint cross-disciplinary ventures. This would demand that all the individuals in the project, regardless of their particular disciplinary affiliations, be trained in the use of similar methodologies, for example, quantitative techniques. However, institutional reward systems frequently do not support this kind of multidisciplinary research.

Since the main concern of this volume is to evaluate the cross-cultural contributions of anthropology to alcohol studies, the basic issue seems to be whether that contribution should be uniquely anthropological in approach, or whether anthropology should focus on cross-disciplinary kinds of concerns. It may be that a particular subdiscipline of anthropology, such as medical anthropology, could provide a kind of two-way interaction between these two concerns.

In weighing and evaluating the various methodological strategies relevant to alcohol studies, each of these approaches should be viewed against the other in comparative perspective. Dual research strategies with both cross-cultural or hologeistic and biological components are possible. There are strengths and weaknesses in both paradigms. On the other hand, an analytic paradigm which focuses not on large-scale cross-cultural comparisons but instead on intracultural variations in particular social systems, might be a more appropriate strategy for certain kinds of research.

There are several critical issues evident in the selections comprising Part 6. Perhaps the most significant one is that some kind of meaningful link-up beween method and theory is necessary. But whether this research should concentrate on substantive theoretical issues — e.g. the link between drinking and interpersonal conflict — or whether it should focus on methodological innovation and sophistication, is a difficult question to resolve. The two are certainly not mutually exclusive, but they clearly present the researcher with different kinds of problems.

Another crucial concern is how the division of labor and cooperation necessary for cross-disciplinary research can best be implemented. The precise relationship of anthropology to other disciplines involved in alcohol studies remains to be clearly defined and put into some kind of workable research framework.

A major concern emerges out of the discussions about method and theory, namely, the whole issue of the uses to which alcohol method and theory are put. Most discussions of method and theory focus on academic intellectual concerns, theory building, causality and explanation, and such, but very infrequently do they focus on problems of practice and application. The area of educational, therapeutic, and rehabilitative alcohol research and application is yet to be clarified in terms of its relationship to the theoretical and methodological pre-occupations of alcohol investigations.

Selden Bacon's concluding remarks at the Chicago conference provided the stimulus for this concern about "theories for whom and theories for what?" It is a major concern of this volume. At least three categories of groups have interests in alcohol: academic disciplines (anthropology, psychology, sociology, etc.), alcohol action groups (treatment programs), and research groups and institutions. All three have their own perspectives, policy statements, and needs; as a result, alcohol studies are a very complicated field of endeavor. What are the relationships between these divergent interests and perspectives? As Selden Bacon pointed out, no one group's needs are paramount over those of the other two, but all three can benefit directly from a cross-cultural perspective. The major problem in bringing together the many diverse perspectives interested in the cross-cultural approach is that of terminology and communication. Also, an idealized theory that seems suitable for anthropological needs may be somewhat impoverished in biomedical terms. This is a critical issue in view of the obvious need for interdisciplinary research involving human biology and sociocultural systems.

There are critical questions to be answered if, in fact, anthropologists are to make any kind of cross-cultural contribution TO alcohol studies and if they are to learn anything FROM alcohol studies. What are the purposes of talking in cross-cultural theoretical and methodological terms within an anthropological context or any other scientific framework? What is the quality of the academic products resulting from the kind of multidisciplinary endeavor referred to above? What does anthropology have to gain from cross-disciplinary research enterprises, and what is it that anthropology can contribute to other disciplines in this regard? What kinds of perspectives, what kinds of new sources of data and information, what kinds of understanding with regard to human alcohol use and its linkages are likely to come from such efforts? How do we evaluate or critically assess the relationship between the various disciplines involved in alcohol studies? What is the output of cross-disciplinary alcohol research in terms of its advantage for the development and maximization of human resources and potential? Clearly, demonstrable linkages between theoretical and methodological notions and the whole issue of human problems stemming from alcohol must be confronted in practical, applied terms for their cross-cultural value in therapy and in building awareness and understanding.

It appears that several new perspectives in alcohol studies are beginning to develop, namely, awareness of a broader cross-cultural conceptual framework, recent methodological innovations, new data and resources, current research projects and funding policies, and the need for cooperative research strategies. New information and sources of information in the following areas are still very much needed by a variety of scholars involved in alcohol studies: anthropological research on behavioral, psychological, and semantic problems; biomedical research on metabolism, racial and ethnic differences in physiological responses to alcohol, and nutritional problems; European research projects and data; and bibliographic and documentation resources.

The multidisciplinary perspective of the conference, reiterated in this volume, is important for anthropology and alcohol studies in these various areas because it generates (1) stimulating new data, ideas, problems, and research designs and techniques; (2) increased awareness of diverse disciplinary interests and enthusiasms; and (3) a challenge to develop much needed cooperative efforts and effective channels of communication.

It is hoped that this volume will help to assess and evaluate current and future cross-cultural alcohol research and help to stimulate greater collaboration between anthropologists and representatives of other disciplines in the developing field of alcohol studies.

PART ONE

*Pioneering Works and Their
Reassessment*

Introduction

The major purpose of the Chicago Alcohol Conference, as originally conceived, was to evaluate what anthropological studies have contributed to our understanding of alcohol, and incidentally to discern what studies of alcohol have contributed to anthropological perspectives. In that connection, it seemed fruitful to review the history of studies that deal with beliefs and behaviors concerning alcohol in non-Western societies, and in cross-cultural perspective. (One review, organized in chronological sequence, appears in the following section of this book; another review, organized in terms of categories that predominate in the international literature on alcohol written by psychologists, psychiatrists, sociologists, physiologists, social workers, and many others who are concerned with a variety of different perspectives, is forthcoming elsewhere.)

Although a few scattered and generally superficial descriptions of drinking and its regulation among populations remote in space and time have appeared throughout preceding centuries, there was little systematic attempt to characterize in any detail such alien behavioral and attitudinal patterns or to show how they related to other aspects of the way of life of which they were a part. In terms of anthropological approaches to alcohol studies, pioneering efforts are not remote in time, nor has their value diminished to the point where "historically important" is a euphemism for "outdated." In fact, this is one realm of social investigation in which some of the pioneers not only survive but are still active, and in which the approaches and insights which characterized their early contributions remain vital and relevant today.

One such pioneer is Ruth Bunzel, whose 1940 paper (see the Heath bibliography in this volume) is not only one of the earliest comparative studies of drinking in cross-cultural perspective, but is also still one of the most complete. She used what has since come to be called "the method of controlled comparison," and showed how different patterns of drinking and drunkenness are shaped by different patterns of child rearing, sex roles, religious beliefs, and a host of other sociocultural variables in two Mesoamerican Indian communities. She integrated psychoanalytic interpretations with ethnographic reporting to yield insights into drinking and drunkenness that still seem relevant to those communities and that are more convincing than many other kinds of analysis and interpretation that have been imposed on data from other groups in the thirty years of anthropological contributions since then. She sought not only to delineate the positive functions of such behavior, but also to understand the social and economic problems that it caused.

As a personal note, it must be mentioned that it is characteristic of Dr. Bunzel that she was hesitant when first approached to participate in the conference, noting how long it was since she had written the paper comparing Chamula and Chichicastenango, and stressing that she had not really intended to study alcohol then nor had she done so in the ensuing years. When she was finally convinced that we wanted specifically to learn about how and why she had written that paper, and what its reception over the years had meant to her, she agreed to take part in the conference. The paper printed here was edited from a taped transcription of the conference session, and graciously approved by her.

The other "pioneering approach" discussed here is the cross-cultural correlational method of alcohol studies. The method itself was introduced by Donald Horton in 1943; although his work became an immediate classic, the method was sharpened in terms of definitions, ratings, indices, and more sophisticated integration of psychological theory by Margaret Bacon and her colleagues, Herbert Barry and Irvin Child. Bacon's paper, printed here, served not only to trace the history of cross-cultural studies of alcohol and their misinterpretation, but also to focus attention on a number of significant correlations that have been virtually ignored to date and that may well provide important leads for further research.

Like her colleague, Bacon chafed a little at the label "pioneer," wondering about the image of the bonnet and oxcart that hardly seemed pertinent in terms of contributions that are not yet ten years old. It is clear, however, that in terms of research, pioneering is more a matter of imagination than seniority, and in this sense Bacon's contribution has been substantial. It promises to be even more so in coming years, in view of her current efforts to prepare a field guide for the study of alcohol, as a partial means of assuring that more, and more comprehensive, data are collected on the subject by nonspecialists who have some familiarity with societies that have not been thoroughly studied. It is only on the basis of the accumulated corpus of fragmentary ethnographic descriptions that the hologeistic method came to be feasible, and her dedication to expanding "the universe of societies" about which we have useful data may have long-range value in making such studies easier and more valid. With all of its limitations, this method of research may come as near to approximating "laboratory conditions" and allowing systematic study of the correlations of variables as does anything that is feasible in the study of human populations.

In summary, with reference to alcohol studies and anthropology, "pioneering works" are not only close to us in time, but they are also still immediately relevant in terms of methods, kinds of data, interpretations, and implications for action. This does not mean that little progress has been made, but that we are fortunate in having had sound and fruitful guidelines offered (however unintentionally) by insightful and imaginative people. The range of topics dealt with at the conference and in this volume fit well with the primary concerns of Bunzel and Bacon — not so much to understand alcohol, as to try to understand human behavior, which sometimes involves, and is affected by, alcohol.

Chamula and Chichicastenango:
A Re-examination

RUTH BUNZEL

I have not revisited either of the two Middle American communities in which I worked several years ago. Nor did I plan to re-study them, although it would be an interesting experience. And I haven't pursued alcohol, alcoholism, or drinking habits as a special research area since then. My original paper happened quite accidentally as a by-product of general ethnographic studies in the two geographic areas. The two research projects were separated by several years, during which time I was in New York and during which time my point of view changed somewhat because of involvement with the 1937 Columbia seminar of psychiatrists, psychoanalysts, and anthropologists. This experience prompted me to look at things quite differently in my subsequent research.

When I was in Guatemala, I did not perceive alcohol or drinking as special problems to be investigated. It just seemed that patterns of drinking were the familiar ones associated with Mexican fiestas. If I had been a little more concerned with drinking as a research problem, as I did become very much later, I would have approached my study quite differently. For example, I would have focused on who drinks, how often, and other things.

In the Mexican village of Chamula, everybody drank whenever they had the opportunity. So there was no problem conducting a detailed drinking study. And in Chamula the drinking pattern was so completely different from anything that we experience in our own society, where we have some knowledge about alcohol use, that it immediately attracted our attention. Here were two societies — Chamula and Chichicastenango — within the same culture area that had completely different drinking patterns. It seemed to me that we had to deal with these differences and look for their cultural context.

Although I have turned to other things since this study was done, my basic concern has always been consistently the same from the time I first went down and studied pottery making. Years later, when someone asks me, "Oh, are you still studying pottery?" I can say, "Look, I've never studied pottery. I was studying human behavior, and I wanted to know how potters felt about what they were doing."

I feel the same way about alcohol. I have never studied alcohol; I have just studied people and their drinking habits as seen in their cultural contexts and the influences behind these habits. This is really what has been my consistent preoccupation, throughout all my years, even after I began dealing with Chinese political habits and behavior. It is not politics that I studied, but human behavior in its cultural context.

I have very little to add to the paper on Chamula and Chichicastenango, except to mention the sorts of things I might have done differently had I gone into the research as a study of drinking. I think I would probably have given the paper a different title if I had been a little more sophisticated. But, again, this was something I did not consider at the time.

The principal point of my study is that drinking, or alcoholism, or whatever you want to call it, is not the same thing in different cultures. It is quite a different entity in Chamula from what it is in Chichicastenango. We cannot deal with drinking in these two cultures as one thing. Alcoholism plays an entirely different role in the lives of the people in the two cultures. An entirely different etiology of drinking is apparent in each of these different areas. That is the major point that I tried to make. Drinking fulfills quite different roles. Principally, in Chichicastenango, drinking is a release from the extreme pressures of surrounding cultures. It is also a way of dealing with the anxieties provoked by these external pressures which, of course, lead to more anxieties in a sort of feedback relationship. In Chamula, however, drinking performs the function of lubricating social relations at a very basic level; you cannot enter into any kind of relationship with another person without first establishing the pattern of sharing a drink. This pattern could be due to infantile experiences.

I want to emphasize again how drinking fits into a much broader context, not leading into studies of alcohol *per se*, but into a concern for human behavior. Since it is a rather extreme form of human behavior, the differences in the ways in which people use drinking as a mechanism show up very clearly.

Cross-Cultural Studies of Drinking: Integrated Drinking and Sex Differences in the Use of Alcoholic Beverages

MARGARET K. BACON

Cross-cultural studies of drinking which have made some attempt at the quantification of variables across a sample of societies have been relatively few in number. The pioneer study making use of this method in the field of alcohol studies was, of course, that of Donald Horton (1943). Horton's monograph was a landmark in a number of different respects. Not only was it the first cross-cultural study of drinking, but it was also a pioneer effort to make a quantitative test of an hypothesis regarding human behavior in a cross-cultural setting.

It is perhaps of some historical interest to note that Horton was not primarily interested in the problems of alcohol. His interest was chiefly methodological. His concern was to test a psychological hypothesis in a sample which consisted of societies, rather than people, as units of variation. His work grew out of his contact with the now famous group of learning theorists who were at Yale University in the late 1930's — Miller, Dollard, Sears, Mowrer, Hull, Marquis, etc. It was also a direct consequence of the founding of the Human Relations Area Files by Murdock. The idea that psychological hypotheses might and should be tested against a universe of the world's peoples, as well as within the population of a single cultural group, received great impetus at that time.

The main hypothesis that Horton chose to test in his cross-cultural study was based on the widespread, popular, clinically supported belief that one of the psychological effects of alcohol consumption was the reduction of anxiety — and that anxiety reduction might therefore be a widespread motive for drinking. If this were true, then it would be expected that societies whose members generally experienced high levels of anxiety might exhibit a higher frequency of drunkenness than societies where the anxiety level was low. In his search for measures of anxiety which might be cross-culturally valid, Horton chose, as is well known, two measures of subsistence insecurity and one of acculturation. These were chosen simply as possible sources of anxiety which might be operative in a sample of preliterate societies and which might also be subject to rough but reliable quantification on the basis of the ethnographic descriptions available in the cross-cultural files. Horton did not intend to suggest that inebriety was specifically related to anxiety about food, as has been implied by some subsequent researchers.

The point can be made then that Horton's work stands as a landmark not only in the field of alcohol research but also in the field of cross-cultural studies in general. Horton's monograph preceded by ten years the now classic study of child training and personality by Whiting and Child (1953) and the area of research stemming from this publication.

Following Horton's study there were no further cross-cultural studies of drinking for nearly two decades. Then in the late 1950's, the second Yale cross-cultural study of drinking was undertaken by Bacon, Barry, and Child, hereafter referred to as the B., B., and C. study.

In the early 1960's, Field (1962) published a cross-cultural study based on a re-analysis of Horton's data and including some of the unpublished ratings of the B., B., and C. study. It should be noted that Field's analysis was not concerned with motives for drinking but rather with possible social organization correlates of sobriety — i.e. social controls of drinking.

The B., B., and C. study was published in 1965 (Child, et al. 1965a, 1965b; Bacon, et al. 1965a, 1965b; Barry, et al. 1965). Since then, McClelland and his colleagues (1966, 1972) have published cross-cultural studies relating ratings of drinking and insobriety from the B., B., and C. study to the word content of translated folktales. These studies have been utilized in the development of a theory relating drinking to the need for power in males.

The 1965 B., B., and C. study was undertaken with several purposes in mind. It was hoped that (1) it might serve as a representative survey of drinking practices as they were reported in the then existing literature of preliterate societies in all areas of the world, and (2) it might provide quantitative comparative measures of various aspects of drinking customs which were felt to be widely present and significant as variables. In brief, the intent was to codify, collect, and roughly quantify a large amount of data on drinking customs in a broad sample of cultural groups, and to make these data available for the testing of hypotheses by other research groups and as a background of cultural variation against which to view the customs of any single group. Another goal was to test an hypothesis regarding relationships between dependency conflict and consumption of alcoholic beverages. Other more incidental aims were largely methodological. The reliability and validity of Horton's findings were checked and certain inadequacies of his procedure were corrected. In Horton's study all ratings were made by Horton alone. As a consequence, there was no check on the reliability of the rating and no control over the possible effects of experimenter bias. The B., B., and C. study sought to correct these methodological defects by making use of two independent raters who made their judgments on ethnographic material extracted verbatim from the original source with all identifying data removed. The ratings were thus done "blind" and could not have been influenced by other incidental knowledge held by the rater, or by any bias held with respect to the hypotheses being tested.

Horton's study was based on 57 societies. The B., B., and C. study involved 139 societies including Horton's original 57. Horton's sample consisted simply of all those societies which had been processed in the cross-cultural files at Yale at that time and which contained sufficient information to make a rating on drunkenness. The B., B., and C. sample was determined by a number of considerations. It was decided to include the Horton sample for purposes of validating his measures of drunkenness along with the new B., B., and C. ones. It was also decided to include as many societies as possible from earlier studies of child rearing so that it would be possible to test the interrelationships of variables of socialization with those of drinking behavior. An attempt was made to choose a worldwide sample and to include only societies that were independent units. A further limitation was encountered in terms of the adequacy of the material on drinking. The resulting sample achieved most of these objectives but was inadvertently somewhat overweighted with regard to the inclusion of African societies.

The results of the B., B., and C. study seem to have been interpreted by the academic community largely in terms of the dependency-conflict hypothesis. There are, however, certain other findings of the study which seem to be of equal significance and there are other data still in the process of analysis. Both of these areas warrant some discussion.

In the original design of the study, information was sought for a total of forty-nine different variables related to the use of alcohol. These covered, for each society, the general aspects of the drinking custom, such as the availability of alcohol, the extent, frequency, quantity, and duration of drinking what and by whom. Information on the contexts of drinking was sought, i.e. religious, ceremonial, household, solitary drinking, etc. Behavior associated with drinking was also noted: sociability, exhibitionism, hostility, rule breaking, extreme behavior, etc. Summary ratings were also made regarding overall consumption of alcohol, frequency of drunkenness, degree of the problems, efforts to procure alcohol, and the attitudes of the society towards drinking and drunkenness, etc.

In considering these findings it should be kept in mind that quantification, in this as in other cross-cultural studies, consists of ratings on a comparative rather than an absolute scale. Thus, a rating of four for, say, frequency of alcohol consumption means that the consumption of alcohol by the typical adult in that society is judged to be about average (on a seven-point scale) for the sample on which the study is based, in this case 139 societies.

The available ethnographic material was, as might be expected, often insufficient to make a reasonably confident rating on all of these variables. When the data were insufficient no rating was made on that variable; when a given variable was rated on fewer than twelve societies it was eliminated from the subsequent analysis.

The final body of data nevertheless consisted of thousands of ratings and the methods of data reduction seemed to be in order. It was decided, therefore, to apply factor analysis to those variables which had been rated by both judges in at least 50 of the 121 societies where the consumption of alcoholic beverages was reported. Nineteen alcohol-related variables met this criterion. When the intercorrelations of these nineteen variables were subjected to factor analysis, four independent dimensions of variation in the use of alcohol were revealed. In descending order of importance these four dimensions were: (1) the Integrated Drinking Factor, (2) the Inebriety Factor, (3) the Hospitality Factor, and (4) the Quantity or General Consumption Factor. These four factors accounted for 80 percent of the total variance.

The discovery of these four basic dimensions of variation in the use of alcohol across a sample of 121 different cultural groups throughout the world makes this finding seem of very considerable significance. It raises the question of the existence and nature of such dimensions for future exploration and elaboration. It provides the beginning of a cultural frame of reference against which to view the drinking practices of any given group.

The delineation of the Integrated Drinking Factor[1] provides an excellent example of the significance of such findings. The meaning of this fac-

[1] The precise definitions of this and all other variables investigated are given in Section V of the B., B., and C. study (Bacon, et al. 1965b).

tor is fairly clearly indicated by the listing of the variables with the highest loading on it, namely, (1) the extent of ritualization of drinking, i.e. the extent to which each act of drinking is surrounded by restrictions as to time, place, material apparatus, way of drinking, etc.; (2) frequency of drinking and quantity consumed in a religious context; and (3) frequency and quantity of public or ceremonial drinking, i.e. drinking related to culturally standardized recurrent rites, ceremonies, celebrations, or assemblies of general social significance and of a public nature, including family ceremonials of public importance such as weddings, name-giving, funerals, work parties, etc.

The emergence of this factor as a dimension of alcohol-related behavior in a sample of societies provides a statistical verification of the significance of this variable which has hitherto been based on intuitive case study methods. For example, Snyder, in his study of Jewish drinking (1958), clearly depicted the manner in which drinking is interwoven into the ceremonial customs of this group. He suggested that the association of alcohol with these socially meaningful activities might be a significance factor in reducing or preventing alcohol-related problems. Similar case studies of drinking in other cultural groups have also made use of this concept or its variations (Bales 1962; Glad 1947; Lolli, et al. 1958). Whether or not this variable demonstrates the interrelationships suggested by these writers, its importance as a factor in drinking behavior is verified by cross-cultural analysis.

The interrelationship of Integrated Drinking with other variables is also revealed by this analysis. One of the most striking relationships is found to be with the presence or absence of drinking in aboriginal times. It seems reasonable to assume that the integration of drinking customs into cultural traditions would be to some degree a function of time. It would be expected, for example, that Integrated Drinking would occur more frequently in groups accustomed to drinking in the aboriginal period than it would in groups where drinking developed only after contact with a dominant culture. The cross-cultural findings strongly confirm this prediction. Of the forty-nine societies with aboriginal drinking, thirty-seven were rated as having Integrated Drinking and only three as definitely lacking it. Of the thirty-five societies which are listed as drinking after contact but not aboriginally, Integrated Drinking was rated as present in only three, and in two of these the ratings were below average.

Integrated Drinking may thus be viewed as a cultural adjustment to drinking, an adaptation that has occurred through time. Consistent with this view is the finding that societies high in Integrated Drinking are also found to have a highly organized and stratified social structure and a subsistence economy which permits the accumulation of food. These features appear to be characteristic of a relatively settled and organized culture. It seems logical that cultural integration of drinking customs would be more likely to occur in this type of society than in one less stable and less well organized.

Societies high in Integrated Drinking also tend to be those which show high cultural pressures toward responsibility and obedience, either during the childhood training period or in adult life. They also show a low expectation of achievement. This pattern of socialization pressures has also been found to be characteristic of societies whose economy permits an accumulation of food.

The interrelationship of Integrated Drinking with other variables of drinking behavior is also important. Societies high in Integrated Drinking show the following characteristics: generalized approval of drinking, widespread participation, and a high rate of alcohol consumption. It woud be expected that in societies where drinking is highly integrated with ceremonial and social life, most of the members of the society would drink and there would be generalized approval of drinking. The fact that such societies also rank high in the rate of consumption of alcohol is interesting and not entirely expected. This finding indicates that a high rate of consumption does not necessarily mean that alcohol is essentially disruptive of social life. A high rate of alcohol consumption is apparently entirely compatible with a pattern of alcohol use which is linked with the positive values of the group. This finding is contrary to the generally accepted belief in our society that a high rate of consumption of alcoholic drinks is, almost by definition, socially threatening.

The variable, Approval of Drunkenness, is also highly correlated with Integrated Drinking. This is of special interest. It would seem logical that a society which ranked high in Integrated Drinking might disapprove of drunkenness as potentially disruptive. However, the finding here suggests rather that societies high in Integrated Drinking are generally accepting of drunkenness. In other words, Snyder's finding (1958) that Jewish customs of drinking unite a strong tendency toward Integrated Drinking with a strong disapproval of drunkenness is not repeated in a larger sample of societies. These two variables are not necessarily linked in this way. The finding is rather that societies with a high ranking in Integrated Drinking usually show a general approval rather than disapproval of drunkenness. The presence of Integrated Drinking certainly does not presuppose the existence of a disapproving attitude toward drunkenness.

The relationship between Integrated Drinking and actual frequency of drunkenness, quite apart from attitudes of approval or disapproval, is also interesting. The correlation between the two in a cross-cultural sample is close to zero. This indicates that these measures are not inter-related, i.e. societies rated high in Integrated Drinking may be rated high, low, or intermediate in frequency of drunkenness. This finding is again somewhat opposed to the implications of Snyder's study (1958) where he related the almost complete absence of alcohol-related problems among the Jews to the high degree of ritualization and cultural integration of their drinking patterns. While this association may hold for Jewish drinking, the generality of the relationship is not supported by cross-cultural findings.

Field's argument (1962), which would seem to predict that an increase in Integrated Drinking would be accompanied by a parallel decrease in frequency of drunkenness, is also not supported by these findings. This is not to suggest that the concept of social control of drinking is unrelated to the Integrated Drinking Factor. Certainly the development through time of culturally prescribed patterns of alcohol use involves social norms, consensus, and concepts of limits and propriety, all of which are a part of social control. The findings here merely mean that the social norms accompanying Integrated Drinking do not necessarily demand sobriety. With Integrated Drinking present, drunkenness may or may not be frequent, may or may not be absent.

Areas for further research with regard to Integrated Drinking are numerous. Questions can be raised as to the patterns of integration of drinking through time and the variable effect of acculturation on societies with and without well-developed integration of drinking customs at the time of contact. The suggested interrelationship of Integrated Drinking and factors of economy is also in need of further exploration.

The whole question of sex differences in the use of alcohol is another field in which cross-cultural findings are pertinent. In anthropological literature, the drinking behavior of women has received relatively little attention. Horton (1943) presented very limited data on sex differences in drinking. The B., B., and C. study seems to represent the first serious attempt to collect cross-cultural evidence on this subject.

In most Western societies women tend to drink less than men; in some cases this difference is quite marked. This frequently observed discrepancy has apparently led to the widespread belief that in all societies men drink more than women. The cross-cultural evidence indicates that this is not true.

According to the evidence from the B., B., and C. study, both men and women drank in 109 of 113 societies where there was sufficient information to make a judgement. Drinking was restricted to one sex in only four societies, and in each of these cases, the men drank and the women did not. A total of fifty-three societies was classified by a third judge as showing evidence of a sex difference in the use of alcohol. The difference was in all cases in the same direction, with men participating to a greater degree than women.

On the other hand, thirty-six societies were classified by the same judge as not showing evidence of any sex difference. And on any particular alcohol-related variable, the majority of societies showed no sex difference in quantitative rating. Clearly, the tendency for men to drink more than women is a frequently observed pattern, cross-culturally, but it is by no means universal. The direction of the difference, when it does occur, does seem to be uniform.

If a comparison is made between the two groups — those with definite evidence of sex differences in drinking and those with no evidence of difference or evidence that the sexes are equal in this respect — such a comparison reveals interesting differences. The most conspicuous difference found was that related to the aboriginal use of alcohol. Alcohol was used aboriginally rather than being introduced post-contact in 81 percent of the societies with a definite sex difference but in only 45 percent of those without evidence of a sex difference. This difference is highly significant statistically. The presence of sex differences in drinking is positively associated not only with the presence of aboriginal drinking but also with Integrated Drinking. The interpretation of these interrelationships is subject to surmise. The fact that men usually participate in ceremonial observances to a greater extent than women may influence the development of sex differences in drinking to the extent that alcohol is involved in such rites.

Two additional findings with respect to sex differences are of interest. Among societies with aboriginal drinking, those with a definite sex difference show: (1) lower scores in the availability of alcoholic beverages and (2) higher scores in the occurrence of extreme hostility. A low score in availability of alcohol beverages generally refers to seasonal restrictions. The tendency for this situation to be found in societies with definite sex differences in drinking might indicate that when the supply of alcohol is limited, men are inclined to reserve most of it for themselves and thus limit the amount that women may drink.

Extreme hostility while drinking tends to be found in men rather than women. It's occurrence in societies with definite sex differences in drinking might be due to a generally more unrestrained expression of aggression by men in societies where there is a general emphasis on difference in sex role. In such societies, women may lack the opportunity to intervene when drunken brawls occur or may not be permitted to do so. Possibly the presence of women in the drinking situation, when it is permitted, i.e. when sex differences are less, operates as an inhibition with respect to the expression of hostility.

This is an interesting finding in view of the interpretation suggested by Field (1962) and by McClelland, et al. (1966, 1972) that male solidarity, masculine domination, etc. leads to increased control of drinking and lower frequency of intoxication. The relationships here are not necessarily contradictory but certainly suggest the complexity of the factors involved in the interaction of variables of social organization and drinking customs.

The whole question of the expression of hostility while drinking is in urgent need of further exploration. Although it has been popularly believed for a long time that alcohol releases aggressive behavior, there seems to have been very little scientific interest in the extent and nature of this interrelationship. As Carpenter and Armenti (1972: 509) have recently pointed out, "...the amount of experimental evidence for opinions about the actions of ethyl alcohol on either sexual behavior or aggression is extremely small." The B., B., and C. study included directions for rating various kinds of behavior while drinking, including the expression of hostility. This material is now in the process of analysis and may provide some cross-cultural evidence pertinent to this question.

In conclusion, it should be emphasized that there is a need for the development of a larger and more uniform body of ethnographic material on drinking for discrete cultural groups. Much excellent material exists, but a great deal is either incomplete or written from a particular frame of reference or in conjunction with a specific set of hypotheses and is therefore fragmentary. Information on certain aspects of drinking may be presented in detail in one ethnography and completely omitted in another. Possibly societies which have been thoroughly investigated from another point of view could be re-studied with regard to their drinking practices. The Six Cultures project might provide an example (Whiting and Child 1953; Whiting 1963). These societies have been extensively studied and a great deal of well-organized data on child rearing, child behavior, social organization, economy, etc. are available. If studies of drinking could be done on these societies, information available in other aspects of these respective groups would be available for analysis.

Also, the need for the development of a "field guide for the study of drinking practices" is clear. Such a publication in fact seems long overdue. If carefully developed by a team of researchers comprising both expertise in ethnographic techniques and understanding of the requirements of data for cross-cultural analysis, such a field guide could be extremely useful as a research instrument. Through its use, a body of data might be developed which would eliminate many of the inadequacies of existing material and greatly increase the scope and validity of comparative studies.

REFERENCES

BACON, M. K., H. BARRY, III, I. L. CHILD
   1965a A cross-cultural study of drinking, II: relations to other features of cultures. *Quarterly Journal of Studies on Alcohol*, supplement 3:29–48.
BACON, M. K., H. BARRY, III, I. L. CHILD, C. R. SNYDER
   1965b A cross-cultural study of drinking, V: detailed definitions and data. *Quarterly Journal of Studies on Alcohol*, supplement 3:78–112.
BALES, R. F.
   1962 "Attitudes toward drinking in the Irish culture," in *Society, culture and drinking patterns*. Edited by D. J. Pittman and C. R. Snyder, 157–187. New York: Wiley and Sons.
BARRY, H., III, C. BUCHWALD, I. L. CHILD, M. K. BACON
   1965 A cross-cultural study of drinking: comparisons with Horton ratings. *Quarterly Journal of Studies on Alcohol,* supplement 3:62–77.
CARPENTER, J. A., N. P. ARMENTI
   1972 "Some effects of ethanol on human sexual and aggressive behavior," in *The biology of alcohol*, volume two. Edited by B. Kissin and H. Begleiter, 509–543. New York: Plenum Press.
CHILD, I. L., M. K. BACON, H. BARRY, III
   1965a A cross-cultural study of drinking, I: descriptive measures of drinking customs. *Quarterly Journal of Studies on Alcohol*, supplement 3:1–28.
CHILD, I. L., H. BARRY, III, M. K. BACON
   1965b A cross-cultural study of drinking, III: sex differences. *Quarterly Journal of Studies on Alcohol*, supplement 3:49–61.
FIELD, P. B.
   1962 "A new cross-cultural study of drunkenness," in *Society, culture and drinking patterns*. Edited by D. J. Pittman and C. R. Snyder, 37–74. New York: Wiley and Sons.
GLAD, D. D.
   1947 Attitudes and experiences of American Jewish and American Irish male youth as related to differences in adult rates of inebriety. *Quarterly Journal of Studies on Alcohol* 8:406–472.
HORTON, D.
   1943 The functions of alcohol in primitive societies: a cross-cultural study. *Quarterly Journal of Studies on Alcohol* 4:199–320.

LOLLI, G., E. SERIANNI, G. M. GOLDER, P. LUZZATTO-FEGIZ
   1958   *Alcohol in Italian culture.* Glencoe, Illinois: Free Press.
MC CLELLAND, D. C., W. DAVIS, R. KALIN, E. WANNER
   1972   *The drinking man: alcohol and motivation.* New York: Free Press.
MC CLELLAND, D. C., W. DAVIS, E. WANNER, R. KALIN
   1966   A cross-cultural study of folk-tale content and drinking. *Sociometry* 29:308–333.
SNYDER, C. R.
   1958   *Alcohol and the Jews.* Glencoe, Illinois: Free Press.
WHITING, B. B.
   1963   *Six cultures: studies of child rearing.* New York: Wiley and Sons.
WHITING, J. W. M., I. L. CHILD
   1953   *Child training and personality: a cross-cultural study.* New Haven: Yale University Press.

PART TWO

The Ethnographic Data Base

Introduction

Any cumulative body of knowledge has a history. There are innovative studies that seem to set precedents for new trends or orientations: in this volume we have referred to them as pioneering studies. Bunzel "pioneered" in 1940; Bacon "pioneered" in 1965. Their reassessments in Part 1 of this collection are exemplary of the fact that many promising ideas and approaches suggested in earlier studies are either misconceived or ignored as new avenues of research are pursued. In both Bunzel's and Bacon's studies, there appear to have been very specific theoretical concerns about alcohol and behavior which prompted their intellectual efforts. While this is certainly true to some extent in most ethnographic field observations, it is more likely that observations on alcohol and behavior are more random, that is, they are important but incidental to some more overriding ethnographic concern or substantive intellectual problem being analyzed and solved.

This section attempts to provide some appraisal of the sources and kinds of cross-cultural data on drinking. Ethnographically, it is not complete in that it does not survey all of the major culture areas of the world. In fact, it does not seem necessary to do this since any ethnographic atlas or compendium of cross-cultural data (such as the Human Relations Area Files) contains data on drinking from all of the reported culture areas. In addition, most scholars who work in particular culture areas and who are interested in data on drinking have built up bibliographies of work done in those areas. Finally, it seems that the problem, as far as the data base is concerned, is not a lack of information; the problem is how these data can be used and whether they are reliable for either theoretical or applied purposes.

What we do include in this section are: a very valuable historical survey of the direction that anthropology and alcohol studies have taken throughout the life history of anthropological science; a much-needed review of Oceania, where alcohol studies as well as alcohol use *per se* are relatively new phenomena; and a review of cultural drinking patterns in Europe, an area much forgotten by anthropologists in their search for the exotic and the non-Western patterns of culture. In this section, we also include two studies by anthropologists in order to suggest how ethnographic research is deriving data on alcohol and behavior from new, nontraditional sources of cultural data, e.g. clinical or therapeutic settings, and how ethnographers are asking questions which have implications for an applied anthropology of alcohol "abuse."

Heath, in his article called "Anthropological perspectives on alcohol: an historical review," provides us with an understanding as to what we mean by an "anthropological perspective" and why alcohol has consistently and widely caught the attention of the anthropologist in his field laboratory, his methods of obtaining data on culturally meaningful behavior, and his theoretical interests. He appropriately reminds us that anthropology, very early in its development, became dependent upon what was happening in other developing disciplines such as psychology, sociology, and physiology. An important feature of Heath's selection is his sense of history and his time-period survey of developments in anthropological concerns in one or another kind of data. Here we can see a developmental history of the germane area of cross-cultural alcohol studies which currently preoccupies a number of us. Finally, Heath takes us through a series of substantive topical areas of study where anthropology has unevenly accumulated a rich, often untapped source of data that are relevant for cross-cultural studies. These topics also have somewhat of a time trajectory in that emphases or fads in one or another area come and go. Out of this kind of careful survey it would seem that we could find some predominant and persisting concerns that characterize much of what anthropology has contributed. It should also suggest new and meaningful syntheses and approaches to data collection and theory.

In the second selection, Marshall reviews a particular culture area in terms of past studies of *kava* and alcohol use in Oceania. He significantly and critically evaluates hypotheses of the few Oceanic scholars, such as Lemert, who have studied variations in *kava* usage and drinking patterns in the Pacific. Most important of all, Marshall points to the woeful lack of alcohol studies in the Pacific and proposes that scholars of that area pay much more attention to alcohol in the immediate years ahead.

Ahlström-Laakso, in her article, surveys some of the limitations of data about European drinking patterns. She critically challenges both survey methods and interpretive conclusions derived from them. What Ahlström-Laakso calls for is a greater concern for discovering variations within countries rather than typing each country for the purpose of comparing one country's type of drinking to that of another. Additionally, she points out that there is both divergence and convergence in national patterns and trends that can be explained in terms of the rapid mobility characteristic of European countries. This should revive an interest in diffusional phenomena, something not alien to anthropological concerns in the past.

As Heath has noted, one of the current trends in anthropology is the primary attention that alcohol is drawing in research. No longer is alcohol only one of a whole array of interesting pieces of cultural behavior that will be woven, at the appropriate place, in a descriptive, holistic ethnography. Rather, it is the central variable to which other pertinent social and cultural data are related. Ablon's article focuses on the qualitative dimensions of family dynamics and the role that alcohol plays in complicating family relations. She suggests a number of avenues of investigation for anthropologists and other social scientists who might be involved in clinical work. Likewise, Ferguson's article is a brief summary of data and conclusions drawn directly from an intensive and prolonged involvement in a Navajo community treatment plan for Indian problem drinkers. While her brief summary of the data and conclusions is interesting, her study is important because it is suggestive of both new sources of data on intracultural variation in drinking style and new possibilities for taking this variation into account in specific treatment modalities.

Anthropological Perspectives on Alcohol: An Historical Review

DWIGHT B. HEATH

There is no doubt that alcohol is the drug most widely used for purposes of "expanding consciousness" by men and women throughout the world. It is probably also the oldest and the most versatile, having served also as food, medicine, narcotic, energizer, and aphrodisiac, in various contexts, during millennia.

Planning this evaluative conference on alcohol studies and anthropology (see the Preface and the Introduction to this volume) provided an appropriate occasion for reviewing in broad perspective the contributions that anthropologists have made in terms of our understanding of alcohol and human behavior, as well as the ways in which alcohol studies have affected the discipline. The subject is far too large and diverse to be analyzed in detail in a single article so I have endeavored here to provide a useful preliminary outline that includes the following: (1) a brief chronological summary of the history of research that deals with patterns of belief and behavior concerning alcoholic beverages; (2) a fairly comprehensive bibliography that reflects the breadth and depth of the diverse and widely scattered literature, written as much by others as by people whose primary professional identification is as anthropologists; and (3) a few suggestions concerning potentially fruitful lines of investi-

As a co-editor of this volume, I have already expressed most of my acknowledgments in the front matter of the book. Special thanks are due to Mie Caudill, Bela Maday, Bill Douglass, and Valerie Ashenfelter for their role in making the conference not only fruitful for all participants but even enjoyable for the organizers as well. René González of Pan-American Health Organization helped me to integrate the conference with ongoing research on alcohol, also under the auspices of NIAAA.

gation that probably deserve further attention. Many of the topics mentioned only briefly here have been developed in more detail in a complementary article (Heath 1974a) addressed to a more multidisciplinary readership; that article is organized in terms of categories that are familiar to those who work on alcohol and other drugs, regardless of their interest in social science, but it would also be useful to many anthropologists.

INTRODUCTION

There are a number of reasons why anthropologists have paid attention to alcohol[1] over the years, although there can scarcely be said to exist any constituency of specialists or any subdiscipline of "alcohol studies." In the first place, it is obvious that a major portion of the work reflects the importance of alcohol in the lives of the world's peoples and the fact that anthropologists are concerned about what matters to the people among whom they study. The best proof of this is the fact that, almost without exception, ethnographic descriptions of drinking[2] patterns have been unexpected by-products of broadly conceived research, rather than reflecting a sharply focused collection of data or testing of hypotheses. Virtually none of the anthropologists whose publications are cited here went to the field with the intention of studying drinking; many, like myself, discovered the importance of our data on alcohol only in the course of analyzing the wealth of diverse data that we had collected. (An important difference between academic generations deserves mention in this context: during the 1970's a number of colleagues have begun specifically to study drinking and several such works are forthcoming.)

Although it has rarely been articulated in these terms, it seems plausible that some special importance attaches to alcohol as the best known and most widely used means of altering human consciousness. It is a natural product and fermentation occurs throughout most of the inhabited

---

[1]   It is probably common knowledge that no people normally drink pure alcohol. Throughout this paper I will use the terms "alcohol," "alcoholic beverages," and "beverage alcohol" interchangeably to refer to drinks in customary usage with whatever distinguishable concentration of ethanol.

[2]   Throughout this paper, as in much of the writing on alcohol, it is a convenient convention to use the word "drinking" not only in the generic sense but also to stand for the more precise but cumbersome phrase "drinking of alcoholic beverages."

world in milk, fruits, vegetables, honey, sap, and other substances that are common. Because of this, it is relatively simple and inexpensive to produce in substantial quantities. Furthermore, alcohol is a food (in the technical sense that it affords calories), but it contains no vitamins, minerals, or other nutrients; however, alcohol does often occur in flavorful association with highly nutritional foods. When used in moderation, it is readily oxidized in the human body and does no lasting damage. In short, there is little reason to wonder why it has, throughout history, been the world's most popular drug.

Despite its widespread natural occurrence, alcohol is almost universally subject to rules and regulations unlike those that pertain to other drinks. Not only are there usually special rules about alcoholic beverages, but the rules tend to have a peculiarly emotional charge. This affective quality relates not only to drinking, but also to drunkenness and drunken comportment. Whether predominant feelings about these are positive, negative, or ambivalent varies from culture to culture, but indifference is rare, and feelings are usually much stronger in connection with alcohol than with respect to other things.

A superficially attractive rationale for studying alcohol in cross-cultural perspective might be the presumption that it offers a degree of control over variables that is rare in behavioral research outside of the laboratory. Unfortunately, reality is much more complex than many imagine. Contrary to popular belief, alcohol is NOT a chemically simple substance and its biophysiological effects on the human body are by no means uniform in detail. It does, however, provide a useful common denominator in the sense that physical reactions to substantial amounts of alcohol are visible and tend to be categorized as distinctive, regardless of how they are evaluated in a particular sociocultural context.

Although feeling runs high, and rules are almost universal, there is little consistency — and even considerable contradiction — among human populations with respect to what feelings and rules are appropriate with respect to drinking, drunkenness, drunken behavior, or even the drunken individual.

For these reasons, the ethnological view has special relevance, with emphasis on a cross-cultural perspective that features controlled comparison of variables as they occur in sociocultural systems throughout time and space. The anthropological approach to the world as a "natural laboratory" has many shortcomings, but it probably comes as near to approximating "the experimental method" as is feasible in dealing with human populations.

RELATIONS TO OTHER PERSPECTIVES

In a sense, alcohol studies constitute an area of concern where multidisciplinary perspectives, and even interdisciplinary collaboration, might be thought to be "natural" or even indispensable. Alcoholic beverages are substances that yield pertinent data, whether they are analyzed in terms of food value, simple ethanol content, or even trace-element composition. These physical factors influence the effects which the beverages have on a drinker both immediately and over a period of many years. Physiology, neurology, and other realms of human biology can offer fruitful insights into the effects of various beverages, various amounts or rates of ingestion, and so forth. Psychology should be able to contribute to our understanding of why people drink, or why they don't drink, or why they drink as they do, and why some who drink similar amounts in similar ways may react very differently, and so forth. Sociological analysis of particular customary drinking patterns or institutions associated with alcohol seems important, especially in view of the fact that drinking is usually primarily a social act and, to a remarkable degree, attitudes and actions associated with drinking are learned and shared within human groups.

In this context, I use the term "anthropological perspectives" in a broad sense, subsuming the wide range of methodological approaches and topical concerns that are included in "anthropology" as that term is used in most North American universities — that is, including cultural and social anthropology, ethnography and ethnology, physical anthropology, archaeology, folklore, and linguistics.

The anthropological emphasis on human groups has tended in recent years to presume regularity within the species with respect to biological and physiological states, potentials, and mechanisms. This has long set ethnographic studies apart from the casual observations of many journalists, administrators, missionaries, and other travelers who have tended to posit "racial" differences as fundamental and causal with respect to many kinds of behavioral and attitudinal variations they observed among human populations. As will be noted below, we may have to temper our rejection of this conventional wisdom somewhat, especially with respect to the "firewater myth." My discussion of anthropological perspectives on alcohol studies therefore emphasizes differences among human populations, without including the full range of physiological, neurological, biochemical, and other "physical" aspects that have to do with the reaction of alcohol on the human body.

Similarly, although many anthropologists have long spoken with considerable pride — whether justifiably or not — about the holistic concerns of their discipline, few would claim universal expertise, even within the behavioral sciences. Academic disciplines are social conventions, to be sure, and no profession has a monopoly on any given subject matter or on conceptual or other approaches to understanding. Nevertheless, there are significant differences — in terms of general emphases — between the perspectives of anthropologists and other social scientists.

In common with psychology, for example, there is a concern with motivations, personality, character, and similar features — but the anthropological perspective tends to focus on understanding the mode and range of variation within a population, rather than emphasizing the idiosyncratic features of individuals or life trajectories.

In common with sociology, there is a concern with social groups, categories, and norms, and there are also similar methods, theories, and units of analysis — but the anthropological perspective tends to focus on nonliterate and other non-Western societies and on peasant components of Western societies. During recent years, an increasing number of anthropologists have studied modern urban systems, including their own; the contrast is that few sociologists have studied other kinds of systems.

In common with history and classics, there is a concern with attempting to understand what happened in the past, using a variety of documents, both written and unwritten, together with numerous other kinds of evidence — but the anthropological perspective tends to focus on nonliterate and non-Western groups, or on the "grass roots" portions of more complex societies, people whose workday lives are not otherwise depicted.

In common with other linguists and philologists, anthropological linguists are concerned with the form, meaning, and history of verbal and other forms of communication — but the anthropological perspective tends to focus on unwritten languages of primitive peoples and argots, slang, or common usages that rarely attract the attention of many other scholars.

There are of course many and exciting exceptions to each of the stereotypical statements in the previous paragraphs, but the contrasts made between typically anthropological concerns and those of other disciplines have a reality in terms of what people who call themselves anthropologists are doing. They reflect the aptness of Kluckhohn's characterization of anthropology as "the science of leftovers."

The admittedly traditional bias that is reflected in this characterization of "anthropological perspectives" should not be construed as reflecting my view of what is most important or most promising in terms of teaching and research, but rather as a rough outline of the parameters that seem relevant to an understanding of the interrelations of anthropology and alcohol studies in historical perspective. In the course of summarily reviewing what has been done over the years in terms of the traditional anthropological emphases, I will also point out significant areas in which interdisciplinary collaboration has already been effected, and some of the approaches from other fields that appear to hold special promise for arriving at a fuller and better understanding of the manifold patterns of belief and behavior that cluster around alcohol.

AN HISTORICAL PERSPECTIVE

Whenever one attempts to comprehend what people have thought about a given topic, one of the most effective ways to start is by ranging the available records in roughly chronological sequence and attempting to discern themes or patterns that conveniently characterize the material at various periods. Obviously, this is a highly impressionistic procedure; it would be difficult to explain consistently and rigorously the processes of discrimination that are involved and so it would be fallacious to try to justify or defend the relevance (much less the validity) of such an enterprise. Nevertheless, it has proven to be of heuristic and pedagogical value, so the following chronological outline of anthropological studies of alcohol is offered as a simple expository and descriptive tool. I have found it helpful as a pioneering attempt at surveying this broad and varied literature, and hope that others may also.

Before 1850

Alcohol has long been a subject to which people paid special attention and about which some people wrote, in both descriptive and evaluative terms. Though few of the things written before 1850 could be called "anthropological" in any meaningful sense, many of them constitute relevant source material which lends itself to discussion in terms of the concepts and approaches of the discipline. In general, I refer to a few scattered descriptions of "exotic" drinking patterns and a larger corpus of rules about drinking that demonstrate how long alcohol has been subject to special regulations.

There are many who call Tacitus "the father of ethnography," and some would even say that his generalizations about drinking patterns among the Teutonic/Germanic peoples still ring true today. Among the earliest Egyptian papyri, a father's counsel to his son includes a warning that too much beer might prompt him to say things he would regret. More than 4,000 years ago, the Code of Hammurabi included such consumer-protection features as price controls and standard measures for drinks as well as regulations for wine sellers. Pliny listed 116 wines encountered in his travels and noted that beer was the commonplace beverage of "barbarians." Darius, Phillip, and Alexander of Macedon were notorious alcoholics and Tiberius Claudius Nero earned the nickname "Biberius" — all at a time when watered wine was the typical beverage of all classes of people. The role of wine in religion was widespread and the fact that prescriptions and proscriptions are spelled out in considerable detail implies early recognition of the values and dangers of alcohol.

Spokesmen of the so-called "great religions" have been no more consistent in their concern with alcohol than have secular leaders. Ascetic Protestantism is a recent phenomenon; there are some rules but no negative statements about alcohol in the Bible. Similarly, in Islam the prescription of abstinence postdates the Koran, but sectarian variation has developed over the centuries with respect to this as well as other forms of behavior.

For material on drinking prior to 1850, an incredibly rich fund of primary sources remains to be exploited. A few secondary articles which reflect the quality and range of data that are available include the following. Some of the material on ancient Egypt and the Near East has been synthesized by Crothers (1903), Cornwall (1939), Modi (1888); with reference to ancient India an abundant literature has been reviewed by Mitra (1873), Prakash (1961), and Ravi-Varma (1950), among others. A variety of studies on classical circum-Mediterranean antiquity are available in Rolleston (1927) and McKinlay (all works listed); Biblical and old Jewish patterns are described and analyzed by many scholars, including Danielou (1949), Fenasse (1964), Goodenough (1956), Keller (1970), Jastrow (1913), and Raymond (1927).

The accounts of missionaries are often rich in descriptive detail; this refers not only to "fundamentalist" Protestants who were scandalized by sensual indulgence, but also to Jesuits, Franciscans, and a wide range of others whose reports often convey alarm in an almost academic and objective tone. As early as 1639, Archbishop Cardenas threatened to excommunicate anyone who sold alcoholic beverages to Indians in his episcopate in Peru (cited in de Lejarza 1941); the *Jesuit relations* have been searched systematically for data on drinking among Indians in northeastern North America (Dailey 1968). Early compilations that might be considered regional ethnohistories of alcohol were written by missionaries (e.g. Wheeler 1839; de Belmont 1840).

Other positive contributions to alcohol studies prior to 1850 include Kant's functional interpretation of the already remarkable sobriety of Jews (1798), calling it in effect a collective defense in the face of pre-existing prejudice. Few other attempts were made at analyzing alien drinking patterns, but historical and worldwide descriptive summaries were compiled early (e.g. Medical Practitioner 1830; Morewood 1838).

1850–1899

From the middle of the nineteenth century, occasional authors offer what might be considered "anthropological perspectives" on alcohol studies in the broad sense discussed here. A few more ethnological and ethnohistorical surveys of drinking patterns were compiled, some with ambitiously worldwide scope, others attempting to relate contemporary patterns to classical or primitive antecedants. These are generally "armchair scholarship," representing enormous library research but providing little detailed documentation of specific behavior.

Despite these limitations, these early efforts are noteworthy for the degree to which some attempt to relate the data on drinking to a broader conceptual context. For example, Buckland's (1878) brief survey is not just a pastiche of "quaint and curious customs"; in discussing methods of preparation, he suggests what we might now call a naively diffusionistic view and he also proposes a grand evolutionary scheme. Eddy's title (1887) might lead some to dismiss the book, unseen, as just a temperance tract, but it is an unusually detailed and well-documented survey of the role of alcohol in various cultures. Bourke offers an ethnographic description of Mexican Indian distillation (1893) and argues for its pre-Columbian antiquity (1894). The conclusion in an historical review of drunkenness and its cures has a curiously timely ring: "treat him as a patient labouring under a baffling and inveterate disease" (Brown 1898: 297).

1900–1924

In the first quarter of the twentieth century, a few colonial administrators and health officers wrote truly ethnographic studies which included abundant information on alcohol in contemporary primitive cultures within their jurisdictions, often emphasizing technology and/or ritual. Historical and ethnographic surveys continued and a few incipient "review articles" appeared. As before, the intellectual climate of the times is reflected in alcohol studies.

An encyclopedic compilation by Emerson (1908) is richly detailed but lacks citation of sources. A.E. Crawley (1912) was similarly summary; Bose (1922) traced historical and scriptural references to wine in ancient India; and Crothers (1903) dealt with Egypt and Chaldea.

Harford's (1905) title is misleading inasmuch as he compiled survey data only from Africa and India. Ray (1906), Vanderyst (1920), and Roth (1912) reported in considerable detail on methods of manufacture that they observed in various areas; the symbolic and ritual uses and meanings of alcohol beverages in several cultures were described by Kircher (1910) and Jochelson (1906), who also reflected the contemporary concern with *materiel* in his detailed comments on wooden drinking vessels; and by Preuss (1910) who also recorded songs.

Cheinisse's (1908) espousal of Durkheim's *anomie* as a "cause" of alcoholism led him to wonder about Jewish "immunity"; Feldman (1923) offered one of the earliest discussions of various theories about differential rates of alcoholism and opposed the eugenicists' plea that alcoholics be banned from having children.

1925–1934

During this decade, the emphases did not differ significantly from those of the previous twenty-five years, except that there was more attention paid to the scholarly conventions of reporting and citing one's sources of data, and a few efforts appeared which came close to modern standards of historical and ethnographic writing.

Cherrington's multi-volume encyclopedia (1925–30) is an ambitious compilation including much of anthropological relevance. The *Kulturkreis* approach is reflected in Seekirchner's (1931) survey of African drinking. A couple of studies of Indian-white relations in the United States paid special attention to the role of alcohol (MacLeod 1928; Frederikson 1932).

One study of this period, Hellman's (1934) study of beer brewing in a South African "native yard," is remarkable on several counts. It is an early effort in "urban anthropology"; the positive and negative aspects of drinking are weighed equally; the role of ethnicity in a multitribal setting is analyzed; and the significance of women's roles is clearly specified in sociocultural context.

Following the repeal of Prohibition, people in the United States began to recognize that it is legitimate to discuss alcohol without moralizing or being preoccupied with trying to ameliorate social problems. A number of alcoholics "came out of the closet" with the founding of Alcoholics Anonymous. The Yale Center of Alcohol Studies was established and brought together experts in several disciplines in a context that moved toward mutually fruitful collaboration and lent a new air of scientific, academic respectability to work with alcohol and alcoholics. Throughout the world, a variety of more sophistocated social science approaches were brought to bear on beliefs and behavior centering on alcohol.

The volume of relevant literature expanded significantly during this period, so that I will mention only a small sample of the books and articles which were selected to include those which have had a lasting impact on alcohol studies and also a few that offer unusual perspectives.

One of the latter is Banks' account of drinking among five different tribes on Sarawak (1937); one of the earliest comparative studies based on observation, it shows a striking gradient in frequency of drinking and drunkenness. La Barre's (1938) survey of native American beers combines typological and culture-area approaches; one of the most ambitious efforts at reconstructing historical trait distributions is Bruman's (1940) delineation of drink-areas in New Spain.

Bunzel's (1940) pioneering study comparing patterns in Chamula (Mexico) and Chichicastenango (Guatemala) set a new standard for ethnographic reporting in terms of showing how alcohol relates to the broader sociocultural context. This paper has broader importance in anthropology — in terms of systematic approach using what later came to be called "controlled comparison" and her explicit integration of psychoanalytic concepts and discussion of child-rearing practice — with respect to the adult institutions. It is important to keep in mind (as she describes elsewhere in this volume) that she never set out to study "alcohol" or "drinking" as such, but that this milestone contribution was merely a by-product of her profound concern with understanding human behavior. She anticipated many of the key questions that have subsequently been raised with respect to drinking in non-Western cultures: the relation of drunken behavior to personality, the relation of social structure to child training, the disruptive (or dysfunctional) consequences of drinking as well as the positive functions that it serves, and so forth.

S. D. Bacon (1943) offered guidelines for a sociological approach to alcohol which serve as well for anthropologists. The role of cultural ambivalence in relation to problem drinking was stressed by Myerson (1940a) in ways that have subsequently been somewhat elaborated (e.g. by Mizruchi and Perrucci 1962; E. Blacker 1966) but not significantly discredited.

At this time also, the Cross-Cultural Survey (subsequently Human Relations Area Files) was organized at Yale University by Murdock and his associates as an imaginative and ambitious compendium of data on the human experience throughout space and time. One of those rare instances when a doctoral dissertation had a broad impact within an academic discipline occurred when a student of sociology used the Survey to test a few simple hypotheses about the interrelations of psychological factors and cultural patterns. In terms of alcohol studies, the published version of his thesis gained immediate notoriety because of his straightforward and unequivocal conclusion that "...*the primary function of alcoholic beverages in all societies is the reduction of anxiety*" (Horton 1943:223; emphasis in original). In terms of anthropology, the effort was also important as the first large-scale "cross-cultural" (or "hologeistic") study in which statistical analysis of the correlation of particular cultural features in a large sample of sociocultural systems was used to test explicit "theorems." Horton's contribution has so often been condensed, abridged, and summarized that more about it shall not be repeated here, except to note that Margaret Bacon's paper elsewhere in this volume very aptly characterizes many of the ways in which it was misunderstood and unjustly criticized; a self-styled "third generation" of students interested in refining what is now called "the hologeistic method" has also justifiably pointed out a variety of misjudgments in that pioneering effort.

1945–1954

The increased pace and sophistication of social science research that followed World War II is reflected, in part, in anthropological contributions to alcohol studies. A few cultural anthropologists offered fairly detailed descriptions of drinking patterns in various parts of the world; many of the articles show an increasing emphasis on the cultural context and analysis of meanings.

Bales's (1946) comparison of Irish and Jewish patterns of alcohol use and alcoholism went beyond description of customs, including a typology of attitudes toward alcohol and a sociocultural interpretation of excessive drinking. Both the typology and the interpretation have been used — often with only minor adaptation — by many authors with reference to a wide variety of groups around the world.

The importance of cultural variation became increasingly recognized by people other than anthropologists, especially as the World Health Organization (1951, 1952) wrestled with the thorny problem of attempting to define "alcoholism" in a way that would be meaningful among the various member states of the United Nations. Anderson, et al. (1946) introduced an historical perspective in looking at drinking in nonliterate societies; and distributional studies on a continental scale were offered by Driver (1961) for North America and by Cooper (1949) for South America.

Psychoanalytic perspectives became more fully integrated with structural-functional approaches during these years (e.g. Devereux 1948; Viqueira and Palerm 1954). Non-Western literate peoples were studied by anthropological methods (e.g. Yamamuro 1954; Barnett 1955; Carstairs 1954); Carstairs's contribution is also useful in exploring relations of alcohol to other drugs and different drinking patterns among castes within a community in India. The *American Anthropologist* carried a symposium with the titillating, but not wholly representative title, "Did man live by beer alone?" (Braidwood, et al. 1953).

1955–1959

The output of publications on alcohol, using anthropological perspectives, gained momentum; it was twice as great during these five years as in the preceding decade and a few books appeared that focused on drinking in sociocultural context. More anthropologists undertook to describe and interpret drinking patterns in several areas and comparisons of different ethnic groups within pluralistic communities became more commonplace. Time-depth was also more often introduced than was the case in previous works on the topic.

In a sense, review articles by Trice and Pittman (1958) and by Ullman (1958) signaled that sociocultural approaches had clearly become accepted as relevant to the understanding of alcoholism. Lolli, et al. (1958) used an unusual combination of research methods to get data on the relation of alcohol to total diet among a large sample of Italians and Italian-Americans; Snyder (1958) reviewed Jewish sobriety. Among the first to show sustained cross-cultural interest in alcohol studies were Lemert (in Oceania and northwestern North America), the Honigmanns (in Arctic

America), Jellinek, and a few others; Popham and Bruun strove, from different starting points, to demonstrate the complementarity of socio-logical and anthropological approaches.

More rigorous historical studies appeared during this period (e.g. Goodenough 1956; Hoffman 1956); an unusual effort in ethnohistory was the analysis of the role of pulque as depicted in Mexican codices (Gonçalves de Lima ca. 1956). An anthology by McCarthy (1959) includes a considerable amount of anthropological material; Lemert's work (1956, 1958, 1962, 1964a, 1964b, 1965, 1967, 1969) combines solid ethno-graphic reporting with conceptualizing about deviance. Social organiza-tion is a focus of many studies (e.g. Berreman 1956; Pozas Arciniegos 1957; Heath 1958; Simmons 1959; and others). A wide variety of other studies provides insights into many important topics, such as small group dynamics (Bruun 1959), alcohol as a means of achieving religious experi-ence (Carpenter 1959), distribution of technology (Hartmann 1958), drunkenness in relation to acculturation stress (Hawthorn, et al. 1957).

1960–1964

The volume of publications on anthropology and alcohol doubled again during this period, including a couple of anthologies on alcohol which are heavily anthropological in content. The *American Anthropologist* published a symposium on alcohol and culture (Spindler 1964) and the range of methods and concepts applied to the subject continued to ex-pand markedly.

The Tri-Ethnic Research Project at the University of Colorado in-troduced an unprecedented degree of methodological rigor and con-ceptual specificity in comparing drinking (and other forms of deviant behavior) in a study of Spanish-American, Anglo-American, and Ute groups in the southwestern U.S.; a number of preliminary papers issued during these years were influential although the monograph did not ap-pear until 1968 (Jessor, et al. 1968).

Horton's cross-cultural methods were tested and sharpened by Field (1962:58), who emphasized features of social organization: "...drunkenness in primitive societies is determined less by the level of fear in a society than by the absence of corporate kin groups with stabil-ity, permanence, formal structure, and well-defined functions." Klaus-ner (1964) also used the cross-cultural correlational approach (in an ad-mittedly statistically unsophisticated manner), with a very different con-clusion, emphasizing religious symbolism.

Increasingly during this period, attention was paid to change, not merely in long-term historical perspective, but also in terms of acculturation and short-term variation in drinking practices and beliefs (e.g. Madsen 1964; Leis 1964; Heath 1965; Whittaker 1962–1963; and others). Not only did people look at the ways in which customary drinking patterns change in context of cultural contact; but acculturation was often cited as a causal factor in excessive drinking. For some observers the concern was with "cultural stress," with others the crucial problem was "cultural deprivation"; a few even referred to "anomie."

Frake's (1964) essay brought componential analysis into the wide variety of anthropological tools used to look at alcohol around the world. More studies emphasized the significance of ambivalence in predisposing people toward having problems with alcohol (e.g. Mizruchi and Perrucci 1962). McCord, et al. (1960), on the basis of long-term studies of individual life trajectories, proposed that conflict over dependency is crucial in the etiology of alcoholism; Barry, Bacon, and Child found strong cross-cultural support for that view (M. Bacon, et al. 1965a, 1965b, Barry, et al. 1965, and Child, et al. 1965a, 1965b).

A book by Washburne (1961) brought together data on drinking in a number of primitive societies; the anthology compiled by Pittman and Snyder (1962) introduced the cultural perspective to a much broader readership, while Roueché's popular account (1960) may have served to correct a few of the widespread misconceptions about alcohol among intelligent laymen.

The volume of relevant material published during this period was so great that any sampling must omit some excellent contributions, but among the outstanding sources with an anthropological perspective are, among others, du Toit on acculturation (1964), unusually comprehensive analyses of how alcohol fits with other aspects of culture (Kennedy 1963; Sangree 1962; Netting 1964; and others), Lemert's continuing (1962, 1964a, 1964b, 1965, 1967, 1969) contributions on a variety of forms and meanings of drinking among several groups in Oceania and Jellinek's (1960) wide-ranging treatise.

1965–1969

Three unrelated events could each be interpreted, in a sense, as signalling that alcohol had reached a degree of acceptance as a topic for anthropological research during the late 1960's — or that anthropological data and approaches had reached a degree of acceptance as pertinent to alcohol studies. None of these events was so construed at the time, I am sure, but it is striking to note, in this kind of historical perspective, that 1965 saw the publication of an article on "Alcohol and culture" in *Current Anthropology* (Mandelbaum, et al. 1965), with "CA treatment" by discussants. Also in that year, a special supplement to the *Quarterly Journal of Studies on Alcohol* was devoted to the cross-cultural research on drinking of Child, et al. (1965a, 1965b), M. Bacon, et al. (1965a, 1965b), and Barry, et al. (1965). The third event was the publication of a substantial bibliography on culture and alcohol studies (Popham and Yawney 1966), with a revised edition only a year later.

The literature on anthropological perspectives about alcohol continued to proliferate and to reflect a variety of new approaches as well as some refinement of traditional ones. A symposium on drinking in Latin America was organized by Dobyns at the American Association for the Advancement of Science meetings; anthropologists engaged in collaborative research on drinking patterns in a variety of contexts (e.g. Ferguson, all works listed; Kunitz, et al. 1969; Levy, et al. 1969; Graves, all works listed). MacAndrew and Edgerton (1969) imaginatively used ethnographic and ethnohistorical sources to demonstrate convincingly that drunken comportment is learned; they also provided a global hypothesis that drunkenness may be useful in providing "time out" from normal social expectations. McClelland, et al. were publishing the research, using a variety of methods, that subsequently (1972) was compiled as a unitary formulation about drinking in very different terms, emphasizing the value of alcohol in making men feel powerful.

Chafetz and Demone (1962) revised their popular book on alcoholism with more emphasis on sociocultural dimensions. Cavan (1966) applied fieldwork techniques to the description and analysis of behavior in urban American bars. A number of ethnographic studies in other parts of the world incorporated discussions of change (e.g. Hamer 1965; Honigmann and Honigmann 1968; Lomnitz 1969a); interethnic relations (e.g. Hurt and Brown 1965; Ogan 1966; Lurie 1971) and even proxemics (Csikszentmihalyi 1968). Pittman's (1967) anthology is heavily anthropological as are Reader's (1967) and E. Blacker's (1966) impressive review articles. As is the case with reference to the previous decades, I should emphasize that the small sample of specific citations that occur in this text necessarily omits a number of excellent contributions; the appended list of references should be studied by interested students, inasmuch as it includes a number of books and articles that are not discussed in this brief historical sketch.

1970's

The increasing recognition of the mutual relevance of anthropology and alcohol studies is forcefully attested by this volume and by the conference from which it grew. At the conference, it became clear that among a new generation of anthropologists, a few have even set out with the intention of studying beliefs and behaviors connected with alcohol, using a variety of techniques. Their works are forthcoming (e.g. Everett, Waddell, Schaefer, and Topper).

Beyond the academic realm, a variety of new approaches to alcohol have been undertaken by the National Institute of Alcohol Abuse and Alcoholism, within the U.S. Department of Health, Education, and Welfare. The Institute is funding research but it is also active in several ventures that have not been tried on a large scale before. Among these, for example, is a comprehensive "clearinghouse" service which significantly facilitates communication about alcohol and widespread educational programs through mass media. With respect to ethnic groups within this diverse country, NIAAA has also helped in the establishment of a number of experimental programs for prevention and treatment of alcoholism, using personnel and approaches of the individual "subculture" treatment groups (especially Indian tribes).

Instead of attempting to summarize the exciting developments of this period, it seems appropriate to just mention a few of the new directions. Linguistic analysis, in relation to cognitive categories, is being rigorously applied (e.g. Hage 1972; Spradley 1970; Topper, this volume). Epidemiological approaches yield unforeseen cross-national uniformities (de Lint, Schmidt) and hologeistic (cross-cultural correlational) studies on alcohol are being used on a large scale (Schaefer, this volume). Further studies of alcoholics and of social problems in other cultures are being provided, as well as new applications of anthropological approaches (cf. Kunitz, Levy, Ferguson, and others).

Controversy over the social responsibility of scholars is swirling around the revival of the "firewater myth." It has long been a widespread piece of folk wisdom that Indians and other Mongoloids have a lower tolerance to alcohol and react to it more strongly. That bit of folk wisdom, however, has been generally rejected by scientists throughout most of the twentieth century. In recent years, however, fragmentary evidence suggests that significant racial differences in the rate of metabolism may exist (e.g. Fenna, this volume; Wolff 1972, 1973). Many anthropologists are alarmed at the degree to which these findings have been adopted by politicians and others; the threat of "racist" reactions has prompted them to express reservations about the publication of such material on the basis of limited data.

The work of McClelland, et al. was revised and brought together (1972) in a volume that provided another universal psychodynamic theory to account for drinking. Through a series of imaginative experiments involving projective tests, content analysis of folklore, role playing, and several other techniques, they muster evidence to support their conclusion

... that the alcoholic experience has a common core for men everywhere and that they drink to get it. While individuals in different cultures embroider and interpret the experience in different ways, and while it is more marked for distilled liquors than for wine or beer, the experience centers everywhere in men on increased thoughts of power which, as drinking progresses, becomes more personal and less socialized and responsible. And societies and individuals with accentuated needs for personalized power are most likely to drink more heavily in order to get the feeling of strength they need so much more than others. (McClelland, et al. 1972: 336).

The complementarity of the "power theory" and the Barry-Bacon-Child "dependency theory" is discussed elsewhere in this volume.

It would be pretentious in this context to project probable lines of research and action that may build upon the interaction of alcohol studies and anthropology; in a very real sense, that is what the rest of this book is about.

SELECTED REFERENCES

In a review of this nature and scope, it seems appropriate to indicate the range of works that were sought out and considered relevant to the broad topic, as well as those that were specifically cited in the text. The following list, then, includes all references used in the preparation of this article, many of which are devoid of conceptual or theoretical content but all of which contribute in some measure to anthropological perspectives on alcohol.

Titles are given in the original language only; place of publication is mentioned for those journals that might be confused with others of the same name, or that might be difficult to locate without such information. For historical purposes, books and articles are cited in their initial publication; in those instances where significant revision has been made, the most recent edition is also indicated. Unauthored articles are alphabetized under the name of the responsible source. A few unpublished sources are listed because they deal with topics or approaches that are not fully represented in the published literature.

In the great majority of cases, references were verified through examination of the original publication; in a few instances, I have seen only copies of the text of the article, so that bibliographic data on the inclusive source may be incomplete. This bibliography was completed in September 1973; I would welcome additional pertinent references.

AALTO, P.
    1955   Alkoholens ställning i Indiens klassiska kultur. *Alkoholopolitik* 18(2):32–46.
ABLON, J.
    1975   "Family behavior and alcoholism," in *Cross-cultural approaches to the study of alcohol: an interdisciplinary perspective.* Edited by M. W. Everett, J. O. Waddell, and D. B. Heath. World Anthropology. The Hague: Mouton.
ADANDÉ, A.
    1954   Le vin de palme chez les Diola de la Casamance. *Notes africaines* 61:4–7. Dakar.
ADLER, NATHAN, DANIEL GOLEMAN
    1969   Gambling and alcoholism: symptom substitution and functional equivalents. *Quarterly Journal of Studies on Alcohol* 30:733–736.
ADRIAENS, S.-L., F. LOZET
    1951   Contribution à l'étude des boissons fermentées indigenes au Ruanda. *Bulletin agricole du Congo belge* 42:933–950.
AGUILAR, GERMAN Z.
    1964   Suspension of control: a sociocultural study on specific drinking habits and their psychiatric consequences. *Journal of Existential Psychiatry* 4:245–252.
AHLFORS, U. G.
    1969   *Alcohol and conflict: a qualitative and quantitative study on the relationship between alcohol consumption and an experimentally induced conflict situation in albino rats.* Alcohol Research in Northern Countries 16. Helsinki: Finnish Foundation for Alcohol Studies.
AIYAPPAN, A.
    n.d.   "Alcohol and anxiety in Orissa, India." *Alcohol Science and Society.*
    1945   *Journal of Studies on Alcohol.* New Haven, Connecticut.
ALHAVA, A.
    1949   Väkijuomaolojen erikoisluonne Lapíssa. *Alkoholiliikkeen Aikakauskirja* 12:35–37.
ALLARDT, ERIK
    1956   Alkoholvanorna på landsbygden i Finland. *Alkoholpolitik* 19:73–77.
    1957   "Drinking norms and drinking habits," in *Drinking and drinkers.* Edited by E. Allardt, et al. Finnish Foundation for Alcohol Studies 6. Helsinki.
ALLARDT, E., et al.
    1957   *Drinking for drinkers.* Finnish Foundation for Alcohol Studies 6. Helsinki.

ALMEIDA, V. MANUEL
1962   Investigacíon clínica sobre la evolución del alcoholismo. *Revista de Neuro-psiquiatría* 25:97–122. Lima.

América Indígena
1954   El alcohol y el indio. *América Indígena* 14:283–285.

AMERICAN MEDICAL ASSOCIATION
1956   *Manual on alcoholism.* Chicago: American Medical Association. (Revised edition 1967.)

ANDERSON, BARBARA G.
1969   How French children learn to drink. *Transaction* 5:20–22.

ANDERSON, R. K., J. CALVO, G. SERRANO, G. PAYNE
1946   A study of the nutritional status and food habits of Otomi Indians in the Mezquital Valley of Mexico. *American Journal of Public Health* 36:883–903.

ANDO, HARUHIKO, ETSUKO HASEGAWA
1970   Drinking patterns and attitudes of alcoholics and nonalcoholics in Japan. *Quarterly Journal of Studies on Alcohol* 31:153–161.

ANGROSINO, MICHAEL V.
1974   *Outside is death. Alcoholism, ideology and community organization among the East Indians of Trinidad.* Wake Forest University, Overseas Research Center, Medical Behavioral Science Monograph. Winston-Salem, N.C.

ARRIOLA, JORGE LUÍS
1962   "Introducción al estudio (del) alcoholismo como problema social," in *Primera reunión regional centroamericana sobre alcoholismo.* Guatemala: Patronato Antialcohólico de Guatemala.

AUERSPERG, A. P., A. DERWORT
1962   Beitrag zur vergleichenden Psychiatrie exogener Psychosen vom soziokulturellen Standpunkt. *Nervenarzt* 33:22–27.

BACON, MARGARET K., HERBERT BARRY, III, IRVIN L. CHILD
1965   A cross-cultural study of drinking, II: Relations to other features of culture. *Quarterly Journal of Studies on Alcohol*, supplement 3:29–48.

BACON, MARGARET K., HERBERT BARRY, III, IRVIN CHILD, CHARLES R. SNYDER
1965   A cross-cultural study of drinking, V: Detailed definitions and data. *Quarterly Journal of Studies on Alcohol*, supplement 3:78–111.

BACON, SELDEN D.
1943   Sociology and the problems of alcohol: foundations for a sociological study of drinking behavior. *Quarterly Journal of Studies on Alcohol* 4:399–445.
1945   "Alcohol and complex society," in *Alcohol, science, and society. Journal of Studies on Alcohol.* New Haven. (Revised in 1962 in *Society, culture, and drinking patterns.* Edited by David J. Pittman and Charles R. Snyder. New York: John Wiley and Sons.)
1955   Current research on alcoholism, V. Report on the section on sociological research. *Quarterly Journal of Studies on Alcohol* 16:551–564.

1958   *Understanding alcoholism.* Annals of the Academy of Political and Social Science 315. Philadelphia.
1973   The process of addiction to alcohol: social aspects. *Quarterly Journal of Studies on Alcohol* 34:1–27.

BADDELEY, FELIX J.
1966   "African beerhalls." Unpublished thesis, School of Architecture, University of Cape Town.

BAIRD, E. G.
1944–1948   The alcohol problem and the law. *Quarterly Journal of Studies on Alcohol* 4:535–556; 5:126–161; 6:335–383; 7:110–162, 271–296; 9:80–118.

BAKER, JAMES L.
1959   Indians, alcohol and homicide. *Journal of Social Therapy* 5:270–275.

BALDUS, H.
1950   Bebidas e narcóticos dos índios do Brasil: sugestões para pesquisas etnográficas. *Sociologia* 12:161–169. São Paulo.

BALES, ROBERT F.
1946   Cultural differences in rates of alcoholism. *Quarterly Journal of Studies on Alcohol* 6:480–499.

BANAY, RALPH S.
1945   Cultural influences in alcoholism. *Journal of Nervous and Mental Diseases* 102:265–275.

BANKS, E.
1937   Native drink in Sarawak. *Sarawak Museum Journal* 4:439–447.

BARD, JEFFREY, CHRISTOPHER MARE, CHARLES WILLIAMS, IVAN WOLPAW
1955   "Effect of intra-group competition on alcohol consumption in primitive cultures." Unpublished manuscript.

BARNETT, MILTON L.
1955   "Alcoholism in the Cantonese of New York City: an anthropological study," in *Etiology of chronic alcoholism.* Edited by O. Diethelm. Springfield: Charles Thomas.

BARRERA VÁSQUEZ, A.
1941   El pulque entre los mayas. *Cuadernos Mayas* 3. Mérida, Mexico.

BARRY, HERBERT, III
1968   Sociocultural aspects of addiction. *The Addictive States* 46:455–471.

BARRY, H., III, CHARLES BUCHWALD, IRVIN L. CHILD, MARGARET K. BACON
1965   A cross-cultural study of drinking, IV: Comparisons with Horton ratings. *Quarterly Journal of Studies on Alcohol,* supplement 3: 62–77.

BEALS, RALPH I.
1932   *The comparative ethnology of northern Mexico before 1750.* Berkeley: University of California Press.

BEAUBRUN, MICHAEL H.
1967   Treatment of alcoholism in Trinidad and Tobago, 1956–1965. *British Journal of Psychiatry* 113:643–658.
1968   Alcoholism and drinking practices in a Jamaican suburb. *Alcoholism* 4:21–37.

1971 "The influence of socio-cultural factors in the treatment of alcoholism in the West Indies," in *29th International Congress on Alcoholism and Drug Dependence*. Edited by L. G. Kiloh and D. S. Bell. Sydney, Australia: Butterworths.

BEAUBRUN, MICHAEL H., HEDY FIRTH
1969 "A transcultural analysis of Alcoholics Anonymous: Trinidad/London." Paper presented at the meeting of the American Psychiatric Association, Ocho Rios, Jamaica.

BEIDELMAN, THOMAS O.
1961 Beer drinking and cattle theft in Ukaguru: intertribal relations in a Tanganyika chiefdom. *American Anthropologist* 63:534–549.

BEJARANO, JORGE
1950 *La derrota de un vicio: origen e historia de la chicha*. Bogotá: Iqueima.

BELLMANN, HERBERT
1954 Die Destillation bei den Naturvölkern. *Wissenschaftliche Zeitschrift der Friedrich Schiller Universität* 3:179–185.

BERNIER, G., A. LAMBRECHT
1960 Etude sur les boissons fermentées indigènes du Katanga. *Problèmes sociaux congolais* 48:5–41.

BERREMAN, GERALD D.
1956 Drinking patterns of the Aleuts. *Quarterly Journal of Studies on Alcohol* 17:503–514.

BETT, W. R., et al.
1946 Alcohol and crime in Ceylon: a preliminary communication [and discussion]. *British Journal of Inebriety* 43:57–60.

BISMUTH, H., C. MENAGE
1960 "Alcoolisation du Niger; . . . du Sénégal; . . . d'Haut Volta; . . . des états de langue française de l'Afrique occidentale; aspects de l'alcoolisation du Dahomey; aperçu de l'alcoolisation de la Guinée." Multigraphed. Paris: Haut Comité d'Etude et d'Information sur l'Alcoolisme.

BLACKER, EDWARD
1966 Sociocultural factors in alcoholism. *International Psychiatry Clinics* 3(2):51–80.

BLACKER, HERETH
1971 Drinking practices and problems abroad: the Isle of Reúnion. *Journal of Alcoholism* 6(2):61–63.

BLEICHSTEINER, ROBERT
1952 Zeremoniale Trinksitten und Raumordnung bei Turko-Mongolischen Nomaden. *Archiv für Völkerkunde* 6–7:181–208.

BLEVANS, STEPHEN A.
1967 "A critical review of the anthropological literature on drinking, drunkenness, and alcoholism." Unpublished M. A. thesis. University of Washington.

BLOCK, MARVIN A.
1965 *Alcoholism: its facets and phases*. New York: John Day.

BLOM, FRANS
1956 On Slotkin's "Fermented drinks in Mexico." *American Anthropologist* 58:185–186.

BLOOM, JOSEPH D.
1970 Socio-cultural aspects of alcoholism. *Alaska Medicine* 12:65–67.

BLUM, RICHARD H., EVA M. BLUM
1964 Drinking practices and controls in rural Greece. *British Journal of Addiction* 60:93–108.

BLYTH, W.
1972 "Transcultural studies in alcoholism in a rural catchment area as pertaining to three cultures: white Americans, American Negroes, American Indians." Multigraphed.

BOALT, GUNNAR
1961 *A sociological theory of alcoholism*. International Bureau Against Alcoholism, Selected Articles 4. Lausanne.

BOSE, DHIRENDRA K.
1922 *Wine in ancient India*. Calcutta: K. M. Connor.

BOURGUIGNON, ERIKA E.
1964 Comment on Leacock's "Ceremonial drinking in an Afro-Brazilian cult." *American Anthropologist* 66:1393–1394.

BOURKE, JOHN G.
1893 Primitive distillation among the Tarascoes. *American Anthropologist*, old series 6:65–69.
1894 Distillation by early American Indians. *American Anthropologist*, old series 7:297–299.

BOYER, L. BRYCE
1964 "Psychological problems of a group of Apaches: alcoholic hallucinosis and latent homosexuality among typical men," in *The psychoanalytic study of society*, volume three. Edited by W. Muensterberger and S. Axelrad. New York: International Universities Press.

BRAIDWOOD, ROBERT J., et al.
1953 Symposium: did man once live by beer alone? *American Anthropologist* 55:515–526.

BRODY, HUGH
1971 *Indians on Skid Row*. Northern Science Research Group. Department of Indian Affairs and Northern Development Publication 70–72. Ottawa.

BROWN, DONALD N.
1967 "Patterns of heavy drinking at Taos Pueblo, New Mexico." Paper presented at Southwestern and Rocky Mountain Division, American Asssociation for the Advancement of Science, Tucson.

BROWN, WILLIAM L.
1898 Inebriety and its "cures" among the ancients. *Proceedings of the Society for the Study of Inebriety* 55:1–15.

BROWNLEE, FRANK
1933 Native beer in South Africa. *Man: Journal of the Royal Anthropological Institute*, old series 33:75–76.

BRUMAN, HENRY J.

1940 "Aboriginal drink areas in New Spain." Unpublished Ph.D. dissertation, University of California.

1944 Asiatic origin of the Huichol Still. *Geographical Review* 34:418–427.

BRUNN, KETTIL

1959 Den sociokulturella backgrunden till alkoholismen. *Alkoholpolitik* 22:54–58.

1959 Significance of role and norms in the small group for individual behavioral changes while drinking. *Quarterly Journal of Studies on Alcohol* 20:53–64.

BRUUN, KETTIL, RAGNAR HANGE

1963 *Drinking habits among northern youths.* Finnish Foundation for Alcohol Studies Publication 12. Helsinki.

BUCKLAND, A. W.

1878 Ethnological hints afforded by the stimulants in use among savages and among the ancients. *Journal of the Royal Anthropological Institute* 8:239–254.

BUCKLEY, JOSEPH, ANGELO P. FURGIULE, MAUREEN J. O'HARE

1967 The pharmacology of kava. *Journal of the Polynesian Society* 76:101–102.

BUNZEL, RUTH

1940 The role of alcoholism in two Central American cultures. *Psychiatry* 3:361–387.

BUSCH, CARLOS E.

1952 Consideraciones médico-sociales sobre la chicha. *Excelsior* 217: 25–26. Lima.

CAGOL, A.

1936 A note on Bapedi beverages. *Primitive Man* 9:32.

CAHALAN, DON, IRA H. CISIN, HELEN M. CROSSLEY

1969 *American drinking practices: a national study of drinking behavior and attitudes.* Rutgers Center of Alcohol Studies Monograph 6. New Brunswick, New Jersey.

CALDERÓN NARVAEZ, GUILLERMO

1968 Consideraciones acerca del alcoholismo entre los pueblos prehispánicos de México. *Revista del Instituto Nacional de Neurología* 2(3):5–13.

CAPPELL, HOWARD, C. PETER HERMAN

1972 Alcohol and tension reduction: a review. *Quarterly Journal of Studies on Alcohol* 33:33–64.

CARPENTER, EDMUND S.

1959 Alcohol in the Iroquois dream quest. *American Journal of Psychiatry* 116:148–151.

CARPENTER, JOHN A., NICHOLAS P. ARMENTI

1972 "Some behavioral effects of alcohol on man," in *The biology of alcoholism*, volume two. Edited by B. Kissin and H. Begleiter. New York: Plenum Press.

CARSTAIRS, G. M.
1954   Daru and bhang: cultural factors in the choice of intoxicant.
Quarterly Journal of Studies on Alcohol 15:220–237.

CAVAN, SHERRI
1966   Liquor license: an ethnography of bar behavior. Chicago: Aldine.

Central African Journal of Medicine
1958   Native liquors in Southern Rhodesia. Central African Journal of
Medicine 4:558–559.

CHAFETZ, MORRIS E.
1964   Consumption of alcohol in the Far and Middle East. New England Journal of Medicine 271:297–301.

CHAFETZ, MORRIS E., HAROLD W. DEMONE, JR.
1962   Alcoholism and society. New York: Oxford University Press.
(Revised edition 1965.)

CHASSOUL, M., CHARLES HEATH, DWIGHT B. HEATH
n.d.   "Research on drinking patterns in several communities of Costa
Rica." In preparation.

CHATTOPADHYAY, A.
1969   The ancient Indian practice of drinking wine with reference to
kathasaritsagara. Journal of the Oriental Institute 18:145–152.
Baroda.

CHEINISSE, L.
1908   La race juine, jouit-elle d'une immunité à l'égard de l'alcoolisme?
Semaine Médicale 28:613–615.

CHERRINGTON, ERNEST H., editor
1925–1930   Standard encyclopedia of the alcohol problem, volumes one
to six. Westerville, Ohio: American Issue.

CHILD, IRVIN L., MARGARET K. BACON, HERBERT BARRY, III
1965a   A cross-cultural study of drinking, I: descriptive measurements
of drinking customs. Quarterly Journal of Studies on Alcohol,
supplement 3:1–28.

CHILD, IRVIN L., HERBERT BARRY, III, MARGARET K. BACON
1965b   A cross-cultural study of drinking, III: sex differences. Quarterly
Journal of Studies on Alcohol, supplement 3:49–61.

CHOPRA, R. N., G. S. CHOPRA, J. C. CHOPRA
1942   Alcoholic beverages in India. Indian Medical Gazette 77:224–232,
290–296, 361–367.

CHU, GEORGE
1972   Drinking patterns and attitudes of rooming-house Chinese in San
Francisco. Quarterly Journal of Studies on Alcohol, supplement
6:58–68.

CINQUEMANI, DOROTHY K.
n.d.   "Research on drinking and alcoholism in Middle America." In
preparation.

CLAIRMONT, DONALD H.
1962   Notes on the drinking behavior of the Eskimos and Indians in the
Aklavik area: a preliminary report. Ottawa: Northern Coordination and Research Centre, Department of Northern Affairs and
National Resources.

1963   *Deviance among Indians and Eskimos in Aklavik.* Ottawa: Northern Coordination and Research Centre, Department of Northern Affairs and National Resources.

CLAUDIAN, J.
1970   "History of the usage of alcohol," in *International encyclopedia of pharmacology and therapeutics,* section twenty, volume two. Edited by J. Tremolières. Oxford: Pergamon Press.

CLEMMESEN, C.
1958   Oversigt over alkoholproblemet på Grønland. *Ugeskrift for Laeger* 120:1374–1379.

COFFEY, T. G.
1966   Beer Street; Gin Lane: some views of 18th-century drinking. *Quarterly Journal of Studies on Alcohol* 27:669–692.

COLLARD, J.
1962   Drug responses in different ethnic groups. *Journal of Neuropsychiatry* 3:5114–5121.

COLLINS, THOMAS
1970   "Economic change and the use of alcohol among American Indians." Paper presented at the Annual Meeting of the American Anthropological Association, San Diego.

1974   "Variance in northern Ute drinking." Unpublished manuscript, University of Utah.

COLLINS, THOMAS, JOHN DODSON
1972   "Arapahoe, Shoshone, and Ute drinking behavior: a comparative analysis." Paper presented at the Annual Meeting of the American Anthropological Association, Toronto.

COLLIS, C. H., P. J. COOK, J. K. FOREMAN, J. F. PALFRAMAN
1971   A search for nitrosamines in East African spirit samples from areas of varying oesophageal cancer frequency. *Gut* 12:1015–1018. London.

1972   Cancer of the oesophagus and alcoholic drinks in East Africa. *Lancet* (1):441.

COLLOCOTT, E. V.
1927   Kava ceremonial in Tonga. *Journal of the Polynesian Society* 36:21–47.

COMMISSION TO STUDY ALCOHOLISM AMONG INDIANS
1956   *Report to the United States Department of the Interior, Bureau of Indian Affairs.* Washington, D.C.

CONGER, JOHN J.
1951   The effects of alcohol on conflict behavior in the albino rat. *Quarterly Journal of Studies on Alcohol* 12:1–29.

1956   Reinforcement theory and dynamics of alcoholism. *Quarterly Journal of Studies on Alcohol* 17:296–305.

CONNELL, K. H.
1962   Illicit distillation: an Irish peasant industry. *Historical Studies* 3:58–91.

COOPER, JOHN M.
1949 "Stimulants and narcotics," in *Handbook of South American Indians, 5: The comparative ethnology of South American Indians.* Edited by J. H. Steward. Bureau of American Ethnology Bulletin. Washington, D.C.

CORNWALL, EDWARD E.
1939 Notes on the use of alcohol in ancient times. *Medical Times* 67:379–380.

CRAWLEY, A. E.
1912 "Drinks, drinking," in *Encyclopaedia of religion and ethics,* volume five. Edited by J. Hastings. New York: Charles Scribner's Sons.

CRAWLEY, ERNEST
1931 *Dress, drink, and drums.* London: Methuen.

CROTHERS, T. D.
1903 Inebriety in ancient Egypt and Chaldea: *Quarterly Journal of Inebriety* 25:142–150.

CSIKSZENTMIHALYI, MIHALY
1968 A cross-cultural comparison of some structural characteristics of group drinking. *Human Development* 11:201–216. Basel.

CURLEY, RICHARD T.
1967 Drinking patterns of the Mescalero Apache. *Quarterly Journal of Studies on Alcohol* 28:116–131.

CUTLER, HUGH C., MARTIN CARDENAS
1947 Chicha: a native South American beer. *Harvard University Botanical Museum Association Leaflet* 13:33–60.

CUTTER, HENRY S. G.
1964 Conflict models, games, and drinking patterns. *Journal of Psychology* 58:361–367.

CUTTER, HENRY S. G., JOHN C. KEY, EMIL ROTHSTEIN, WYATT C. JONES
1973 Alcohol, power, and inhibition. *Quarterly Journal of Studies on Alcohol* 34:381–389.

DAILEY, R. C.
1964 *Alcohol and the Indians of Ontario: past and present.* Addiction Research Foundation Substudy 1:20–64.
1966 *Alcohol and the North American Indian: implications for the management of problems.* Addiction Research Foundation Substudy 2:20–66.
1968 The role of alcohol among North American Indian tribes as reported in the Jesuit relations. *Anthropologica* 10:45–59.

DANIELOU, JEAN
1949 *Les repas de la Bible et leur signification.* Paris: La Maison Dieu.

DA PIEDADE, J., H. AYATS, H. COLLOMB
1971 Aspects socio-culturels de l'alcoolisme au Sénégal. *Alcoholism* 7:104–108. Zagreb.

DAVIS, WALTER
1972 "Sociocultural factors in black alcoholism." Unpublished manuscript.

DAVIS, WILLIAM N.
  1972 "Drinking: A search for power or nurturance?" in *The drinking man*. Edited by D. McClelland, W. Davis, R. Kalin, and E. Wanner. New York: Free Press.

DE ALBA, MARTÍNEZ
  1926 The maguey and pulque. *Mexican Folkways* 2(4):12–15.

DE BELMONT, FRANCOIS V.
  1840 *Histoire de l'eau-de-vie en Canada*. Quebec: Société Litteraire de Québec.

DE FELICE, PH.
  1936 *Poisons sacrés, ivresses divines*. Paris: Albin Michel.

DE HAAS, S. J., C. JONKER
  1965 "Horton's hypothese getoetst." Unpublished manuscript.

DE LEJARZA, FIDEL
  1941 Las borracheras y el problema de les conversiones en Indias. *Archivo Ibero-Americano* 1:111–142, 229–269.

DE LINT, JAN, WOLFGANG SCHMIDT
  1970 *The epidemiology of alcohol*. Addiction Research Foundation Substudy 12–10 and 4–70. Toronto.
  1971 Consumption averages and alcoholism prevalence: a brief review of epidemiological investigations. *British Journal of Addiction* 66:97–107.

DEFER, B.
  1969 Variations épidémiologiques de toxicomies associées à des contacts de culture. *Toxicomanies* 2:9–18. Quebec.

DESAI, A. V.
  1965 "An exploratory survey of drinking in Suraf and Bulsar community." Unpublished manuscript. Department of Psychology, S.B. Garda College, Navsari, India.

DEVENYI, PAUL
  1967 *Sociocultural factors in drinking and alcoholism*. Clinical Division Substudy 17–1967. Toronto: Alcoholism and Drug Addiction Research Foundation of Ontario.

DEVEREUX, GEORGE
  1948 The function of alcohol in Mohave society. *Quarterly Journal of Studies on Alcohol* 9:207–251.

DIEHL, J. R.
  1922 Kava and kava drinking. *Primitive Man* 5:61–68.

DOBYNS, HENRY F.
  1965 "Drinking patterns in Latin America: a review." Paper presented at the Annual Meeting of the American Association for the Advancement of Science, Berkeley, California.

DOUGHTY, PAUL L.
  1971 The social use of alcoholic beverages in a Peruvian community. *Human Organization* 30:187–197.

DOUYON, E.
  1969 Alcoolisme et toxicomanie en Haiti. *Toxicomanies* 2:31–38. Quebec.

DOXAT, JOHN
1971   *Drinks and drinking: an international distillation.* London: Ward Locke.

DOZIER, EDWARD P.
1966   Problem drinking among American Indians: the role of socio-cultural deprivation. *Quarterly Journal of Studies on Alcohol* 27: 72–87.

DRIVER, HAROLD E.
1961   Abstract of "Alcoholic beverages in North America." *Indiana Academy of Science* 64:50–51.

DROWER, E. S.
1966   *Water into wine: a study of ritual idiom in the Middle East.* London: John Murray.

DUBE, K. C.
1972   Drug abuse in northern India. *Bulletin on Narcotics* 24:49–53.

DUMMETT, RAYMOND E.
1973   "The social impact of the European liquor trade on the Akan of Ghana: an interdisciplinary study." Paper presented at the IXth International Congress of Anthropological and Ethnological Sciences, Chicago.

DU TOIT, BRIAN M.
1964   Substitution: a process in culture change. *Human Organization* 23:16–23.

EDDY, RICHARD
1887   *Alcohol in history, an account of intemperance in all ages: together with a history of the various methods employed for its removal.* New York: National Temperance Society and Publication House.

EFRON, VERA
1970   "Sociological and cultural factors in alcohol abuse," in *Alcohol and alcoholism.* Edited by R. E. Popham. Toronto: University of Toronto Press.

EIS, G.
1961   Altdeutsche Hausmittel gegen Trunkenheit und Trunksucht. *Medizinische Monatsschrift* 15:269–271. Stuttgart.

ELWIN, VERRIER
1943   *Maria murder and suicide.* Bombay: Oxford University Press.

EMERSON, EDWARD R.
1908   *Beverages past and present: an historical sketch of their production, together with a study of the customs connected with their use,* two volumes. New York: G. Putnam's Sons.

ERIKSSON, K., K. KÄRKKÄINEN
1971   Pullo ja tölkkijatteen Kasaantriminen luontoon Suomessa uvonna. 1970. *Alkoholipolitiika* 36:175–186.

ERLICH, VERA S.
1965   Comment on David Mandelbaum's "Alcohol and culture." *Current Anthropology* 6:288–289.

ERVIN, A. M.
1971   *New northern townsmen in Inuvik.* Mackenzie Delta River Project 5. Ottawa: Department of Indian Affairs and Northern Development.

ESCALANTE, FERNANDO
n.d.   "Yaqui drinking groups," in *Indian drinking in the Southwest.* Edited by M. W. Everett and J. O. Waddell. In preparation.

EVERETT, MICHAEL W.
n.d.   " 'Drinking' and 'trouble': the Apachean experience," in "Indian drinking in the Southwest." Edited by M. W. Everett and J. O. Waddell. In preparation.

EVERETT, MICHAEL W., CARLA BAHA, EDWIN DECLAY, MARILYN R. ENDFIELD, KAREN SELBY
1973   "Anthropological expertise and the 'realities' of White Mountain Apache adolescent drinking." Paper presented at the Society for Applied Anthropology Annual Meeting, Tucson.

EVERETT, MICHAEL W., JACK O. WADDELL, *editors*
n.d.   *Indian drinking in the Southwest an anthropological perspective.* In preparation.

EZELL, P. H.
1965   "A comparison of drinking patterns in three Hispanic cities." Paper presented at the Annual Meeting of the American Association for the Advancement of Science, Berkeley, California.

F., H.
1933   Chikaranga cocktails. *Nada* 11:116–117. Salisbury.

FALLDING, H.
1964   The source and burden of civilization, illustrated in the use of alcohol. *Quarterly Journal of Studies on Alcohol* 25:714–724.

FELDMAN, W. M.
1923   Racial aspects of alcoholism. *British Journal of Inebriety* 21:1–15.

FELICIANO, R. T.
1926   Illicit beverages. *Philippine Journal of Science* 29:465–474.

FENASSE, J. M.
1964   La Bible et l'usage du vin. *Alcool ou santé* 63:17–28.

FERGUSON, FRANCES N.
1965   "A community treatment plan for Navajo problem drinkers and a few words about the role of drinking in Navajo culture." Paper presented at the Southwestern Anthropological Association Meeting, Los Angeles.

1966   "The peer group and Navajo problem drinking." Paper presented at the Southern Anthropological Association Meeting, New Orleans.

1968   Navajo drinking: some tentative hypotheses. *Human Organization* 27:159–167.

1970   A treatment program for Navajo alcoholics: results after four years. *Quarterly Journal of Studies on Alcohol* 31:898–919.

1972   "A 'stake in society,' deviance and conformity: an explanation of response to an alcoholism treatment program." Unpublished Ph.D. dissertation, Department of Anthropology, University of North Carolina.

1972   "Change from within and without: Navajo Indians' response to an alcoholism treatment program." Paper presented at the International Congress of Americanists Meeting, Rome.

n.d.   "Navajo drinking: an aspect of culture conflict." Research in progress.

FIELD, PETER B.
1962   "A new cross-cultural study of drunkenness," in *Society, culture, and drinking patterns*. Edited by D. J. Pittman and C. R. Snyder. New York: John Wiley and Sons.

FORT, JOEL
1965   "Cultural aspects of alcohol (and drug) problems," in *Selected papers presented at the 27th International Congress on alcohol and alcoholism*, volume one. Lausanne: International Bureau against Alcoholism.

FOUGUET, PIERRE
1965   Alcool et religions. *Revue d'alcoolisme* 11:81–92.

FRAKE, CHARLES O.
1964   How to ask for a drink in Subanun. *American Anthropologist* 66(6, 2):127–132.

FREDERIKSON, OTTO F.
1932   *The liquor question among the Indian tribes in Kansas. 1804–1881*. Bulletin of the University of Kansas 33. Lawrence, Kansas.

FRØLUND, BJARKE
1965   "Drinking patterns in Zambiza (Pichincha)," in *Drinking patterns in highland Ecuador*. Edited by Eileen Maynard, et al. New York.

GALANG, RICHARDO C.
1934   Pangasi: the Bukidnon wine. *Philippine Magazine* 31:540.

GALLAGHER, ORVOELL R.
1965   Drinking problems of the tribal Bihar. *Quarterly Journal of Studies on Alcohol* 26:617–628.

GANDHI M. K.
1952   *Drink, drugs, and gambling*. Ahmedabad: Navajivan.

GARCÍA-ALCARAZ, AGUSTÍN
1972   El maguey y el pulque en Tepetlaoxtoc. *Comunidad* 7, 38:461–474. Mexico City.

GEARING, FRED
1960   "Toward an adequate therapy for alcoholism in non-Western cultures: an exploratory study of American Indian drinking." Unpublished manuscript, Department of Anthropology, University of Washington.

GEERTZ, CLIFFORD
1951   "Drought, death, and alcohol in five southwestern cultures." Unpublished manuscript. Department Social Relations, Harvard University.

GELFAND, MICHAEL
  1966   Alcoholism in contemporary African society. *Central African Journal of Medicine* 12:12–13.
  1971   The extent of alcohol consumption by Africans: the significance of the weapons at beer drinks. *Journal of Forensic Medicine* 18:53–64.
GEÑIN, ALEXIS M. A.
  1924   *La cerveza entre los antiguos mexicanos y en la actualidad.* Mexico.
GHOSH, SAMIR K.
  1973   "Alcohol and alcoholism in the North-East Frontier area." Paper presented at the IXth International Congress of Anthropological and Ethnological Sciences, Chicago.
GILDER, D. D.
  1921   Drink in the scriptures of the nations. *Anthropological Society of Bombay* 12:172–189.
GLAD, D. D.
  1947   Attitudes and experiences of American-Jewish and American-Irish male youth as related to differences in adult rates of inebriety. *Quarterly Journal of Studies on Alcohol* 8:406–472.
GLATT, M. M.
  1969   Hashish and alcohol "scenes" in France and Great Britain 120 years ago. *British Journal of Addiction* 64:99–108.
GLOVER, EDWARD
  1932   Common problems in psycho-analysis and anthropology: drug ritual and addiction. *British Journal of Medical Psychology* 12: 109–131.
GOLDMAN, IRVING
  1963   *The Cubeo: Indians of the northwest Amazon.* Illinois Studies of Anthropology 2. Urbana.
GÓMEZ HUAMÁN, NILO
  1966   Importancia social de la chica como bebida popular en Huamanga. *Wamani* 1(1):33–57.
GÓMEZ, JOSUÉ
  1914–1915   Chichismo: estudio geneal, clínico, y anatomopatológico de los efectos de la chicha en la clase obrera de Bogotá. *Repertorio de Medicina y Cirujía* 5:302–320; 366–379; 424–440; 483–497; 540–559; 588–; 652–677; 6:179–. Bogotá.
GONÇALVES DE LIMA, OSWALDO
  1956   *El maguey y el pulque en los códices mexicanos.* Mexico City: Fondo de Cultura Económica.
GOODENOUGH, ERWIN R.
  1956   *Jewish symbols in the Geco-Roman period, 5–6: fish, bread, and wine.* Bollingen Series 37. New York: Pantheon Books.
GÓRSKI, J.
  1969   Alkohol u kultury i obyczaju. *Problemy Alkoholizmu* 17(7–8): 10–11.
GRACE, V.
  1957   Wine jars. *Classical Journal* 42:443–452.

GRACIA, M. F.
  1973   "Analysis of incidence of alcoholic intake by Indian population in one state of U.S.A. (Montana)." Paper presented at the IXth International Congress of Anthropological and Ethnological Sciences, Chicago.

GRANT, A. P.
  1963   Some observations on alcohol consumption and its results in Northern Ireland. *Ulster Medical Journal* 32:186–191.

GRAVES, THEODORE
  1967   Acculturation, access, and alcohol in a tri-ethnic community. *American Anthropologist* 69:306–321.
  1970   The personal adjustment of Navajo Indian migrants to Denver, Colorado. *American Anthropologist* 72:35–54.
  1971   "Drinking and drunkenness among urban Indians," in *The American Indian in urban society*. Edited by J. O. Waddell and O. M. Watson. Boston: Little, Brown.

GREGSON, RONALD E.
  1969   "Beer, leadership, and the efficiency of communal labor." Paper presented at the American Anthropological Association Meeting, New Orleans.

GREMEK, M. D.
  1950   Opojna pića i otrovi antiknih Ilira. *Farmaceutskik Glasnik* 6:33–38. Zagreb.

GUIART, JEAN
  1956   *Un siècle et demi de contacts culturels à Tanna, Nouvelles Hébrides*. Publications de la Société des Océanistes 5. Paris.

GUNSON, NIEL
  1966   On the incidence of alcoholism and intemperance in early Pacific missions. *Journal of Pacific History* 1:43–62.

HAAVIO-MANNILA, E.
  1959   Alkoholens roll vid byslagsmålen i Finland. *Alkoholpolitik* 22:16–18.

HAGE, PER
  1972   "A structural analysis of Munchnerian beer categories and beer drinking," in *Culture and cognition: rules, maps, and plans*. Edited by J. P. Spradley. San Francisco: Chandler.

HAMER, JOHN H.
  1965   Acculturation stress and the functions of alcohol among the forest Potawatomi. *Quarterly Journal of Studies on Alcohol* 26:285–302.
  1969   Guardian spirits, alcohol, and cultural defense mechanisms. *Anthropologica* 11:215–241.

HANSEN, EDWARD C.
  1971   "From political association to public tavern: two phases of urbanization in rural Catalonia." Unpublished manuscript.

HARFORD, CHARLES F.
  1905   Drinking habits of uncivilized and semi-civilized races. *British Journal of Inebriety* 2:92–103.

HARRISON, B. H., B. TRINDER
  1969   Drink and sobriety in an early Victorian country town: Banbury 1830–1869. *English Historical Review*, supplement 4:1–72.

HARTMAN, LOUIS F., A. L. OPPENHEIM
  1950   *On beer and brewing techniques in ancient Mesopotamia*. Baltimore: American Oriental Society.

HARTMANN, GÜNTHER
  1958   *Alkoholische Getränke bei den Naturvölkern Südamerikas.* Berlin: Frei Universität Berlin.
  1968   Destillieranlagen bei südamerikanischen Naturvölkern. *Zeitschrift für Ethnologie* 93:225–232.

HARTOCOLLIS, P.
  1966   Alcoholism in contemporary Greece. *Quarterly Journal of Studies on Alcohol* 27:721–727.

HARWOOD, ALAN
  1964   "Beer drinking and famine in a Safwa village: a case of adaptation in a time of crisis." Paper presented at East African Institute of Social Research Conference, Kampala.

HASAN, KHWAJA A.
  1964   Drinks, drugs, and disease in a north Indian village. *Eastern Anthropologist* 17:1–9.
  1965   Comment on David Mandelbaum's "Alcohol and culture." *Current Anthropology* 6:289.

HAVARD, V.
  1896   Drink plants of the North American Indians. *Bulletin of the Torrey Botanical Club* 23:33–46.

HAWTHORN, H. B., C. S. BELSHAW, S. M. JAMIESON
  1957   The Indians of British Columbia and alcohol. *Alcoholism Review* 2(3):10–14.

HAYS, TERENCE E.
  1968   "San Carlos Apache drinking groups: institutional deviance as a factor in community disorganization." Paper presented at the American Anthropological Association Meeting, Seattle.

HEATH, DWIGHT B.
  1952   "Alcohol in a Navajo community." Unpublished A. B. thesis. Department of Social Relations, Harvard College.
  1958   Drinking patterns of the Bolivian Camba. *Quarterly Journal of Studies on Alcohol* 19:491–508.
  1964   Prohibition and post-repeal drinking patterns among the Navajo. *Quarterly Journal of Studies on Alcohol* 25:119–135.
  1965   Comment on David Mandelbaum's "Alcohol and culture." *Current Anthropology* 6:289–290.
  1971   Peasants, revolution, and drinking: interethnic drinking patterns in two Bolivian communities. *Human Organization* 30:179–186.
  1974a "A critical review of ethnographic studies of alcohol use," in *Recent advances in alcohol and drug studies*, volume two. Edited by R. J. Gibbins, Y. Israel, H. Kalant, R. E. Popham, W. Schmidt, and R. Smart. New York: John Wiley and Sons.

1974b Anthropological studies of alcohol in Latin America: a review. *Acta Psiquiátrica y Psicológica de América Latina.*

HEILIZER, FRED
1964 Conflict models, alcohol, and drinking patterns. *Journal of Psychology* 57:457–473.

HELGASON, T.
1968 Rapport från Island: alkoholismens epidemiologi. *Alkoholfrågan* 62:219–230.

HELLMANN, ELLEN
1934 The importance of beer-brewing in an urban native yard. *Bantu Studies* 8:38–60.

HENDERSON, NORMAN B.
1967 Cross-cultural action research: some limitations, advantages, and problems. *Journal of Social Psychology* 73:61–70.
1972 "Indian problem drinking: stereotype or reality?" Paper presented at the American Psychological Association Meeting, Honolulu.

HERRERO, MIQUEL
1940 Las viñas y los vinos del Perú. *Revista de Indias* 1(2):111–116.

HES, J. P.
1970 Drinking in a Yemenite rural settlement in Israel. *British Journal of Addiction* 65:293–296.

HICKMAN, RICHARD C.
n.d. "Demonstration tri-cultural alcoholism treatment program in Santa Fe, New Mexico." Research in progress.

HIPPLER, ARTHUR E.
1973 Fundamentalist Christianity: an Alaskan Athabascan technique for overcoming alcohol abuse. *Transcultural Psychiatric Review* 10:173–179.

HIRSH, JOESPH
1953 Historical perspectives on the problem of alcoholism. *Bulletin of the New York Academy of Medicine* 29:961–971.

HIRVONEN, K.
1969 Antiikin alkoholijoumat. *Alkoholipolitiikka* 34:138–142, 191–194, 244–248, 300–305.

HOCKING, R. B.
1970 Problems arising from alcohol in the New Hebrides. *Medical Journal of Australia* 2:908–910.

HOFF, EBBE C.
1958 *Cultural aspects of the use of alcoholic beverages.* New Hampshire State Department of Health, Division on Alcoholism. Publication 22. Concord.

HOFFMAN, M.
1956 *5000 Jahre Bier.* Berlin: Alfred Metzner.

HOLLOWAY, ROBERT
1966 *Drinking among Indian youth: a study of the drinking behaviour, attitudes, and beliefs of Indian and Metis young people in Manitoba.* Winnipeg: Alcohol Education Service.

HOLMBERG, ALLAN R.
   1971   The rhythms of drinking in a Peruvian coastal mestizo com-
          munity. *Human Organization* 30:198–202.

HONIGMANN, JOHN J.
   1963   Dynamics of drinking in an Austrian village. *Ethnology* 2:157–
          169.
   1965   Comment on David Mandelbaum's "Alcohol and culture." *Cur-
          rent Anthropology* 6:290–291.
   1971   "Alcohol in its cultural context." Paper presented at Interdisci-
          plinary Symposium on Alcoholism, Washington, D.C.

HONIGMANN, JOHN J., IRMA HONIGMANN
   1945   Drinking in an Indian-white community. *Quarterly Journal of
          Studies on Alcohol* 5:575–619.
   1965   How Baffin Island Eskimos have learned to drink. *Social Forces*
          44:73–83.
   1968   *Alcohol in a Canadian northern town.* Chapel Hill: Institute for
          Research in Social Science, University of North Carolina.

HORTON, DONALD J.
   1943   The functions of alcohol in primitive societies: a cross-cultural
          study. *Quarterly Journal of Studies on Alcohol* 4:199–320.

HORWITZ, JOSÉ, JUAN MARCONI, GONZALO ADIS CASTRO, editors
   1967   *Bases para una epidemiología del alcoholismo en América latina.*
          Buenos Aires: Fonda para la Salud Mental.

HOWAY, F. W.
   1942   The introduction of intoxicating liquors amongst the Indians of
          the northwest coast. *British Columbia Historical Quarterly* 6:157–
          169.

HRDLIČKA, A.
   1904   Method of preparing Tesvino among the White River Apaches.
          American Anthropologist 6:190–191.

HURT, WESLEY R., RICHARD M. BROWN
   1965   Social drinking patterns of the Yankton Sioux. *Human Organiza-
          tion* 24:222–230.

HUTCHINSON, BERTRAM
   1961   Alcohol as a contributing factor in social disorganization: the
          South African Bantu in the nineteenth century. *Revista de Anthro-
          pologia* 9:1–13. São Paulo.

INTERNATIONAL LABOR OFFICE
   1953   "Alcoholism and the mastication of coca in South America," in
          Indigenous populations. Geneva: International Labor Office.

IRGENS-JENSEN, OLAV
   1970   The use of alcohol in an isolated area of Norway. *British Journal
          of Addiction* 65:181–185.

IRISH NATIONAL COUNCIL ON ALCOHOLISM
   n.d.   "Research on endogenous depression and alcoholism in Ireland."
           Research in progress.

JACKSON, CHARLES
   1970   "Some situational and psychological correlates of drinking be-
          havior in Dominica, W. I." Paper presented at the American An-
          thropologcial Association Meeting, San Diego.
JACOBS, WILBUR R.
   1950   *Diplomacy and Indian gifts: Anglo and French rivalry along the
          Ohio and Northwest frontiers, 1748–1763.* Palo Alto: Stanford
          University Press.
JACOBSEN, ERIK
   1951   "Alkohol als soziales Problem," in *Rauschgifte und Genussmittel.*
          Edited by K. O. Møller. Basel: Benno Schwabe.
JARVIS, D. H.
   1899   *Report of the cruise of the U.S. Revenue Cutter Bear, and the
          overland expedition for the relief of the whalers in the Arctic
          Ocean.* House Document 511 (56th Congress, Second Session,
          volume ninety-three). Washington, D.C.: U.S. Government Print-
          ing Office.
JASTROW, MORRIS, JR.
   1913   Wine in the Pentateuchal codes. *Journal of the American Oriental
          Society* 33:180–192.
JAY, EDWARD J.
   1966   Religious and convivial uses of alcohol in a Gond village of
          middle India. *Quarterly Journal of Studies on Alcohol* 27:88–96.
JAY, MAURICE
   1971   L'évolution de l'alcoolisme à la Réunion. *Alcool ou santé* 104:
          32–38.
JEFFREYS, M. D. W.
   1937   Palm wine among the Ibibio. *Nigerian Field* 22:40–45.
JELLINEK, E. M.
   1952a Alkoholbruket sasom en Folksed. *Alkoholpolitik* 15:36–40.
   1952b Phases of alcohol addiction. *Quarterly Journal of Studies on Al-
          cohol* 13:673–684.
   1957   The word and its bottle. *World Health* 10:4–6.
   1960   *The disease concept of alcoholism.* New Haven: Hillhouse Press.
   1961   *Drinkers and alcoholics in ancient Rome.* Addiction Research
          Foundation Substudy. Toronto.
   1965   *The symbolism of drinking: a cultural-historical approach.* Addic-
          tion Research Foundation Substudy. Toronto.
JESSOR, R., T. GRAVES, R. C. HANSON, S. I. JESSOR
   1968   *Society, personality, and deviant behavior: a study of a tri-ethnic
          community.* New York: Holt, Rinehart and Winston.
JESSOR, R., H. B. YOUNG, E. B. YOUNG, G. TESI
   1970   Perceived opportunity, alienation, and drinking behavior among
          Italian and American youth. *Journal of Personality and Social
          Psychology* 15:215–222.
JILEK-AAL, L.
   1972   "Alcohol and the Indian-white relationship: the function of Alco-
          holics Anonymous in Coast Salish society. Unpublished M. A.
          thesis, University of British Columbia, Vancouver.

JOCHELSON, W.
1906 "Kumiss festivals of the Yakut and the decoration of Kumiss vessels," in *Boas anniversary volume*. Edited by B. Laufer. New York: Stechert.

JOHNSTON, THOMAS F.
1973 Musical instruments and practices of the Tsonga beer-drink. *Behavior Science Notes* 8:5–34.

JONES, M. C.
1968 Personality correlates and antecedents of drinking patterns in adult males. *Journal of Consulting and Clinical Psychology* 32: 2–12.

JONSSON, ERLAND, TOM NILSSON
1972 *Samnordisk undersökning av vuxna mäns alkoholvanor*. Stockholm: Centralförbundet för alkohol-och narkotikaupplysning.

JOSEPH, ALICE, ROSAMUND SPICER, JANE CHESKY
1949 *The desert people*. Chicago: University of Chicago Press.
Journal of American Medical Association.
1954 Alcohol intoxication in Indians. *Journal of American Medical Association* 156:1375.

JUHAZ, P., R. FRATER
1971 Alcohol consumption and alcoholism in a rural [Hungarian] community. *Alcoholism* 7:93–95. Zagreb.

JUPP, G. ALEX
1971 Social-cultural influences on drinking practices. *Brewers Digest* 46:76ff.

KALANT, HAROLD
1969 "Problems of alcohol and drugs: relationships and non-relationships from the point of view of research," in *Proceedings of the 28th International Congress on Alcohol and Alcoholism*, volume two. Edited by M. Keller and T. G. Coffey. Highland Park, New Jersey: Hillhouse Press.

KALIN, RUDOLF, WILLIAM N. DAVIS, DAVID C. MC CLELLAND
1966 "The relationship between use of alcohol and thematic content of folktales in primitive societies," in *The general inquirer*. Edited by P. J. Stone, et al. Cambridge, Mass.: M.I.T. Press. (Revised edition in David C. McClelland, et al., Cross-cultural study of folk tale content and drinking. *Sociometry* 29(1972):308–333.)

KANT, IMMANUEL
1798 *Anthropologie in pragmatischer Hinsicht*. Königsberg: F. Nicolovius.

KAPLAN, BERT
1962 "The social functions of Navaho 'heavy drinking.'" Paper presented at the Society for Applied Anthropology Meeting, Kansas City.

KEARNEY, MICHAEL
1970 Drunkenness and religious conversion in a Mexican village. *Quarterly Journal of Studies on Alcohol* 31:132–152.

KEEHN, J. D.
1969   Translating behavioral research into practical terms for alcoholism. *Canadian Psychologist* 10:438–446.
1970   Reinforcement of alcoholism: schedule control of solitary drinking. *Quarterly Journal of Studies on Alcohol* 31:28–39.

KEIRN, SUSAN E.
n.d.   "Urban African biculturalism: stress and adaptation." Research in progress.

KELBERT, M., L. HALE
1965   *The introduction of alcohol into Iroquois society.* Addiction Research Foundation Substudy 1-k and H-65. Toronto.

KELLER, MARK
1958   Beer and wine in ancient medicine. *Quarterly Journal of Studies on Alcohol* 19:153–154.
1962   Definition of alcoholism. *Quarterly Journal of Studies on Alcohol* 21:125–134. (Revised version in *Society, culture, and drinking patterns.* Edited by David J. Pittman and Charles R. Snyder. New York: John Wiley and Sons. 1962.)
1966   Alcohol in health and disease: some historical perspectives. *Annals of the New York Academy of Sciences* 113:820–827.
1970   The great Jewish drink mystery. *British Journal of Addiction* 64: 287–296.

KELLER, MARK, *editor*
1966–   *International bibliography of studies on alcohol,* three volumes, to be continued. New Brunswick: Rutgers Center of Alcohol Studies.

KENNEDY, JOHN G.
1963   Tesguino complex: the role of beer in Tarahumara culture. *American Anthropologist* 65:620–640.

KERKETTA, KUSHAL
1960   Rice beer and the Oraon culture: a preliminary observation. *Journal of Social Research* 3:62–67. Ranchi.

KERMORGANT, A.
1909   L'alcoolisme dans les colonies françaises. *Bulletin de la Société de Pathologie Exotique et de ses Filiales* 2:330–340.

KIM, YONG C.
1972   *A study of alcohol consumption and alcoholism among Saskatchewan Indians: social and cultural viewpoints.* Regina: The Research Division, Alcoholism Commission of Saskatchewan.

KINSEY, BARRY A., LORNE PHILLIPS
1968   Evaluation of anomy as a predisposing or developmental factor in alcohol addiction. *Quarterly Journal of Studies on Alcohol* 29: 892–898.

KIRCHER, KARL
1910   Die sakrale Bedeutung des Weines im Alterum. *Religionsgeschichtliche Versuche und Vorarbeiten* 9(2).

KLAUSNER, SAMUEL Z.
1964   Sacred and profane meanings of blood and alcohol. *Journal of Social Psychology* 64:27–43.

KLINE, JAMES A., ARTHUR C. ROBERTS
n.d.   A residential treatment program for American Indian alcoholics. *Quarterly Journal of Studies on Alcohol*. Expected 1974.

KNUPFER, G.
1960   Use of alcoholic beverages by society and its cultural implications. *California's Health* 18:9–13.

KOPLOWITZ, I.
1923   *Midrash Yayin Veshechor: Talmudic and Midrashic exegetics on wine and strong drink*. Detroit.

KRIGE, E. J.
1932   The social significance of beer among the Balobedu. *Bantu Studies* 6:343–357.

KUBODERA, I.
1935   Ainu no Kozoku, Sake no Jozo Oyobi Sono Saigi. *Minozokugaky Kenkyu* 1:501–532.

KUNITZ, STEPHEN J., JERROLD E. LEVY, MICHAEL W. EVERETT
1969   Alcoholic cirrhosis among the Navajo. *Quarterly Journal of Studies on Alcohol* 30:672–685.

KUNITZ, S. J., J. E. LEVY, C. L. ODOROFF, J. BOLLINGER
1971   The epidemiology of alcoholic cirrhosis in two southwestern Indian Tribes. *Quarterly Journal of Studies on Alcohol* 32:706–720.

KUTTNER, ROBERT E., ALBERT B. LORINCZ
1967   Alcoholism and addiction in urbanized Sioux Indians. *Mental Hygiene* 51:530–542.

LA BARRE, WESTON
1938   Native American beers. *American Anthropologist* 40:224–234.
1946   Some observations on character structure in the Orient, I: the Chinese, Part 2. *Psychiatry* 9:375–395.
1956   Professor Widjojo goes to a Koktel Parti. *New York Times Magazine* December 9:17ff.

LA GRAVIÈRE, EMMANUEL
1957   The problem of alcoholism in the countries and territories south of the Sahara. *International Review of Missions* 46(183):290–298.

LANE, EDWARD W.
1883   *Arabian society in the Middle Ages*. London: Chatto and Windus.

LANGNESS, L. L., LAWRENCE HERRIGH
1964   "American Indian drinking: alcoholism or insobriety." Paper presented at the Mental Health Research Meeting, Fort Steilacoom, Washington.

LANU, K. E.
1956   *Control of deviating behavior: an experimental study on the effect of formal control over drinking behavior*. Finnish Foundation for Alcohol Studies Publication 2. Helsinki.

LARNI, M.
1960   Kinesiska dryckesseder. *Alkoholpolitik* 23:116–118.

LEACOCK, SETH
1964   Ceremonial drinking in an Afro-Brazilian cult. *American Anthropologist* 66:344–354.

LEAKE, CHAUNCEY, MILTON SILVERMAN
1966   *Alcoholic beverages in clinical medicine.* Cleveland: World.

LEDERMANN, SULLY, *editor*
1956–1964   *Alcool, alcoolisme — alcoolisation.* Institut National d'Etudes Démogaphiques. Travaux et Documents Cahiers 29 and 41. Paris: Presses Universitaires de France.

LEE, ROSE H., EPHRAIM MIZRUCHI
1960   "A study of drinking behavior and attitudes toward alcohol of the Chinese in the United States." Unpublished manuscript.

LEIBOWITZ, J. O.
1967   Acute alcoholism in ancient Greek and Roman medicine. *British Journal of Addiction* 62:83–86.

LEIS, PHILLIP E.
1964   Palm oil, illicit gin, and the moral order of the Ijaw. *American Anthropology* 66:628–638.

LELAND, JOY
1973   *The firewater myth: alcohol addiction among North American Indians.* New Brunswick, N.J.: Rutgers Center of Alcohol Studies.
n.d.   "Indian alcohol users: an insiders' view." In preparation.

LEMERT, EDWIN M.
1954   Alcohol and the Northwest Coast Indians. *University of California Publications in Culture and Society* 2:303–406.
1956   Alcoholism and the sociocultural situation. *Quarterly Journal of Studies on Alcohol* 17:306–317.
1958   The use of alcohol in three Salish tribes. *Quarterly Journal of Studies on Alcohol* 19:90–107.
1962   Alcohol use in Polynesia. *Tropical and Geographical Medicine* 14:183–191.
1964a   Forms and pathology of drinking in three Polynesian societies. *American Anthropologist* 66:361–374.
1964b   Drinking in Hawaiian plantation society. *Quarterly Journal of Studies on Alcohol* 25:689–713.
1965   Comment on David Mandelbaum's "Alcohol and culture." *Current Anthropology* 6:291.
1967   Secular use of kava in Tonga. *Quarterly Journal of Studies on Alcohol* 28:328–341.
1969   "Socio-cultural research on drinking," in *28th International Congress òn Alcohol and Alcoholism*, volume two. Edited by Keller and T. Coffey. Highland Park, New Jersey: Hillhouse Press.

LENDER, MARK
1973   Drunkenness as an offense in early New England: a study of "Puritan" attitudes. *Quarterly Journal of Studies on Alcohol* 34: 353–366.

LENOIR, RAYMOND
1925   "Les fêtes de boisson," in *Compte-rendu de la XXIe session, deuxième partie. Congrès internationale des américanistes.* Museum, Göteborg.

LEVY, JERROLD E., STEPHEN J. KUNITZ
  1971   Indian reservations, anomie, and social pathologies. *Southwestern Journal of Anthropology* 27:97–128.
LEVY, JERROLD E., STEPHEN J. KUNITZ, MICHAEL W. EVERETT
  1969   Navajo criminal homicide. *Southwestern Journal of Anthropology* 25:124–152.
LEVY, ROBERT I.
  1966   Ma'ohi drinking patterns in the Society Islands. *Journal of the Polynesian Society* 75:304–320.
  n.d.   "Drinking among the Newars of Nepal." In preparation.
LEYBURN, J. C.
  1944   Native farm labor in South Africa. *Social Forces* 23:133–140.
LICKISS, J. NORELLE
  1971   Alcohol and aborigines in cross-cultural situations. *Australian Journal of Social Issues* 6:210–216.
LIEBER, CHARLES S.
  1972   Metabolism of ethanol and alcoholism: racial and acquired factors. *Annals of Internal Medicine* 76:326–327.
LINDNER, PAUL
  1933   El secreto del "soma," bebida de los antiguos indios, y persas. *Investigación y Progreso* 7:272–274.
LITTLE, MICHAEL A.
  1970   Effects of alcohol and coca on foot temperature responses of Highland Peruvians during a localized cold exposure. *American Journal of Physical Anthropology* 32:233–242.
LITTMANN, GERARD
  1965   "Some observations on drinking among American Indians in Chicago," in *Selected papers presented at 27th International Congress on Alcohol and Alcoholism*, volume one. Lausanne: International Bureau Against Alcoholism.
  1970   Alcoholism, illness and social pathology among American Indians in transition. *American Journal of Public Health* 60:1769–1787.
LOBBAN, MARY C.
  1971   Cultural problems and drunkenness in an Arctic population. *British Medical Journal* 1:344.
LOEB, EDWIN M.
  1943   Primitive intoxicants. *Quarterly Journal of Studies on Alcohol* 4:387–398.
  1960   "Wine, women, and song: root planting and head-hunting in Southeast Asia," in *Culture and history*. Edited by S. Diamond. New York: Columbia University Press.
LOLLI, GIORGIO
  1955   Alcoholism as a medical problem. *Bulletin of the New York Academy of Medicine* 31:876–885.
LOLLI, GIORGIO, EMIDIO SERRIANI, GRACE M. GOLDER, PIERPAOLO LUZZATIO-FEGIZ
  1958   Alcohol in Italian culture: food and wine in relation to sobriety among Italians and Italian Americans. *Yale Center of Alcohol Studies Monograph* 3. New Haven.

LOMNITZ, LARISSA

1969a Patrones de ingestión de alcohol entre migrantes mapuches en Santiago. *América Indígena* 29:43–71.

1969b Función del alcohol en la sociedad mapuche. *Acta Psiquiátrica y Psicológica de América Latina* 15:157–167.

1969c Patterns of alcohol consumption among the Mapuche. *Human Organization* 28:287–296.

1973 Influencia de los cambios políticos y económicos en la ingestión del alcohol: el caso mapuche. *América Indígena* 33:133–150.

LONG, JOSEPH K.

n.d. "Drinking and witchcraft as indices of tension in Latin American." In preparation.

LUBART, J. M.

1969 Field study of the problems of adaption of Mackenzie Delta Eskimos to social and economic change. *Psychiatry* 32:447–458.

LUCIA, SALVATORE P., *editor*

1963 *Alcohol and civilization*. New York: McGraw-Hill.

LUNDBERG, GRETA

n.d. "Sociocultural change and drinking patterns in British Honduras." In preparation.

LURIE, NANCY O.

1971 The world's oldest on-going protest demonstration. North American Indian drinking patterns. *Pacific Historical Review* 40:311–332.

LUTZ, H. F.

1922 *Viticulture and brewing in the ancient Orient*. Leipzig: J. C. Heinrichs.

MAC ANDREW, CRAIG, ROBERT B. EDGERTON

1969 *Drunken comportment: a social explanation*. Chicago: Aldine.

MACCOBY, MICHAEL

1965 El alcoholismo en una comunidad campesina. *Revista de Psicoanálisis, Psiquiatría y Psicología* 1:38–64.

1972 "Alcoholism in a Mexican village," in *The drinking man*. Edited by D. McClelland, W. Davis, R. Kalin, and E. Wanner. New York: Free Press.

MAC LEOD, WILLIAM C.

1928 *The American Indian frontier*. New York: Alfred A. Knopf.

1930 "Alcohol: historical aspects," in *Encyclopedia of the social sciences*, volume one. Edited by E. R. A. Seligman and A. Johnson. New York: Macmillan.

MADSEN, WILLIAM

1964 The alcoholic Agringado. *American Anthropologist* 66:355–361.

1965 Comment on David Mandelbaum's "Alcohol and culture." *Current Anthropology* 6:291–292.

1973 "Alcoholics Anonymous as a crisis cult." Paper presented at National Institute on Alcoholism and Alcohol Abuse Conference, Washington.

1973 *The American alcoholic: the nature-nurture controversy in alcoholic research and therapy*. Springfield, Ill.: Charles C. Thomas.

MADSEN, WILLIAM, CLAUDIA MADSEN
1969 The cultural structure of Mexican drinking behavior. *Quarterly Journal of Studies on Alcohol* 30:701–718.

MAHA PATRA, SHRI S. K.
n.d. "Alcohol and alcoholism among the tribal communities in Orissa, India." In preparation.

MAIL, PATRICIA D.
1967 "The prevalence of problem drinking in the San Carlos Apache." Unpublished M.P.H. thesis, Yale University Medical School.

MALEN, VERNON D.
n.d. "Value orientation and alcoholism on the Pine Ridge Sioux Reservation." In preparation.

MANDELBAUM, DAVID G., et al.
1965 Alcohol and culture, with CA comment. *Current Anthropology* 6:281–294.

MANGIN, WILLIAM
1957 Drinking among Andean Indians. *Quarterly Journal of Studies on Alcohol* 18:55–66.

MARCONI, JUAN
1969 Barreras culturales en la comunicación que afectan el desarrollo de programas de control y prevención del alcoholismo. *Acta Psiquiátrica y Psicológica de América Latina* 15:351–355.

MARROQUÍN, JOSÉ
1943 Alcoholismo entre los aborígenes peruanos. *Crónica Médica* 60: 226–231. Lima.

MARTINDALE, DON, EDITH MARTINDALE
1971 *The social dimensions of mental illness, alcoholism, and drug dependence.* Westport, Conn.: Greenwood.

MARTÍN DEL CAMPO, RAFAEL
1938 El pulque en México precortesiano. *Universidad Nacional Autónoma de México. Anales del Instituto de Biología* 9:5–23.

MASSERMAN, J. H., K. S. YUM
1946 An analysis of the influence of alcohol on experimental neurosis in cats. *Psychosomatic Medicine* 8:36–52.

MAYNARD, EILEEN
1965 "Drinking patterns in the Colta Lake Zone (Chimborazo)," In *Drinking patterns in highland Ecuador.* Edited by E. Maynard, B. Frøland, and C. Rasmussen. Cornell University, Department of Anthropology.
1969 Drinking as part of an adjustment syndrome among the Oglala Sioux. *Pine Ridge Reservation Bulletin* 9:35–51.

MAYNARD, EILEEN, BJARKE FRØLAND, CHRISTIAN RASMUSSEN, editors
1965 *Drinking patterns in highland Ecuador. Andean Indian community research and development program.* Cornell University, Department of Anthropology.

MC CALL, GRANT
n.d. "Drinking patterns of Basques in Europe." In preparation.

MC CARTHY, ROBERT G., *editor*
   1959   *Drinking and intoxication: selected readings in social attitudes and controls.* Glencoe, Ill.: Free Press.
MC CLELLAND, DAVID C., WILLIAM N. DAVIS, RUDOLF KALIN, ERIC WANNER
   1966   *The drinking man.* New York: Free Press.
   1972   A cross-cultural study of folk tale content and drinking. *Sociometry* 29:308–333.
MC CLOY, SANDRA G.
   n.d.   "Drinking patterns and religion in the Outer Hebrides." In preparation.
MC CORD, WILLIAM, JOAN MC CORD, JON GUDEMAN
   1960   *Origins of alcoholism.* Palo Alto: Stanford University Press.
MC FARLAND, R. A., W. H. FORBES
   1936   The metabolism if alcohol in man at high altitudes. *Human Biology* 8:387–398.
MC GLASHAN, N. D.
   1969   Oesophageal cancer and alcoholic spirits in central Africa. *Gut* 10:643–650. London.
MC GUIRE, MICHAEL T., STEFAN STEIN, JACK H. MENDELSON
   1966   Comparative psychosocial studies of alcoholic and non-alcoholic subjects undergoing experimentally induced ethanol intoxication. *Psychosomatic Medicine* 28:13–25.
MC KINLAY, ARTHUR P.
   1939   The "indulgent" Dionysius. *Transactions of the American Philosophical Association* 70:50–61.
   1944   How the Athenians handled the drink problem among their slaves. *Classical Weekly* 37:127–128.
   1945   The Roman attitude toward women's drinking. *Classical Bulletin* 22:14–15.
   1948a Temperate Romans. *Classical Weekly* 41:146–149.
   1948b Early Roman sobriety. *Classical Bulletin* 24:52.
   1948–1949   Ancient experience with intoxicating drinks: non-Classical peoples; non-Attic Greek states. *Quarterly Journal of Studies on Alcohol* 9:388–414; 10:289–315.
   1949   Roman sobriety in the later Republic. *Classical Bulletin* 25:27–28.
   1950a Bacchus as health-giver. *Quarterly Journal of Studies on Alcohol* 11:230–246.
   1950b Roman sobriety in the early Empire. *Classical Bulletin* 26:31–36.
   1951   Attic temperance. *Quarterly Journal of Studies on Alcohol* 12: 61–102.
   1953   New light on the question of Homeric temperance. *Quarterly Journal of Studies on Alcohol* 14:78–93.
MC NAIR, CRAWFORD N.
   1969   *Drinking patterns and deviance in a multi-racial community in northern Canada.* Addiction Research Foundation Clinical Division Substudy 32–1969. Toronto.
MEARS, A. R. R.
   1942   Pellagra in Tsolo district. *South African Medical Journal* 16:385–387.

MEDICAL PRACTITIONER
1830 *Notices respecting drunkenness, and of the various means which have been employed in different countries for restraining the progress of that evil.* Glasgow: William Collins.

Medical Tribune and Medical News
1972 Unusual intoxication laid to GI fermentation. *Medical Tribune and Medical News* 13, 43:23.

MEDINA, C. E., J. MARCONI
1970 Prevalencia de distintos tipos de bebedores en adultos mapuches de zona rural en Cautín. *Acta Psiquiátrica y Psicológica de América Latina* 16:273–285.

MERRY, JULIUS
1966 The "loss of control" myth. *Lancet* (1):7449, 1257–1258.

MESA Y P., S.A.
1959 Historia del alcohol y el alcoholismo en Europa y en América. *Orientaciones Médicas* 8:107ff. Medellín.

METZGER, DUANE G.
1964 "Interpretations of drinking performances in Aguacatenango." Unpublished Ph.D. dissertation, Department of Anthropology, University of Chicago.

METZGER, DUANE G., GERALD WILLIAMS
1963 "Drinking patterns in Aguacatenango: code and content." Unpublished manuscript.

MIDGLEY, J.
1971 Drinking and attitude toward drink in a Muslim community. *Quarterly Journal of Studies on Alcohol* 32:148–158.

MILES, J. D.
1965 *The drinking patterns of Bantu in South Africa.* National Bureau of Educational and Social Research Series 18, Department of Education, Arts, and Sciences. Johannesburg.

MITRA, BÁBU RA'JENDRALA'LA
1873 Spirituous drinks in ancient India. *Journal of the Asiatic Society* 43:1–23. Bengal.

MIZRUCHI, EPHRAIM H., ROBERT PERRUCCI
1962 Norm qualities and differential effects of deviant behavior: an exploratory analysis. *American Sociological Review* 27:391–399.

MODI, JIVANJI JAMSHEDJI
1888 *Wine among the ancient Persians.* Bombay: Bombay Gazette Steam Press.

MOHATT, GERALD
1972 "The sacred water: the quest for personal power through drinking among the Teton Sioux," in *The drinking man.* Edited by D. McClelland, W. Davis, R. Kalin, and E. Wanner. New York: Free Press.

MONTELL, G.
1937 Distilling in Mongolia. *Ethnos* 2:321–332.

MONTOYA Y F., J. B.
1903 El alcoholismo entre los aborígenes de Antioquia. *Anales de la Academia de Medicina* 12:132. Medellín.

MOORE, MERRILL
   1948   Chinese wine: some notes on its social use. *Quarterly Journal of Studies on Alcohol* 9:270–279.

MORA, CARLOS FEDERICO
   1962   "Problemas psicológicos peculiares al aborígen Guatemalteco," in *Primera reunión regional centroamericana sobre alcoholismo.* Guatemala: Patronato Antialcohólico de Guatemala.

MOREWOOD, SAMUEL
   1838   *A philosophical and statistical history of the invention and customs of ancient and modern nations in the manufacture and use of inebriating liquors.* Dublin: William Curry, Jun, and William Carson.

MOROTE BEST, EFRAÍN
   1952   Chicha. *Impulso* 1(3):1–6.

MOSSMAN, BEAL M., MARIO D. ZAMORA
   1973   "Culture-specific treatment for alcoholism." Paper presented at the IXth International Congress of Anthropological and Ethnological Sciences, Chicago.

MUELLE, JORGE C.
   1945   La chicha en el distritio de San Sebastián. *Revista del Museo Nacional* 14:144–152. Lima.

MYERSON, ABRAHAM
   1940a Alcohol: a study on social ambivalence. *Quarterly Journal of Studies on Alcohol* 1:13–20.
   1940b The social psychology of alcoholism. *Diseases of the Nervous System* 1:43–50.

NAGLER, MARK
   1970   *Indians in the city: a study of the urbanization of Indians in Toronto.* Ottawa: Canadian Research Centre for Anthropology, St. Paul University.

NEGRETE, J. C.
   1970   Les attitudes envers le comportement des alcooliques: étude comparative dans trois sous-cultures québécoises. *Toxicomanies* 3: 193–212. Quebec.
   1973   "Factores socio-culturales en el alcoholismo." Paper presented at Curso International sobre Alcoholismo, San José, Costa Rica.
   n.d.   Cultural influences on social performance of chronic alcoholics: a comparative study. *Quarterly Journal of Studies on Alcohol.*

NELSON, G. K., L. NOVELLIE, D. H. READER, H. REUNING, H. SACHS
   1964   *Psychological, nutritional, and sociological studies of Kaffir beer.* Johannesburg Kaffir Beer Research Project. Pretoria: South African Council for Scientific and Industrial Research.

NETTING, ROBERT MC C.
   1964   Beer as a locus of value among the West African Kofyar. *American Anthropologist* 66:375–384.

NEWELL, W. H.
   1947   The kava ceremony in Tonga. *Journal of the Polynesian Society* 56:364–417.

New Mexico Association on Indian Affairs Newsletter
1956   The liquor problem among Indians of the Southwest. *New Mexico Association on Indian Affairs Newsletter* (July).

Newsletter of Southwestern Association on Indian Affairs
1959   Drinking and Indian problems. *Newsletter of Southwestern Association on Indian Affairs* (January).

NIDA, EUGENE A.
1959   Drunkenness in indigenous religious rites. *Practical Anthropology* 6:20–23.

NISSLY, CHARLES M.
n.d.   "Chicha in Peru." In preparation.

NORELLE-LICKISS, J.
1971   Social deviance in aboriginal boys. *Medical Journal of Australia* 58:460–470.

NORICK, FRANK A.
1970   Acculturation and drinking in Alaska. *Rehabilitation Record* 11(5):13–17.

OGAN, EUGENE
1966   Drinking behavior and race relations. *American Anthropologist* 68:181–187.

O'LAUGHLIN, BRIDGET
1973   "Mbum beer-parties and structures of production and exchange in an African social function." Unpublished Ph.D. dissertation, Department of Anthropology, Yale University.

OTELE, ACHILLE
1959   Les boissons ferementées de l'Oubangui-Chari. *Laision* 67:34–42. Brazzaville.

OWEN ROGER C.
n.d.   "Alcohol consumption and use in several Brazilian population segments: an evolutionary approach." In preparation.

PACHECO E SILVA, A. C.
1959   Intoxicación crónica en América Latina. *Revista Psiquiátrica Peruana* 2:159–181.

PAREDES, ALFONSO, LOUIS JOLYON WEST, CLYDE COLLINS SNOW
1970   Biosocial adaptation and correlates of acculturation in the Tarahumara ecosystem. *International Journal of Social Psychiatry* 16:163–174. London.

PARK, PETER
1962   "Problem drinking and role deviation: a study of incipient alcoholism," in *Society, culture and drinking patterns*. Edited by D. J. Pittman and Charles R. Snyder. New York: John Wiley and Sons.
1973   Developmental ordering of experiences in alcoholism. *Quarterly Journal of Studies on Alcohol* 34:473–488.

PARKIN, D. J.
1972   *Palms, wine, and witnesses: public spirit and private gain in an African farming community*. San Francisco: Chandler.

PASCAL, G. R., W. O. JENKINS
  1966 On the relationship between alcoholism and environmental satis-
        factions. *Southern Medical Journal* 59:698–702.

PATNAIK, N.
  1960 Outcasting among oilmen for drinking wine. *Man in India* 40:1–7.

PATRICK, C. H.
  1952 *Alcohol, culture, and society*. Duke University Sociological Series
        8. Durham, North Carolina.

PELTO, P. J.
  1960 "Alcohol use in Skolt Lapp society." Paper presented at American
        Ethnological Society Meeting, Stanford, California.

  1963 "Alcohol use and dyadic interaction." Paper presented at North-
        eastern Anthropological Association Meeting, Ithaca, New York.

PENDERED, A.
  1931 Kubika wawa: beer making. *Nada* 9:30. Salisbury.

PERISSE, J., J. ADRIAN, A. RERAT, S. LABERRE
  1959 Bilan nutritif de la transformation du sorgho en biere: prepara-
        tion, composition, consommation d'une biere du Togo. *Annales
        de la nutrition et de l'alimentation* 13:1–15.

PERTOLD, O.
  1931 The liturgical base of Mahuda liquor by Bhils. *Archiv Orientalni*
        3:400–407. Prague.

PIGA PASCUAL, ANTONIO
  1942a Influencia del uso de las bebidas fermentadas en la primitiva
        civilización egipicia. *Actas y Memorias de la Sociedad Española
        de Antropología, Etnografía, y Prehistoria* 17:61–86.

  1942b La lucha antiacohólica de los españoles en la época colonial.
        Revista de Indias 3:711–742.

PITT, PETER
  1971 Alcoholism in Nepal. *Journal of Alcoholism* 6:15–19. London.

PITTMAN, DAVID J.
  1967 *Alcoholism*. New York: Harper and Row.

PITTMAN, DAVID J., CHARLES R. SNYDER, *editors*
  1962 *Society, culture, and drinking patterns*. New York: John Wiley
        and Sons.

  1965 "Social and cultural factors in drinking patterns, pathological and
        nonpathological," in *Selected papers presented at 27th Inter-
        national Congress on Alcohol and Alcoholism*, Lausanne.

  1971 "Transcultural aspects of drinking and drug usage," in *29th Inter-
        national Congress on Alcoholism and Drug Dependence*. Edited
        by L. G. Kiloh and D. S. Bell. Sydney, Australia: Butterworths.

PLATT, B. S.
  1955 Some traditional alcoholic beverages and their importance in in-
        digenous African communities. *Proceedings of the Nutrition So-
        ciety* 14:115–124.

PLAUT, THOMAS F.
 1967   *Alcohol problems: a report to the nation by the cooperative com-mission on the study of alcoholism.* New York: Oxford University Press.

PODLEWSKI, HENRY, RONALD J. CATANZARO
 1968   "Treatment of alcoholism in the Bahama Islands," in *Alcoholism: the total treatment approach.* Edited by R. J. Catanzaro. Springfield: Charles C. Thomas.

POIRIER, JEAN
 1969   L'alcoolisme Madagascar: données statistiques et problèmes psycho-sociologiques. *Toxicomanies* 2:57–77. Quebec.
 1970   Les problèmes de la consommation du chanvre indien à Madagascar. *Toxicomanies* 3:65–88. Quebec.

POLASCSEK, E., T. BARNES, N. TURNER, R. HALL, C. WEISE, *compilers*
 1972   *Interaction of alcohol and other drugs.* Addiction Research Foundation Bibliography Series 3. Toronto.

POOT, A.
 1954   Le "munkoyo" boisson des indigenes Bapende (Katanga). *Bulletin des séances de l'Institut Royal Colonial Belge* 25:386–389.

POPHAM, ROBERT E.
 1959   Some problems of alcohol research from a social anthropologist's point of view. *Alcoholism* 6(2):19–24.
 1959   Some social and cultural aspects of alcoholism. *Canadian Psychiatric Association Journal* 4:222–229.
 1968   *The practical relevance of transcultural studies.* Addiction Research Foundation Substudy 9-2-70. Toronto.

POPHAM, ROBERT E., *editor*
 1970   *Alcohol and alcoholism.* Toronto: University of Toronto Press.

POPHAM, ROBERT E., CAROLE D. YAWNEY, *compilers*
 1966   *Culture and alcohol use: a bibliography of anthropological studies.* Toronto: Addiction Research Foundation.

POZAS ARCINIEGOS, RICHARDO
 1957   El alcoholismo y la organización social. *La Palabra y el Hombre* 1:19–26.

POZNANSKI, ANDREW
 1956   Our drinking heritage. *McGill Medical Journal* 25:35–41.

PRAKASH, OM
 1961   *Food and drinks in ancient India: from earliest times to ca. 1200 A.D.* Delhi: Munshi Ram Manohar Lal.

PREUSS, K. TH.
 1910   "Das Fest des Erwachens (Weinfest) bei den Cora-Indianern," in *Verhandlungen des XVI Internationalen Amerikanisten-Kongresses*, volume two. Vienna: A. Hartleben.

PRINCE, RAYMOND, ROCHELLE GREENFIELD, JOHN MARRIOTT
 1972   Cannabis or alcohol? Observations on their use in Jamaica. *Bulletin on Narcotics* 24:1–9.

QUARCOO, A. K.
 n.d.   "Alcohol and traditional religions in Ghana." In preparation.

QUICHAUD, J.
  1955   Problèmes médico-sociaux d'outre-mer: l'alcoolisme en Guinée. *Semaine Médicale Professionelle et Médico-Sociale* 31:574–575.

RADOVIC, B.
  1937   Pechenje rakije v nashem narodu. *Glasnik Etnograficheskog Muzea* 55:69–112.

RAMAN, A. C.
  1968   "Cultural factors in alcoholism." Paper presented at International Congress of Mental Health, London.

RAO, M. S. A.
  n.d.   "A religious temperance movement and its impact on a toddy-taping caste in Kerala." In preparation.

RASMUSSEN, C.
  1965   "Drinking patterns in Peguche (Imbabura)," in *Drinking patterns in highland Ecuador*. Edited by E. Maynard, Bjarke Frøland, and Christian Rasmussen. Cornell University: Department of Anthropology.

RAVI-VARMA, L. A.
  1950   Alcoholism in Aurveda. *Quarterly Journal of Studies on Alcohol* 11:484–491.

RAY, R. B. J-C.
  1906   Hindu method of manufacturing spirit from rice. *Journal of the Asiatic Society of Bengal*, new series 2(4).

RAYMOND, I. W.
  1927   *The teaching of the early church on the use of wine and strong drink*. Columbia University Studies in History, Economics, and Public Law 286. New York.

READER, D. H.
  1967   *Alcoholism and excessive drinking: a sociological review*. Psychologia Africana Monograph Supplement 3. Johannesburg: National Institute for Personnel Research.

READER, D. H., J. MAY
  1971   *Drinking patterns in Rhodesia: Highfield African Township, Salisbury*. University of Rhodesia Department of Sociology Occasional Paper 5. Salisbury.

REDDING, CYRUS
  1860   *A history and description of modern wines* (third edition). London: Henry G. Bohn.

REDDY, G. P.
  1971   Where liquor decides everything: drinking subculture among tribes of Andhra. *Social Welfare* 17, 11:4–5.

REICHE, C., CARLOS ENRIQUE
  1970   Estudio sobre el patrón de embriaguez en la región rural altaverapacense. *Guatemala Indígena* 5:103–127.

REICHEL-DOLMATOFF, GERARDO, ALICIA REICHEL-DOLMATOFF
  1961   *The people of Aritama: the cultural personality of a Colombian mestizo village*. Chicago: University of Chicago Press.

RESNIK, H. L. P., LARRY H. DIZMANG
  1971 Observations on suicidal behavior among American Indians. *American Journal of Psychiatry* 127:882–887.

RIBSTEIN, M., A. CERTHOUX, A. LAVENAIRE
  1967 Alcoolisme au rhum: étude de la symptomatologie et analyse de la personalité de l'homme martiniquais alcoolique au rhum. *Annales Médico-Psychologiques* 125:537–548.

RICHARDS, AUDREY I.
  1939 *Land, labour, and diet in Northern Rhodesia: an economic study of the Bemba tribe.* London: Oxford University Press.

RIFFENBERG, A. S.
  1956 Cultural influences and crime among Indian-Americans of the Southwest. *Federal Probation* 10:38–41.

RILEY, JOHN W., JR.
  1946 Sociological factors in the alcohol problem. *Scientific Temperance Journal* 54:67–74.

RILEY, JOHN W., JR., CHARLES F. MARDEN
  1947 The social pattern of alcoholic drinking. *Quarterly Journal of Studies on Alcohol* 8:265–273.

ROBARTS, E.
  1966 Distilling liquors in Tahiti in 1806. *Journal of Pacific History* 1:62.

ROBBINS, MICHAEL C., RICHARD B. POLLNAC
  1969 Drinking patterns and acculturation in rural Buganda. *American Anthropologist* 71:276–284.

ROBBINS, RICHARD H.
  1969 Role reinforcement and ritual deprivation: drinking behavior in a Naskapi village. *Papers on the Social Sciences* 1:1–7.
  1973 Alcohol and the identity struggle: some effects of economic change on interpersonal relations. *American Anthropologist* 75:99–122.

ROCA W., DEMETRIO
  1953 Apuntes sobre la chicha. *La Verdad* 42(2004):3.

RODRÍGUEZ SANDOVAL, LEONDIAS
  1945 Drinking motivations among the Indians of the Ecuadorean Sierra. *Primitive Man* 18:39–46.

ROEBUCK, JULIAN B., RAYMOND G. KESSLER
  1972 *The etiology of alcoholism: constitutional, psychological and sociological approaches.* Springfield, Ill.: Charles C. Thomas.

ROHRMANNN, CHARLES A.
  1972 "Drinking and violence: a cross-cultural survey." Unpublished manuscript.

ROJAS GONZÁLEZ, FRANCISCO
  1942 Estudio histórico-etnográfico del alcoholismo entre los indios de México. *Revista Mexicana de Sociología* 4:111–125.

ROJAS, ULISES, *compiler*
  1960 La lucha contra las bebidas alcohólicas en la época de la colonia. *Repertorio Boyacense* 46:877ff.

ROLLESTON, J. D.
1927   Alcoholism in classical antiquity. *British Journal of Inebriety* 24: 101–120.
1933   Alcoholism in mediaeval England. *British Journal of Inebriety* 31:33–49.
1941   The folklore of alcoholism. *British Journal of Inebriety* 39:30–36.

ROOM, ROBIN
1968   Cultural contingencies of alcoholism: variations between and within nineteenth-century urban ethnic groups in alcohol-related death rates. *Journal of Health and Social Behavior* 9:99–113.

ROTH, WALTER E.
1912   On the native drinks of the Guianese Indian. *Timehri Demerara,* series 3 2:128–134.

ROTTER, H.
1957   Die Bedeutung des alkoholischen Milieus für den Alkoholismus. *Wiener Medizinische Wochenschrift* 107:236–239.

ROUECHÉ, BERTON
1960   *The neutral spirit: a portrait of alcohol.* Boston: Little, Brown.

ROUFS, TIMOTHY G., JOHN M. BREGENZER
1968   "Some aspects of the production of pulque," in *Social and cultural aspects of modernization in Mexico.* Edited by F. Miller and P. Pelto. Minneapolis: University of Minnesota, Department of Anthropology.

RUBINGTON, EARL
1968   The bottle gang. *Quarterly Journal of Studies on Alcohol* 29:943–955.
1971   The language of drunks. *Quarterly Journal of Studies on Alcohol* 32:721–740.

RÜDEN, E.
1903   Der Alkohol im Lebensprozess der Rasse. *Internationale Monatsschrift zur Erforschung des Alkoholismus und Bekämpfung der Trinksitten* 13:374–379.

RUIZ-MORENO, ANÍBAL
1939   La lucha antialcohólica de los Jesuitas en la época colonial. *Estudios* 62:339–352, 423–446. Buenos Aires.

SADOUN, ROLAND, GIORGIO LOLLI, MILTON SILVERMAN
1965   *Drinking in French culture.* Rutgers Center of Alcohol Studies Monograph 5. New Brunswick.

SALONE, EMILE
1907   Les sauvages du Canada et les maladies importies de France au XVIIe et au XVIIIe siècle: la picote et l'alcoolisme. *Journal de la société des Américanistes de Paris,* new series 4:7–20.

SALONEN, A.
1957–1958   Dryckesseder före och efter Muhammed. *Alkoholpolitik* 20:50–52, 81–83, 107–109.

SANDERS, ANDREW
n.d.   "Alcohol and alienation: the Amerindians of the Corentyne River Valley." In preparation.

SANGREE, WALTER H.
1962 "The social functions of beer drinking in Bantu Tiriki," in *Society, culture, and drinking patterns*. Edited by D. J. Pittman and Charles R. Snyder. New York: John Wiley and Sons.

SARGENT, MARGARET J.
1967 Changes in Japanese drinking patterns. *Quarterly Journal of Studies on Alcohol* 28:709–722.
1971 A cross-cultural study of attitudes and behaviour towards alcohol and drugs. *British Journal of Sociology* 22:83–96.

SARIOLA, S.
1954 *Väki juomaksmyksen tutkimussaatio, Helsingfors. Lappi ja vakijuomat.* (English translation 1956.)
1956 Indianer och alkohol. *Alkoholpolitik* 19:39–43.
1961 Drinking customs in rural Colombia. *Alkoholpolitik* 24:127–131.

SAVARD, R. J.
1968 "Cultural stress and alcoholism: a study of their relationship among Navajo alcoholic men." Unpublished Ph.D. dissertation, University of Minnesota.
1968 Effects of disulfiram therapy on relationships within the Navajo drinking group. *Quarterly Journal of Studies on Alcohol* 29:909–916.

SAYRES, W. C.
1956 Ritual drinking, ethnic status, and inebriety in rural Colombia. *Quarterly Journal of Studies on Alcohol* 17:53–62.

SCHAEFER, J. M.
1973a Galton's problem in a hologeistic study of drunkenness. *Behavior Science Notes.*
1973b "A methodological review of holocultural studies in drunkenness." Paper presented at IXth International Congress of Anthropological and Ethnological Sciences, Chicago.
1974 *Drunkenness: a hologeistic treatise.* New Haven: Human Relations Area Files Press.

SCHMIDT, KARL E.
1969 "Some preliminary observations on excessive alcohol consumption in Port Vila." Report to the Resident Commissioners in New Hebrides Condominium.
1970a "Excessive alcohol consumption (E. A. C.) in the New Hebrides and recommendations for its managements, South Pacific Commission." Unpubished manuscript.
1970b "The present state of alcohol and drug consumption in the South Pacific." Paper presented at the 29th International Congress on Alcohol and Drug Dependence, Sydney, Australia.

SCHMIDT, WOLFGANG, ROBERT E. POPHAM
1961 *Some hypotheses and preliminary observations concerning alcohol among Jews.* Addiction Research Foundation Substudy 1-4 and 2–61. Toronto.

SCHREIBER, GEORG
1958 Der Wein und die Volstumsforschung: zur Sakralkultur und zum Genossenrecht. *Rheinische Jahrbuch für Volkskunde* 9:207–243.

SEARS, WILLIAM F., EUGENE L. MARIANI
  1964   "Community treatment plan for Navajo problem drinkers." Santa
         Fe: New Mexico Department of Public Health. Unpublished
         manuscript.
SEEKIRCHNER, A.
  1931   "Der Alkohol in Afrika," in *Atlas Africanus*, volume eight. Edited
         by L. Frobenius and R. von Wilm. Berlin: W. de Gruyter.
SELBY, H.
  1963   *Non-drinking societies.* Institute for the Study of Human Prob-
         lems Manuscript 46. Stanford.
SELTMAN, CHARLES
  1957   *Wine in the ancient world.* London: Routledge and Kegan Paul.
SEREBRO, BORIS
  1972   Total alcohol consumption as an index of anxiety among urbanized
         Africans. *British Journal of Addiction* 67:251–254.
SHALLOO, JEREMIAH P.
  1941   Some cultural factors in the etiology of alcoholism. *Quarterly
         Journal of Studies on Alcohol* 2:464–478.
SHORE, JAMES H., BILLEE VON FUMETTI
  1972   Three alcohol programs for American Indians. *American Journal
         of Psychiatry* 128:1450–1454.
SIEVERS, MAURICE L.
  1968   Cigarette and alcohol usage by southwestern American Indians.
         American Journal of Public Health 58:71–82.
SILICEO PAUER, PAUL
  1920   El pulque. *Ethnos* 2:60–63.
SIMMONS, OZZIE G.
  1959   Drinking patterns and interpersonal performance in a Peruvian
         mestizo community. *Quarterly Journal of Studies on Alcohol*
         20:103–111.
  1960   Ambivalence and the learning of drinking behavior in a Peruvian
         community. *American Anthropologist* 62:1018–1027.
  1968   The sociocultural integration of alcohol use: a Peruvian study.
         Quarterly Journal of Studies on Alcohol 29:152–171.
SINGER, K.
  1972   Drinking patterns and alcoholism in the Chinese. *British Journal
         of Addiction* 67:3–14.
SINGH, SARABIT
  1937   Preparaton of beer by the Loi-Manipuris of Sekami. *Man in In-
         dia* 17:80.
SIVERTS, HENNING
  1972   "Drinking patterns in highland Chiapas," in *A teamwork ap-
         proach to the study of semantics through ethnography.* Edited by
         H. Siverts. Bergen: Universitetsforlaget.
SKOLNIK, JEROME
  1958   Religious affiliation and drinking behavior. *Quarterly Journal of
         Studies on Alcohol* 19:453–470.

SLOTKIN, J. S.
1954   Fermented drinks in Mexico. *American Anthropologist* 56:1089–
        1090.

SMYTHE, DALLAS W.
1966   Alcohol as a symptom of social disorder: an ecological view.
        Social Psychiatry 1:144–151. Berlin.

SNYDER, CHARLES R.
1958   *Alcohol and the Jews: a cultural study of drinking and sobriety.*
        Yale Center of Alcohol Studies Monograph 1. Glencoe, Ill.: Free
        Press.
1958   "Culture and Jewish sobriety: the ingroup-outgroup factor," in
        The Jews: social patterns of an American group. Edited by M.
        Sklare. Glencoe, Ill.: Free Press.

SNYDER, CHARLES R., DAVID J. PITTMAN
1968   "Drinking and alcoholism: social aspects," in *International ency-
        clopedia of the social sciences,* volume four. New York: Macmil-
        lan and Free Press.

SOLMS, H.
1966   Sozio-kulturelle und wirtschaftliche Bedingungen der Giftsuchten,
        des Medikamentenmissbrauches und des chronischen Alkoholis-
        mus. *Hippokrates* 37:184–192.

SOMMER, ROBERT
1969   *Personal space: the behavioral basis of design.* Englewood Cliffs,
        N.J.: Prentice-Hall.

SPAULDING, PHILIP
1966   "The social integration of a northern community: white mythol-
        ogy and Metis reality," in *A northern dilemma: reference papers.*
        Edited by A. K. Davis, Bellingham: Western Washington State
        College.

SPRADLEY, JAMES P.
1970   *You owe yourself a drunk: ethnography of urban nomads.* Boston:
        Little, Brown.

SPINDLER, GEORGE D.
1964   Alcohol symposium: editorial preview. *American Anthropologist*
        66:341–343.

STEINER, CLAUDE
1971   Games alcoholics play: the analysis of life scripts. New York:
        Grove Press.

STEWART, OMER C.
1960   "Theory for understanding the use of alcoholic beverages." Paper
        presented at American Anthropological Association meeting,
        Minneapolis.
1964   Questions regarding American Indian criminality. *Human Orga-
        nization* 23:61–66.

STRAUS, ROBERT, RAYMOND G. MC CARTHY
1951   Nonaddictive pathological drinking patterns of homeless men.
        Quarterly Journal of Studies on Alcohol 12:601–611.

STRÜBING, E.
1960 Vom Wein als Genuss- und Heilmittel in Alterum mit Plinius und Asklepiades. *Ernährungsforschung* 5:572–594.

SUOLAHTI, J.
1956 Statlig Alkoholpolitik i Rom under Kejsartidens Slutskede. *Alkoholpolitik* 19:5–12.

SWANSON, DAVID W., AMOS P. BRATRUDE, EDWARD M. BROWN
1971 Alcohol abuse in a population of Indian children. *Diseases of the Nervous System* 32:835–842.

SZWED, JOHN F.
1966 Gossip, drinking, and social control: consensus and communication in a Newfoundland parish. *Ethnology* 5:343–441.

TADESSE, ESHETÉ
1958 Preparation of Täğ among the Amhara of Šäwa. *Bulletin of Addis Ababa University College in Ethnology and Sociology* 8:101–109.

TAPIA P., ISABEL, JORGE GAETE A., CARLOS MUÑOZ I., SONIA SESKOVITCH, ISABEL MIRANDA, JORGE MINGUELL I., GILBERTO PEREZ P., and GASTON ORELLANA A..
1966 Patrones socio-culturales de la ingestión de alcohol en Chiloé: informe preliminar: algunos problemas metodológicos. *Acta Psiquiátrica y Psicológica de América Latina* 12:232–240.

TAYLOR, WILLIAM B.
n.d. "Research on Indian drunkenness in colonial Mexico." In preparation.

THORNER, J.
1953 Ascetic Protestantism and alcoholism. *Psychiatry* 16:167–176.

TILLHAGEN, C. H.
1957 Food and drink among the Swedish Kalderaša Gypsies. *Journal of the Gypsy Lore Society* 36:25–52.

TITCOMB, M.
1948 Kava in Hawaii. *Journal of the Polynesian Society* 57:105–169.

TOPPER, MARTIN D.
1973 "Navajo culture, 'social pathology,' and alcohol abuse: a broad interpretation." Paper presented at Society for Applied Anthropology Meeting, Tucson.
n.d. "Drinking and adolescence: the Navajo experience," in "Indian drinking in the Southwest." Edited by M. W. Everett and J. O. Waddell. In preparation.

TOULOUSE, JULIAN H.
1970 High on the hawg, or how the Western miner lived, as told by the bottles he left behind. *Great Plains Journal* 4:59–69.

TRICE, HARRISON M., DAVID J. PITTMAN
1958 Social organization and alcoholism: a review of significant research since 1940. *Social Problems* 5:294–306.

UDVALGET FOR SAMFUNDSFORSKNING I GRØNLAND
1961 *Alkoholsituation i Vestgrøland.* København: Dansk Bibliografisk Kontor.

ULLMAN, ALBERT D.
1958   Sociocultural backgrounds of alcoholism. *Annals of the American Academy of Political and Social Sciences* 315:48–54.

UMUNNA, IFEKANDU
1967   The drinking culture of a Nigerian community: Onitsha. *Quarterly Journal of Studies on Alcohol* 28:529–537.

UNITED STATES DEPARTMENT OF HEALTH, EDUCATION, AND WELFARE
1970   *Alcoholism — a high priority health problem: a report of the Indian Health Service Task Force on Alcoholism.* Washington, D.C.: U.S. Government Printing Office.

UNITED STATES DEPARTMENT OF THE INTERIOR
1956   *Report of the Commission to Study Alcoholism Among Indians.* Bureau of Indian Affairs. Washington, D.C.: U.S. Government Printing Office.

VACHON, ANDRÉ
1960   L'eau-de-vie dans la société indienne. *Canadian Historical Association Annual Report*, (1960): 22–32.

VALENZUELA ROJAS, BERNARDO
1957   Apuntes brenes de comidas y bebidas de la region de Carahue. *Archivo Folklórico* 8:90–105.

VALLEE, B. L.
1966   Alcohol metabolism and metalloenzymes. *Therapeutic Notes* 14: 71–74.

VALLEE, FRANK G.
1968   Stresses of change and mental health among the Canadian Eskimos. *Archives of Environmental Health* 17:565–570.

VANDERYST, HYAC
1920   Le vin de palm ou malafu. *Bulletin Argicole du Congo* Belge 8, 11:219–224.

VARLET, F.
1956   Fabrication et composition de l'alcool de Bangul. *Notes Africaines* 71:74–75.

VARMA, S. C.
1959   Problem of drinking in the primitive tribes. *Eastern Anthropologist* 12:252–256.

VASEV, C., V. MILOSAVČEVIĆ
1970   Alkoholizam kod Cigana. *Alkoholizam* 10:47–57. Belgrad.

VATUK, VED PRAKASH, SYLVIA VATUK
1967   "Chatorpan: a culturally defined form of addiction." Unpublished manuscript.

VÁZQUEZ, MARIO C.
1967   La chicha en los países andinos. *América Indígena* 27:265–282.

VEDDER, H.
1951   Notes on the brewing of Kaffir beer in South West Africa. *South West Africa Scientific Society Journal* 8:41–43.

VELAPATIÑO ORTEGA, ALFREDO, ALFREDO GARCÍA BONILLA
n.d.   "Alcohol and drugs in eastern Peru." In preparation.

VIÑAS TELLO, EDUARDO
1951   *La composición química de las diferentes variedades de chicha que se consumen en el Perú.* Lima: Ministerio de Salud Pública y Asistencia Social, Departamento de Nutrición.

VIQUEIRA, CARMEN, ÁNGEL PALERM
1954   Alcoholismo, brujería y homocidio en dos comunidades rurales de México. *América Indígena* 14:7–36.

VOGEL-SPROTT, M. D.
1967   "Alcoholism as learned behavior: some hypotheses and research," in *Alcoholism: behavioral research, therapeutic approaches.* Edited by R. Fox. New York: Springer.

VON HENTIG, H.
1945   The delinquency of the American Indian. *Journal of Criminal Law and Criminology* 36:75–84.

VOSS, HARWIN L.
1961   *Alcoholism in Hawaii.* Honolulu: Economic Research Center.

WADDELL, JACK O.
1973a "For individual power and social credit: the use of alcohol among Tucson Papagos." Paper presented at Society for Applied Anthropology Meeting, Tucson.
1973b " 'Drink, friend!' Social contexts of convivial drinking and drunkenness among Papago Indians in an urban setting," in *Proceedings of First Annual Institute on Alcohol Abuse and Alcoholism.*
1974   "Drinking and friendship: the urban Papago experience," in *Indian drinking in the Southwest.* Edited by M. W. Everett and J. O. Waddell. In preparation.

WANG, RICHARD P.
1968   A study of alcoholism in Chinatown. *International Journal of Social Psychiatry* 14:260–267.

WANNER, ERIC
1972   "Power and inhibition: a revision of the magical potency theory," in *The drinking man.* Edited by D. McClelland, W. Davis, R. Kalin, and E. Wanner. New York: Free Press.

WASHBURNE, CHANDLER
1956   Alcohol, self and the group. *Quarterly Journal of Studies on Alcohol* 17:108–123.
1961   *Primitive drinking: a study of the uses and functions of alcohol in preliterate societies.* New York: College and University Press.
1968   Primitive religion and alcohol. *International Journal of Comparative Sociology* 9:97–105.

WEAVER, D. G., editor
1962   *Alcoholism workshop report, Dec. 1-2, 1962. Window Rock, Arizona.* Gallup, New Mexico: Gallup Indian Community Center.

WEBE, GOSTA
n.d.   "A distributional study of drinking among South American Indians." In preparation.

WECHSLER, H., H. W. DEMONE, JR., D. THUM, E. H. KASEY
1970   Religious-ethnic difference in alcohol consumption. *Journal of Health and Social Behavior* 11:21–29.

WEST, LOUIS J.
   1972   A cross-cultural approach to alcoholism. *Annals of the New York Academy of Sciences* 197:214–216.
WESTERMEYER, JOSEPH J.
   1971   Use of alcohol and opium by the Meo of Laos. *American Journal of Psychiatry* 127:1019–1023.
   1972a Options regarding alcohol use among the Chippewa. *American Journal of Orthopsychiatry* 42:398–403.
   1972b Chippewa and majority alcoholism in the Twin Cities: a comparison. *Journal of Nervous and Mental Diseases* 155:322–327.
WESTERMEYER, JOSEPH J, J. BRANTNER
   1972   Violent death and alcohol use among the Chippewa in Minnesota. *Minnesota Medicine* 55:749–752.
WHEELER, DANIEL
   1839   *Effects of the introduction of ardent spirits and implements of war among the natives of the South Sea Islands and New South Wales.* London: Harvey and Darton.
WHITE, MERVIN F.
   1971   "Drinking behavior as symbolic interaction." Unpublished Ph.D. dissertation, Department of Sociology, University of Kentucky.
WHITEHEAD, PAUL C.
   1972   "Toward a new pragmatic approach to the prevention of alcoholism: a reconciliation of the socio-cultural and distribution of consumption approaches," in *30th International Congress on Alcoholism and Drug Dependence.* Edited by E. Tongue and Z. Alder. Lausanne.
WHITEHEAD, PAUL C., CARL F. GRINDSTAFF, CRAIG L. BOYDELL, *editors*
   1973   *Alcohol and other drugs: perspectives on use, abuse, treatment, and prevention.* New York: Holt, Rinehart and Winston.
WHITTAKER, JAMES O.
   1962—1963 Alcohol and the Standing Rock Sioux tribe. I: The pattern of drinking; II: Psychodynamic and cultural factors in drinking. *Quarterly Journal of Studies on Alcohol* 23:468–479; 24:80–90.
   1966   The problem of alcoholism among American reservation Indians. *Alcoholism* 2:141–146. Zagreb.
WHITTET, M. M.
   1970   An approach to the epidemiology of alcoholism: studies in the highlands and islands of Scotland. *British Journal of Addiction* 65:325–339.
WILKINSON, RUPERT
   1970   *The prevention of drinking problems: alcohol control and cultural influences.* New York: Oxford University Press.
WILLIAMS, ALLAN F.
   1966   Social drinking, anxiety, and depression. *Journal of Personality and Social Psychology* 3:689–693.
WILSNACK, SHARON C.
   1972   "Psychological factors in female drinking." Unpublished Ph.D. dissertation, Social Relations, Harvard University.

WILSON, GEORGE C.
   1963   *Drinking and drinking customs in a Mayan community*. Cornell-Columbia-Harvard-Illinois Summer Field Studies Program in Mexico, Harvard University.

WITKIN, HERMAN A., STEPHEN A. KARP, DONALD GOODENOUGH
   1959   Dependence in alcoholics. *Quarterly Journal of Studies on Alcohol* 20:493–504.

WOLCOTT, HARRY F.
   n.d.   The African beer gardens of Bulawayo: intergrated drinking in a segregated society. Rutgers Center of Alcohol Studies, Monograph. New Brunswick, N.J.
   n.d.   "Feedback influences on fieldwork, or, a funny thing happened on the way to the beer garden," in *Urban man in Southern Africa*. Edited by C. Kileff and W. Pendleton.

WOLFF, PETER H.
   1972   Ethnic differences in alcohol sensitivity. *Science* 175 (4020):449–450.
   1973   Vasomotor sensitivity to alcohol in diverse Mongoloid populations. *American Journal of Human Genetics* 25:193–199.

WORLD HEALTH ORGANIZATION, EXPERT COMMITTEE ON MENTAL HEALTH
   1951   *Report of the first session of the Alcoholism Subcommittee*. World Health Organization Technical Report Series 42. Geneva.
   1952   *Second report of the Alcoholism Subcommittee*. World Health Organization Technical Report Series 48. Geneva.

WRIGHT-ST. CLAIR, R. E.
   1962   Beer in therapeutics: an historical annotation. *New Zealand Medical Journal* 61:512–513.

YAMAMURO, BUFO
   1954   Notes on drinking in Japan. *Quarterly Journal of Studies on Alcohol* 15:491–498.
   1958   Japanese drinking patterns: alcoholic beverages in legend, history, and contemporary religions. *Quarterly Journal of Studies on Alcohol* 19:482–490.
   1964   Further notes on Japanese drinking. *Quarterly Journal of Studies on Alcohol* 25:150–153.
   1968   Origins of some Japanese drinking customs. *Quarterly Journal of Studies on Alcohol* 29:979–982.

YAWNEY, CAROLE D.
   1967   *The comparative study of drinking patterns in primitive cultures*. Addiction Research Foundation Substudy. 1–Y–67. Toronto.
   1969   Drinking patterns and alcoholism in Trinidad. *McGill Studies in Caribbean Anthropology Occasional Papers* 5:34–48.

YOUNGER, WILLIAM
   1966   *Gods, men, and wine*. New York: World.

ZENTNER, HENRY
   1963   Factors in the social pathology of a North American Indian society. *Anthropologica* 5:119–130.

ZINGG, ROBERT M.
   1942   The genuine and spurious values in Tarahumara culture. *American Anthropologist* 44:78–92.

A Review and Appraisal of Alcohol and Kava Studies in Oceania

MAC MARSHALL

Oceania and most of North America are the world's two major culture areas known not to have had alcoholic beverages at the time of European contact. An extensive literature on alcohol use and abuse among North American Indians in the post-contact period has developed (see Heath, this volume), but there have been very few investigations of drinking behavior among Pacific islanders. In reviewing this neglected aspect of social science research in the Pacific, it is hoped that the demonstration of how much is NOT known regarding the place of alcohol in the cultures of Oceania and in Pacific history will inspire others to gather data on these important subjects.[1] At the same time, certain topics relating to alcohol in the islands that are particularly ripe for study will be recommended.

Although all Pacific islanders lacked alcoholic beverages at contact, many of them did possess a beverage which, like alcohol, was imbued with important symbolic meanings and surrounded by myriad rules and regulations regarding its consumption. Variously known as *kava*, *'ava*, *kawa*, *'awa*, *hoi*, *wati*, *sakau*, and *yangona*, this infusion prepared from the root of *Piper methysticum* has attracted much attention in the

I would like to thank the Center for the Study of Man at the Smithsonian Institution for financial assistance in attending "Alcohol Studies and Anthropology: An Evaluative Conference," and the Graduate College of the University of Iowa for an Old Gold Summer Faculty Research Fellowship under tenure of which some of the research reported here was completed.
[1] This survey covers all papers published in English that deal specifically with alcohol use among Pacific islanders; no attempt has been made to treat those sections of ethnographies or other works where only brief mention is made of alcohol use.

literature, beginning with the first European explorers who ventured into the area. While a review of all published works mentioning *kava* is beyond the scope of this brief paper, I shall discuss some of the more important *kava* literature, particularly where it affords useful perspective on or contrast with alcohol consumption in Oceania.

With the single exception of Edwin Lemert, a sociologist with long-standing research interests in alcohol studies, no investigator has set out specifically to study alcohol and culture in the Pacific. Lemert's pioneering work has pointed out a number of interesting problems for further research, but even his valuable studies suffer from certain shortcomings. By his own account Lemert (1962a, 1964b) spent approximately thirteen months in the Pacific during 1959–1960, nine of which were devoted to a study of interethnic differences in uses of alcohol among employees of eleven sugar plantations on the "Big Island" of Hawaii. The remaining four months were spent traveling and gathering data on drinking behavior in Western Samoa, the Society Islands, and the Cook Islands. This research has resulted in a paper on "Drinking in Hawaiian plantation society" (Lemert 1964b) and two other papers based on his four-month trip elsewhere in Polynesia (Lemert 1962b, 1964a).

Lemert's discussion of Hawaiian plantation drinking patterns is only marginally of interest to most students of Pacific cultures. This is because the bulk of his paper is concerned with immigrant ethnic groups employed on the plantations, e.g. Caucasians, Portuguese, Puerto Ricans, Japanese, and Filipinos. Some data on "Hawaiians" are included and, while these are interesting for comparison with the other ethnic groups studied, the sample of fifty individuals is very small; and as Lemert himself notes (1964b, reprint edition 1967: 165), it is a biased sample as well since over one half of the individuals were Mormons. No indication is given in the paper as to how the ethnic category "Hawaiian" was determined (physical appearance? a certain percentage of Polynesian Hawaiian blood? self-identification?), and this further limits its usefulness.[2] If we ignore these problems, however, Lemert found that "Hawaiians" led all the other ethnic groups statistically in beginning to drink alcoholic beverages by age fifteen, even though "Hawaiians" had the highest percentage of individuals who either had never drunk or who had drunk at one time but no longer did so.[3]

[2]   The same problem applies to the other ethnic groups Lemert discusses. This issue needs to be given particular attention by researchers conducting such studies in Pacific plural societies such as Hawaii or Fiji. For a discussion of this problem see Petersen (1969).

Lemert found that "Hawaiians" generally were willing to drink a variety of alcoholic beverages although ". . . the drinks they mentioned indicate an ethnic preference for beverages of moderate rather than high alcoholic content" (1964b, reprint edition 1967: 162). It appears from his account that Lemert could classify Hawaiian drinking as essentially "festive" drinking along with that of Tahitians (1962b: 185, 1964a, reprint edition 1967: 176–177, 1964b, reprint edition 1967: 165). Thus he says of Hawaiian drinking that

. . . it still tends to perpetuate older festive patterns, taking place at *luaus* and house parties, sometimes days or weeks in duration, at which dancing and singing are essential ingredients of the occasions (1964b, reprint edition 1967: 165).

. . . the seeming capricious disregard of work and family responsibilities for periods of indulgence actually may be part of an older festive pattern of drinking by Hawaiians, which serves to reaffirm older, esoteric, Polynesian values which center around psychic rapport (1964b, reprint edition 1967: 172).

Perhaps the most valuable contribution of this paper for future studies of alcohol and culture in the Pacific is Lemert's effort to discuss the influence of interethnic contacts on drinking practices. With regard to the "Hawaiians" in his sample, Lemert attributes the offering of an alcoholic beverage as a sign of hospitality to their co-mingling with Caucasians from early days. In similar fashion, the influences of the different colonial powers who have held sway over Oceanic peoples, each with their own peculiar cultural patterns regarding alcohol, may be expected to have resulted in different attitudes on the part of the various Pacific peoples who fell under their rule. Other Pacific plural societies besides Hawaii, such as Tahiti, Fiji, and New Caledonia, likewise provide logical bases for the diffusion and intermixing of different drinking styles.

In 1962 Lemert published a comparative paper treating "Alcohol use in Polynesia," based on his trip to Tahiti, Samoa, and the Cooks. This paper, in a revised form, later received wider attention from social scientists when it was published as part of a special "Alcohol Symposium" in the *American Anthropologist* (Lemert 1964a). Taken together, these two articles by Lemert contain a number of exemplary

---

[3] Lemert attributes this to a high percentage of Mormons in his "Hawaiian" samples: "Specifically nine out of 11 Hawaiians who had never used alcohol, and eight out of 14 who had given up drinking, were Mormons" (1964b, reprint edition 1967: 165).

leads which others dealing with the subject in the Pacific would do well to follow up. First, Lemert has devoted considerable attention to historical factors that have influenced present-day drinking behavior in the islands. Second, in the tried and true fashion of Pacific anthropological studies, Lemert has employed Pacific island cultures as a "laboratory" for a study in controlled comparison. Finally, on the basis of his comparative study, Lemert has attempted to identify some general patterns of drinking in the societies he investigated. It remains for others to show whether these patterns are distributed more widely in the Pacific, or whether they are in need of revision.

Lemert (1962b, 1964a) develops three patterns of drinking which he associates with major cultural values, aspects of social structure, and historical circumstances in Polynesia. These are "festive" drinking for Tahiti, "ritual-disciplined" drinking for the Cooks, and "secular" drinking for Samoa.

Hypothesizing that festive drinking was the earliest form of consuming alcoholic beverages in Polynesia (1962b: 184), Lemert argues that drinking was incorporated into feasting and was accompanied by group singing, chanting, dancing, and occasionally "promiscuous sexual pairings."

In the face of pressure from the missions and colonial political controls, Lemert suggests that festive drinking was supplanted by ritual-disciplined drinking on some of the Islands, notably Atiu in the Cooks (1962b: 185–186), Rarotonga and Aitutaki (1964a, reprint edition 1967: 178), and the Marquesas (1962b: 186). Such drinking in so-called "bush beer schools" is characterized by the leadership of a steward and brewers who exercise control over who drinks, the amount drunk, and the behavior of those who drink, while abstaining from drinking themselves.

Ascribing the secular drinking of Samoans at least in part to conditions of continuous prohibition (1964a, reprint edition 1967: 179), Lemert discusses this as an unpatterned, nonritualized, nonfestive "... device through which individuals in group settings find release for a variety of unintegrated feelings and impulses" (1964a, reprint edition 1967: 178–179).

Given this typology of festive, ritual-disciplined, and secular drinking, Lemert develops an argument that Tahitian festive drinking is well integrated with the basic values of Society Islanders, e.g. kinship hospitality, and "psychic rapport overtly symbolized by collective eating, singing, dancing, and sexual communion" (1964a, reprinted edition 1967: 180–181). The ritual-disciplined drinking of the Cooks is seen as somewhat less well integrated with basic cultural values, and the secular drinking of Samoa is believed to ". . . directly threaten or destroy the cherished values which are central to the *fa'a Samoa*, the 'Samoan way' " (1964a, reprint edition 1967: 182–183). Paralleling the relative integration of drinking into the value systems of these three Polynesian societies, Lemert describes only mild interpersonal aggression during drinking in Tahiti (1964a, reprint edition 1967: 180), greater aggressiveness in the Cooks (1964a, reprint edition 1967: 182), and striking, sometimes wanton violence in Samoa (1962b: 188–189, 1964a, reprint edition 1967: 182–183).

Against this historical and typological backdrop, Lemert parades what he believes to be the functions of Polynesian drinking (1962b: 186–189). These functions are: (1) to increase confidence in the face of foreign intervention and culture change and to release aggressive impulses against alien power groups; (2) to dissipate tension and anomie for persons at "stress points" in the culture; (3) to recruit labor for certain kinds of work; (4) to increase psychic rapport and in-group solidarity; and (5) to overcome shyness and release inhibitions in sexual encounters.

Although Lemert cautions in regard to his festive-ritual-disciplined-secular drinking typology that, "These do not exhaust all forms of drinking in the areas but rather call attention to what I regard as the dominant patterns" (1964a, reprint edition 1967: 176), the net effect of his articles is to pair a particular society with a particular pattern of drinking. While such crude categorizations may be helpful as a first approximation, it is obvious that they run roughshod over the almost certain intracultural variation that occurs.[4] A more thorough investigation should examine systematically the effect of variables such as age, sex, religion, location (urban port town versus rural hinterland), education, and employment history on drinking behavior and drunken comportment. In addition, it is apparent that Lemert spent only a brief time in Tahiti, Samoa, and the Cooks which hardly was sufficient to gain an in-depth view of the place of alcohol in these societies. Adding to this problem was his presumed lack of fluency in the local languages which restricted both his potential informants and the kinds of data he could collect.

---

[4] For example, in regard to an urban Tahitian neighborhood in Papeete, Kay (1963: 350) writes: "Spending connected with leisure activities is another variable item in Manuhoe budgets. Probably the major dimension of variation is the drinking pattern of the various members of the household. Whereas in one or two households a third or more of the entire monthly expenditure may be for beer and wine, there are households whose members are complete teetotallers."

In spite of these criticisms, Lemert has gathered a very useful array
of data upon which later workers can build. Among the interesting
matters he raises that should be investigated further in Oceania are the
relation between kind of beverage consumed and type of drinking; the
relation between patterns of *kava* drinking and patterns of alcohol
consumption (see below); the relation between colonially imposed prohibition restrictions and type of drinking; the implications of alcohol
consumption for relations between the sexes and between members of
the same sex; the relation between status rivalry, political factionalism,
and drinking; the relation between participation in a wage-work econ-
onmy and drinking behavior; the association between drunkenness and
criminal acts; the effects of mission policies on drinking patterns and
frequencies; the association between cycles of work and play and
drinking; the connection between diet and values on eating and obesity
and absence of organic pathology deriving from excessive alcohol
consumption (e.g. cirrhosis of the liver); and the role played by guilt
in excessive alcohol consumption. Quite obviously Lemert has laid a
solid groundwork for more detailed analyses of alcohol and culture in
the Pacific islands.

Inspired at least in part by Lemert's efforts, Levy (1966) and Ogan
(1966) have contributed further to our understanding of the place of
alcohol in contemporary Oceania.

Writing about the drinking behavior of the *ma'ohi* or traditionally
oriented inhabitants of the Society Islands, Levy finds his observations
to be in agreement with Lemert's generalizations for Tahiti.[5] This is
important because Levy's observations derive from an intensive study
of Tahitian personality and culture lasting approximately two years.
In addition, Levy was fluent in the Tahitian language. Knowing this, it
is not surprising that Levy's account of *ma'ohi* drinking provides a
great deal more historical and ethnographic detail than was possessed
before.

Recognizing the biases that often tinge historical accounts of native
drinking in the Pacific, Levy cautions against the uncritical acceptance
of these early sources. But even a critical reading of these materials
convinces him that "... there seem to have been throughout the nineteenth century evidences of demoralization and extensive drunkenness

---

[5]   Blacker's conflicting remarks (1971: 63) on Tahitian drinking seem wholly without foundation. For example, he says: "... there is much public drunkenness and
scenes of violence are frequent ... the aim is to get completely drunk as quickly
as possible. Alcoholism among minors is another problem...." Nowhere does
Blacker indicate the evidence on which these assertions are based.

which were not evident during the early 1960's . . ." (1966: 308). At the time of his fieldwork, Levy argues that a new balance — an integrated "neo-Polynesian" culture — had developed with the Tahitianized Protestant church as its focus. In the face of rapidly accelerating changes occurring in the Society Islands by the mid-1960's, e.g. tourism, the building of an international airport, and the development of a French nuclear weapons testing site at Mururoa, however, Levy (1966: 308) presents the following hypothesis:

It seems most likely that these changes will be associated with a disruption of the interactional and psychological patterns conducive to restrained drinking, and that a significant increase in socially and personally disruptive drinking may once more be expected.

Since changes of the sort Levy mentions are occurring throughout the Pacific along with incipient urbanization (South Pacific Commission 1967; Spoehr 1963), an excellent opportunity exists to investigate the disruptive and excessive drinking presumed to accompany rapid change. The presumption of personal and social "disorganization" in the face of urbanization or modernization seems to be an empirical question for investigation. Along with this, it may be the case that drinking behavior is as "organized" or as "disorganized" in the rural outer island communities as it is in the port towns of the Pacific.

Especially valuable in Levy's article are the brief comparisons he makes between drinking in Piri, a rural community on Huahine, and drinking as it occurs in the urban center of Papeete. In addition, Levy offers data on preferred beverages, drinking histories, sexual differences in drinking, drunken comportment, and *ma'ohi* interpretations of their own drinking. In a concluding section on the "psychodynamics of *ma'ohio* drinking" Levy argues that the personal motives for drinking are gratified by low-level intoxication, that there are few if any motives to drink to achieve high and prolonged levels of intoxication, and that moderate drinking accords well with Tahitian socialization practices and attitudes toward helpless dependency.

Levy (1969) has published a related article on Tahitian aggression management which underscores his observation that contemporary Tahitians are basically non-violent, gentle, and controlled. At several points in this article, he makes reference to drinking and aggression, and in every instance it is clear that violent fighting and destruction are NOT part of Tahitian drunken comportment (Levy 1969: 363, 364, 366–369).[6]

[6] It is worth pointing out that Levy's report of Tahitian drinking supports the central thesis of MacAndrew and Edgerton's recent book that consumption of

It is to be hoped that other researchers working in the Pacific will emulate Levy's examination of local perception of drinking, community controls of drunkenness, and the effects of socialization and adult personality on drinking practices.

Ogan's brief communication (1966) on alcohol use among the Nasioi of Bougainville in the Solomon Islands explores the manner in which race relations are affected by, and reflected in, drinking behavior. Colonially imposed prohibition had just been removed on his arrival in 1962. According to Ogan (1966: 183) the official segregation and other social barriers encountered by the Nasioi led him to view ". . . Europeans as constituting a domineering, threatening, depriving force." This situation resulted in resentment and condemnation of Europeans by the Nasioi.

Most Nasioi drinking occurred among young men with a smattering of education whose behavior was interpreted by Ogan as an effort to demonstrate equality with Europeans. Wherever possible, the strongest alcoholic beverage obtainable was sought. Drinking by young men (under age thirty-five) sometimes occurred at *singsing* or "secular feasts" to the accompaniment of singing, dancing, and eating. More often, however, small groups of from two to eight young men would pool their resources and buy liquor which they would drink off by themselves on the fringe of the community. Such drinking bouts led men to lurch and fall down, vomit, or urinate in public, fall into their own filth, assault non-human objects, argue with each other, and on rare occasions engage in brawls. Ogan makes clear that such behavior contradicts Nasioi values, but he explains such drunken comportment as fulfilling two psychological functions. On the one hand, he argues that ". . . since liquor is so strongly associated with Europeans, drinking enables these men to act out a kind of fantasy of themselves as Europeans . . ." (1966: 187). In the second place, he echoes Horton's hypothesis (1943) that the function of alcoholic beverages is to reduce anxiety, when he states that ". . . the obvious gap remaining between the desired and the actual social situation generates tensions which can be discharged in drunkenness and the extreme behavior associated with it . . ." (Ogan 1966: 187).

The connection between race relations and drinking (e.g. colonially imposed prohibition laws) needs to be explored in greater depth for other Pacific societies. It seems likely that historians and ethnohistorians

---

alcoholic beverages does not automatically lead to changes in comportment in which people behave in ways they would find unthinkable when sober (MacAndrew and Edgerton 1969).

will be able to make important contributions in this area which will complement reports such as Ogan's. For example, Ralston's recent paper (1971) on race relations in nineteenth-century Pacific port towns makes tantalizing mention of taverns and grog shops on Samoa and Fiji which were patronized by members of the local community as well as foreigners. Further investigation of historical sources should reveal much generally unknown information on interethnic contacts and drinking relationships during the early contact period (e.g. Wheeler 1839). Likewise, historians can do much to illuminate the role of missions in helping shape Oceanic attitudes toward both alcohol and *kava*. O'Brien (1971), for instance, discusses missionary efforts on Ponape to ban the drinking of alcohol and *kava* as part of their program to gain political power. He notes:

The attack on *kava* was much more than the general missionary dislike of alcohol. The missionaries were far less concerned with prohibiting coconut toddy or rum. *Kava* was singled out for special attention because of the important position it held (in the system of political tribute) in native society (1971: 55).[7]

Observations like this raise intriguing questions such as: was the prohibition imposed by the colonial administrators in most parts of the Pacific an effort to "save the native from vice," a move based on fear of violence from "drunken savages," or an assertion of simple political power?

The most thoroughgoing attempt so far to address a question on the place of alcohol in Pacific history is a penetrating paper by Gunson (1966). Gunson's focus is on missionaries in the Pacific (primarily in Tahiti) during the late eighteenth and nineteenth centuries and their attitudes toward consumption of alcoholic beverages. It is clear from his account that there were considerable differences of opinion among church leaders and between denominations on whether imbibing was a sin and on whether prohibition was a blessing. Gunson also makes clear the influence that developments in the metropolitan powers had on the church's stance toward alcohol use in the Pacific by missionaries and converts alike. That the arduous conditions under which the early missionaries labored were conducive to heavy alcohol use by some of them is apparent, but Gunson goes on to note that the spread of the

---

[7]   For similar examples from elsewhere in the Pacific, compare Gunson (1966: 60): "In 1862, when the Rev. Joseph Waterhouse instituted a policy of teetotallism in Fiji, he included *kava*, the honored ceremonial drink of Polynesia, amongst the proscribed beverages, viewing it as the 'opium' of Fiji." Gatty says (1956: 242): "*Kava* used to be grown in Tubuai, but the missionaries came in 1882 and forbade the drink."

temperance movement resulted in negligible "alcoholism" among missionaries by the 1850's.

Hocking (1970) has attempted a brief reassessment of the social problems associated with alcohol use in the New Hebrides since prohibition was lifted in 1962. His data show that 60 percent of all criminal convictions were "crimes due to liquor" and that over 75 percent of men charged with liquor offenses were age thirty or younger. Schmidt (1969, 1970a, 1970b) has prepared recommendations for the management of "excessive alcohol consumption" in the New Hebrides in connection with his work as mental health specialist for the South Pacific Commission. Like Hocking, Schmidt views young, employed male wage earners in the port town of Vila as the major "problem drinkers." Reminiscent of Ogan's suggestion (1966) that Nasioi drink in imitation of Europeans, Schmidt holds the same to be true for New Hebrideans. Schmidt also offers the interesting observation that a link exists between cargo cults and excessive alcohol consumption:

... in the cults the concrete ritual followed is believed to bring the 'cargo.' In the same way, if one drinks alcoholic beverages like the Europeans do, one could expect to acquire their other characteristics such as a certain amount of wealth and status (1970b: 19).

This postulated relationship might repay further investigation by a future worker in the area.

Among the many recommendations Schmidt offers for controlling "the alcohol problem" in the New Hebrides is the increased propagation and commercial production of *kava* as a competitor to alcoholic beverages. The relationship between alcohol and *kava* drinking in the Pacific is of some significance and warrants discussion here, along with a summary of what is known of the pharmacological effects of *kava* on the human body. At the same time, mention will be made of the geographical distribution of *kava* drinking in Oceania, and some of the anthropological literature describing the *kava* ceremony will be discussed.

Two excellent survey articles have appeared in recent years which summarize the knowledge of the chemistry, pharmacology, and physiological activity of *Piper methysticum* (Hansel 1968; Keller and Klohs 1963). In addition, there is Gatty's thorough discussion (1956) of the planting, cultivation, and marketing of the shrub. First, since there appears to be some confusion on this point (e.g. Lurie 1971: 322–323), it should be noted that *kava* is neither fermented nor alcoholic. The active pharmacologic agents of *kava* appear to be a series of alpha-pyrones, e.g. kawain, methysticum, yangonin, dihydromethysticum, and dihydrokawain.[8] These *kava* constituents have the following physiological effects: diuretic, soporific, anticonvulsant, spasmolutic, analgesic, and local anesthetic properties; muscle relaxation which does not affect consciousness or volition; intensification of barbituate narcosis; and active anticycotic properties useful in the treatment of various skin diseases (Hansel 1968). Recognizing the pharmacologic capabilities of *kava*, Pacific island peoples have long employed the drug in traditional medical remedies as well as using it as a social and ceremonial beverage.

Kava is or was cultivated generally throughout the high islands of Polynesia (except New Zealand and Easter Island), in Fiji and scattered other localities in Melanesia, and on Ponape and Kusaie in Micronesia (Fischer 1957; Gatty 1956; Lemert 1967). Gatty notes that rich soil and good drainage are necessary for growing *kava* and this doubtless accounts for its absence on most Pacific atolls. The plant also is known to grow wild in New Guinea (Gatty 1956), on Palau (Yuncker 1959), and possibly on Yap and in the Marianas.[9]

Stemming from his earlier work on alcohol use in Polynesia, Lemert (1967) has provided us with the only contemporary account comparing alcohol and *kava* use in Oceania. Focusing on the nonritual, social use of *kava* and alcohol in Tonga, Lemert pays particular attention to the differences in comportment surrounding ingestion of these two substances.[10] *Kava* parties usually occur in a family setting at the home of an unmarried girl, and normally are initiated by the young men present. Conviviality, conversation, gossip, singing, and sometimes dancing characterize the proceedings. Disorderliness at *kava* parties seldom if ever occurs according to Lemert. Finding himself in agreement with "the general outlines" of the Beagleholes' description (1941) of secular use of *kava* in the Tongan village of Pangai, Lemert is not completely satisfied with their presentation because it "... fails to explain why *kava* rather than other beverages continues to function as an integrating

[8] This matter is still of some controversy among pharmacologists. Buckley, et al. (1967) hold that alpha-pyrones, e.g. methysticum, may not be the important constituents of *kava* because they are not water-soluble. Instead, they have provisionally identified a water-soluble amorphous solid which they have called F_1 on which they are conducting furhter experiments (see Buckley, et al. 1967; Furguile, et al. 1965; O'Hara, et al. 1965).

[9] It is of interest that a close relative of *Piper methysticum* — *Piper betle* — is cultivated on Yap, Palau, and the Marianas where betel chewing is widespread. Yuncker (1959: 91) observes that, "Betel chewing has not developed to any extent in Polynesia, where the *Piper methysticum* beverage called *kava* apparently takes its place."

[10] It is not clear whether Lemert's research in Tonga formed part of his earlier trip through Polynesia (1959-1960), or whether he visited Tonga separately at a later time.

force in Tongan life" (1967, reprint edition 1967: 190). In trying to explain this, Lemert points out the different effects that intoxication with alcohol and *kava* have on Tongan comportment. Whereas alcohol makes most Tongans aggressive and whets the sexual appetite, *kava* has just the opposite results. Lemert (1967, reprint edition 1967: 194–195) types the drinking of alcoholic beverages in Samoa: a "secular" pattern of alcohol use, unintegrated with basic cultural values, is postulated for both of these island groups. Having drawn this contrast between alcohol and *kava* use in Tonga, Lemert (1967, reprint edition 1967: 191) explains the persistence of secular *kava* drinking in the following way:

If the effects I have chosen to assign to *kava* are valid they immediately speak of a clear superiority over alcohol as a social reagent at least in certain sociocultural contexts. The inhibition of two kinds of impulses or motivations most likely to be socially disruptive, namely sex and aggression, together with a kind of dissociation of the psychic processes ... may explain the special utility which *kava* has had for Polynesian social interaction.

Scholars working elsewhere in the Pacific where both *kava* and alcohol are consumed would do well to examine Lemert's conclusions to see if they apply more widely. The fact that *kava* bars now operate in Tonga, Fiji, Ponape, and possibly elsewhere, alongside bars dispensing alcoholic beverages, needs to be looked at carefully. Is comportment following *kava* drinking different in a bar room setting than in a family or community setting? What happens to people's comportment when alcohol and *kava* are both consumed? Does imbibing alcohol convey certain important intercultural or interpersonal messages that drinking *kava* does not?[11] We know surprisingly little about the secular role of *kava* in the Pacific today.

We know a good deal more about the ritual or ceremonial use of *kava*, however. Tonga has received the greatest attention in the literature beginning with Pratt's short description (1922) and concluding with Newell's detailed examination (1947) of the place and meaning of the *kava* ceremony in Tongan culture. Margaret Titcomb has presented us (1948) with an admirable survey and organization of the scattered references to *kava* use in Hawaii and Firth has given a characteristically lucid account (1970: 199–232) of the religious meaning of the *kava* ritual on Tikopia. Numerous other discussions of the *kava* ceremony are to be found in the anthropological literature — especially for

---

[11]   Cf. Lurie (1971) who explores the "message" communicated by North American Indian drinking practices.

western Polynesia — but it is beyond the scope of this paper to enumerate them here.

What, then, is known of the place of alcohol in Pacific cultures and cultural history? As this quick survey makes clear, very little. A start has been made for Polynesia with the works of Lemert, Levy, and Gunson laying a solid foundation upon which others can build. Although we do have a few reports for island Melanesia (Hocking, Ogan, Schmidt), Ogan's paper (1966) is the only effort to examine alcohol use in this diverse area from an anthropological perspective. There is nothing currently available in the social science literature dealing explicitly with alcohol consumption and attendant behaviors either for the island of New Guinea or for Micronesia.[12] There are signs, however, that this situation may soon be changing.[13] Hopefully, this demonstration of the woeful lack of data on this important subject will stimulate those embarking on research in the Pacific during the 1970's to pay attention to alcohol. Not only will such studies contribute to questions of academic interest and importance, but they will also provide a solid data base upon which policy-makers may draw in formulating solutions to alcohol-related problems in the islands.

[12]   MacAndrew and Edgerton (1969: 25-29) use data from Ifaluk Atoll in the Caroline Islands in support of their argument that alcohol use does not automatically release aggressive and sexual impulses. While their central thesis appears viable, their choice of Ifaluk as an example is questionable. Examination of their original sources reveals that every one of their quotations pertaining to alcohol use and drunken comportment (1969: 27-29) is drawn from a series of off-the-cuff remarks that can hardly be taken as adequate information on these matters. Furthermore, none of the authors on whom they rely was truly conversant in the Ifaluk dialect, and all of these men were on the atoll for only a few months and were concerned with research problems having almost nothing to do with drinking. Thus not much is known about Ifaluk drunken comportment and this example underscores the need for in-depth, scientific investigations of drinking phenomena in Micronesia.
[13]   For example, a government sponsored pilot study of alcohol abuse in several of the port towns of the United States Trust Territory of the Pacific Islands, conducted by an economic and social development consulting firm, is scheduled to be carried out during autumn 1973. Moreover, a working session on "Alcohol and *Kava* Use in the Pacific" has been organized by the author for the Third Annual Meeting of the Association for Social Anthropology in Oceania (ASAO) to be held in March 1974. Ethnographic studies of alcohol and/or *kava* use on Ponape, Tonga, Kapingamarangi, Hawaii, Rarotonga, Palau, Losap, Etal, and Namoluk have been promised.

REFERENCES

BEAGLEHOLE, E., P. BEAGLEHOLE
   1941   "Pangai village in Tonga," in *Memoirs of the Polynesian society,*
          volume eighteen. Wellington: The Polynesian Society.

BLACKER, H.
   1971   Drinking practices and problems abroad, 2: Tahiti. *The Journal of*
          Alcoholism 6:63.

BUCKLEY, J. P., A. R. FURGUILE, M. J. O'HARA
   1967   The pharmacology of kava. *Journal of the Polynesian Society*
          76:101–102.

COLLOCOTT, E. E. V.
   1927   Kava ceremonial in Tonga. *Journal of the Polynesian Society*
          36:21–47.

FIRTH, R.
   1970   *Rank and religion in Tikopia.* Boston: Beacon Press.

FISCHER, J.
   1957   *The eastern Carolines.* New Haven: Human Relations Area Files.

FURGUILE, A. R., W. J. KINNARD, M. D. ACETO, J. P. BUCKLEY
   1965   Central activity of aqueous extracts of *Piper methysticum* (kava).
          Journal of Pharmaceutical Sciences 54:247–252.

GATTY, R.
   1956   Kava — Polynesian beverage shrub. *Economic Botany* 10:241–249.

GUNSON, N.
   1966   On the incidence of alcoholism and intemperance in early Pacific
          missions. *Journal of Pacific History* 1:43–62.

HANSEL, R.
   1968   Characterization and physiological activity of some kava constit-
          uents. *Pacific Science* 22:293–313.

HOCKING, R. B.
   1970   Problems arising from alcohol in the New Hebrides. *The Medical*
          Journal of Australia, volume two (57th year), 20:908–910.

HORTON, D.
   1943   The functions of alcohol in primitive societies: a cross-cultural
          study. *Quarterly Journal of Studies on Alcohol* 4:199–320.

KAY, P.
   1963   Aspects of social structure in a Tahitian urban neighborhood.
          Journal of the Polynesian Society 72:325–371.

KELLER, F., M. W. KLOHS
   1963   A review of the chemistry and pharmacology of the constituents
          of *Piper methysticum. Lloydia* 26:1–15.

LEMERT, E. M.
   1962a The stuttering and social structure in two Pacific Island societies.
          Journal of Speech and Hearing Disorders 27:3–10. (Reprinted
          1967 in *Human deviance, social problems and social control,* by
          Edwin M. Lemert 146–153. Englewood Cliffs, New Jersey: Pren-
          tice-Hall.)
   1962b Alcohol use in Polynesia. *Tropical and Geographical Medicine*
          14:183–191.

1964a Forms and pathology of drinking in three Polynesian societies. *American Anthropologist* 66:361–374. (Reprinted 1967 in *Human deviance, social problems, and social control*, by Edwin M. Lemert, 174–186. Englewood Cliffs, New Jersey: Prentice-Hall.)

1964b Drinking in Hawaiian plantation society. *Quarterly Journal of Studies on Alcohol* 25:689–713. (Reprinted 1967 in *Human deviance, social problems and social control*, by Edwin M. Lemert, 154–173. Englewood Cliffs, New Jersey: Prentice-Hall.)

1967 The secular use of kava — with special reference to Tonga. *Quarterly Journal of Studies on Alcohol* 28:328–341. (Reprinted 1967 in *Human deviance, social problems and social control*, by Edwin M. Lemert, 187–196. Englewood Cliffs, New Jersey: Prentice-Hall.)

LEVY, R.
1966 Ma'ohi drinking patterns in the Society Islands. *Journal of the Polynesian Society* 75:304–320.

1969 "On getting angry in the Society Islands," in *Mental health research in Asia and the Pacific*. Edited by William Caudill and Tsung-Yi Lin. Honolulu: East-West Center Press.

LURIE, N. O.
1971 The world's oldest on-going protest demonstration: North American Indian drinking patterns. *Pacific Historical Review* 40:311–332.

MAC ANDREW, C., R. B. EDGERTON
1969 *Drunken comportment: a social explanation.* Chicago: Aldine.

NEWELL, W. H.
1947 The *kava* ceremony in Tonga. *Journal of the Polynesian Society* 56:364–417.

O'BRIEN, I. E.
1971 Missionaries on Ponape: induced social and political change. *The Australian National University Historical Journal* 8:53–64.

OGAN, E.
1966 Drinking behavior and race relations. *American Anthropologist* 68:181–188.

O'HARA, M. J., W. J. KINNARD, J. P. BUCKLEY
1965 Preliminary characterization of aqueous extracts of *Piper methysticum* (kava, kawa kawa). *Journal of Pharmaceutical Sciences* 54:1021–1025.

PETERSEN, W.
1969 The classification of subnations in Hawaii: an essay in the sociology of knowledge. *American Sociological Review* 34:863–877.

PRATT, REV. M. A. R.
1922 A kava ceremony in Tonga. *Journal of the Polynesian Society* 31:198–201.

RALSTON, C.
1971 The pattern of race relations in 19th century Pacific port towns. *Journal of Pacific History* 6:39–59.

SCHMIDT, K. E.
1969 "Some preliminary observations on excessive alcohol consump-

tion in Port Vila." Report to the Resident Commissioners, South Pacific Commission.

1970a "The present state of alcohol and drug consumption in the South Pacific." Paper presented at the Twenty-Ninth International Congress on Alcoholism and Drug Dependence, Sydney, Australia.

1970b *Excessive alcohol consumption (E.A.C.) in the New Hebrides and recommendations for its management.* Noumea: South Pacific Commission.

SOUTH PACIFIC COMMISSION

1967 *Urban problems in the South Pacific.* South Pacific Commission Technical Paper 152. Noumea: South Pacific Commission.

SPOEHR, A., *editor*

1963 *Pacific port towns and cities.* Honolulu: Bishop Museum Press.

TITCOMB, M.

1948 Kava in Hawaii. *Journal of the Polynesian Society* 57:105–171.

WHEELER, D.

1839 *Effects of the introduction of ardent spirits and implements of war among the natives of the South Sea Islands and New South Wales.* London: Harvey and Darton.

YUNCKER, T. G.

1959 Piperaceae of Micronesia. *Occasional Papers of the Bernice P. Bishop Museum* 22:83–108. Honolulu.

European Drinking Habits:
A Review of Research and Some
Suggestions for Conceptual Integration
of Findings

Alcohol consumption is heavily concentrated in Europe, where only 13 percent of the total population of the world accounts for about one half of the consumption of intoxicating beverages (Sulkunen 1973). Together with this high consumption level are some striking differences in per capita consumption, ranging from a minimum of three liters in Iceland to a high in France of nearly seventeen liters of absolute alcohol per year. At the same time, the Scandinavian countries as a whole form a fairly homogeneous area in Europe in that their level of alcohol consumption falls noticeably below the level prevailing in the rest of the continent — an average of five liters per person per year. Even within such similar cultures, however, there are variations. The Danes and the Swedes drink more than the Finns and the Norwegians.

Such differences, coupled with the generally high alcohol consumption, offer great possibilities for understanding drinking behavior through the comparative method. While what might be termed a cross-cultural description has, to some extent, been attempted from time to time, it seems that much more analytic material can be gleaned from European studies than are presently available at present. In order for this to be possible, however, researchers in the field should consider two important aspects of such an undertaking: (1) the current state of knowledge through European statistics and alcohol studies on drinking behavior, and (2) the importance of developing concepts concerning alcohol intake that aid in comparing variations between and within countries in such a way as to point out the significance of what is known as well as further avenues of investigation. Both of these points will be discussed below.

THE CURRENT STATE OF STATISTICS AND KNOWLEDGE ON DRINKING BEHAVIOR IN EUROPE

Examination of international statistics on alcohol consumption usually aims at determining the degree of alcohol use in different countries. That is, there is a tendency to limit comparisons by classifying countries primarily in terms of the amounts of liquor consumed or, correspondingly, in terms of the kinds of liquor used most. A picture of a "typical" wine-drinking country or a "typical" small-consumption country is thus formed and an assumption is made that the variations in drinking habits within classes are, if not quite insignificant, at least considerably less marked than those between the classes.

We know that both the statistics on alcohol consumption and studies of drinking behavior are full of errors. The validity of consumption statistics has only begun to be investigated (Sulkunen 1973). The sources of errors in studies of drinking behavior have been given attention at various times (for example, Makela 1971b). There are, however, certain empirical facts that indicate flaws existing in consumption statistics. First of all, unregistered consumption of alcohol (homemade intoxicating beverages, imported liquor not included in the statistical records, and the ingestion of alcohol not intended to be taken internally) is estimated to amount to about one-third of the officially recorded consumption in Norway and as much as one-fifth in Finland (Bruun 1972). In spite of this unrecorded addition, neither country's total consumption reaches the Danish or Swedish level, let alone that of the central European nations.

Secondly, the proportionate number of alcohol users in the Scandinavian countries is conspicuously different from that in the countries of central and southern Europe. Whereas 44 percent of the women and 10 percent of the men interviewed in France in 1956 had not drunk a drop DURING THE PREVIOUS DAY (Sadoun, et al. 1965: 35), in 1969, 36 percent of the Finnish women and 8 percent of the men had correspondingly refrained from touching alcohol DURING THE PREVIOUS YEAR (Makela 1970b: 18). Within the Nordic sphere, again, the percentage of teetotalers is the lowest in Denmark and the highest in Norway and Finland (Jonsson and Nilsson 1972). The per capita consumption of alcohol and the numbers of teetotalers are not, however, in direct proportion. In Great Britain the per capita consumption is about 1.5 times as high as in Finland, but the ratio of men practicing abstinence for a whole year is not lower, at least in London (Edwards, et al. 1972). On the other hand, drinking alcoholic beverages is a less strictly masculine activity in England than in Finland; only 10 percent of the women in London are reported to be teetotalers compared with the far higher Finnish figure of 36 percent.

The statistics on alcohol consumption do have their uses, however. First of all, they provide information on the patterns of consumption and their division into different categories. Also, there are indications that the per capita consumption of alcohol is positively correlated with the rate of liver cirrhosis mortality (de Lint and Schmidt 1968) and, further, that the distribution of consumption is generally skewed.

It should also be emphasized that considerable variation in patterns of alcohol consumption occur within any given country; homogeneity within any country is more often the exception than the rule. For instance, only part of the population in some countries uses alcohol, while a large portion of the alcohol consumed is concentrated in a small segment of the population.

Upon discovering a country whose per capita consumption of alcohol is low and the proportion of teetotalers is high, a researcher is easily tempted to surmise that the use of alcohol is concentrated in a small part of the population. In some cases this is indeed true, but internal variations deserve consideration. In Finland, for instance, alcohol consumption is divided unevenly among individuals: 10 percent of the male population account for 53 percent of the total consumption of alcohol by men, and 10 percent of the female population accounts for no less than 72 percent of the total consumption by women (Makela 1971a, 1971b). In France, where the per capita figure is four times as high as in Finland, alcohol consumption is highly concentrated also but the concentration is not as striking as in Finland: 16 percent of the men consumed 42 percent of the total amount of alcohol ingested by all Frenchmen and 14 percent of the women drank 55 percent of all the alcohol consumed by the women of France (Sadoun, et al. 1965: 35). Thus external similarities may mask internal differences.

Notwithstanding the fact that the use of alcohol is much more common in France than in Finland, the purpose of drinking in both countries appears to be to get drunk. In France a widespread tolerance of alcohol intoxication was found in a recent survey, along with the view that heavy drinking is a mark of virility (Sadoun, et al. 1965). Correspondingly, the majority of the inhabitants of the Finnish capital considers occasional unrestrained drinking more desirable than restrained regular drinking (Allardt 1957). By contrast, Italians have been found to regard the use of alcohol with a good deal of indifference. They seem to look upon it as part and parcel of everyday life and they emphasize the nutritional value of alcohol (Lolli, et al. 1958). This attitude does not prove, however, that a state of intoxication is not held by Italians, too, to have a certain inherent value. Further research might find that intoxication is also taken for granted.

The wish to get drunk can be detected in the very drinking procedures themselves. Although the total consumption of alcohol varies in the different Scandinavian countries, ingestion with the specific aim of getting "tipsy" and the frequency of drunkenness are practically equivalent in all these countries. On the other hand, drinking situations in which the amounts of alcohol ingested at any one time are so small as not to cause intoxication are conspicuously more common in Denmark and Sweden than in Finland and Norway (Jonsson and Nilsson 1972). It is precisely this more abundant "extra small consumption" paralleling consumption aimed at producing intoxication that raises the per capita annual consumption in Denmark and Sweden above the Finnish and Norwegian levels. In Finland and Norway, then, alcohol is ingested more frequently to make the head swim than as a nightcap or to add a festive touch to a meal.

Unfortunately, few systematic or detailed empirical data are available from other countries on the frequency of drinking sessions and on consumption aimed at producing inebriation. From various sources we learn, however, that 21 percent of Frenchmen polled, and correspondingly 3 percent of the French women, admitted to drinking too much "fairly often." At the same time, 66 percent of these men and 43 percent of the women reported having rarely imbibed excessively (Sadoun, et al. 1965). In the light of distribution of alcohol consumption, it has been correspondingly estimated that 7 percent of the adult population are excessive drinkers — more than 20 centiliters of pure alcohol per day (Lederman 1956). Again, in the Netherlands 17 percent of the sample population acknowledged to interviewers having drunk excessively at some time (Gadourek, et al. 1963: 452). It is possible that these figures fall short of the true amounts, although people are known to exaggerate in both directions.

Some are accustomed to admiring Italian drinking customs. Although the Italians drink large amounts of alcohol each year, their manner of drinking nevertheless appears to be marked by moderation rather than aimed at achieving a state of intoxication as in northern Europe. This routine observation seems to be borne out by survey results. The evidence at hand, however, has such large gaps that we can not really be sure yet that Italians do not get drunk just as often, if not oftener, than their fellow Europeans up north. In any case, the rate of mortality from cirrhosis of the liver is about five times as high in Italy as in Finland, though, it is true, almost twice as low as in France (de Lint and Schmidt 1968). In the survey of Italian drinking habits, the frequency of excessive drinking was estimated by applying a subjective definition of drunkenness, as set forth by the researchers as follows:

... by intoxication here is meant an ingestion of alcoholic beverages which led to some significant changes in feeling, thinking or acting of the subject – a change which, because of its nature, has not been forgotten even though it had no consequences, or only slight ones (Lolli, et al. 1958: 83).

It is highly likely that in a permissive culture, like the Italian, the "per mil boundary" of intoxication is much higher than in cultures where the prevailing attitude toward alcohol is negative or ambivalent. More empirical studies of drunkenness are therefore needed.

The definition of drunkenness is, however, a very difficult problem. The per mil limit provides a means of making comparisons but its applicability depends on each individual's drinking background and habits. If, again, the definition of drunkenness is applied to behavioral changes, we find ourselves getting involved with drinking situations and the drunken person's role (MacAndrew and Edgerton 1969).

The quality, consistency, and intensity of detail of drinking behavior studies vary dramatically from country to country also. Traditionally, all the Scandinavian countries have striven to eliminate the consumption of alcohol or at least bring about a drastic reduction of consumption. It is therefore understandable that drinking habits have been studied more systematically in the Nordic group of nations than in countries where the production and distribution of alcohol are not under centralized control and where alcohol not only brings the state tax revenue but is an important factor in commercial and industrial life and a noteworthy export article. Research in the Nordic countries (excepting Denmark) has been going on without interruption, resulting in the accumulation of consistent categories of data over periods of time. Additionally, in Norway and Finland alcohol research has been institutionalized.

Studies of drinking habits elsewhere in Europe have been of a more sporadic nature but in many instances also quite extensive, dealing with other habits and practices besides the use of alcohol, such as tobacco smoking (Gadourek 1963), dining customs in general and the drinking of milk in particular (Lolli, et al. 1958), or drinking of every description involving both alcoholic and nonalcoholic beverages (Sadoun, et al. 1965). Consideration of data in light of these differences will greatly aid analytic comparisons of this rich store of research results.

IMPORTANT CONCEPTS FOR COMPARING VARIATIONS IN DRINKING BEHAVIOR

Studies of drinking behavior have been done by individuals in each country with little or no consideration *vis-à-vis* coordinating efforts or accumulating new research on that of the past. What is needed in order to more completely mine the wealth of information contained in these studies are some overriding or general concepts into which diversely described findings can be categorized. Three such concepts are suggested here for consideration, although obviously these by no means exhaust the possibilities. The first is the integration-segregation continuum or dimension. It will be illustrated by data on drinking as an accompaniment to meals and the setting selected for drinking in various countries. The second concerns the variations and interplay in the balance of informal and formal social control of drinking. The third assesses the effect of cultural diffusion through mass media and travel on drinking patterns and preferences. Available studies offering findings that might be categorized by these concepts and possibilities for future research are discussed below.

Cultural Differences in Integration or Segregation of Alcohol Consumption

More interesting than comparing per capita consumption statistics is investigating the integrative role drinking plays in various cultures. In discussing the degrees of integration of drinking with other social behavior in a culture, only countries in their entirety as homogeneous entities, with but few exceptions, will be considered. In so doing it must be recognized that in any given country any single drinking pattern actually can exist. There are various patterns which differentiate, for instance, social classes and the sexes. Subcultures probably also add to these divergencies. However, much can be learned by examining the various so-called "marginal distributions," or the total picture in a country and the place of drinking behavior within it.

ALCOHOL AS IT IS INTEGRATED WITH MEALS   The integration of alcohol with everyday activities can be understood in part by describing how alcoholic beverages are consumed with meals. Only in Sweden, of all the Scandinavian countries, is alcohol used fairly frequently in connection with meals. More than three-quarters of the men interviewed in Stockholm had eaten a meal when they drank their most recent drink. In the other Nordic capitals the corresponding figure was about 50 percent, though it depended on the beverage in question. In Copenhagen and Oslo dining does not accompany alcoholic drinks with equal frequency. This applies to "hard" liquors along with lighter drinks. But in Helsinki wine or beer drunk alone is less common than taken in connection with meals (Jonsson and Nilsson 1972: 44). In Helsinki the ingestion of wine alone without a meal is a consequence of the cheap price of wine in comparison with other alcoholic beverages. Wines have been found to be a special favorite of thrifty alcoholics (Ahlström-Laakso 1970).

Drinking alcoholic beverages during meals is not customary in the Netherlands either. Only about 2 percent of the Dutch drink during their hot meal (Gadourek 1963: 451). The use of alcohol is not connected with eating in London, either, but apparently rather with togetherness and "hanging around." This finding did not come from a survey especially concerned with the subject of drinking with meals. Apparently the matter of drinking in a public house was spontaneously mentioned by nearly two-thirds of the men excepting those belonging to the two uppermost social classes (Edwards, et al. 1972: 84). In Poland, where the main source of alcohol is vodka, alcohol consumption with meals is uncommon but social drinking is frequent (Swiecicki 1963).

Drinking can also be quite detached from everyday social activities and reserved for separate occasions in countries where it is not concomitant with meals. The concentration of drinking situations and alcohol consumption within the space of a few days of the week is one aspect of this phenomenon. In Finland, for example, of all the alcohol ingested by men, 65 percent is consumed during the three days of the weekend and 38 percent on Saturday alone (Makela 1969: 128). In Copenhagen consumption is distributed more evenly over the week (Jonsson and Nilsson 1972: 46). In the Netherlands some 42 percent of the drinking is done over the weekend, Saturday being the specially favored day (Gadourek 1963: 452). In London also the weekend exerts a strong influence on drinking.

It is interesting to note that, even though in many countries the heaviest drinking is done over the weekend, its concentration on a particular day varies from country to country. Thus in London drinking does not reach as sharp a peak on Saturdays as it does, for instance, in Finland. However, in London the second most favored drinking day is Sunday, whereas in Finland, Friday competes on equal terms in this respect with Sunday (Edwards, et al. 1972: 83). It would be interesting to know the reason for this difference. Does the Englishman's observance of the Sabbath, for instance, involve a visit to the neighborhood pub?

In France, on the other hand, all the alcoholic beverages taken by women are consumed in accompaniment with lunch or dinner. Additionally, a substantial part of the alcohol used by French men is drunk during some meal. Here, however, the differences between the types of drinks were found to be clear-cut. The rank order of preference was approximately four-fifths of all cider, three-quarters of all wine, two-thirds of all beer, and one half of all distilled spirits — but no aperitifs whatsoever were taken with meals. In France, therefore, alcohol is largely if not exclusively used as a food chaser. For instance, if individual consumption rather than beverage-type is considered, more than one-third of the men and one-tenth of the women in France drink frequently between meals. Further, 15 and 5 percent of men and women, respectively, admit to frequent use (Sadoun, et al. 1965: 46, 104).

In Italy drinking is connected with eating even more closely than in France. Seventy percent of the men and 94 percent of the women claimed to drink exclusively with food and at regular meal times. Moreover, serving alcoholic beverages with meals was reported to be associated with the consumption of moderate quantities of alcohol. Of those men whose alcohol consumption represented less than 10 percent of the total daily caloric intake, 74 percent drank exclusively with meals. Of those whose alcohol consumption provided more than 10 percent of the total caloric intake, 64 percent drank exclusively with meals (Lolli, et al. 1958: 71).

Considering the connections between eating meals and drinking alcoholic beverages, it should also be remembered that the importance of meals varies in each culture. In Italy the eating of meals is to a high degree a social activity, one having an inherent worth, an integrating function. Only 10 percent of the men and 8 percent of the women were found by the survey to eat their evening meals customarily alone (Lolli, et al. 1958: 107). In Finland, by contrast, eating is conspicuously less of a social ritual. Finns look upon mealtime as an unavoidable part of their daily routine. In the preparation and eating of meals, the Finns spend less time than the Italians.

PICKING THE PROPER PLACE TO DRINK   To what extent, then, is the use of alcohol a segregated activity? A clear majority of the drinking sessions among Finns takes place in private premises and less than a quarter of them in restaurants. The restaurant institution is fairly foreign to Finns. Over half the Finns visit a restaurant less than once a year (Partanen 1970). Yet in Finland alcohol consumption in restaurants accounts for a larger share of the total consumption than it does in Sweden and Norway. The explanation for this lies in the fact that it is the heavy consumer who is the mainstay of the Finnish restaurants; only 10 percent of the Finnish population accounts for 80 percent of the visits to restaurants and for even a larger percentage of the alcohol consumed in them (Partanen 1970). Similarly, Swedes drink alcoholic beverages primarily when visiting the homes of friends or when entertaining guests. However, the main Swedish consumers of alcohol are also the chief patrons of restaurants (Nilsson and Svensson 1971: 131). In Copenhagen, by contrast, as much as one-third of the drinking takes place at work and the use of alcohol at home is a notably less frequent occurrence than in the other Scandinavian capitals (Jonsson and Nilsson 1972: 40). Likewise, in the Netherlands the use of alcohol can be described as a "home activity," where roughly half the population of that country generally confines its drinking to the household (Gadourek 1963: 452).

In London, quite the same as Finland and Sweden, enjoying restaurant service belongs primarily to the style of life pursued by the upper class. The institution of the English pub, however, rests mainly on the support of the middle and lower social classes. The pub is the preferred place of drinking "usually" or "always" for about 60 percent of classes III, IV, and V, but no more than 37 percent of classes I and II (Edwards, et al. 1972: 84). Correspondingly, a larger proportion of the members of the upper social classes than of the lower groups favor the ingestion of alcohol in home surroundings.

In France, the social functions of the English pub are performed by the cafe. Nearly one-third of the men and one-twentieth of the women in that country visit a cafe every day or several times a week for a drink. Like the British pub, the French cafe is the accepted meeting place of members of the lower economic groups. In nearly every community most of the workers have no other place to spend their leisure time (Sadoun, et al. 1965: 91–92). The Italian survey gives no information about the preferred places for drinking, nor does it throw light on the extent to which Italians dine in restaurants. Thus this important comparison cannot be made as yet.

The Interplay Between Formal and Informal Social Control

In discussing the toleration and control, both formal and informal, of drinking and drunkenness in a culture, attention must first be drawn to normative attitudes as well as actual behavior.

Finns have won a reputation for a particularly strong Finnish thirst, for a reckless manner of quenching it, and for seeking an escape from routine cares in drink with a splendid disregard for the consequences. The concept of the "Finnish booze head" is played up not only in magazines and popular literature but also by research scholars who took it seriously as early as the 1940's (Verkko 1949). The "booze head" concept has been used not only to describe reality but also to support the validity of temperance ideology in its applicability to Finns. Additionally, the concept of the hard-drinking Finn has even been looked upon as something to brag about a little; a parallel to the Finnish style is found in the reckless sousing of the Irish. A contrast is found mainly in the restrained and civilized way in which Jews and Italians take alcohol.

The release of aggression through drinking as observed among Scandinavians and Anglo-Saxons, especially the Finns and the Irish, has been explained in the light of the ambivalence of their cultures. In the attitudes toward the use of alcohol, expressions of both categoric rejection and outright idealization of drunkenness prevail side by side (Pittman 1964). Owing to this ambivalence, no universal norms applicable to the use of alcohol have evolved but only norms propagated by small groups (Bruun 1959). When alcohol is discussed in small groups in special situations, such discussions do not result in creating norms, that is, norms to be passed on from generation to generation.

Reflecting the absence of informal norms, for example, is the fact that formal social control of drunkenness is created through statutory machinery. These legislated controls are necessary because the informal control deriving from some generally accepted norm concerning this behavior is virtually nonexistent. This is shown, for instance, in an investigation recently made to find an explanation for the fact that Helsinki has a rate of arrests for drunkenness from seven to thirteen times higher than Copenhagen, despite the fact that the actual frequency of drunkenness is only slightly higher in the Finnish capital than in the Danish capital (Bruun 1969). The answer to this apparent contradiction was that the control machinery set up in the two cultures has a very different meaning in each. The values upheld in Helsinki as the basis for the social control of drunkenness favor such control.

They emanate from the community and emphasize public security, the maintenance of order, and esthetic considerations. The values applied in the control system in Copenhagen reflect community opposition to control, quite contrary to Helsinki. With community-oriented values absent in the Danish milieu, individually oriented values become predominant (Ahlström-Laakso 1971). Another way of putting it is that in Denmark, unlike the situation in Finland, general informal norms governing the act of drinking do exist. The Danes control drunkenness and its consequences in this way and start at an early stage of the entire cycle, that is, with the actual drinking situation itself.

Altogether too little is known about the informal norms and informal social control regulating drinking. When researchers investigating the Italian alcohol culture emphasize the significance of meals in the regulation of drinking, they have only described an end product. More crucial to knowledge about control of drinking behavior than whether it accompanies meals is to learn how such informal norms governing drinking arise and how they are incorporated into the culture as a custom. As yet, it is not known what kinds of control mechanisms exist in the Italian case, nor is anything known about their dynamic operations. Before the Italian wine culture and the Finnish dining table can be integrated, the conceptual similarities and differences in the informal control system of each situation must be known.

The Investigation of Changes in Drinking Habits Due to
Cultural Diffusion

In most studies, when drinking habits are investigated the culture is regarded always as given. Nowadays cultural interchange is probably so lively that its flux cannot help but influence drinking habits and customs, and this is a subject that bears investigation. The influence of mass communications and mass tourism is becoming conspicuous. For instance, Finnish tourists learn to drink wine on holiday trips to Majorca. At present, however, it is not known exactly how this new knowledge or its variants are integrated with old habits. In Finland new statistics on alcohol consumption indicate that light beverages are on the way to usurping the traditional preference for hard liquors. This apparent trend has been hailed as a positive development. But research surveys reveal that the light drinks have become favorite beverages of alcoholics because they are relatively inexpensive (Ahlström-Laakso 1970; Makela 1970c). This fact, in addition to the cultural diffusion mentioned above, accounts for their increased sale. Correspondingly, when international trade in alcoholic beverages takes a place alongside the traditional domestic production, its effects are probably also reflected in drinking behavior.

Correspondingly, it is known that after the removal of restrictions on the sale of medium beer in 1969 (the sales network for this beverage was expanded from approximately 103 retail stores run by the Alcohol Monopoly to all food shops), medium beer did not usurp the market of the traditionally favored distilled liquors, but merely took a place beside them (Makela 1970a). Details of the situation, however, are still obscure and consideration of it raises questions: will, for instance, two different types of drinking situations evolve in time or will some synthesis gradually emerge? Alternatively, it is known that when a certain behavior pattern marks a culture, new habits resembling the old in their function are fairly easily grafted on the existing pattern. This occurred in a Finnish rural community where a malt beverage tradition had prevailed. The local alcoholics switched from "Pilsner" (very light beer) to medium beer. On the other hand, in another community where this malt beer tradition had not developed, medium beer took its place alongside the previously favored drinks (Ahlström-Laakso 1972).

Epidemiological alcohol studies carried out from time to time have the important function of acting as a gauge for the alcohol or temperance situation. Parallel studies are also needed, however, to bring to light the substantive content of the changes taking place and the processes by which they occur.

REFERENCES

AHLSTRÖM-LAAKSO, S.
  1970   *Alkoholistien alkoholinkayttotavoista* [Drinking habits of alcoholics]. Alkoholipoliittisen Tutkimusliatoksen Tutkimusseloste 57.
  1971   Arrests for drunkenness — two capital cities compared. *Scandinavian Studies in Criminology* 3:89–105.
  1972   "The effects of a slight change in alcohol restrictions on the drinking habits of alcoholics." Paper presented at the Thirtieth International Congress on Alcoholism and Drug Dependence, Amsterdam.
ALLARDT, E.
  1957   "Drinking norms and drinking habits," in *Drinking and drinkers.* Finnish Foundation for Alcohol Studies 6. Helsinki.
BRUUN, K.
  1959   *Drinking behavior in small groups.* Helsinki.
  1969   The actual and the registered frequency of drunkenness in Helsinki. *British Journal of Addiction* 64:3–8.

1972 *Alkoholi: käytto, vaikutukset ja kontrolli* [Alcohol: its use, effects and control]. Helsinki.

DE LINT, J., W. SCHMIDT
1968 The distribution of alcohol consumption in Ontario. *Quarterly Journal of Studies on Alcohol* 29:968–973.

EDWARDS, G., J. CHANDLER, C. HENSMAN
1972 Drinking in a London suburb. Correlates of normal drinking. *Quarterly Journal of Studies on Alcohol*, supplement 6:69–93.

GADOUREK, I., *et al.*
1963 *Riskante gewoonten en zorg eigen welzijn* [Hazardous habits and human well-being]. Groningen.

JONSSON, E., T. NILSSON
1972 *Samnordisk undersökning av vuxna mans alkoholvanor* [Joint Nordic survey of drinking habits among adult males]. Central-förbundet för alkohol — och narkotikaupplysning (CAN).

LEDERMANN, S.
1956 *Alcool, alcoolisme — alcoolisation*, volume one. Paris.

LOLLI, G., E. SERIANNI, G. M. GOLDER, P. LUZATTO-FEGIZ
1958 *Alcohol in Italian culture*. New Brunswick, N.J.: Rutgers Center of Alcohol Studies.

MAC ANDREW, C., R. B. EDGERTON
1969 *Drunken comportment*. Chicago: Aldine.

MAKELA, K.
1969 *Alkoholinkayton viikkorytmi* [The weekly rhythm in the use of alcohol]. Alkoholipoliittisen Tutkimuslaitoksen Tutkimusseloste 46.

1970a Juomiskertojen useus nautittujen juomien ja maaran mukaan en-nen ja jalkeen lainuudistuksen [The frequency of drinking occa-sions according to consumed beverages and quantities before and after the new liquor laws]. *Alkoholipolitiikka* 35:246–255.

1970b Uusi alkoholilainsaadanto ja raittiden lukumaara [The new alco-hol legislation and the number of abstainers]. *Alkoholiksymys* 38:18–23.

1970c Ammatin arvostus, tulot ja alkoholijuomien käytto. [Occupational prestige of profession, income and the use of alcohol] *Alkoholiky-symys* 38:125–148.

1971a Concentration of alcohol consumption. *Scandinavian Studies in Criminology* 3:77–88.

1971b "Measuring the consumption of alcohol in the 1968-69 alcohol consumption study," in *Oy Alko Ab. Social Research Institute of Alcohol Studies*, volume two. Helsinki.

NILSSON, T., P. G. SVENSSON
1971 *Svenska folkets alkoholvanor och alkoholattityder* [Drinking hab-its and attitudes among Swedish people]. RUS (Riksundersöknin-gen), Statens Offentliga Utredningar.

PARTANEN, J.
  1970   *Asiakastutkimus 1968. ravintolakäyntien tiheytta ja suhtautumista ravintoloihin kartoittavan tutkimuksen tulokset* [Clientele study, 1968. Findings of the pilot study on the frequency of restaurant visits and the attitude toward restaurants]. Alkoholipoliittisen Tutkimuslaitoksen Tutkimusseloste 53.

PITTMAN, D. J.
  1964   "International overview: social and cultural factors in drinking patterns, pathological and non-pathological," in *Selected papers presented at the 27th International Congress on Alcohol and Alcoholism*, volume one: *Alcoholism as a cultural question*, 1–13.

SADOUN, R., G. LOLLI, M. SILVERMAN
  1965   *Drinking in French culture*. New Brunswick, N.J.: Rutgers Center of Alcohol Studies.

SULKUNEN, P.
  1973   Alkoholijuomien tuotannosta jja kulutuksesta [On the production and consumption of alcoholic beverages]. *Alkoholipolitiikka* 37: 111–117.

SWIECICKI, A.
  1963   *Struktura spożycia napojów alkohowych w. polsce*. Warsaw.

VERKKO, V.
  1949   *Lahimmaisen ja oma henki* [One's own life and that of one's fellow men]. Jyväskylä.

Family Behavior and Alcoholism

JOAN ABLON

As a consequence of the realization that the early stereotype of the alcoholic as a homeless derelict was an erroneous and unrealistic one, a florescence of literature dealing with family-related aspects of alcoholism has appeared during the last twenty years. While the number of papers is substantial, the authors, issues, and orientations are limited. The literature on the alcoholic family typically has presented two divergent viewpoints: (1) a psychological emphasis on specific pathological characteristics of the personalities of the two spouses, and (2) a sociological emphasis on interaction between family members. Few papers have combined the two approaches. The most persistent subject that has been explored has been the personality and role of the wife of the alcoholic in relation to the inception and maintenance of her husband's excessive drinking patterns. Little attempt has been made to tie family behavior in alcoholism into the substantial body of theory and data dealing with other forms of family crisis and stress. Rarely has any reference to the larger sociocultural context within which the family exists been presented. This paper will review the literature on alcoholism and the family and suggest areas that have been neglected and new directions which hold promise for future research.

Bailey (1961: 82) noted that early sampling of subjects taken largely from arrested inebriate and certain hospitalized populations tended to present a view of alcoholics as a group of "undersocialized, poorly integrated individuals, comprising homeless derelicts, chronic offenders,

The research for this paper was supported in part by the National Institute of Mental Health, United States Public Health Service, Grant nos. MH-21552 and MH-08375.

and the mentally ill." The alcoholic was regarded as a loner with few social ties. Later studies were based on middle- and upper-class non-psychotic samples from hospitals and outpatient clinics; alcoholics were recognized to have married to the same extent as urban males and females of comparable age but to exhibit a significantly higher separation and divorce rate. Bacon, in one of the earliest papers on alcoholism and the family (1945), argues that excessive drinking patterns are more incompatible with marriage than with any other societal institution because these patterns effectively preclude the close interpersonal relations that constitute the essence of the marital association.

THE WIFE OF THE ALCOHOLIC

Initial clinically oriented studies pictured the wife as a disturbed pathological personality with dependency conflicts and complex needs that directed her to choose as a husband an alcoholic or someone with a personality type susceptible to alcoholism (if it were not full blown at time of marriage), and further to maintain the excessive drinking patterns. It was suggested that if the husband began to improve, many wives exhibited their own form of emotional disorder (Futterman 1953; Lewis 1954; Whalen 1953; MacDonald 1956; Price 1945). A common pattern was that of a woman with great dependency needs, yet who chose a man unable to meet them. She then castigated him for not being able to meet her conflicting dependency needs. Her vested psychological interests were evidenced when his achievement of sobriety commonly caused her to decompensate psychologically or physically. She could maintain her own adequacy only at his expense.

A contrasting point of view was presented in the works of Jackson (1954, 1958, 1962), who focused on how the family as a total unit adjusted to alcoholism. From her careful and systematic observations of Al-Anon Family Groups in Seattle over nearly a decade, Jackson presented in various papers a natural history of the phases of the alcoholic process for the family. Jackson organized her data on the experiences of member wives into a stable chronology of seven stages representing family behavior in the alcoholic process: (1) attempts to deny the problem; (2) attempts to eliminate the problem; (3) disorganization; (4) attempts to reorganize in spite of the problem; (5) efforts to escape the problem; (6) reorganization as part of the family; (7) recovery and reorganization of the family (Jackson 1954). Jackson was skeptical that current pathological characteristics of the wife could be hypothesized to constitute a set personality type and to have existed in the pre-drinking or pre-marriage period. She presented the alternative suggestion that the particular "pathological" behavior constellations exhibited by the types of wives suggested by Whalen and others might represent these women as they coped in particular ways appropriate to stresses of the respective stages:

> ... that women undergoing similar experiences of stress, within similarly unstructured situations defined by the culture and reacted to by members of the society in such a manner as to place limits on the range of possible behavior, will emerge from this experience showing similar neurotic personality traits. As the situation evolves some of these personality traits will also change. Change has been observed in the women studied which correlates with altered family interaction patterns (Jackson 1954: 586).

Jackson noted that in her work with Al-Anon members she found very few women who decompensated when their husbands achieved sobriety. The findings of other researchers later supported this statement.

Lemert (1960), following Jackson's search for a fixed sequence of events by looking at five sample groups of wives in a California city, added a rich socioeconomic dimension to his data that is characteristically lacking in the literature. These groups were derived from: (1) city commitments to the state hospital, (2) public welfare agency clients, (3) divorce court, (4) police probation cases, and (5) Al-Anon groups. He suggested that family behavior must be seen in the larger cultural context in which it occurs. Family members may perceive and react to differing events in large part depending on socioeconomic factors. The meaning and functions of the same events (such as isolation, frequency of sexual relationships, conflict over children) for the subjects may depend on their socioeconomic status. Lemert could not find a common sequence of events in family adjustment; rather, he found that events tended to cluster in general stages of early, middle, and late adjustment. While several researchers have, in passing, commented on the social class of their samples, few have emphasized this as it affects attitudes or motivation for treatment.

James and Goldman (1971) attempted to integrate Jackson's stages of family adjustment within five reasonably distinct and persistent styles of coping behavior that had been identified by Oxford and Guthrie (1968). Among their other findings, James and Goldman noted that the coping styles of wives in their sample changed over time as did their related problems, and all wives in the sample used more than one style of coping. While cautioning against causal theories, the authors concluded that the results of their study seem to favor Jackson's view that the wife's behavior and current coping style may be caused by the current stage of the husband's drinking, rather than a situation in which the "wife's fixed personality pathologies caused the husband's pliable personality to change via alcoholism which then allows her to employ her latent coping mechanism" (James and Goldman 1971: 380).

Bailey (1961: 90) cogently summarized the two points of view presented above:

Research on alcoholism and marriage has been based on one of two hypotheses: (a) that women with certain types of personality structure tend to select alcoholics or potential alcoholics as mates in order to satisfy unconscious needs of their own, and that these needs require the continued drinking of the husband; (b) that women undergoing similar experiences of stress will, as a result, manifest many neurotic traits in common. While no one denies that the spouse of the alcoholic is seriously disturbed by the time she reaches an identifiable source of help or community intervention, there is a basic question as to whether her disturbance antedates the partner's alcoholism or stems from it. Logically, the two hypotheses need not be mutually exclusive, yet their implications for treatment, for public education and for the future direction of research are very different.

A few years later, Bailey (1963b) reported on new research published or in progress that presented more evidence that a conceptualization of a unitary personality for wives of alcoholics is not tenable. Even if pathology could be shown for a contemporary period, it was difficult indeed to assume the wife had chosen a man destined for alcoholism, since more recent studies indicated that a minority of alcoholics were drinking to excess at the time of marriage (Jackson 1954; Bailey 1965; James and Goldman 1971). Clifford (1960) and Lemert (1960), on the other hand, stated that a majority or even all of their subjects knew about their prospective husband's problems. Lemert found that those men who had drinking problems before marriage showed a much higher incidence and higher frequency of dependency attributes than those whose problems developed later (Lemert 1962).

Kogan and Jackson in the 1960's produced a series of papers investigating a variety of aspects of personality of the wives of alcoholics. These aspects included emotional disturbance, role expectations, and perceptions of their spouses and themselves. Kogan, et al. (1963) reported a comparison of MMPI responses of wives of alcoholics who belonged to Al-Anon and to a control group of wives who had no alcoholism problem in their families. While significantly more wives of alcoholics showed evidence of disturbance in personality function than did the comparison group, the total number of disturbed subjects was less than half on any measure, hence the investigators did not feel

that generalization was warranted. They noted that the type of disturbance found was highly variable and that no particular personality type
could be distinguished. They concluded that a static concept of the
"wife of the alcoholic" was inappropriate (Kogan, et al. 1963: 237).

Bailey, et al. (1962) and Corder, et al. (1964) likewise found relatively little difference indicating marked neurotic or disturbed behavior
between samples of wives of alcoholics and wives of non-alcoholics.

Kogan and Jackson (1965b, 1965c) explored both early life experience and current stress situations of wives of alcoholics and concluded
that complex multivariate relationships must be considered in order to
understand disturbance. Women who experienced the dyad of an inadequate mother and an unhappy childhood appeared to experience
more personal stress and to marry men who were alcoholic or became
alcoholic.

Kogan and Jackson (1965a) further tried to differentiate between
types of current stress situations, categorizing some as impersonal
(financial, legal) as opposed to personal (dealing with interrelationships
in the family), and found that personal stress situations contributed
more to current disturbance in the wives. One finding that might be
noted was that there were no basic personality differences found between wives whose husbands continued to drink and those who had
achieved sobriety.

In contrast, Clifford (1960) reported from a New York clinic sample
that he was able to find identifiable differences in certain attitudes of a
group of wives whose husbands had stopped drinking in contrast to a
group whose husbands were active alcoholics. Six basic attitudes toward
the role of alcoholism and toward the alcoholic in the wife's life were
chosen for study: (1) the effect on the family; (2) the wife's acceptance
of personal responsibility; (3) her attitudes and feelings about a possible
cure for her husband's alcoholism; (4) her sense of social adequacy;
(5) her concept of social status; and (6) her concept of her indispensa-
bility to the welfare of the alcoholic. Clifford noted that all of the
women in both groups had a history of alcoholism in their families and
also a premarital awareness of their husband's alcoholism. Clifford's
findings are dramatic in being so clear-cut but it would be helpful to
know more about his methodology. His report is written in sweeping
terms that suggest unanimity on all counts in the differential group.
This contrasts with the complexities in response that almost all other
researchers report.

Bailey, et al., in a New York sample (1965), found a pattern of "un-
natural" attitudes toward drinking, i.e. excessive drinking or total ab-

stinence in 79.2 percent of parents of women who married alcoholics, in contrast to 54.2 percent of parents of comparison groups. Clifford (1960) stated that all of the subjects in his study had a history of alcoholism in their families. Unfortunately, little data are available on this very significant aspect of the wives' early life experiences.

HUSBANDS OF WOMEN ALCOHOLICS

There is a dearth of material available on husbands of alcoholic women in contrast to the substantial number of studies dealing with wives of male alcoholics. Jellinek (1960) estimated that women constitute one sixth of the alcoholic population of the United States. Belfer, et al. (1971) quoted figures ranging from one fifth to one half. The latter figure would place the female alcoholic population at close to 4.5 million. Discussions with community agency personnel indeed suggest that a liberal estimate is indicated. Female alcoholics often are able to maintain low social visibility compared to their male counterparts, chiefly for economic reasons. The housewife who drinks at home may sooner or later become obvious in her habits to her family but still may maintain a facade before her friends and the larger community.

Lisansky (1957, 1958) reported on two samples of female and male alcoholics from a Connecticut prison farm and from an outpatient clinic in New York. Significant differences appeared in the comparison of women from these two samples, differences that in large part may well result from corresponding differences in socioeconomic status. The clinic sample represented a typically middle-class population, while the prison farm sample included women of a lower socioeconomic status.

Lisansky noted that a somewhat larger percentage of the women than of the men had married (87 percent compared to 80 percent). The proportion of women and of men outpatients who married and who remained single was about the same as in the general population, but sizable and statistically highly significant differences occurred between alcoholics and the general population in proportions of separation and divorce. A predominance of alcoholics married other alcoholics. Relatively little data were given on husbands of female alcoholics but among the women, one third had had, or had at the time of the study, husbands who also were problem drinkers. There was a tendency for women to be married to men much older than themselves.

The prison farm women had a higher incidence of divorce, separation, and death in their families. Their problem drinking had begun at an earlier age and their marriages were characterized by more conflict and instability than those of the outpatient women. Husbands of the prison farm women were often physically abusive, unemployed, or irregularly employed and were heavy drinkers. Some also were in jail. These women frequently supported unemployed husbands or boyfriends. Their marriages gave them very little economic or emotional security. The outpatient women, while secure in such more obvious aspects of their marriages, were conflicted in other ways. More than twice the number of outpatient women than prison farm women were raising their own children (77 percent compared to 35 percent).

Lisansky's study suggested that women's drinking more often related to, and was triggered by, specific life events than was the case for the males sampled. The women's problematic marriages then might contribute to their drinking patterns. Belfer, et al. (1971) stated that they found no association between marital status and any definable group of alcoholic women, but they did not deny that marital status may be an important contribution to the total picture even though not a "sufficient cause."

Fox (1956: 11) reported from her psychiatric practice experience that compared to wives of male alcoholics, husbands of alcoholic women are less accepting of their wives' drinking patterns and more apt to leave "an alcoholic wife whom they feel they can no longer love." Women have a greater tendency to mother and nurse a sick husband, while men are less willing to learn about alcoholism as an illness. Cultural norms allow more freedom for drinking among males, making alcoholism a less acceptable form of behavior among women. Unlike many wives, who are dependent on their husbands for subsistence, men can more easily opt for the economic independence that goes with separation.

Fox (1962) presented a typology of husbands of alcoholic women somewhat reminiscent of Whalen's typology of wives of male alcoholics, mentioning such types as the long-suffering martyr, the punishing, sadistic male, the dependent male, and others. These she differentiated from the "normal" man who "finds" himself with an alcoholic wife.

INTERACTION IN THE ALCOHOLIC MARRIAGE

During the 1950's little research was published that examined the contemporary dynamics of the dyadic relationship between spouses or interrelationships within the total family unit. One glimpse into the nature of marital relationships in the conflicted alcoholic family was reported in a group of articles included in a symposium published in the *American Journal of Orthopsychiatry* in 1959. A major failing of previous research had been the lack of control groups and a tendency to look at each spouse as a bundle of pathological characteristics with little sensitive examination of the marital interaction. This symposium, entitled "The interrelatedness of alcoholism and marital conflict," contained three papers (by Bullock and Mudd, Ballard, and Mitchell) that reported research with couples, in some instances using both alcoholic and nonalcoholic conflicted families.

Bullock and Mudd (1959) reported a high degree of conflict in the couples observed. While the wives regarded the husbands' drinking as the main difficulty in their relationships, the husbands presented a variety of complaints about the attitudes and behavior of their wives. Conflict was of long duration and was reported to have existed in the premarital relationship in more than half the cases. Personality problems and difficult family backgrounds of both partners appeared to be important factors.

Ballard (1959) reported on MMPI results from experimental alcoholic families and control nonalcoholic families. His paper is of particular interest for several reasons. His data suggested that the conflicted alcoholic family is not unique when compared to its nonalcoholic, conflicted counterpart in our society. Secondly, Ballard's conclusions represent an early emphasis on the marital unit with ongoing interaction and continuing feedback and reaction rather than focusing only on the specific individual pathologies of individual members. Ballard described the personality features of both spouses which interacted in complementary fashion to bring unconscious gratifications to the other. Each had a stake in maintaining the status quo established by the drinking behavior. He pointed out the complex reasons why the alcoholic conflicted marriage was less amenable to therapeutic intervention than the nonalcoholic conflicted marriage.

A series of papers, which implicitly or explicitly regarded the interaction between spouses or the total family unit as a necessary functional context for the understanding of the individual alcoholic's drinking pattern, began to appear in the 1960's.

Ewing and Fox (1968) suggested that the family homeostasis is the perpetuator of drinking problems and that this homeostasis must be changed if the drinking is to be controlled. They also noted that the wives tend to have personality dynamics similar to those of their husbands. The wife copes with her own unacceptable dependency wishes by adopting the mastery of the family when the husband's excessive drinking patterns cause him to drop responsibilities.

Indeed, it appears that in alcoholic marriages a homeostatic mechanism is established which resists change over long periods of time. The behavior of each spouse is rigidly controlled by the other. As a result, an effort by one person to alter his typical role behavior threatens the family equilibrium and provokes renewed efforts by the spouse to maintain the status quo (Ewing and Fox 1968: 88).

In treatment, the wife's appreciation of her dependency needs and acceptance of some responsibility for the husband's drinking must accompany real changes in marital roles. Reciprocal role changes in self-defeating interactions must occur if the existing homeostasis is to be changed.

Steinglass, et al. (1971a, 1971b), working within an explicit systems approach, presented a specific model of several dimensions for use in analysis of the family in alcoholism, and described the clinical application of this model in several treatment situations involving dyads of family members. The authors present the clearest statement in the literature describing the manner in which family members are involved in an ongoing alcoholic bargain which functions for the maintenance of the system, and how the untangling of the elements of this system may be useful for the therapist.

Steinglass, et al. suggest that family members as component parts of a system "manipulate" other members and adjust their behavior as is necessary to maintain a complementary relationship of psychopathology, needs, strengths, cultural values, etc. within the family (Steinglass, et al. 1971b: 405). This maneuvering is necessary for the ongoing existence of the family group as a functioning system. Drinking behavior may operate in either of two forms: the drinking behavior of one member may serve as a symptom or expression of stress or strain created by conflicts within the system. In this way the drinking may serve, as it were, as an escape valve for such stress. Or drinking may constitute an integral part of one of the working programs within the system. In this form it might serve unconscious needs of family members in its effect on such areas as role differentiation or the distribution of power.

The model presented here forms a bridge between the psychological and sociological theories presented previously by explaining two differing functions of drinking, both occurring for the maintenance of the ongoing family system. The authors (Steinglass, et al. 1971b) suggest that the specific role that alcohol plays in maintaining family systems must be carefully understood before any therapeutic intervention is planned.

The systems approach indicates that the "drinking system" rather than the individual alcoholic should be considered as the appropriate basic unit of clinical research. As noted by Ewing and Fox (1968), Steinglass, et al. (1971a, 1971b) point out the significance of the efforts of the system to maintain itself:

From a systems point of view, it is the protection of the functioning system itself that takes precedence over the individual concerns or needs of the members of the system. If the continuation of therapy implies a threat to the integrity or functioning of the system, then therapy will probably be rejected as an alien and dangerous force. It would seem, then, that the task of the therapist is to effect the desirable changes without appearing as an imminent threat to the ongoing system.

Ward and Faillace (1970) presented an even more comprehensive "system's view" of pathological drinking patterns. They described basically circular self-perpetuating behavior maintained to preserve an equilibrium that involves the alcoholic, his family, his employer, and community helpers. The authors suggested that three levels of inter-action systems must be considered: (1) that of the complex deter-minants of behavior within the individual; (2) that of the small group system of family behavior and response; and (3) that of the larger sociocultural context.

Ward and Faillace (1970) discussed patterns of family behavior, such as denial or punishment, that the wife may employ on herself and toward the alcoholic. These patterns serve to produce homeostasis in the family and are of a complementary and circular nature. Any actions that may require behavioral changes throughout the family system may be avoided at all costs. Thus the wife may resist change in the status quo to prevent the stress caused by disruption of existing equilibrium within the family. This system's view explains stress and symptoms exhibited by wives of recovering or recovered alcoholics from a structural-functional approach rather than by linking resistance to the specific individual pathology of the wife.

Ward and Faillace (1970) suggested that the action of extra-family community helpers in like manner may covertly serve to maintain drinking behavior because of the complementary persecution, rescue, or forgiveness needs of the helping system.

Steiner (1971) elaborated on Berne's exposition (1964: 73–81) of the transactional analysis position on alcoholism. Steiner considered alcoholism as a script or life plan for self-destruction. The individual may make an early decision — often forced and immature — which influences and predicts the rest of his life. For this decision he must have a script to follow. Steiner described three distinctive games alcoholics play: "Drunk and Proud," "Lush," and "Wino." The actions of the alcoholic put those around him in the position of being foolish and full of blame. The games differ in their dynamics, aims, and the roles taken by the significant others of the alcoholic or the community caregivers who allow the game-playing to continue. Roles suggested are Patsy, Dummy, Rescuer, Persecutor, and Connection. The importance of each of the roles in maintaining the game is discussed and the changes that must be made in these roles to thwart the drinker's game are explained. (For an interesting parallel analysis, see the Al-Anon brochure, "Alcoholism, a merry-go-round named denial," Al-Anon Family Group Headquarters 1969. This particular piece of literature is one of their most popular items.) Steiner's view also appeared in an article (1969) that met with considerably conflicting responses from other clinicians.

Gorad, working within an "interpersonal-interactional" framework (1971), explored the nature of styles of communication used by alcoholics and their wives by matching a sample of alcoholic married couples with a sample of nonalcoholic control couples in an interactional game-playing situation. He found that the alcoholic couples used "one-up" messages significantly more than did nonalcoholic couples. Gorad concluded that the alcoholic uses a responsibility-avoiding style of communication when drunk or sober for gaining control, while the wife uses a more direct responsibility-accepting style of communication. Alcoholics are competitive in the sense that by using this style of communication they attempt to gain for themselves a "one up" position in relationships. Control, then, may be sought through passive, dependent-appearing techniques, as well as through action, independence, and aggression which are the more commonly used modes. Because the alcoholic uses indirect, nonaggressive techniques, he characteristically is not seen as competitive. Gorad suggested that this may explain the frequent depiction of the alcoholic as withdrawn, dependent, and submissive, while the wife appears as dominant and controlling because of her direction. In reality they are equal in their competition for control.

Kogan and Jackson (1963), exploring role perceptions of wives of alcoholics, found that they perceived themselves as hyperfeminine, submissive, and wanting to be led and managed more than did wives of non-alcoholics. These perceptions are contrary to the view frequently found in the literature that wives of alcoholics often have strong dominance needs that require them to select a passive dependent spouse. The portrait of the wife as dominant has been described by the spouse (Mitchell 1959) and frequently by clinicians. Reality needs that cause the wives to overtly assume practical responsibilities within the household no doubt enter strongly into the creation of the image of the powerful wife.

Cork, in a paper suggesting treatment approaches (1964), listed and discussed characteristics of the alcoholic which most vitally affect family life. These characteristics are functionally and interactionally oriented in that they determine the nature of ongoing relationships within the family group, the employment situation, and significant social networks.

THE CHILDREN OF ALCOHOLICS

Bacon (1945), Newall (1950), Fox (1956, 1962), Cork (1964), Jackson (1962), Bailey, et al. (1965), and Chafetz, et al. (1971) have discussed the destructive effects that an alcoholic parent has on the development of the children in the household. Fox's comprehensive discussion (1962) covered virtually every consideration from the etiological factors leading to alcoholism in early life to the complexity of interrelationships that obtain in the alcoholic family. She emphasized parent-child relations and presented a detailed consideration of how the development of the personality of the child is complicated in this problem family situation.

Children of alcoholics suffer significant problems of identification and modeling. Their view and expectations of sex and family roles may be sorely distorted. They may reject the alcoholic or may take on many of his characteristics. Fighting and dissension between parents mar the children's perspective on marital relationships and may force them to take a position *vis-à-vis* conflicting parents. They have particular problems in defining their own identity and self worth. As they become sensitive to the larger social world around them, they may react with great shame and humiliation, often becoming withdrawn and isolated from their peers. Family agency personnel today stress the prevalence of drug-related problems among these children.

Bailey, et al. (1965) found that children of alcoholics exhibited more negative behavioral symptoms than did the children in the control groups of non-alcoholic families. The children of alcoholics were more frequently identified by the New York Social Service Exchange clearance as having problems than were children in the other groups.

Chafetz, et al. (1971) cited some sources suggesting that children of alcoholics fare worse in symptomatology than children of non-alcoholics and others that find little evidence of ill health. They reported their own study of a sample of children of alcoholics in a child guidance center whom they compared to children of non-alcoholics. They did not find great differences in negative effect on health. They did, however, point out the "distinct and deleterious social consequences" for such a child with respect to his potential socialization problems: "The major dissimilarities have to do with the effect of an alcohol problem in a parent on the functioning of the family as a social unit and on occurrences in the child's life which may represent impediments to becoming a socialized adult" (Chafetz, et al. 1971: 696). Family disruption was frequent, as was a relatively high incidence of problems in school and with the law.

Bacon (1945) and Jackson (1958, 1962) have pointed out that the presence of children may intensify the problems of the alcoholic. Cognizance of failure in the responsibilities of parenthood, and related guilt, may present added pressure for excessive drinking.

Day, in a succinct review article entitled "Alcoholism and the family" (1961), listed characteristic parent-child relationships in the family of orientation that have been suggested as crucial in the etiology of male alcoholism. She discussed the effects of alcoholism in the family on children and emphasized the critical links between family process and aspects of etiology.

FACTORS AFFECTING FAMILY ACTIONS IN REGARD TO THE ALCOHOLIC PROBLEM

Bailey, et al. (1962) and Jackson and Kogan (1963) focused on types of action taken by wives of alcoholics. Bailey and associates looked at three groups of wives: (1) a group who had separated from or divorced from their spouses; (2) a group who were living with active alcoholics; and (3) a group whose husbands had achieved sobriety. They found that families who had separated had experienced extensive patterns of economic inadequacy and pathological behavior with physical violence involved. Wives who stayed with an active alcoholic had experienced less stressful situations than those who had separated. There was less job loss, fewer young children, less infidelity, and less trouble with the police. In general, these wives had suffered fewer serious behavioral consequences.

Those wives whose husbands were sober at the time of the study were of higher economic status. The wives shared a concern about economic security and upward economic and social mobility. It was suggested that the anxiety over economics may have exerted a constructive force in the husband's recovery. These wives were the most isolated from friends and community professional resources. Interestingly, those women who had the best outcomes had least often been subjects of community concern.

Although the wives tested scored higher in psychophysiological disturbances than a representative sample of New York women, the differences were relatively slight except for those wives who were living with an active alcoholic. These women exhibited the highest scores on psychopathology, which may suggest that they were women who had greater basic emotional distress than those who terminate their marriages or support their husband's recovery. However, the other groups — those women who had separated and those whose husbands were now sober — reported that they too had exhibited significantly higher symptomatology when their husbands were actively drinking. These findings support the point of view presented by Jackson (1954) that the early clinical reports might well have focused on symptomatic reaction to stress that was stage specific and time limited rather than reflective of long-standing basic pathology.

Jackson and Kogan (1963) studied help-seeking patterns in wives who attended Al-Anon groups in Seattle. The average Al-Anon member had tried 4.5 caregivers before coming to Al-Anon. The authors found that help-seeking was a patterned activity with psychological and social correlates. The nature and effectiveness of available community resources were likewise of significance. They investigated the variety and kinds of help sought and the perceived effectiveness of these resources for the women. In this pithy article, Jackson and Kogan touched on a number of significant issues of importance to the researcher and the clinician. They found that in congruence with societal values that stress family independence and urge families to try to help themselves before seeking outside help, most indeed did initially try. However, the greater the hardship experienced by the family, the more help was sought. Lower-class families, as Lemert noted (1960), sought help earlier and more fequently than did middle-class families. The former also experienced more hardship in terms of economic inadequacy, physical violence, and infidelity.

Jackson and Kogan discussed in this paper (1963) a variety of issues surrounding conditions and circumstances for divorce. In keeping with the findings of Bailey, et al. (1962), they noted that the divorced differ significantly in having experienced greater hardship in economics, violence, and infidelity than those who did not divorce. As also noted by Bailey, et al., the families of recovered alcoholics had sought significantly less help from a smaller number of professionals over a briefer period of time. Once help was sought, it was used more effectively and there was less trial and error in approaches to community resources. This might suggest greater initial family strength. In support of Jackson's early work on the stages of alcoholism for the family unit, they found that the precipitating crisis of threatened divorce may be correlated with motivating the alcoholic to stop drinking. Those women who divorced and who attempted divorces fell into categories of greater emotional health more frequently than those who had made no such attempt.

In summary, Jackson and Kogan suggested that a prominent characteristic of the help-seeking careers of these families was the existence of fluctuating definitions of the nature of the problem combined with complex social and psychological factors.

TREATMENT

Families of alcoholics have sought help or "treatment" from a wide range of community caregivers — clergy, physicians, private mental health professionals of all persuasions, and various community service agencies. Emphatic feelings of failure have been mutual on the part of clients and caregivers. Clients argue that professionals do not understand their particular pernicious problem. Clinicians characteristically have felt that in their experience the wives of alcoholics are highly defensive and resistent to introspection and change and that their problems are almost as refractory to treatment as those of their alcoholic spouses. Thus much of the literature available on treatment approaches is not only cautious in its reporting but commonly pervaded with pessimism. This literature deals primarily with experiments in group therapy with wives and with family casework. A small number of writings discuss family therapy and Al-Anon groups.

The appearance in recent years of papers dealing with the alcoholic family in professional journals other than the *Quarterly Journal of Studies on Alcoholism* constitutes a hopeful step forward, reflecting a growing concern for the subject and an acknowledgment of its prevalence, as well as providing an opportunity for exposure to materials to professionals in a broader range of medical and caregiving fields.

GROUP THERAPY   The early group therapy papers reported on experimental groups, describing the group process and suggesting possible alternative formats for future endeavors (which it was hoped might be more successful). By and large, traditional analytic approaches were not effective. Most clinicians stated they felt the groups had been of positive consequence for participants despite the wives' poor attendance, initial resistance to facing their role in the alcoholic's drinking patterns, and a host of other difficulties (Burton 1962; Cork 1956; Ewing and Fox 1968; Gliedman, et al. 1956; Igersheimer 1959; MacDonald 1958; Pattison, et al. 1965; Pixley and Stiefel 1963). Some clinicians who ran groups for wives concurrently with their treatment endeavors with the alcoholic husbands noted that the parallel participation of wives in separate groups benefited the alcoholic in his treatment process (among these clinicians were Ewing and Fox, Gliedman, Pattison, and Pixley and Stiefel).

For an overview of issues and process in contrasting group modalities, the reader is directed to Pixley and Stiefel (1963) and Pattison, et al. (1965). Pixley and Stiefel presented a more traditional psychoanalytic approach toward group experience and discussed the evolution of the group process toward an analytic model. Pattison, et al. (1965) described experimental short-term group efforts in lieu of a traditional psychoanalytic approach. They emphasized certain significant socioeconomic class factors that contributed to the acceptance or rejection of the modes of treatment offered.

Meeks and Kelly (1970) reported on a project with five families in family therapy as a post-hospitalization treatment program. The nonalcoholic spouse initially was seen individually while the alcoholic was hospitalized. The authors emphasized the significance of involving the total family in the treatment process. The families showed evidence of improved relationships and healthier communication between members. Likewise, changes were noted in drinking behavior of the alcoholic patients.

CASEWORK   Bailey (1963a) shared her extensive casework experience in a paper that cogently discussed the present and continuing problems of the wife of the alcoholic. Her philosophical approach eclectically recognized the need for both reality-based therapy and some degree of depth analysis of the client's problems:

Social workers must use both the psychoanalytic theories and the sociological stress theories, blending them flexibly as appropriate in each case. The strength or weakness of a person's underlying personality influences his response to stress; some persons break down more easily than others. Stress theory, however, provides a useful framework for working with the wife of an alcoholic, regardless of the configuration of her personality. No one who has worked with such a wife will deny that she is seriously upset by the time she arrives at a potential source of help and treatment. The diagnostic question is whether her personality disturbance antedates her husband's alcoholism and indeed her marriage, or whether it is at least in part a result of the stresses inherent in living with an active alcoholic. The treatment implications of these two theories are quite different. The first point of view suggests a focus on direct treatment of the wife's underlying problems — an approach that has not been notably successful. If, on the other hand, the wife's disturbance is regarded as even partly a response to stress, the caseworker's efforts will be directed either toward modifying or removing the stress situation or toward enabling the wife to adapt to it with less anxiety and hostility. The wife of an alcoholic often responds favorably to this approach. She becomes able to function more comfortably and may eventually motivate her husband to seek help, so that in a real sense the husband and wife recover together from alcoholism.

Admittedly, the wife whose emotional problems are deep-seated will not respond to this approach. The point to be emphasized is that in the beginning phase of casework, it is almost impossible to make an adequate differential diagnosis. Though the worker should certainly be alert to diagnostic clues, he may be more effective initially if he works directly with the stress situation presented by the wife and postpones judgment on the degree of underlying disturbance (Bailey 1963a: 275).

Bailey (1968) and Cohen and Kraus (1971) have presented two comprehensive and thoughtful volumes that discuss salient issues and considerations in all aspects of the process of casework with the alcoholic family. Bailey's volume is a report of a training course conducted by the staff of the Alcoholism Programs of the Community Council of Greater New York. Cohen and Kraus (1971) described in detail the theoretical underpinnings and operations of an experimental program carried out in Cincinnati.

AL-ANON FAMILY GROUPS   Al-Anon Family Groups constitute an effective self-help, nonprofessional modality of group therapy and group education. Al-Anon Family Groups are fellowships of spouses, relatives, and friends of alcoholics who have banded together to solve the common problems encountered in living with an alcoholic. At present more than 5,000 Al-Anon Family Groups exist throughout the world, yet little is known about these groups by community caregivers and even less by the general public.

The dynamics of the Al-Anon process work through a mixture of educational and operational principles that must be accepted and assimilated by the member if she is to change her attitudes and behavior (Al-Anon Family Group Headquarters 1965, 1966; for analysis see Ablon 1973). The acceptance of one basic didactic lesson and several operational principles are paramount in the Al-Anon process: the basic didactic lesson is that alcoholism is a disease of the body and of the mind. The acceptance of the disease concept removes many burdens of hostility, guilt, and shame from the member and from her spouse if she passes this teaching onto him.

The operational principles involve changes in attitudes and behavior in the members and are based on a revised set of the "Twelve Steps" taken from Alcoholics Anonymous. The principles revolve about the goals of loving detachment from the alcoholic and acceptance of the fact that his drinking patterns cannot be changed by the Al-Anon member or by any person except himself. A second basic goal is the re-establishment of the self-esteem and independence of the member. She must take her own personality inventory and work on improving her own life and that of her children and her household. Ideally, the actions of the alcoholic are not discussed in meetings.

The group process is characterized by sharing rather than confrontation. Through the candid sharing of emotional reactions, experiences, and strategies for coping with common problems encountered in living with an alcoholic, the member is drawn into a process of self-examination and, usually, a change for the better in her own coping abilities.

Bailey (1965, 1968), Jackson (various papers), and, more briefly, Pattison, et al. (1965) perhaps have presented the most materials on Al-Anon that are available in the literature. Jackson's rich contributions to the literature resulted from data collected through a decade of participant observation and interviewing with Al-Anon members.

Bailey (1965) briefly but cogently described the process and compared attitudes of Al-Anon members with non-Al-Anon wives of alcoholics. She found that the majority of Al-Anon members defined alcoholism as a mental and physical illness; in contrast, non-members regarded it as a mental disturbance. Likewise, Al-Anon wives less frequently expressed moralistic attitudes toward alcoholism. Al-Anon members stated that they had found the groups of more help than any other form of aid sought. They had gained self-understanding in relation to their husband's drinking and the likelihood of the husband's achieving sobriety was increased by the wife's participation in Al-Anon.

Most clinicians who report on therapy with wives of alcoholics comment on their resistance to looking at their own role in the drinking patterns as a chief stumbling block in treatment of any sort. Jackson noted from her experiences in Al-Anon groups that in the nonthreatening context of Al-Anon groups, members readily expressed concern about "their sanity."

Bailey and Jackson's writings as well as Pattison's briefer reference to Al-Anon suggest two points to be noted. Al-Anon women tend to be relatively well educated and of the middle class. They may be more motivated for a variety of reasons to expend greater efforts to salvage their marriage. Bailey (1963a, 1968) suggested that professionals have moved too rapidly in trying to explore underlying problems. Bailey has made pragmatic use of Al-Anon process and operationally her own suggested professional casework principles (1963a, 1968) closely follow those of Al-Anon. Bailey (1963a, 1965, 1968) and Cohen and Kraus (1971) have pointed up the potential value of using Al-Anon as a supplement to professional treatment.

Al-Ateen groups for children of alcoholics have been discussed briefly (Bailey 1968). Al-Ateen, too, works on a self-help principle of peers sharing common problems. The few agency personnel who have had occasion to work with children attending these groups laud their effectiveness.

OVERVIEW: WORK TO BE DONE The evolution of research on the family and alcoholism may be traced through several distinct phases. Initially, there appeared a series of clinical studies documenting the pathology of the spouse. This florescence of papers was followed by a series by Jackson and her associates that constituted a rebuttal to the chief thrust of the earlier studies that focused on the wife as the causal factor in the husband's drinking patterns. A primary component of this rebuttal was the exploration of various aspects of the personality of the wife through psychological tests, rather than relying on impressionistic interviews at specific crisis periods when the wife logically might be expected to be highly agitated. Wives of alcoholics were compared with "normal" non-alcoholics' wives and significant differences in disturbance were not identified. The work of Jackson and Kogan presented evidence that the concept of a unitary "personality of the wife of the alcoholic" was untenable. A second and highly significant dimension of Jackson's research was sociological in its orientation and placed emphasis on the adaptation of the total family to stress caused by the existence of alcoholism in the household. This orientation drew attention to alcoholism as a total family problem and family disease.

Papers focusing on interaction between spouses began to appear in 1959 but there have been relatively few of these since. In more recent years, such papers have implicitly or explicitly been based on functional systems and interactionist theories. Steinglass, Weiner, and Mendelson's consideration of the family as a system, and Ward and Faillace's broader overview of alcoholism as it involves the individual, his family, and the larger community presented perhaps the most sophisticated statements in the literature aside from the earlier foundation-building works of Jackson. Steinglass, Weiner, and Mendelson proposed a long-awaited articulate model lending itself to significant implications for treatment. Ward and Faillace took into consideration all aspects of the drinker's environment, both as they function in regard to him and in terms of the internal workings of the respective systems that may determine this functioning, independent of the actual reality needs of the specific alcoholic individual. Brief as this article is, it contains the directions for a great many areas of research that are essentially as yet untouched.

Bailey (1961), Jackson (1962), and Day (1961) have emphasized the need for conceptually broad studies that integrate the psychological and sociological approaches. Researchers and clinicians in this field by and large have found the psychological approach to be more congenial to their training and experience and thus have accepted and focused on the personal pathology of the individual or of the two spouses, at the expense of looking to a multivariate approach combining individual personality characteristics with interpersonal interactions within the family and significant social network, and with the more diffuse and broader socioeconomic context within which the individual and the family exist. It is of interest that the multivariate approach has been suggested in recent literature in relation to the problem drinker (Cahalan 1970; Jessor, et al. 1968; United States Department of Health, Education, and Welfare 1971), yet largely ignored in studies of the response of his family or the significant other factors in his environment.

While the importance of sociocultural factors as one significant determinant in stimulating or maintaining drinking behavior has been considered by many investigators (for example, Cahalan, et al. 1969; Pittman 1967; Snyder 1962; Ullman 1958; and Bales 1946), the role of these factors in family attitudes toward the drinker or in modes of coping with the problem drinker by his spouse and significant others has been given scant attention.

The great majority of the studies reviewed in this paper have made little or no comment on the sociocultural context within which their subjects exist. The attitudes and drinking patterns of their extended family, friendship circle, fellow churchgoers, and of the larger society play a great part in the attitudes of family members toward the alcoholic and in their actions in relation to him. Jackson (various papers), Lisansky (1957), Lemert (1960), Bailey (1965), and Pattison, et al. (1965) have discussed the significance of the socioeconomic membership of their subjects in relation to their differential responses to questionnaires, testing, or treatment modalities. Lemert (1960) primarily emphasized the need for exploration in this area of differential perception of problems, but detailed research focused on the specific sociocultural or socioeconomic variables in wife and family response have yet to appear.

Another related area largely ignored in the consideration of family response is the extra-family dimension involving prevalent sociocultural attitudes toward alcoholism and how they effect the nature of the available sources of help. These may play a primary role in the development of attitudes maintained by the family and in determining what options for action they will or can take in regard to their problem. Hansen and Hill (1964) presented a classification of various family crises with the possible related community response, i.e. the attitudes and actions that community caregivers display in response to respective types of stress situations. Again, it has been primarily Jackson who has given attention to the role of the prevailing cultural attitudes toward specific alcohol-related family problems and toward the types of aid available to the family. Jackson (1962) noted that a chief complication for the family is a lack of cultural guidelines for family response to this specific problem other than a generic categorization of the excessive drinking as deviant behavior. Such a labeling process then invokes shame and stigma in family members that contribute further to an already sensitive crisis situation.

Comparable in importance to the drinking history of the alcoholic "regularly sought by caregivers" might be the history of the help-seeking of the spouse and other family members. The area of help-seeking and community response to the needs of the family has been given relatively little consideration in regard to how this has affected the progression of the problem. Unsuccessful attempts in the help-seeking career of the spouse often contribute to the anti-professional attitudes found among wives who dismiss help-seeking endeavors with professional caregivers as futile.

Another important gap in research efforts is apparent in the lack of studies tying the specific alcoholic-related crisis syndrome to the existing body of theory dealing with family and community behavior in a variety of crisis situations. Researchers on the alcoholic family consistently have been parochial in their conceptualization, seldom turning to outstanding available and relevant literature. Only Jackson (1958, 1962) and Steinglass, et al. (1971b) have pointed up the similarities of family system dysfunction in alcoholism to those reported by other researchers for families in other forms of crisis.

Various papers by Hill (1958) and Hansen and Hill (1964), for example, offer a wealth of theoretical considerations for comparison. Hill (1958) classified alcoholism as an intra-family stressful event involving "demorale-ization" of the family, because its role patterns are disturbed. He noted that the family succeeds as a family chiefly on the basis of the adequacy of the role performance of its members. When role patterns are changed and equilibrium is disturbed the crisis is incurred. Hill offered suggestions to the caregiver who works with families in crisis. He notes that a chief consideration is to keep the total family context in mind. In the case of families in crises of demoralization, this consideration is of particular significance. He suggested a list of family characteristics that are conducive to good adjustment to crisis. The researcher and clinician might well use these as indicators or variables of family strength or viability in an exploration of the total configuration of the alcoholic family.

Spiegel (1957), Parad and Caplan (1960), and Riskin (1963) have presented methodologies for studying families in crisis: all of these are appropriate for the consideration of the alcoholic family. Riskin (1963: 344) presented a theoretical model for studying the family in crisis which utilized a clear systems approach:

The family is viewed as an ongoing system ... it tends to maintain itself around some point of equilibrium which has been established as the family evolves. The system is a dynamic, not a static, one. There is continuous process of input into the system, and thus a continuous tendency for the system to be pushed away from the equilibrium point. The input may be in the form of an external stress such as a job change, war, or depression; or it may be an internal stress such as the birth of a new child, a death, or a biological spurt such as the onset of puberty. Over a period of time, the family develops certain repetitive, enduring techniques or patterns of interactions for maintaining its equilibrium when confronted by stress; this development tends to hold whether the stress be internal or external, acute or chronic, trivial or gross. These techniques, which are assumed to be characteristic for a given family, are regarded as homeostatic mechanisms. In the above description, the family is described somewhat analogously to an individual with his drives, defences, character traits, and ego functions. However, these concepts differ from classical psychoanalytic ones in that they refer primarily to interpersonal organizations of behavior rather than to internal mechanisms.

Although a few works reviewed above such as those of Jackson, Ewing and Fox, Steinglass, Weiner and Mendelson, and Ward and Faillace have employed such concepts as offered by Hill and Hansen, Riskin, Parad and Caplan, or Spiegel, by and large researchers have not taken advantage of the rich body of theory on the problem family that exists.

NEW AREAS OF SAMPLING FOR FUTURE RESEARCH

The studies available in the literature typically focused on relatively small cohort samples (six to fifty persons) of women taken from out-patient clinic caseloads, Al-Anon Family Groups, family service centers, and in a few cases prison or probation populations. They may accordingly represent the most desperate, the most motivated, or the most coerced family members available to researchers. It is important that the fact of sample bias be noted. How representative such small samples from specialized agency or self-help groups are in relation to the millions of "hidden" casualties of alcoholic marriages is questionable.

One approach to overcome such sampling bias would be intensive, in depth holistic studies of "normal" families in various categories of risk as indicated by survey research data such as that of Cahalan (1970). The prevalence of hidden alcoholic problems may be encountered in the course of such intimate exploration. Likewise, more comparative studies with conflicted though non-alcoholic families are needed. Still another approach would be to focus on the alcoholism component in problem families who come to the attention of caregivers with other presenting problems, and to examine how this specific element relates to other areas of marital discord. Alcoholism frequently either is presented as the only problem (which ideally, when taken care of, would "settle" all other problems) or is carefully hidden because it is perceived as an insignificant symptom of other deeper problems.

A chief goal of future research must be the charting of an eclectic comprehensive approach that views alcoholic-related problems as not totally unique to the class phenomenon of family crisis. Furthermore, the details of alcohol-related problems must be explored holistically and in depth, taking into account potentially significant psychological, social, and cultural characteristics of all family members. Only such a comprehensive approach gives appropriate cognizance to the reality that alcoholism is a multi-faceted affliction which crucially affects the family as a total unit and each member as an interacting part of that unit.

REFERENCES

ABLON, J.
   1973   Al-Anon Family Groups: impetus for learning and change through the presentation of alternatives. *American Journal of Psychotherapy.*
AL-ANON FAMILY GROUP HEADQUARTERS
   1965   *Al-Anon faces alcoholism.* New York: Al-Anon Family Group Headquarters.
   1966   *Living with an alcoholic.* New York: Al-Anon Family Group Headquarters.
   1969   *Alcoholism: a merry-go-round named denial.* New York: Al-Anon Family Group Headquarters.
BACON, S. D.
   1945   "Excessive drinking and the institution of the family," in *Alcohol, science and society.* Edited by *Quarterly Journal of Studies on Alcohol,* 223–238. New Haven: Yale Summer School of Alcohol Studies.
BAILEY, M. B.
   1961   Alcoholism and marriage: a review of research and professional literature. *Quarterly Journal of Studies on Alcohol* 22(1).
   1963a   The family agency's role in treating the wife of an alcoholic. *Social Casework* 44(5).
   1963b   "Research on alcoholism and marriage," in *National Conference on Social Welfare, Columbus, Ohio.* Edited by Social Work Practice. Columbus, Ohio: National Conference on Social Welfare.
   1965   Al-Anon family groups as an aid to wives of alcoholics. *Social Work* 10(1):68.
   1968   *Alcoholism and family casework.* New York: The Community Council of Greater New York.
BAILEY, M. B., P. W. HABERMAN, H. ALKSNE
   1962   Outcomes of alcoholic marriage: endurance, termination or recovery. *Quarterly Journal of Studies on Alcohol* 23:610.
BAILEY, M. B., P. W. HABERMAN, J. SHEINBERG
   1965   "Distinctive characteristics of the alcoholic family," in *Report of the Health Research Council of the City of New York.* New York: The National Council on Alcoholism.
BALES, R. F.
   1946   Cultural differences in rates of alcoholism. *Quarterly Journal of Studies on Alcohol* 6(4):480.
BALLARD, R. G.
   1959   The interaction between marital conflict and alcoholism as seen

through MMPI's of marriage partners. *American Journal of Orthopsychiatry* 29(3):528.

BELFER, M. L., R. I. SHADER, M. CARROLL, J. S. HARMATZ
1971   Alcoholism in women. *Archives of General Psychiatry* 25(6):540.

BERNE, E.
1964   *Games people play*. New York: Grove Press.

BULLOCK, S. C., E. H. MUDD
1959   The interaction of alcoholic husbands and their non-alcoholic wives during counselling. *American Journal of Orthopsychiatry* 29(3):519.

BURTON, G.
1962   Group counselling with alcoholic husbands and their non-alcoholic wives. *Marriage and Family Living* 24(1):56.

CAHALAN, D.
1970   *Problem drinkers*. San Francisco: Jossey-Bass.

CAHALAN, D., I. CISIN, H. M. CROSSLEY
1969   *American drinking practics: a national survey of behavior and attitudes*. Rutgers School of Alcohol Studies, Monograph 6. New Brunswick, New Jersey.

CHAFETZ, M. E., H. T. BLANE, M. J. HILL
1971   Children of alcoholics. *Quarterly Journal of Studies on Alcohol* 32(3).

CLIFFORD, B. J.
1960   A study of the wives of rehabilitated and non-rehabilitated alcoholics. *Social Casework* 41(1):457.

COHEN, P. C., M. S. KRAUS
1971   *Casework with wives of alcoholics*. New York: Family Treatment Association.

CORDER, B. F., A. HENDRICKS, R. F. CORDER
1964   An MMPI study of a group of wives of alcoholics. *Quarterly Journal of Studies on Alcohol* 25(3):551.

CORK, R. M.
1956   Casework in a group setting with wives of alcoholics. *Social Worker* 14:1.
1964   "Alcoholism and the family." Paper presented at the Alcoholism and Drug Addiction Research Foundation Annual Course, May 1964. University of Western Ontario, Ontario.

DAY, B. R. D.
1961   Alcoholism and the family. *Marriage and Family Living* 23(3):253.

EWING, J. A., R. E. FOX
1968   "Family therapy of alcoholism," in *Current psychiatric therapies*, volume eight. Edited by J. H. Masserman, 86–91. New York: Grune and Stratton.

FOX, R.
1956   "The alcoholic spouse," in *Neurotic interaction in marriage*. Edited by V. W. Eisenstein, 148–168. New York: Basic Books.
1962   "Children in the alcoholic family," in *Problems in addiction: alcohol and drug addiction*. Edited by W. C. Bier, 71–96. New York: Fordham University Press.

FUTTERMAN, S.
1953   Personality trends in wives of alcoholics. *Journal of Psychiatric Social Work* 23(1):37.

GLIEDMAN, L. H., H. T. NASH, W. L. WEBB
1956   Group psychotherapy of male alcoholics and their wives. *Diseases of the Nervous System* 17(3):90.

GORAD, S. L.
1971   Communication styles and interaction of alcoholics and their wives. *Family Process* 10(4):475.

HANSEN, D. A., R. HILL
1964   "Families under stress," in *Handbook of marriage and the family*. Edited by H. T. Christensen, 782–819. Chicago: Rand McNally.

HILL, R.
1958   Generic features of families under stress. *Social Casework* 39(2, 3):139.

IGERSHEIMER, W. W.
1959   Group psychotherapy for non-alcoholic wives of alcoholics. *Quarterly Journal of Studies on Alcohol* 20(1):77.

JACKSON, J. K.
1954   The adjustment of the family to the crisis of alcoholism. *Quarterly Journal of Studies on Alcohol* 15(4).

1958   Alcoholism and the family. *Annals of the American Academy of Political and Social Science* 315:90.

1962   "Alcoholism and the family," in *Society, culture, and drinking patterns*. Edited by D. J. Pittman and C. R. Snyder, 472–492. New York: Wiley.

JACKSON, J. K., K. L. KOGAN
1963   The search for solutions: help seeking patterns of families of active and inactive alcoholics. *Quarterly Journal of Studies on Alcohol* 24(3):449.

JAMES, E., M. GOLDMAN
1971   Behavior trends of wives of alcoholics. *Quarterly Journal of Studies on Alcohol* 32(2).

JELLINEK, E. M.
1960   *The disease concept of alcoholism*. New Jersey: Hillhouse Press.

JESSOR, R., T. D. GRAVES, R. C. HANSON, S. L. JESSOR
1968   *Society, personality, and deviant behavior*. New York: Holt, Rinehart and Winston.

KOGAN, K. L., W. E. FORDYCE, J. K. JACKSON
1963   Personality disturbance in wives of alcoholics. *Quarterly Journal of Studies on Alcohol* 24(2).

KOGAN, K. L., J. K. JACKSON
1963   Role perceptions in wives of alcoholics and of non-alcoholics. *Quarterly Journal of Studies on Alcohol* 24(4):627.

1965a Alcoholism: the fable of the noxious wife. *Mental Hygiene* 49(3): 428.

1965b Some concomitants of personal difficulties in wives of alcoholics and non-alcoholics. *Quarterly Journal of Studies on Alcohol* 26(4):595.

1965c Stress, personality, and emotional disturbance in wives of alcoholics. *Quarterly Journal of Studies on Alcohol* 26(3):486.

LEMERT, E. M.
  1960 The occurrence and sequence of events in adjustment of families to alcoholism. *Quarterly Journal of Studies on Alcohol* 21(4):679.
  1962 Dependence in married alcoholics. *Quarterly Journal of Studies on Alcohol* 23(4):590.

LEWIS, M. L.
  1954 The initial contact with wives of alcoholics. *Social Casework* 35:8.

LISANSKY, E. S.
  1957 Alcoholism in women: social and psychological concommitants, I: Social history data. *Quarterly Journal of Studies on Alcohol* 18(4): 588.
  1958 The woman alcoholic. *Annals of the American Academy of Political and Social Science* 315:73.

MAC DONALD, D. E.
  1956 Mental disorders in wives of alcoholics. *Quarterly Journal of Studies on Alcohol* 17(2):282.
  1958 Group psychotherapy with wives of alcoholics. *Quarterly Journal of Studies on Alcohol* 19:125–132.

MEEKS, D. E., C. KELLY
  1970 Family therapy with families of recovering alcoholics. *Quarterly Journal of Studies on Alcohol* 31(2):399.

MITCHELL, H. E.
  1959 Interpersonal perception theory applied to conflicted marriages in which alcoholism is and is not a problem. *American Journal of Orthopsychiatry* 29(3):547.

NEWALL, N.
  1950 Alcoholism and the father image. *Quarterly Journal of Studies on Alcohol* 11(1):92.

OXFORD, S., S. GUTHRIE
  1968 "Coping behavior used by wives of alcoholics: a preliminary investigation." Abstract from the International Congress on Alcoholism. *Proceedings of the 28th Congress,* page 97.

PARAD, H. J., G. CAPLAN
  1960 A framework for studying families in crisis. *Social Work* 5(3):3.

PATTISON, E. M., P. COURLES, R. PATTI, B. MANN, D. MULLEN
  1965 Diagnostic therapeutic intake groups for wives of alcoholics. *Quarterly Journal of Studies on Alcohol* 26(4):605.

PITTMAN, D. J.
  1967 *Alcoholism.* New York: Harper and Row.

PIXLEY, J. M., J. R. STIEFEL
  1963 Group therapy designed to meet the needs of the alcoholic wife. *Quarterly Journal of Studies on Alcohol* 24(2):304.

PRICE, G. M.
  1945 A study of the wives of 20 alcoholics. *Quarterly Journal of Studies on Alcohol* 5(4):620.

RISKIN, J.

1963   Methodology for studying family interaction. *Archives of General Psychiatry* 8(4).

SNYDER, C. R.

1962   "Culture and Jewish sobriety. The in-group-out-group factor," in *Society, culture and drinking patterns*. Edited by D. J. Pittman and C. R. Snyder, 188–225. New York: Wiley and Sons.

SPIEGEL, J. P.

1957   The resolution of role conflict within the family. *Psychiatry* 20(1):1.

STEINER, C. M.

1969   The alcoholic game. *Quarterly Journal of Studies on Alcohol* 30(4):920.

1971   *Games alcoholics play*. New York: Grove Press.

STEINGLASS, P., S. WEINER, J. H. MENDELSON

1971a Interactional issues as determinants of alcoholism. *American Journal of Psychiatry* 128(3):55.

1971b A systems approach to alcoholism, a model and its clinical application. *Archives of General Psychiatry* 24(5).

ULLMAN, A.

1958   Sociocultural backgrounds of alcoholism. *Annals of the American Academy of Political and Social Science* 315:48.

UNITED STATES DEPARTMENT OF HEALTH, EDUCATION, AND WELFARE

1971   *The first special report to the United States Congress on alcohol and health*. Human Series and Mental Health Administration, National Institute of Mental Health, NIAAA, Washington, D.C.

WARD, R. F., G. A. FAILLACE

1970   The alcoholic and his helpers. *Quarterly Journal of Studies on Alcohol* 31(3):684.

WHALEN, T.

1953   Wives of alcoholics: four types observed in a family service agency. *Quarterly Journal of Studies on Alcohol* 14(4):632.

Similarities and Differences Among a Heavily Arrested Group of Navajo Indian Drinkers in a Southwestern American Town

FRANCES N. FERGUSON

The tendency to stereotype classes of drinkers has often been remarked upon. Indeed, where drinking groups gather regularly, common features are apparent. Less obvious, perhaps, are the differences which exist among members of such groups. This paper will record some similarities and differences within a group of heavily-arrested Navajo Indian drinkers in a small southwestern American city from 1964 to 1968.[1]

While Navajo drinkers are the subject of this study, by no means does this suggest that there are more heavy drinkers among Navajos than in other populations with access to alcohol. Kunitz, et al. (1969) found death rates from Laennec's (alcoholic) cirrhosis somewhat lower among Navajos than among the United States population at large. It is true, however, that some Navajo drinkers tend to be conspicuous when they drink in town or outside border bars. The public (outdoor) nature of their drinking and the frequency of visible drunkenness are modes of alcohol consumption deviant in modern middle-class society and hence associated with arrest. Such drinking often leads to serious consequences in the area such as fatal accidents as indicated in the New Mexico State Police Records, 1963–1973, and prolonged illness as shown in the records of the United States Public Health Service Indian Hospital (Gallup, New Mexico) for the same period.

The research for this paper was supported by the National Institute of Mental Health Grant MH-01389, A Community Treatment Plan for Navajo Problem Drinkers, Gallup, New Mexico; and National Institute for Alcohol Abuse and Alcoholism Special Research Fellowship MH-12477.
[1] "Heavily arrested" is defined as 10 or more alcohol-related arrests. Many of the 110 men had well over 40 arrests, and one or two had more than 100.

This study focuses upon a group of 110 Navajo men, first contacted while in jail for drunkenness or alcohol-related offenses such as stealing the judge's typewriter from the court, being found asleep with a television set in an alley, or (far more serious) stealing and wrecking a friend's pickup truck while both were inebriated. Over a period of one and one-half years, the men had volunteered for an eighteen-mouth National Institute of Mental Health alcoholism treatment program — at first strongly motivated, no doubt, by the chance for freedom given by the associated probation.[2] (See Ferguson 1968, 1970 for details of treatment program, data gathering, plan for evaluation, and results.)

Aggregate arrests for the group of 110 over a period of eighteen months prior to the present arrest amounted to approximately 1,000, revealing that many had been arrested repeatedly during this period.[3] Since the treatment program was a model, destined to terminate at the end of four years,[4] the number of patients was limited. Men in the city jail for drunkenness continued to seek enlistment in the treatment program long after no new patients were accepted. The program had achieved quite a reputation not merely because of the opportunity for probation but also because, with the passage of time, some patients noted for their serious problems with alcohol startled the public by becoming sober and prosperous.

In terms of Navajos being arrested for alcohol-related offenses in town, how representative was this group of 110? Analysis of randomly chosen arrest records of 224 other Navajo men arrested for alcohol-related offenses at comparable times, with measures of comparison confined to number of arrests and locality of residence, revealed that while residence pattern was much the same for both groups, the comparison group was being arrested at only half the rate of the 110 men in this study. It is probable that men in the patient group, being more heavily arrested, were also more apt to be recommended by judge, jailer, police, family, and friends for an interview at the jail. Hence the program tended

[2]   Besides the 110 Navajo men, 11 other Indians were included in the treatment project but omitted from this study. About 90 percent of the persons arrested for alcohol-related offenses in the area were Navajo males, probably due to the proximity of the Navajo Reservation and the fact that the town offered a central location for a dispersed population to gather for sociability as well as marketing. Women were seen much less frequently arrested possibly because police said they did not like to arrest them.

[3]   Patient arrests were reduced from over 1,000 during the eighteen months prior to treatment, to 213 during the eighteen-month treatment period.

[4]   A Navajo Tribal alcoholism treatment program was patterned after the Gallup project and a somewhat similar Fort Deviance project. The tribal program got underway one year before the Gallup project reached its scheduled conclusion.

to fill its quota with the most heavily arrested persons from the very beginning.

SOME COMMON ATTRIBUTES OF PUBLIC DRINKING AMONG NAVAJOS

The public drinking by Navajo males has been well documented[5] (Ferguson 1968; Heath 1964; Kaplan and Johnson 1964; Kluckhorn and Leighton 1962; Levy, et al. 1969; Savard 1968; Topper 1971). It is an activity which often begins in camaraderie, soft-spoken greetings, and handclasps, fostering the renewal of old clan ties and friendships and the discovery of new ones. In this paper we shall focus on urban drinking since it is in town that most of the 110 Navajo men were arrested. Styles of Navajo drinking in town differ to some extent, with younger Navajos more often starting their drinking activities in bars. But men of all ages can be seen participating in small groups outdoors, drifting to other groups when the wine runs out. A man with a pocketful of cash has an opportunity to share the wealth in the form of a bottle of wine, enjoy his own generosity, increase his prestige, and store future social credit. The outdoor gathering of small groups is normal among a people whose dwellings are widely scattered over the 2,400 square mile Navajo Reservation, and who for generations have been moving about with their stock, marking the seasons by reunions under the open sky. One gets the feeling that for Navajos who drink publicly, group identity is enhanced by these drinking occasions which occur in the streets, alleys, and fields of the modern town.[6] Not the least important ingredient of the drinking scene is the excitement generated in limited lives by such occasions.[7] Anything can happen after several hours of sharing bottles. Those drinkers who do not break away from groups and return home have a tendency to "black out." By "black out" is meant continued activity with attendant loss of memory. This "black out" drinking gives *carte blanche* to some drinkers for behavior in which they would seldom engage when sober. Freedom is found in a state of oblivion which many of the drinkers said they sought.

---

[5] Similar drinking has been described for Papago Indians in southern Arizona (Waddell 1971), Chippewa in Manitoba (Koolage 1970), and Naskapi in the Province of Quebec (Robbins 1973).

[6] See also Waddell (1971), Koolage (1970), and Robbins (1973).

[7] Robert A. White explores this in the "Lower class culture of exitement among contemporary Sioux" (1970).

SIM'LARITIES AND DIFFERENCES

Although, in retrospect, there are several other areas of potential interest, those areas which were investigated reveal the presence of a good
deal of variation among the group of 110 Navajo drinkers. This paper
will focus not on the range of variation, not on all the differences which
came to light in the analysis of the data, but instead will touch upon those
features of difference or similarity which seem most salient. Further examination of the data might reveal important features which have been
omitted.

Looking first at age, one finds that the youngest of the 110 Navajo men
was eighteen and the oldest fifty. Over half (55 percent) were under thirty-
five. It appears that the peak of heavy drinking among Navajo males
may occur somewhat earlier than it does among United States males in
general, for whom Cahalan, et al. (1969) found the peak of heavy drinking occurring between the ages of forty-five and forty-nine. Is has been
suggested that heavy drinking is part of the lifestyle of the young Navajo male, a kind of "time out" behavior,[8] a rough-and-ready frontier
style.[9] One can surmise that such a lifestyle would produce evidence of
alcohol problems early in life. However, the age range of the 110 Navajo drinkers reveals that both youth and middle age were represented.

Sixty-two percent of the 110 men had six or more grades of schooling,[10]
while 38 percent had less. Although more of those under thirty-five years
of age had six or more grades (71.5 percent), it is interesting that slightly
more than half the patients thirty-five and over also had six or more
grades. While comparative figures are not available, it is likely that the
group members of age thirty-five and over are as a whole more "educated" than a similar age group in the Navajo male population as a whole.
(It was only after World War II that a push was made for general education for Navajos.) Eighty-two percent of the patients had attended
government or mission boarding schools at some time, a proportion high
in relation to the general Navajo population, although again comparative figures are lacking. This is significant because boarding schools and
their environs are often the scenes of covert drinking among Navajo

[8]   This is a phrase borrowed from MacAndrew and Edgerton (1969).
[9]   Honigmann and Honigmann (1970) describe frontier-style drinking among
Arctic townsmen. Some of the same type of drinking still exists in the western
United States and may have served as a pattern for Indians.
[10]   My designation of sixth grade or more as the dividing line between "educated" and "uneducated" was guided by Vogt's remark (1951) that Navajos were
not indoctrinated with the values of the schools, etc. until they had gone as far as
the sixth grade.

youths. One reason for the preponderance of "educated" persons in the group is probably the fact that, despite the efforts to avoid partiality or bias, the project staff members might have been more apt to talk with English-speaking Navajos at the jail — even though project interpreters were present. With regard to individual differences in education within the group, however, patients ranged all the way from those who spoke no English at all and had never attended school to two who were college graduates.

Patients came from forty-six "communities." These were sometimes located in the city or in reservation towns but more often the "communities" were family sites, a cluster of several small dwellings within a few miles of a trading post. Residences for the group were widely dispersed, some men hailing from as far as ninety miles from the town where arrest occurred. Sixty percent of the patients lived within a twenty-five mile radius of the town, however.[11] The propinquity of the town and the availability of alcohol (still prohibited by the Navajo tribe although often bootlegged on the reservation) very probably are factors for those who lived within a twenty-five mile distance. Interestingly, while fewer in number proportionately, those who lived fifty or more miles from town were being arrested just as often. Quite likely those from afar tended to linger in town and be re-arrested. Sometimes they were seen in town for weeks and months, participating in a "revolving door" pattern.

Not only was locality of residence somewhat varied but type of residence ranged from one-room house or hogan to modern home. While 43 percent of the men lived in one-room dwellings, this was not necessarily indicative of low economic status among Navajos, since an extended family (in which 67 percent of the 110 lived) might include several such dwellings and land-use rights for stock grazing over an area of many acres, with associated prestige. However, it would be surprising if contact with the affluent life style of modern society did not promote a sense of relative deprivation.[12] While type of housing did not necessarily indicate status differences among the 110, and such differences tended to be played down, acquaintance with the men revealed that some belonged to prosperous families who commanded a good deal of power on the reservation while others were in a state of extreme poverty.

Navajo social organization is characterized by membership in unilineal kin groups or clans. Membership in, or association with, sixty-five clans was represented among the group of 110 and clan membership

---

[11]   It is probable that persons living further than fifty miles tended to drink at other border towns.

[12]   This feeling, if present, was seldom expressed.

was claimed by each member of the group. Four clans figured most prominently and proved to be those which had large memberships within thirty miles of the border town. These social bonds are probably a strong factor in promoting heavy drinking, yet they also appeared to be effective in fostering treatment success, when drinking norms were activated.

Thirty-six percent of the 110 patients had been in military service. Again, comparative numbers are lacking, but it is probable that this is higher proportionately than in the Navajo male population group aged eighteen to fifty-five. When they were in the service, the men tended to follow a pattern of drinking heavily when off duty in the company of many other enlisted men. Whether this pattern was acquired in the service or prior to it, one cannot say. As with persons who had six or more grades of education, it is probable that persons with military service would be more apt to speak English well and hence more apt to make contact with the project staff and enlist in the treatment program. Nevertheless, 30 percent of the 110 male Navajo patients spoke English poorly or not at all.

Only 7 percent of the 110 patients were employed at the time of enlistment in treatment which, one might add, included offers of help with finding or regaining employment. Thirty-eight percent had not worked for seven to twenty-six weeks. Sixty-eight percent either became (potentially) permanently employed during treatment or returned to the pursuit of stock-raising or other traditional work in the family context during treatment. Of those employed during treatment, 36 percent were employed in modern jobs, 33 percent were self-employed in traditional and occasional migrant labor, and 31 percent had both full-time modern jobs and traditional economic pursuits as well. The majority of the 110 men had lost previous jobs because of drunkenness, most often because of arrest. One hundred forty-one occupations were represented among past jobs held by the patient group, occupations ranging from laborer to teacher and accountant. Among patients trained for a specific trade, surprisingly few pursued that trade.[13] A tendency to seek jobs on a lower level was observed. Graves (1970), finding a correlation between lack of well-paying employment of Navajos in a large urban area and trouble with the law over drinking, suggests that an important factor in the genesis of alcohol problems is the absence of a well-paying job early in the migrant's stay. However, acquaintance with the Navajo drinkers in the border town revealed that several lost good jobs as a result of their drinking. While reliable data on commensurate pay is

---

[13]   Again, this is an area which invites systematic investigation.

lacking, some of the men said they received the same pay as white men working in the same jobs, while others spoke of exploitation. Generally, there was a variety of past employment and income potential within the group, but occupations on a low pay level were most common.

With regard to marriage, slightly over half of the 110 patients were married or had a recognized marital relationship. About 25 percent said they were not presently living with their wives and a majority had been at least temporarily rejected as a result of the last jailing episode. Graves (1970) found that marriage was associated with freedom from alcohol problems for Navajos in a large urban area, and suggested that marriage might be a preventive factor. However, it was observed that marriage relationships often broke up after prolonged periods of drinking.

As for religion,[14] a topic Navajos do not commonly discuss with non-Navajos, 50 percent of the patients said they had attended Navajo ceremonies during the past year, while 59 percent had attended a Christian church. These categories are not mutually exclusive. Navajos are famous for incorporating attributes of other cultures into their own lives. Ten percent of the men said they had attended peyote meetings, but since this activity was illegal and secretive, more may have done so. With religion, as with most other categories mentioned, variety existed within the patient group.

Ninety percent of the study sample did their drinking in the border town where they were arrested. Seventy-eight percent said wine was the alcoholic beverage they most drank. Sixty-three percent said they gulped down as much as possible each time they took a drink. Fifty-one percent said that they drank between three and four pints of wine a day just previous to the last arrest — although it is difficult to know how this would be ascertained if a state of "black out" existed — or during the ordinary bottle passing. Seventy-seven percent said they had drunk to the point of "black out." Forty four percent said they often drank to unconsciousness. Sixty-two percent had close relatives who drank excessively. Eleven patients had experienced *delirium tremens*.

The above data were gleaned largely from interviews given during five days of intitial hospitalization for the 110 patients. Interviewers were informal and friendly, using the period of interview as an occasion to establish a counseling relationship which in many cases continued for two or more years. During the hospitalization period, a battery of psychological tests, which included the Wechsler Adult Intelligence Test, the Minnesota Multiphasic, the Rorschach, the Thematic Apperception, and

[14] The idea of separating religion into a category apart from actual life is a peculiarity of European (and North American) culture.

the Draw-a-Person, was administered by three staff psychologists. Since there are a variety of ways of imposing categories upon one's social and geographical environment, neither the WAIS nor the MMPI are very useful in a culture strikingly different from the one in which they were devised, but for lack of more appropriate instruments, both were employed. Test results reveal that a low IQ level is highly correlated with lack of formal education, suggesting that actual intelligence in Navajos lacking formal education was not being measured. For this reason the results of the WAIS have been omitted.

The staff psychologists were experienced professionals, able to take into consideration differences in Navajo culture. It is of value to study their individual summary psychological reports on the 110 men. Of the categories which most often appear in these reports, the following are most common: anxiety, 48 percent; depression, 35 percent; feeling of inadequacy, 38 percent; passivity or dependence, 35 percent; rebelliousness or hostility, 29 percent; immaturity, 22 percent. My analysis of Rorschach content reveals that anatomy is seen in 48 percent of protocols, and slightly disturbed responses such as explosions, fighting, etc. occur in 17 percent. It should be kept in mind that the psychological tests were administered in the first five days of treatment when the men may have suffered some lingering effects from hangovers or malnutrition.

The number of times "difficulty with women" appears in the psychologists' summaries is an impressive 59 percent. The TAT's reveal the frequent occurrence of stories in which the woman is telling the recalcitrant male what she feels he ought to do, something which may not be unusual in any society. However, Levy (1965:7) has pointed out the structural inability of the male's position in traditional Navajo culture and the added stress imposed upon the young Navajo male by a modern job, where inlaws often have a claim on his income.

What did the patients themselves say with regard to reasons for their drinking? One young man remarked that he got drunk "to raise hell." When asked why he did not avoid the company of his drinking companions, now that he was in treatment, he replied, "Why, we grew up together; we were rascals together!" A professional Navajo in his thirties said he drank to forget his troubles. An older traditional couple, just out from a few days in jail for drunkenness, were asked why they drank in this way and replied, "One morning we got up and decided to go to town."

It was common to hear patients of all ages talk about the difficulty of refusing drinks offered by friends, a feature of sobriety which appeared to distress them considerably. For Navajos, refusal of hospitality is something of an affront. With nearly all of the 110 men, the sociability of the drinking scene was undeniably a primary factor in the use of alcohol. Indeed, it is easy to overlook the fact that along with the negative aspects of heavy drinking with its associated accidents, illness, and loss, there is a very apparent gain in the bonds of fellowship and assertion of identity, for both the individual and the group, in the drinking scene, particularly in a context where there is social rejection by a larger society. This functional aspect of alcohol has not been neglected in the anthropological literature (Bunzel 1940; Honigmann 1963; Honigmann and Honigmann 1945, 1965; Keller 1966; Madsen 1967; Mandelbaum 1965; Mangin 1957; and others).

DISCUSSION

A population of 110 Navajo Indian men frequently arrested for alcohol-related offenses has been briefly described. An attempt has been made to show that a stereotype fostered by a culturally standardized drinking style would fail to reveal intra-group differences in age, education, location and type of residence, type of employment, and, by implication, degree of aculturation, etc. This group of men included persons accustomed to modern employment and persons who were self-employed in traditional occupations, college graduates and non-English speakers, professionals and laborers, residents of town and country dwellers, older men as well as youths. Points between the extremes which have been used for purposes of illustration were also well represented. A casual profile of a Navajo man with multiple alcohol-associated arrests could not reveal the variety which existed in this group. It is easy to see that a drinking style which is culturally standardized might mask individual differences greater than the similarities.[15] Future studies with more sophistication than this investigation (dating from 1964 to 1968), must be pursued in order to capture the significance of these differences. This brief analysis may serve to point up their importance.

---

[15] Obviously, there is a need to compare the individuals in this heavily arrested group with Navajos who do not get into trouble with the law over alcohol use in order to discover whether there is something which distinguishes those with multiple alcohol-associated arrests from the rest of the population in that area. What social controls, what situations or experiences, what inclinations, and what physiological factors may be operating in the lives of the latter which have protected them from problems with alcohol and which, contrariwise, do not seem to have affected the behavior of the heavily arrested man?

REFERENCES

BUNZEL, R. B.
1940 The role of alcoholism in two Central American cultures. *Psychiatry* 3:361–387.

CAHALAN, D., I. CISIN, H. CROSSLEY
1969 *A national study of drinking behavior and attitudes.* New Brunswick: Rutgers Center of Alcohol Studies.

FERGUSON, F. N.
1968 Navajo drinking: some tentative hypotheses. *Human Organization* 27:159–167.
1970 A treatment program for Navajo alcoholics: results after four years. *Quarterly Journal of Studies on Alcohol* 31:898–919.

GRAVES, T. D.
1970 The personal adjustment of Navajo Indian migrants to Denver. *American Anthropologist* 72:35–54.

HEATH, D. B.
1964 Prohibition and post-repeal drinking patterns among the Navajo. *Quarterly Journal of Studies on Alcohol* 25:119–135.

HONIGMANN, J. J.
1963 Dynamics of drinking in an Austrian village. *Ethnology* 2:157–169.

HONIGMANN, J. J., I. HONIGMANN
1945 Drinking in an Indian-white community. *Quarterly Journal of Studies on Alcohol* 32:575–619.
1965 How Baffin Island Eskimo have learned to use alcohol. *Social Forces* 44:73–83.
1970 *Arctic townsmen: ethnic backgrounds and modernization.* Ottawa: Canadian Research Centre for Anthropology, Saint Paul University.

KAPLAN, B., D. JOHNSON
1964 The social meaning of Navajo psychopathology and psychotherapy, in *Magic, faith and healing: studies in primitive psychiatry today.* Edited by Ari Kiev. London: The Free Press of Glencoe.

KELLER, M.
1966 Alcohol in health and disease: some historical perspectives. *Annals of the New York Academy of Sciences* 133:820–827.

KLUCKHORN, C., D. C. LEIGHTON
1962 *The Navajo* (revised edition). New York: The American Museum of Natural History.

KOOLAGE, W. W.
1970 "Adaptation of Chippewyan Indians and other persons of native background in Churchill, Manitoba." Unpublished Ph.D. dissertation, University of North Carolina, Chapel Hill.

KUNITZ, S. J., J. E. LEVY, M. EVERETT
1969 Alcoholic cirrhosis among the Navajo. *Quarterly Journal of Studies on Alcohol* 30:672–685.

LEVY, J. E.
  1965   Navajo suicide. *Human Organization* 24:308–315.
LEVY, J. E., S. J. KUNITZ, M. EVERETT
  1969   Navajo criminal homicide. *Southwestern Journal of Anthropology* 25:124–149.
MAC ANDREW, C., R. B. EDGERTON
  1969   Drunken comportment: a social explanation. Chicago: Aldine.
MADSEN, W.
  1967   "Acculturation and drinking patterns in a Mexican village." Unpublished manuscript.
MANDELBAUM, D. G.
  1965   Alcohol and culture. *Current Anthropology* 6:281–294.
MANGIN, W.
  1957   Drinking among Andean Indians. *Quarterly Journal of Studies on Alcohol* 18:55–66.
ROBBINS, R. H.
  1973   Alcohol and the identity struggle: some effects of economic change in inter-personal relations. *American Anthropologist* 75: 99–122.
SAVARD, R. J.
  1968   Effects of disulfiram therapy on relationships within the Navajo drinking group. *Quarterly Journal of Studies on Alcohol* 29:909–916.
TOPPER, M. D.
  1971   "Alcohol and the young Navajo man: a study in drinking and culture change." Mimeographed. Evanston, Ill.: Northwestern University.
VOGT, E. A.
  1951   *Navajo veterans.* Papers of the Peabody Museum of American Archeology and Ethnology 4(1). Harvard University.
WADDELL, J. O.
  1971   "Drink, friend! social contexts of convivial drinking among Papago Indians in an urban setting." Paper presented at the First Annual Alcoholism Conference of the National Institute on Alcohol Abuse and Alcoholism, June 25-26. Washington, D. C.
WHITE, R. A.
  1970   "The lower class culture of excitement among contemporary Sioux," in *The modern Sioux: social systems and reservation culture.* Edited by Ethel Nurge, 175-197. Lincoln, Neb.: University of Nebraska Press.

PART THREE

Historical Approaches

Introduction

There was a time in anthropology, as a review of Heath's article will show, that a historical or ethnohistorical perspective was legitimately credible. In the concern for discovering functions or statically isolating institutional structures in very specific time settings in the field, historical concerns were written off by eminent ethnographers as "conjectural." Likewise, the sometimes all too overwhelming influences of psychology, behaviorism, and statistical research methods, in spite of their undeniable value, have blinded us to what we should have learned earlier, namely, the necessity and value of a diachronic perspective. We frequently talk of intercultural variation or intracultural variation as if these were static or time-bound dimensions. What of temporal variations in intercultural and, especially, intracultural regularities that we are able to discern in our synchronic accounts of cultural patterns?

Lomnitz's article on historical patterns of Mapuche alcohol consumption is demonstrative of a badly needed dimension in alcohol studies. In the best of ethnohistorical tradition, she documents and analyzes the shifting regularities of alhohol-consumption patterns of Mapuche Indians over 400 years, tracing the social and cultural factors precipitating new and stabilizing patterns. More studies of this type are badly needed for all parts of the world.

The remaining two articles by anthropologists native to their areas of research, while lacking both the time scope and detail of Lomnitz's study, are similarly historical. Obayemi, who has combined both archeology and ethnology in his Nigerian studies, traces "pre-colonial" and "transitional" patterns of alcohol use, both in terms of the technology of production and social and cultural usages. One can detect his concern for reporting both intracultural variation (the private and public contexts) at single points in time and the impact of British colonial influences in altering or modifying these variable patterns. Through this diachronic perspective, on the other hand, one can see persisting patterns. Velapatiño Ortega briefly explores the influx of new groups into areas traditionally occupied by native societies and traces the variations within and modifications of drinking patterns among these groups.

Alcohol and Culture: The Historical Evolution of Drinking Patterns Among the Mapuche

LARISSA LOMNITZ

Most human societies utilize conscience-modifying agents, particularly ethyl alcohol in the form of fermented or distilled beverages; but the use of these agents is specified by norms and values which vary according to each culture. If social structure represents the context of human behavior, it is of great consequence to understand how, and to what extent, the patterns of alcohol ingestion are determined by sociocultural factors. Before any given behavior pattern can be set apart as DEVIANT an understanding of its function within the culture is essential.

Thus an analysis of the medical etiology and pathology of alcoholism is not sufficient, nor is it adequate to treat alcohol addiction in the individual as if it were only and primarily a matter of choice. The contribution of anthropology to alcohol studies is seen in the recognition that alcohol ingestion represents a part of the SOCIAL behavior of man and that its analysis cannot be taken separately from an analysis of the culture as a whole.

The great variability of cultural norms which affect alcohol use emerges as one of the insights gained from the anthopological approach to alcohol studies. This insight has been obtained basically by applying structuralist-functionalist models to different societies. In brief, the method consists in developing first a holistic understanding of the social structure on its own terms, "from the inside," so to speak. Next, the place of alcohol consumption in the sociocultural context is determined and the interaction between drinking behavior and other aspects of social life in the system are studied. Finally, the specific function assigned to alcohol within the social system is discovered. For historical as well as methodological reasons, these anthropological studies have been carried out primarily among small social groups belonging to peasant or so-called "primitive" societies.

The methods and techniques which have been developed and perfected under these field conditions should be applied to alcohol studies in modern complex societies. The very size of the human groups involved seems at first to represent a formidable obstacle to the phenomenological approach of anthropologists; hence unsystematic data gathering has been open to question at the level of complexity which is characteristic, say, of a large modern city. It is my belief, however, that the holistic approach of social anthropology remains valid in all social situations, no matter how complex. Structuralist-functionalist models, utilized in conjunction with techniques borrowed from other social sciences such as sociology, psychology, and demography, can represent today a useful methodological framework for alcohol studies in complex societies. Once the norm and function of alcohol intake have been determined in a given society, it could become possible to discuss the meaning of deviation and the adoption of preventive and corrective measures relating to alcoholism.

In this paper, the evolution of drinking patterns among the Mapuche is studied on the basis of a longitudinal cross-section of Mapuche culture during the past 400 years. The turning point in the cultural history of the Mapuche people occurred in the sixteenth century, when the Spanish conquered northern and central Chile. The function of alcohol within the social organization at that time may be inferred from Spanish colonial writers. The history of frontier warfare and periodic uprisings leading up to the final "pacification" of the Arauco Territory by the Republican Army in the 1880's was reflected in the socioeconomic structure: periods of social crisis tended to produce the secularization and disorganization of the pattern of alcohol usage, while periods of re-grouping and stabilization reflected a regularization of the norms and values which relate to drinking.

However, after each major crisis there were adaptive changes in social structure which entailed some modifications in the drinking pattern. The initial pattern of social and ritual alcohol consumption was affected by the introduction of trade and barter and resulted in new variations, including drinking at the trading posts and frontier towns. This new trend was institutionalized by the culture in terms of social norms and values which served the purpose of inter-reservation contacts.

A similar adaptive process will be described among Mapuche migrants to large cities during the present decade: an initial period of disorganization accompanied by increased alcohol intake is followed by stabilization, as the migrant succeeds in replacing the functions of his former rural community with new, urban-centered social structures. One result of this process is the "drinking circle," a typically urban institution which tends to take over certain emotional and socioeconomic functions formerly centered in the rural community.

METHODOLOGY

This study is based on fieldwork among Mapuche migrants in Santiago and among Mapuche peasants in two reservations of Cautín Province, Chile, during the period from August 1967 to May 1968. Participant observation techniques were used mainly on the reservation, while the urban migrants were studied by means of unstructured interviews with forty-seven informants. These in-depth interviews were spaced over a period of several months and were continuously checked against the literature on Mapuche culture (Faron 1961, 1964; Munizaga 1960, 1961; Cooper 1946).

The ethnohistory of alcohol consumption has been based on a search and analysis of historical sources. For the sixteenth century, we have used all available chronicles and particularly the outstanding *Cautiverio feliz* [A happy captivity] by de Pineda y Bascunan (1967). The author, a young Spanish soldier, was captured in the Indian Wars around 1590 and spent nearly a year as personal captive of a Mapuche family in a region which had not yet been penetrated by the Spanish. The book contains a detailed ethnographic account of Mapuche daily life with sympathetic descriptions of the economy, norms, values, and social organization. References to alcohol consumption occur on nearly every page of this extensive work. For the subsequent centuries, texts by Chilean historians as well as the original sources which were utilized by these authors have been used. The specific references are given at the appropriate places. Unfortunately, Spanish sources of the seventeenth through the nineteenth centuries tend to be hostile or patronizing, and descriptions of alcohol consumption are centered around the more visible symptoms of social disorganization. Nevertheless it was possible to infer the evolution of drinking patterns because of the abundance of historical materials and thanks to the help of our Mapuche informants.[1]

---

[1] I am particularly indebted to Lorenzo Aillapan, author of a book on the experiences of a Mapuche migrant, who served as informant and guide to his home reservation.

A BRIEF HISTORICAL SKETCH

The Mapuche people are best known for their tenacious resistance to foreign invaders, first to the Inca armies of Tupac Yupanqui in the fifteenth century and later to the Spanish and Chilean armies through the end of the nineteenth century. Tupac Yupanqui extended the Inca Empire to the Maule River and introduced Peruvian crops and cultural elements. In 1535 Diego de Almagro succeeded in crossing the Atacama Desert and Spanish domination extended southward in succeeding years. In 1542 Pedro de Valdivia founded Santiago. The first large-scale Mapuche rebellion occurred in 1562, when the Indians succeeded in expelling the Spanish from much of the invaded territory (Cooper 1946: 69).

The Indian Wars of the succeeding centuries have been analyzed by Jara (1961: 60). The Mapuche population, decimated by epidemics and by migration to the Andean highlands or to Argentina, were faced with rebellion or enslavement as branding of the "hostile Indians" had been expressly authorized by the Crown. The Mapuche war chiefs gradually evolved a system of guerilla tactics combined with periodic uprisings. Nevertheless the Indian frontier was rolled back. The eighteenth century saw the formation of a mestizo working class, causing the landowners to lose interest in Mapuche slave labor (Korth 1968: 227). More than a century of relative peace followed, in which alcohol became an important item of trade. The Republic, proclaimed in 1810, brought an end to slavery; but the white pressure on Mapuche lands was intensified. These lands were purchased at "ridiculous prices or bartered against articles dear to the Indians, such as baubles, wine or spirits" (Guevara 1902: 147). Toward 1850 an important German immigration was settled in the Araucania. The result of these developments was the uprisings of 1869 and 1880 which were put down by the Chilean army. A large emigration to Argentina occurred after 1884; the remaining Mapuche were confined to reservations. The Indian Treaty was signed in 1888, thus settling the fate of the previously recognized Mapuche nation.

Around 1920 the Mapuche population was estimated at 30,000; at present it has begun to rise again. There are an estimated 500,000 Mapuche living on nearly 3,000 reservations and in the larger towns or cities; the Mapuche urban population is estimated at 15 to 20 percent of the total (Lipschutz 1971:993-4). The Indian Treaty is still in force; under this law, the Mapuche are wards of the government and sale of reservation lands to non-Indians is forbidden. Each Mapuche family had received a hereditary land grant under the Treaty; today these lands (which were not selected among the best) have become totally inadequate for subsistence.

As a melancholy footnote to the history of the Mapuche nation, we translate the final dispatch by Colonel Saavedra after putting down the 1880 rebellion: "Mr. President, Angol was taken without a fight. Let me assure you that, minor incidents aside, the occupation of Arauco will cost us nothing, except for the wine and the music" (Navarro 1909:88, 97).

SOCIAL ORGANIZATION IN THE SIXTEENTH CENTURY

The Mapuche, or "people of the land," represent the largest division in the Araucanian cultures of southern South America. In the sixteenth century the Mapuche territory was loosely divided into four regions or *butanmapus*, the coast, the central valley, the foothills, and the Andes. Each *butanmapu* contained a number of provinces or *aillarehues*; an *aillarehue* was divided into several *rehues* or lands with a population of 400 to 1,000 individuals each. The population of a *rehue* was dispersed: a small group of huts, called a *pichicavi*, contained a patrilineal lineage or *kuga*. These lineages were polygamous and generally patrilocal; each hut or *ruca* was the dwelling of a wife with her descendants (Ramírez 1831:30; Farón 1961:453).

The Mapuche people never had a central political organization. The sociopolitical system was based on the territorial units. Each small locality elected a chieftain, usually the oldest or most powerful man of the lineage. Later the position of chieftain became hereditary and fell always on the first-born male. The authority of the chieftains was based on persuasion and respect: they had no formal disciplinary powers. Regional war chiefs or *toquis* were elected in wartime, but their authority was restricted to warfare and terminated at the end of the hostilities. There was no other authority at the tribal or super-tribal level. The election of a war chief was a major social occasion. The population of several *rehues* participated in these feasts, which conferred great social prestige on the host, usually a powerful and rich chieftain. The convocation was made through a special emissary of this chieftain, called a *huelquen*. Large quantities of food and drink were served at these assemblies, which have been vividly described by de Pineda y Bascunan (1967:67, 101, 111–113, 169–173).

The Mapuche economy in the sixteenth century was entirely based on gardening, hunting, gathering, and llama breeding. Agriculture was limited to corn, potatoes, beans, chile peppers, a variety of oats, and several fruits. The gardens were cultivated according to family needs. Gathering was an important economic activity and included 75 to 100 different varieties of plants, such as the wild berries which were used in the preparation of fermented beverages. Further references on social organization and traditional economy of the Mapuche may be found in historical and modern references (Ramírez 1831; Farón 1961, 1964; Ovalle 1888; de Tejillo 1923; de Najera 1889; de Lovera 1865; Cooper 1946; Latcham 1936). Detailed descriptions of Mapuche culture in general, and of the peculiar ethic-religious system in particular, are too fragmentary for the sixteenth century and will be dealt with at a later point in this paper.

DRINKING PATTERNS OF THE SIXTEENTH CENTURY

According to the frequent and detailed descriptions by de Pineda y Bascunan (1862:52, 71, 134, 170, 202, and many others) occasions for drinking might be classified according to the size of the drinking group and their level of social integration. These occasions ranged from the daily consumption in the family circle to large gatherings of tribes. One such *cahuin* described by de Pineda y Bascunan lasted for three or more days and involved 12,000 to 14,000 people.

The importance of alcohol to the Mapuche culture was correctly gauged by Spanish chroniclers, as shown by the following list of drinking occasions: "at the time of cultivation, at sowing time and harvest, on building their houses and for house warming, for curing their sick and burying their dead, on welcoming and hosting of friends, on celebrating their marriages, their games, or their diversions, and, what is more, in the important affairs of peace and of war" (Córdoba y Figueroa 1862:27). Drinking among the Mapuche was an eminently social act and was mandatory at all kinds of gatherings, no matter how solemn or how formal.

Apparently, the amount of alcohol consumption was limited only by the availability of drink. Women drank less than men because of their domestic duties; however, once food was served and the men no longer required their services, they would drink as heartily as the others. It seems that children and adolescents of either sex participated freely and without any moral restraint. The social ritual of drinking has been well described: "The custom is never to drink by oneself, rather one toasts to one's neighbor, who in turn toasts to another neighbor and passes the jar around" (Ovalle 1888:151). No single reference to solitary drinking among the Mapuche is to be found.

Four types of alcoholic beverages have been described for the sixteenth century: of strawberries, of apples, of oats, and of corn. These beverages were and are collectively known as *chicha,* Strawberry *chicha* was the most highly prized; corn *chicha* was the strongest; and oat *chicha* was the most common. *Chicha* was kept in "bottle" jars or in large size jars or *tinajones*. For the *cahuin* described by de Pineda y Bascunan, the consumption was "400 tinajones or 4,000 bottle jars, and it was hardly enough." At a funeral, there were twenty to thirty bottle jars for about 200 people. On being received as guests in a hut, "a jar of *chicha* was put before each of us; once emptied they brought others which they kept setting before us. As the news of our arrival spread other neighbors came and brought many jars of *chicha*" (de Pineda y Bascunan 1862: 200, 250; 1967:67–68, 119–128, 160–165).

De Pineda y Bascunan evidently enjoyed such occasions as much as his hosts, although he claims to have retained a degree of sobriety. The effects of *chicha* depended on the amounts consumed. The larger festivities took place in the open. At first, conversation became animated and less restrained; then people began to laugh, to shout, and to dance. Dancing and drinking continued as long as *chicha* was available. The onset of drunkenness was marked by fighting among men or between husbands and wives, and by indiscriminate sex acts. Drunkenness was equally prevalent among adults, adolescents, and children.

Hospitality required the offering of *chicha*: de Pineda y Bascunan mentions that he once stayed with a family so poor that they had to borrow *chicha* for welcoming a guest. The pattern of a welcome was always the same: the guest was seated before the fireplace while the host toasted and distributed the jars of *chicha* among those present. Conversation began among the men, while the women prepared the food. If many neighbors joined the party a major feast of dancing and drunkenness might ensue. Organized feasts at the clan or region level were more formal and more structured: such feasts included funerals, *mingacos* [collective labor], weddings, competitions of *chuecha* [a game which had a religious connotation], and war gatherings. These feasts added to the prestige of the host in proportion to the expense in food and drink that was served. Far from being subjected to social sanctions, drinking was considered a positive, socially desirable behavior; it was the indispensable vehicle of interpersonal contact and integration of social units at all levels. As such, it was greatly valued, and its misuse for purely selfish pleasure was apparently quite unknown.

EFFECTS OF SOCIAL DISORGANIZATION: THE EIGHTEENTH CENTURY

After the initial 100 years of contact with the Spanish, the seriously dec-imated Mapuche population attempted a re-grouping on the basis of a state of permanent guerilla warfare. The Indian frontier along the Bío-Bío River was the site of constant surprise raids by Mapuche war par-ties and Spanish slavers. Trading posts at the frontier forts were the principal points of contact between the two cultures.

Together with the use of money, the consumption of wine and distilled alcoholic beverages spread into Mapuche territory from the trading posts. Towards the beginning of the eighteenth century, Spanish traders penetrated Indian territory in order to barter for cattle; their wares in-cluded weapons, *anil*, combs, wine, and spirits. The intensity of war-fare receded, and the Indians began to visit the trading posts with their produce, chiefly cattle and woolen blankets. This commerce expanded gradually, and much later (in the nineteenth century), the Mapuche had developed an active trade with Argentina, where they sold their blankets and silverware. In Argentina they bought cattle which they drove into Chile over the high passes in order to benefit from higher prices in the frontier towns.

Mapuche purchases in the Chilean frontier outposts included especial-ly alcohol. The use of wine and hard liquor represented a fundamental change in the Mapuche patterns of alcohol consumption. The Mapuche ceased to depend on gathering or gardening for their alcohol supply; also the visits to the frontier trading posts meant that consumption was no longer restricted to feasts or other social occasions. This departure from the traditional pattern was of considerable consequence, as can be seen in present-day reservation patterns of alcohol consumption. It was a direct consequence of the Spanish conquest and of the intercultural contact which ensued.

The increasing adoption of wine and hard liquor by the Mapuche may be seen as an effect as well as a further cause of social disorganization. Because of the long period of warfare, drinking had become a means of psychological escape; this fact in turn accelerated the decadence of tra-ditional norms and values. It was no longer a matter of reinforcing or reaffirming social cohesion at each of the levels of Mapuche society, but rather a compensation for the destruction of the traditional way of life and its frames of reference. The process of social disorganization pro-duced a noticeable increase in alcohol consumption and the appearance of a social pathology of drinking, which evidently had not been present in the original pattern. Public drunkenness in the streets of the towns and the spectacle of single Indians helplessly lying about in a state of intoxication are often-mentioned aspects of frontier life from the eighteenth century onwards (Guevara 1902:147).

SPOLIATION: THE NINETEENTH CENTURY

Independence from Spain and the proclamation of the Chilean Republic hardly improved the lot of the Mapuche. Particularly after 1840, the government actively pursued a policy of colonization of Araucania, using Chilean and German colonists. New towns sprang up over the Indian territories and the virgin lands of the Mapuche became objects of greed and speculation.

Several travelers and historians have recorded the manner in which the Mapuche were "legally" despoiled. In all the public bars of Araucania, colonists treated the Indians to one drink after another and then made them sign over their lands. The favorite victims of these sharp dealers were Indians who were known to be addicted to alcohol, it being an easy matter to convince them to trade their lands against small sums of money, or against a few barrels of brandy. Such were the methods which caused the speedy degeneration of a once functional and socially useful drinking pattern (Smith 1914:148; Inalaf 1945:72; Guevara 1902: 393).

However, the encroachments of the colonists also caused new resentments which finally led to a renewed resistance against the white man. The rebellions of 1869, 1874, and 1880 were the last desperate attempts of the Mapuche war chiefs to regain their cultural and territorial independence. But it was too late. As we have seen, these uprisings merely served as a pretext for crushing the nominal independence of the Mapuche nation. The spoliation was made official by the Treaty of 1888 which confined the Indians to reservations while all the better lands were in the hands of non-Mapuche colonists.

It is hardly surprising to find that social disorganization as well as alcoholism reached unprecedented proportions among the Mapuche after the 1884 disaster (Guevara 1929:300). Yet the vitality of Mapuche culture overcame the trend towards disintegration. The relative isolation and shelter afforded by the reservation became a factor of consolidation, as the Mapuche learned to come to terms with their new political realities. A new pattern of alcohol consumption also began to emerge.

In 1968 reservations were peasant communities of the corporate type commonly found in the highlands of Peru and Middle America (Wolf 1955: 452–471). Such peasant communities have the following features in common: marginal land occupancy, reliance on traditional hand techniques, low productivity, a unifying political-religious system, minimal social differences within the group, and the prohibition of land sales to outsiders. In addition, the Mapuche pattern of settlement is unusually scattered as families tend to live in mutual isolation. A typical family property contains two or three *rucas* decked with steep straw roofs; each *ruca* is assigned a specific purpose as sleeping house, kitchen, and so on. On the reservation the distance between families may be less than a kilometer but the properties are fenced off and contact is minimal.

The principal crops are wheat, potatoes, beans, peas, and chile peppers. Most properties also contain a small apple orchard which provides the fruit for making *chicha*. Some cattle, sheep, pigs, geese, and chickens are raised on a small scale. In most reservations the wheat harvest is barely adequate to feed the population through early winter; potatoes are the staple for the remainder of the year. Scarcity of food drives increasing numbers of young Mapuche to seek a better livelihood in the cities.

DRINKING PATTERNS ON THE RESERVATION: RITUAL FESTIVALS

Reservation Mapuche were found to consume alcohol on three kinds of occasions: (1) ritual festivals, (2) visits to town, and (3) assorted informal situations. In general a wide tolerance of alcohol consumption prevailed, but there was a stern rejection of nonsocial drinking, which virtually amounted to intolerance of addiction.

Ritual drinking occasions included festivities of Chilean and Mapuche origin, e.g. religious festivals of the Catholic and Mapuche calendars. Among the latter is the *guillatun* or annual fertility rite; an example of the former is St. Sebastian's Day on January 20, a major celebration which comes after the first harvest but before the main wheat harvest. Some lesser Catholic festivals are Palm Sunday, the Cross of May, St. John's Day, and Christmas. Most of the Mapuche festivals are related to the life cycle: they include the *rucan* or housewarming feast and above all the *awin* or funeral feast. *Chueca* competitions have been largely replaced by soccer and horse racing, although the elements of competition and betting between two reservations are still present, along with the feasting.

The *awin* is a good example of a Mapuche festival, as it appears to be the most persistent tradition on the reservation. Any reservation may have several funerals in an average year. The funeral of an important man may last for a full week, but even a poor man will get a decent feast with the assistance of the community. As soon as death seems near, someone is sent to town to buy one or more 100-liter barrels of wine and several animals are slaughtered. A *huelquen* [messenger] is sent out immediately to convene relatives and friends from neighboring reservations. The ritual begins on the evening of the death with speeches which recount the life of the deceased and his ancestor. Catholic prayers may follow. Food is served every two hours, day or night, and the wine glasses are filled continuously. There are many toasts "to him who is gone," and "may he bring us luck." Jokes are told to "keep from crying."

People arrive continually from the more distant places but no one must leave before the feast is over. New arrivals greet ceremonially each of those present and inquire about the dead person — what he ate, what he said, and what he dreamt before he died. These questions are relevant to the cause of death especially since sorcery is involved. Feasting continues for three days, as the early arrivals take occasional naps. Heavy drinking is mandatory according to an informant:

Tradition holds that the Mapuche man should lose consciousness in order to feel close to the dead . . . . There is much talk when there is not enough to drink. People exclaim, "How is this possible — such an important person and no wine when one has got to get drunk." The idea is to lose consciousness as if to be with the dead person and keep him company in the other world.

On the morning of the third day the body is removed for burial. This is another opportunity for speechmaking by expert orators, who use many rhetorical figures to stir the audience and to make people weep. For instance, they may address the deceased to wish him a safe journey to the other side and to point out that he will soon be united again with his parents and other relatives; or they may grieve that "no more shall you hear the song of the bird and the wind." Burial follows and people linger to eat and drink beside the grave. It is worth pointing out that the funeral traditions have remained practically unchanged since the sixteenth century, judging from many available references (e.g. de Pineda y Bascunan 1862; Cooper 1946:734; Farón 1964:81–93; Treutler 1958: 326–329). The observance of these traditions has become a central criterion of affiliation to the Mapuche culture wherever Mapuche live in close contact with non-Mapuche. Those who maintain their identity as Mapuche will drop everything to follow the call of a funeral.

Chueca is a game similar to hockey, played in three-day tournaments between two communities. Each team is supported by his shaman *(machi)* who chants and beats the nad-drum pleading for the victory of the community. There is much betting, eating, drinking, and dancing, and people spend the night on the spot. The semi-sacred field used for *chueca* is also used for other Mapuche or Catholic festivities and the pattern of feasting is remarkably similar. Shed-like open roofs decked with foliage are erected in the field for protection against the weather; these *ramadas* have become typical of popular festivities throughout Chile. Thus the popular celebration of Independence Day (September 18) in the Parque Cousino of Santiago had until very recently most of the typical features of a Mapuche feast.

In the reservation most festivities, of whatever origin, are actually connected with either the agricultural cycle or with the life cycle. Thus St. Sebastian's is the summer festival, while Christmas falls too early at the beginning of the harvest. Palm Sunday marks the late harvest and the christening of children. Holy Cross Day ("the Cross of May") marks the blessing of the fields after sowing. St. John's is the beginning of winter and the end of the agricultural cycle. There are no festivals in winter but in October the spring festivals *(guillatun)* are held in the more traditional communities. Each celebration is associated with different drinking traditions: wine and freshly brewed *chicha* in summer, strong fermented *chicha* in fall, and *muday* made from wheat under low fermentation in winter.

Alcohol is also regarded as food. A voluntary participant in a cooperative labor feast *(mingaco)* may consume four to five liters of alcoholic drink while working. Wine or *chicha* is mixed with toasted wheat flour *(chupilca)* and is served by the women throughout the appointed task. After completion of labor there is dancing, singing, and drinking throughout the night. *Chupilca* is also a favorite food of women and children throughout the year.

VISITS TO TOWN

Mapuche farmers from neighboring reservations visit market towns, sometimes once or twice a week, in order to sell their produce and make purchases. Before driving home on their oxcarts they stop for a drink at one or another of the numerous taverns. They never drink alone; instead those who have some cash treat their friends. "Partners" for sharing drinks are easily found in town; any Mapuche bystander will do.

Thus a tradition has come about which regards surplus cash as a resource to be shared among friends in the form of alcohol. After completing his purchases and finding some money left over, a young farmer was overheard saying, "This is for drinking: now let's find myself a partner." Some male Mapuche take pride in having friends and getting drunk on every single market day. Women may occasionally accompany their husbands to town and may join in drinking. Usually the peasants have not had breakfast on market days and a little alcohol has powerful physiological effects. Says a town resident: "Then they walk out drunk. This happens every ten to fifteen days. When they go to town they would rather get drunk than spend money on food which they can get at home."

While this pattern is not acknowledged by the Mapuche, it undoubtedly plays a part in breaking the monotony of reservation life and accounts for much of the attraction of the market towns. Drinking has become an important form of sharing and a vehicle for establishing contacts with Mapuche from other reservations. Said one Mapuche man: "Nobody goes to town just for drinking. Rather, it is for business. But one cannot help running into friends."

INFORMAL OCCASIONS FOR DRINKING

Perhaps the single most characteristic attitude of the Mapuche towards drinking is the total rejection of the lone drinker. Drinking is an eminently social act, a mark of hospitality or friendship. Turning down an offer of drink is a grave slight. An offer of drink is the standard welcome of a visitor or the usual response on meeting an acquaintance. It is the normal form of sociability. Therefore, the act of drinking alone is not merely abnormal, it is astonishing and absurd. Such cases are extremely rare.

Informal occasions for drinking may arise spontaneously: when someone brings a bottle of wine, when there is *chicha* left, when the weather is too hot or too cold. On a Sunday afternoon, "When there is nothing else to do, the men will get together to pitch a game of *tejo* and to get drunk just for fun and to while the day away." In such a society, abstinence rather than drinking is considered a social problem: teetotalers are assumed to be stingy or proud. Worse, they are immediately suspect because of their unwillingness to let down their guard in the presence of friends.

DRINKING PATTERNS AMONG MAPUCHE URBAN MIGRANTS

Young Mapuche men and women tend to migrate singly; initially they are welcomed at the homes of city relatives who assist them in finding a job and getting to know other Mapuche migrants. Typically, the Mapuche tend to form a close subculture within the city. They practice endogamy and tend to cluster in the same working places. They prefer a certain neighborhood park and they form the patronage of certain restaurants and dance halls (Lomnitz 1969:46, 49).

The loss of their social group of reference initially causes a disorderly and dysfunctional increase of alcohol intake among many Mapuche migrants. They tend to drink whenever they have cash and whenever they see a bar. Gradually they learn to resist the lure of urban drinking opportunities and to bring some money home for their urban needs. About this time, the traditional role of their rural group of reference is partially taken over by a new structure, the DRINKING CIRCLE. This is a strictly urban institution and its composition is entirely male.

In the larger cities, and particularly in Santiago, the Mapuche migrants find their access to jobs to be restricted to the lesser paid, less secure, and less desirable types of labor. In 1969 many Mapuche worked as bakers because bakery help was hired on a nightly basis, working conditions were poor, and there was no social security of any kind. Every evening groups of Mapuche gathered at the baker's union for the night's assignment. After a while, each boss tended to have his own "regulars"; these Mapuche were usually relatives and friends. After getting their pay in the morning, they would go to the nearest bar and drink until their earnings were gone. Bakery help occupied the lowest social status in the Mapuche community and many of them were new arrivals who had not yet fully adjusted to the city and the language. According to the Union of Bakery Workers, about 65 to 70 percent of all bakers were Mapuche, but most of them were unaffiliated. Only 30 percent of the union membership were Mapuche. Understandably, this situation caused some resentment among union officials and membership.

Eventually, some Mapuche migrants tended to move upward into better jobs (construction workers, waiters, industrial labor), and their alcohol intake became stabilized at or below the norm of their Chilean coworkers. Yet the male drinking circle remained their main group of reference. These groups usually meet on payday and usually on Fridays between 6 and 11 P.M. Each drinking circle patronizes a given bar. The activity consists exclusively of playing dice or dominoes and drinking;

the average amount is two liters of wine per person per evening. Often two or three men will stay on after most of their friends have gone and drink to intoxication. The drinking group may gather again on Saturday afternoon, after watching or participating in a sports event. Drinking may continue through Sunday morning. In general, this pattern is not essentially different from the established drinking pattern among the Chilean working class.

A special study was made among a group of Mapuche belonging to Protestant fundamentalist sects popularly known as *canutos*. Some of them were converted by the territorial missions on their reservation; others joined in the city. In all cases, abstinence from alcohol is the trait which sets them apart from other Mapuche. Apparently the Mapuche Protestant seeks a community with well-defined norms and values to replace his group of reference on the reservation; at the same time, he is rejected by his ethnic group because he refuses to join a drinking circle. Since many missions are made up of a majority of Mapuche membership who established an intense relationship of mutual assistance, their adjustment to the city is often very rapid and successful. Converts are taught to bring their wives and children into the congregation and to exert a proselytizing influence in work and deed wherever they go. As a result, *canuto* families tend to be better off economically as earnings are invested in the household which would otherwise be spent on alcohol. Also, affiliation with a Protestant group is equivalent to a testimonial of sobriety and honesty with many employers. In general, it seems that about 90 percent of Mapuche Protestants are completely abstentious while the remainder are either recidivists or extremely moderate drinkers.

DRINKING NORMS AND DRINKING VALUES

The norms and values associated with alcohol intake can best be understood within the cultural context of the particular society to which the drinker belongs. Mapuche social cohesion is based on a strong cultural identity; this identity is outwardly displayed by the use of the Mapuche language and adherence to a moral code.

Farón (1964:124–127) has described the ethic-religious system of the Mapuche. This system, amounting to an ideology or world view, is an interpretation of events in terms of a sacred struggle between the forces of good and evil. Human action is conceived as magical control of good or evil spirits. Thus all events in human life, including illness and death, are held to be due to spiritual causes which may be controlled by sorcery. But sorcery requires knowledge, in particular a familiarity with the habits and weaknesses of the person to be harmed. Hence the persons closest to the victim are the ones most likely to have caused the harm.

Recognition of the ultimate reality of evil is therefore an essential component of Mapuche identity, which dramatizes his allegiance to his cultural heritage. The Mapuche is permanently torn between the need for human solidarity and the fear of personal intimacy. This basic conflict is reflected in Mapuche social structure, mythology, norms, and values. The importance of festivities may reside in an effort to periodically conciliate the opposing drives for and against socialization, to call a truce in the struggle between good and evil. Such a truce is necessarily ephemeral, a fact which partly explains its orgiastic character.

The social variable termed *confianza* (Lomnitz 1971) becomes an essential factor of social intercourse among the Mapuche. *Confianza* between two individuals exists to the extent that fear of mutual harm can be neutralized. Social distance is obviously a major component of *confianza,* but it is ambiguous since close relatives or neighbors are simultaneously the best potential friends and the most dangerous potential enemies. Therefore, *confianza* needs to be established gradually and repeatedly by furnishing mutual proof of goodwill. An important test of *confianza* is the sharing of experiences. Alcohol plays an important part in spiritual communion as it abolishes the mental defenses that have been erected around the world. A man in a state of drunkenness is held to be incapable of dissembling or of scheming, hence an invitation to drink is tantamount to a challenge to depose all weapons. A refusal to share a drink is an implied aggression, since it reveals a desire to keep one's guard high. Such a man is not tolerated in a drinking group, as he could easily take advantage of the unrestrained openness and weakness of his companions while they are under the influence of alcohol.

Thus while social isolation, as reflected in the dispersed pattern of settlement and the use of watchdogs and fences between neighbors, is a normal precaution against envy and sorcery, the offer and acceptance of alcohol have become a vehicle of social contact in almost all its forms. In Mapuche culture it may be said that "people who drink together stay together." Drinking is communion of souls which extends even to the dead, as we have seen in the *awin* or the funeral feast. All available historical data agree with the conclusion derived from participant observation in the sense that alcohol consumption in Mapuche culture has an important social function in lowering the threshhold of interpersonal aggression and serving as a catalyst of social cohesion.

Mapuche norms and values related to drinking may be interpreted consistently in terms of this cultural context. Let us first summarize the norms and values which have remained unchanged since the sixteenth century to date:

1. Alcoholic beverages are normally consumed in a masculine group, never in private. Female drinking is incidental but male drinking is a part of the masculine role.
2. The act of drinking is a social act; it must be preceded by a TOAST, i.e. an invitation which is at the same time an offer and a challenge.
3. A failure to accept a drink is interpreted as an unfriendly act.
4. A failure to offer alcohol is considered a serious breach of hospitality on the part of a host.
5. Alcohol is consumed in gatherings of all kinds and sizes, from the daily family meal to the large collective feasts.
6. The giving of alcohol confers highly prized prestige on the giver.

As a general comment it may be noted that it is considered quite unseemly for each person to pay for his own drinks, especially when drinking in the city is involved. Frequently, there may be some dispute about who will be allowed to pay for the next round. While an element of reciprocity is undoubtedly present in many cases, any overt reference to such an expectation would be offensive. Quite the contrary, paying the bill is felt to be a privilege.

On the reservation, alcohol is a normal part of the diet from infancy. Small children take alcohol in the form of *chupilca*, i.e. stirred in toasted wheat flour and sugar. It is also taken as a general purpose remedy. Children are restrained from fear of bodily harm in participating with adults in the major collective drinking bouts; but this restraint ceases to be effective once the parents are drunk. Groups of children huddle together to drink on the sly, among friends, in a pattern remarkably similar to that of the adults.

In adolescence, drinking becomes an important mark of sharing among pairs or small groups of close friends, usually male. Drinking is a mark of manhood: "It is said that the man who does not drink is like a woman; a man must drink until he becomes unconscious." Yet the young man is still under the control of his father. He is free to drink and treat others only after he reaches manhood. In the reservation, this occurs at age eighteen when he must enlist in military service. At this point he is usually allowed to represent his father in all manner of transactions, including sales and purchases in the market town.

Young bachelors drink less than married men because a married man is the head of his household and "does as he pleases." He is a fully re-sponsible member of the community and has outgrown the authority of his father. The amount of alcohol intake appears to increase with age, or possibly the threshhold of tolerance decreases too. Old men may get drunk as often as they please, without being criticized or scorned.

The evolution of drinking norms has been rather different in respect to women. At the time of the Spanish conquest, there was no substantial difference between male and female drinking norms. Women drank less because of their domestic role; but on extra-domestic occasions, such as participation as guests in festivals, they drank in the same manner as the men. On the reservation the norm was that a wife should drink with her husband to "keep him company" but should not get drunk herself. Her moderation is supposed to set an example for the children. As an actual fact this norm is frequently transgressed. Drunkenness on the part of the mother may later be rationalized by her son as resulting from her being forced to drink by her father.

Among Mapuche migrants, there is a decreased tolerance of drink-ing by women. There is no female equivalent to the urban drinking circle. Women will share a drink to be sociable, but habitual drinking in a wom-an, or drinking to excess, is strongly censured. The evolution of female drinking norms among the Mapuche may be attributed to Spanish cultur-al influences. An informant pointed out that Mapuche women in the city "drink just like the Chilean women do," i.e. to be sociable in mixed company and without ever reaching intoxication. Obviously, there is here an interplay of cultural and social factors which it would take a great deal of research to untangle.

Mapuche values in relation to drinking are predominantly positive. Drinking is accepted as a normal attribute of masculinity and as a man-datory vehicle of sociability. Lone drinking for the sake of drinking is regarded with scorn, disgust, or disbelief. It is important to emphasize that drinking is valued for the sake of friendship and that any cynical suggestion about pretexts for alcohol consumption is rejected. Thus, res-ervation Mapuche uniformly agree that drinking in the market towns is accidental, "because I have many friends from all over." The idea that a Mapuche peasant goes to town because he likes to drink is dis-missed. "It is a mark of fellowship among friends," nothing more.

Generosity and sociability, as expressed in treating others to a drink, are highly valued. For the same reason, there is disapproval of the "bad drinker" (*weshamollufe*) who becomes aggressive when intoxicated. The ideal drinker is one who can maintain his dignity and his good fel-lowship to the last: "when he is drunk he goes quietly home to sleep it off."

Abstinence is criticized as stinginess or pride. However, nondrinking Mapuche who belong to the Protestant sects are increasingly being tolerated, especially in the city, although social intercourse between drinking and nondrinking Mapuche is still very limited. Some guilt feelings in relation to alcohol consumption are undoubtedly present in many Mapuche today: possibly they may be due to missionary influence, and to a realization of the role of alcohol as a weapon of the *huinca* [white man] in overcoming the military resistance of the Mapuche nation. Said an old woman on a reservation: "In the old days, a Mapuche was pure and drank only *muday.*" Another informant asserts: "The *huinca* brought liquor just to get the Mapuche any way he wanted and take his land away." The historical contradiction implied by this attitude reveals an incipient value conflict, which may be consequential in determining the eventual assimilation of the Mapuche to Chilean culture.

It is already apparent that Mapuche urban migrants have adopted the Chilean working-class norms and values with respect to alcohol consumption. Even in the case of the heavy-drinking bakers, a non-Mapuche observes: "Mapuche bakers drink like bakers, not like Mapuche." Adoption of the new norm is preceded by a period of uncontrolled drinking; this pattern has been observed throughout Mapuche history during periods of social disorganization. Thus a tendency toward alcohol addiction may be correlated with a relaxation or a change in the Mapuche system of norms and values.

CONCLUSIONS

Tolerance of alcohol consumption among the Mapuche, in amounts which may be considered "excessive" by Western medical standards, must be viewed within the context of Mapuche cultural evolution during the last 400 years. The ethical and philosophical system of the Mapuche contains an implicit conflict between fear of human society and the need for socialization, which is partly resolved with the aid of alcohol.

The following factors have remained constant throughout known Mapuche history, as far as their pattern of alcohol intake is concerned: (a) the social function of alcohol; and (b) its explicit connection with the masculine role.

Factors which have evolved or changed during the process of cultural and social interaction between the Mapuche and the white man include the following: (a) drinking in bars (of the market towns or cities), rather than in the home or in the community festivals; (b) new ritual drinking occasions of non-Mapuche origin; (c) certain changes in the female drinking norms which reveal a new ambivalence about alcohol consumption; and (d) the use of new, more powerful types of alcoholic beverages which are not brewed in the home.

The permanence, or nonpermanence, of each of these factors can be explained on the basis of the specific function of social cohesion assigned to alcohol in Mapuche culture. This conclusion is in agreement with the hypothesis proposed by Farón (1961) in the sense that Mapuche cultural evolution is the result of an adaptive process which tends to conserve its basic structure unaltered. In other words, the Mapuche way of drinking as a SOCIAL ACT BETWEEN MALES has survived the periods of crisis and disorganization in Mapuche society because it is essential to the social structure.

On the other hand, the changes in the patterns of drinking can be explained as concessions to the dominant Chilean culture which do not affect the basic function of alcohol as a lubricant of the wheels of social contact. The strong feeling of uniqueness and distinctness of the Mapuche people has often been remarked on by Mapuche and non-Mapuche alike; this stubborn allegiance to a separate national identity rests largely upon a combination of solidarity and fear. Alcohol promotes *confianza* among men who already share the same cultural background: it eliminates the ever-present fear of envious plots and therefore it promotes solidarity.

Influence of the dominant culture on Mapuche drinking patterns is a two-way street. It is true that drinking patterns of urban Mapuche migrants are practically identical to those of the Chilean working class, but it is also true that the working-class drinking pattern in Chile has a strong Mapuche flavor. Members of the Chilean middle class display a more European pattern, featuring moderate alcohol consumption with meals and the appearance of the pathological lone drinker, in contrast with the orgiastic male drinking circle which is characteristic of the working class and the Chilean peasantry. The values attached to drinking among these broad strata of the Chilean population are substantially the same as those which de Pineda y Bascunan (1862) described among the sixteenth-century Mapuche. Drinking in Chile today continues to have a positive semi-sacred connotation, through its long association with an institutionalized ritual of male friendship.

REFERENCES

COOPER, J.
1946 "The Araucanians," in *Handbook of South American Indians*, volume two. New York: Cooper Square. Also published as Bureau of American Ethnology Bulletin 143. Washington, D.C.

CÓRDOBA Y FIGUEROA, P.
1862 *Historia de Chile*. Colección de Historiadores de Chile, volume two. Santiago.

DE LOVERA, P. M.
1865 *Crónicas del Reino de Chile*. Colección de Historiadores de Chile, volume four. Santiago.

DE NAJERA, A. G.
1889 *Desengaño y reparo de la guerra del Reino de Chile*. Colección de Historiadores de Chile, volume fifty-four, part two. Santiago.

DE PINEDA Y BASCUNAN, F. N.
1862 *El cautiverio feliz y razón de las guerras dilatadas en Chile*. Colección de Historiadores de Chile, volume three. Santiago.
1967 *El cautiverio feliz de Pineda y Bascunan*. Edited by A. Gonzáles. Santiago: Zig-Zag.

DE TEJILLO, S.
1923 *Restauración del estado de Arauco* (facsimile edition). Quito.

FARÓN, L.
1961 *Mapuche social structure*. Urbana: University of Illinois Press.
1964 *Hawks of the sun*. Pittsburgh: University of Pittsburgh Press.

GUEVARA, S. T.
1902 *Historia de la civilización de la Araucania*, volume three. Santiago: Imprenta Barcelona.
1929 *Historia de Chile: Chile prehispánico*. Santiago.

INALAF, N. J.
1945 *Rol económico, social y político del indígena en Chile*. Santiago.

JARA, A.
1961 *Guerre et société au Chili*. Institut des Hautes Etudes de l'Amérique Latine. Paris: Université de Paris.

KORTH, E.
1968 *Spanish policy in colonial Chile*. Stanford: Stanford University Press.

LATCHAM, R.
1936 *La agricultura precolombina en Chile y países vecinos*. Santiago.

LIPSCHUTZ, A.
1971 El movimiento indigenista latino-americano en el marco de "La ley de la tribu" y de la "Ley de la gran nacion". *América Indígena* 31:4. Mexico City.

LOMNITZ, L.
1969 Patrones de ingestión de alcohol en migrantes Mapuches en Santiago. *América Indígena* 31(1). Mexico City.
1971 *Reciprocity of favors among the urban middle class of Chile*. Studies in Economic Anthropology. Edited by G. Dalton. Washington, D.C.: American Anthropological Association.

MUNIZAGA, C.
   1960   *Vida de un araucano.* Santiago: Centro de Estudios Antropoló-
          gicos de la Universidad de Chile.
   1961   *Estructuras transicionales en la migración de los araucanos de
          hoy a la cuidad de Santiago de Chile.* Santiago: Notas del Centro
          de Estudios Antropológicos de la Universidad de Chile.
NAVARRO, L.
   1909   *Crónica militar de la conquista y pacificación desde el año 1885
          hasta completa incorporacion al territorio nacional,* volume one.
          Santiago.
OVALLE, A. C.
   1888   *Histórica relación del Renio de Chile.* Colección de Historiadores
          de Chile, volumes twelve and thirteen. Santiago.
RAMÍREZ, F. J.
   1831   "Cronicón sacro-imperial de Chile." Unpublished manuscript.
SMITH, R.
   1914   *Los araucanos.* Santiago: Imprenta Universitaria.
TREUTLER, P.
   1958   *Andanzas de un alemán en Chile.* Santiago: Editorial del Pa-
          cífico.
WOLF, E.
   1955   Types of Latin American peasantry: a preliminary discussion.
          American Anthropologist 57:452–471.

Alcohol Usage in an African Society

ADE M. U. OBAYEMI

Although there are many general studies on the cultures of the Yoruba-speaking people of Nigeria, Dahomey, and Togo in West Africa (Johnson 1921; Fadipe 1970; Ojo 1966; Bascom 1969; Forde 1951), those Yoruba-speaking groups who inhabit the northeasternmost portion of Yoruba territory, namely, the Oworo, Abinu, Ikiri, and Ijumu, when not almost completely omitted, are given scant attention. This tendency in the literature illustrates one factor which is not often comprehended — the fact that there are few points on which the generalizations about the culture and history of the other Yoruba would be applicable to these more obscure groups. It is important to bear this in mind as the role alcohol has played in the pre-colonial culture of these people and the present trends in alcohol usage in their "transitional" society are discussed. While the methods of production of palm wine might be the same, the social functions of alcohol in general among these frontier groups cannot be matched point for point with those of the other Yoruba where other variations in practice are obvious.

The acquaintance of the African with intoxicants or stimulants either existing in natural form like plants or requiring some processing has an unknown antiquity. Some well-known ones like the kola nut (*Cola acumunata, C. nitida*, etc.) are regular stimulants gathered from the trees which bear these fruits. Among the northeast frontier Yoruba, namely, the Oworo, Abinu, Owe, Ikiri, Igbede, and the other Ijumu village areas, most of the alcoholic drinks had been obtained from two unrelated sources. At Ufe (Iffe), one of the village areas, alcoholic drinks in general are known as *u-un mumu* (literally, "that which is drunk"). In this usage, water or fluid medicines are never included. The pre-colonial sources of *u-un mumu* were the oil palm tree (*Eleais guineensiss*), and more recently the rafia palm as well as the guinea corn (sorghum).

Okpe (Ope), the oil palm tree, is a prominent member of the local natural vegetation and is recognized as the single most important plant of the local environment. Besides the two types of basic oils it yields, and besides its other products which are used for house roofing, fencing, baskets, brooms, rope making, fuel, and in ritual, the oil palm tree produces *emu*, the white palm wine of which two varieties are known. *Emu aron* is obtained from the erect tree, while *iju* is tapped from the fallen or felled tree. In the pre-colonial Ijumu and Abinu societies, the tapping of the oil palm tree for wine was not a full-time occupation and most adult males up to the age of forty or fifty could, in theory, tap palm wine. But in practice only a proportion, averaging from three to five out of ten, engaged in this part-time job in addition to their agricultural pursuits. In spite of this lack of full-time preoccupation with palm wine tapping, it is an activity with well-defined, specialized tools and equipment. The tool kit of a "climber or a tapper of the oil palm tree" includes the *ugba* [climbing rope], made from three lengths of the palm frond fibre (*ikon*) woven together to make a thick rope two to three meters long, the *akeke okpe* [a special trimming axe], the *ava* [a very sharp U-ended tapping knife made by the blacksmiths], and *edere* [oval-shaped, long, thin gourds tied to the palm trees to collect the sap via a short, hollow reed which is fashioned into a type of funnel to prevent leakages]. On the ground, the palm wine tapper keeps at his depot (*uho*) a pot or some pots in which he pools the wine from many trees, stores the wine (overnight or until dusk), his calabash funnels, his sieves, and the collecting gourds which he carries up and down the trees.

The same palm tree will supply one or more outlets daily for weeks in succession and some trees give palm wine for many months during the year. One gallon or more per tree per day is not unusual. This method, which is by far the most popular or "noble" among the Ijumu, Abinu, and other groups, has the great advantage of not destroying the tree, and thus the same tree can be tapped by succeeding generations. The climbing rope can be dispensed with for the very young palm trees (*omolokpe*) because the tapping points just around the circle where the fronds branch out are accessible to a man standing on the ground. But most wine-yielding trees have heights averaging five to eight meters from the ground level, and some up to 12 meters or more are climbed and tapped. The one disadvantage of this method is that the palm tree has to be climbed twice a day, in the morning and towards evening, using the same method by which the ripe bunches of oil-bearing palm nuts are cut down. It is not an uncommon experience for people to fall from these heights, leading to death or to permanent physical disability.

The method of tapping for *iju* has the advantage of keeping the tapper on the ground. But this means that the palm tree has to be felled. Whether felled deliberately or pulled down by storms, etc. the tapping of *iju* is a waste of assets. Once the wine runs out the dead tree cannot be made to produce again. The product of the two methods is the identical white palm wine, but the *iju* is locally regarded as inferior. One of the reasons frequently given by *iju* abstainers is that it is injurious to the health in various ways.

In the pre-colonial economy, in which full-time specialization in nonagricultural pursuits was rare, palm wine, like food crops, was not sold. Most adult males owned some palm trees which they tapped for themselves or allowed younger relations to exploit. Palm wine was a favorite drink usually consumed after the daily labors on the farm. In the local folklore, the yield from a tree for the first few days is known to contain very little (if any) alcohol. It is very sweet because of a high sugar content. This is usually turned over to women and children since it rarely intoxicates. As the wine matures, the alcohol content increases and water may be added to dilute the drink for general consumption. The *emu ogidi* [pure or concentrated palm wine] is today reserved for the chiefs, elders, priests, or special people. But it is said that in the past it was uncommon to dilute palm wine with water. Palm wine could be preserved as *okusa* overnight and could be mixed with freshly tapped wine to obtain a higher alcohol content. While it is conceivable that palm wine could be kept two or more nights, it was considered improper and unnecessary to drink *emu* which has lost its fresh taste.

Another alcohol beverage, *otin*, is still produced from grains of guinea corn (*eka*) through a process extending over several days. The grains are kept moist and warm until they begin to show signs of germination at which time they are crushed or ground into a coarse paste that is filtered and boiled in big pots for hours. The cooled liquid then receives the fermenting yeast (*oje*) and the brownish beer is the end product. The brewing of *otin* is primarily a woman's occupation, just as the tapping of palm wine is a man's. As in palm wine tapping, there are no exclusive or full-time brewers of *otin*, although experts did exist, and still do, because in some situations the *otin* does not ferment agreeably. Hence success as a brewer could be a matter of qualifications.

The pre-colonial drinking habits of the Ijumu, Abinu, etc., in their informal content, can be described from recorded traditions and as they survive today. Generally speaking more *u-um mumu* is consumed during the dry season months when there is less activity on the farm. This is also the time when the majority of the festivals are held, namely, the second burials are performed or title-taking ceremonies held. In the private or personal routine, a man goes early in the day to collect the wine which has accumulated overnight from all the palm trees he is tapping at the time. This often occurs on his way to work on the farm, which may be situated near or around these trees. He "tastes" the wine and shares some of it with passers-by or companions, and carries some of the *emu* to work. He refreshes himself with small quantities of wine at intervals or at meal time. Taken in this context palm wine is purely functional; it acts as a reliever of fatigue and helps to increase output by reducing consciousness of the heat of the sun.

At work, palm wine is not consumed in enough quantity to intoxicate but it does induce a sleepy feeling. At the close of the work day in late afternoon, the returning farmer makes the evening round of the trees to collect the daytime yield. Adding this to whatever remained from the morning, he retires to a communal gathering place nearer home, usually a clearing under a few shade trees, to drink with other returning farmers who may or may not have their own palm wine. A variety of other activities takes place here; baskets are made, hoes and other wooden implements are carved, bows and arrows (and now guns) may be repaired and tested, small game skinned or roasted, etc., all before the last stage of the journey home is completed about sunset. Such activities and the fact that the evening is still to come make drunkenness more remote.

A certain (fixed) quantity of palm wine is reserved for the head of the extended family, the oldest man, his brothers, and other elders who have retired from the farm long before sunset. Their presence on the farm is little more than for inspection and general tidying up. They spend more time in the village attending to village affairs or individually acting as diviners and medicine men, making themselves available to callers from within and without the village. An old man usually drinks very little, often taking token draughts presented by several of his children or grandchildren before turning over the rest to the members of the household, including women. An old man can use palm wine to entertain late callers and, since he sleeps very little, might sip alone far into the night.

Thus in the context of private life, palm wine occupies a place in the regular "diet" like food and water. As such it is neither particularly moral nor immoral to drink or to abstain from drinking. When taken to the point of intoxication, the effects are obvious: output at work is reduced, and sleep is induced. Purely functional uses of *emu* in traditional societies include consuming it directly as medicine (against measles in children) or as a popular medical agent for washing down powdered medicine (*agunmu*) to combat ailments like dysentery.

[margin note: medicine]

The far more formal usage of *u-un mumu*, either *otin* or *emu*, is in those areas of communal life where these are not merely desirable but are officially demanded as essentials. There are definite social, religious, political, and economic situations which elevate alcohol usage to institutional demands. A man who has been promised a girl, whom he eventually expects to marry, will present the lineage group of his parents-in-law with kola nuts, "pour" pots of *u-un mumu* in favor of the paternal and maternal relations of the girls, and present loads of choice yams and other service in token of his gratitude. The initiation into full membership of the society as an adult, *ogun* among the Ijumu and *ide* or *iro* among some Abinu, also involves the presentation of at least a pot of *u-un mumu*. The taking of, and confirmation in, a chiefly title includes among its requirements the presentation of some pots of *u-un mumu* as well as the drinks that go into the general feasting and entertainment accompanying the occasion. Part of the expenses of funeral rites, especially the second or formal and official burials, is the provision of many pots (*oru*) or *u-un mumu*, as custom demands.

[margin note: Social rites]

In all of these, at least in the past, no provisions were made for substitutions with regard to the *u-un mumu*. Each of these stated demands for drinks has an established procedure for presentation, acceptance, sharing and consumption. All of the "departments" or components of the state, living and dead, have fixed shares and a well-rehearsed order of procedures. The *olu* or *oba* [king], the chiefs in order of importance, the ancestors collectively, as visibly represented by *egungun* (the word often translates as 'masquerade'), state drummers, non-titled adults, the women (mothers, obvious or otherwise), paternal relations (*omoba*), maternal relations (*omoye*), etc., have their clearly defined places. In accordance with the gravity or solemnity of the occasion, it is clear that the celebrant or aspirant seeks out the best *emu* and/or *otin* as befits the event. The *u-un mumu* is presented in standard containers that are usually pots; the *oga* and *agba* are examples which survive.

The *agba* is the largest of the pots manufactured in the area, and the four which survive at Ufe were made before the nineteenth century. They hold, on the average, up to 100 liters. Apart from the obligatory extras which go into the unofficial entertainment of guests, the presentation of drinks is essentially part of the "feasts of state."

One principle in the acceptance of these gifts is that however excellent the quality of the *u-un mumu*, however graceful and polite the presentation, and however expensive or difficult to procure, objections are raised against quality, quantity, etc., and the gifts are officially rejected. After prolonged delays, often lasting many hours during which the celebrant or incumbent and his relations plead for the acceptance of the *u-un mumu* and other presents, these are grudgingly received. Cases of final rejection are very rare. The humbled aspirant will then express his gratitude and make reparations through fines or other presents for previous misdeeds or misdemeanors. The principle behind the total lack of any official compliments is that no gift, payment, or fine, however expensive or excellent, and ample, is good enough to match the winning of a wife, the granting of a title, or the institutional elevation of the interred to full ancestral status. For these, one must carry the feeling or the acknowledgment of the insufficiency of his means alone for the honors or benefits thereby received. Considered in this light, popularized descriptions like "bride price" or "buying of a title" are contextually untenable, at least in terms of the traditional Ijumu practice. The procedure of presenting the *u-un mumu* and of its acceptance is a dramatization of the insufficiency of visible "payments" for a bride, for a title, or for the ancestors to come, in the form of the *egungun*. This is, however, not to deny the sense of achievement and the legitimate pride that belongs to the bridegroom, the initiated, the taker of a title, or the one "burying" his father or mother.

The sense of achievement is well expressed by the requirements for *ogun* [initiation into full manhood]. At Ufe, it was the custom not just to fill the *agba* to the brim with *u-un mumu* of the brightest quality, but to pour more and more drinks in to make it overflow and run along the ground for a distance of about 6 meters. It was only then that the competence of the aspirant to "fill the *agba*" was conceded, and it was only after this that he could plead for its acceptance. Even if his effort was subsequently belittled, and grudgingly accepted as described above, he could claim the legitimate pride and contentment of having achieved what the non-initiated had not been able to do. At the same time, he would be conscious of the fact that in spite of his feat, he had to plead for its acceptance, an interesting balance of pride against a sense of insufficiency.

The occasions of public celebrations, such as title-taking, funerals for important people, and festivals, are usually those when the society sanctions or creates the conditions for drunkenness or drunken behavior. There is thus a social disposition for the acceptance of drunken behavior which takes many forms. Vomiting, even in public, is condoned and, although it might embarrass relatives and friends, this is accepted as one normal outlet for drunkenness. The singing of profane songs or dirty jokes, often of a sexual bias, is excused. Quarreling or even fighting under the influence of alcohol on such occasions is common but, unless it results in serious physical harm or damage to property, is overlooked as *uja emu* [drink-induced quarrel], and exchanges of insults are normally ignored, especially since the parties will not remember them when they regain soberness. In case of violent or other behavior considered extraordinary, even for a drunken person, sobriety is hastened by forcing honey, palm oil, or lime orange down his throat. Finally, drunkenness usually finds an enjoyable outlet in the public dancing to music which is an important aspect of any local festivities.

Such occasions of public festivities apart, it is difficult to determine the reality or rarity of alcoholism as a social problem in pre-colonial society. Oral traditions emphasize the social discipline of a rigid routine centered on work on the farm. This reduces the hours of leisure when one might indulge in excessive alcohol consumption. Other restraining influences were that (1) *emu* and *otin* are regular nutrients which, like food and water, should not be taken in excess, and (2) the fact that being a subsidiary, though specialized, pursuit, alcohol production is limited to what a man can safely combine without prejudice with his normal output on the farm. It is also apparent that alcoholism is looked upon with social disfavor.

There is an *aro* [folktale] in which a woman used *u-un mumu* to overcome her husband's determination not to reveal a deep-seated secret — not unlike the story of Samson and Delilah in some points, the moral of which, though it varies from narrator to narrator, is that one should beware of inquisitive women and drinking (to the extent that one loses control of his mind). Another criticism of drunkenness comes from the scathing attack of an *ogun* or *igonre* song:

O hun gha-gha-gha h'orikpo
  a s'arun emu kpo
ẹ gba gọnrun gha lọwọ ẹ
  a a s'on'ogun ko.

He lies stiffly on the bed
  his drunkard's mouth displayed
Seize our bow from him
  He is not the type that can fight in a war.

In the songs, where virtues in relation to alcohol are cited, these refer to production and possession, not consumption. One of the *obdloo* of Ufe is greeted in the *ogun* songs like this:

ab'arun kpękpę rofin-rofin
o jo da j'o dun k'ęlęja mu.
. . . . he of the keen tapping stick
who tapped the agreeable (wine) for the great to drink.

Descriptions like *a n'otin, n'emu* [rich in *otin* and *emu*] or *omo el'emu kun edere* [he whose palm tree fills his gourds/kegs] are common.

The twentieth century coincides with the imposition of British colonial rule on these people, with their inclusion in the larger Nigerian political system. This development has meant the introduction of a wider range of economic opportunities than had been available before 1900. Christianity came with its own message of salvation and in many ways came to challenge traditional concepts and values and to present opposition to areas of social life which contradict the Biblical position or which the foreign missionaries and their local collaborators do not understand. The beginning of Western education and of wage labor extended the contact of people geographically and mentally. The Western tendency toward individualism, as generally contrasted with the communalism which had prevailed, began to appear. With all these changes, the society modified itself theoretically according to its understanding and interpretation of the new features although in reality, the social adjustments were more pragmatic than anything else.

As far as the use of alcohol was concerned, it was not an important issue in the conflicts between Christian preachings and social practice. Alcohol was rather ennobeled by its well-established place in the entertainments at Christmas, Easter, and Christian harvests, funerals, and other ceremonies. The Anglican (C.M.S.), Methodist, and Baptist churches in the area did not have an alcoholism problem to deal with, partly because alcoholism had not been a social problem and the "normal" usage of alcoholic drinks, as we indicated above, was too well integrated to become a dilemma overnight. The "pagan" festivals and the "pagan" aspects of title-taking and funeral ceremonies were denounced by the Christians, and they withdrew themselves from these aspects of social life, rejecting the *u-un mumu* which came within these contexts. But they accepted their shares of drinks served on the farm or outside "pagan" contexts. A second and third generation of Christians, however, modified the terms of their participation in the communal usage of alcohol, thus blurring the lines along which the earliest local Christians (ca. 1904 to ca. 1930) made their discriminations between what was "pagan" and what was acceptable.

As the new economy increased its inroads into the traditional societies of the Ijumu and Abinu, with its encouragement of cash-crop production and wage labor, the time budget of the pre-colonial era was considerably readjusted. There was the creation of more leisure as the number of hours spent on the farm decreased, and Sundays were observed as work-free days. These changes, together with the abandonment of the scattered hamlet pattern of settlement for bigger nucleated settlements, led to demands for diversions, refreshments, and means of entertainment. Increased alcohol consumption was one response. Another contributory factor was that the increased contact of a wide politico-economic system introduced to the Ijumu, Abinu, and their neighbors other brands of drinks hitherto unknown, or at least uncommon, in their area. Such drinks include *ogogoro* (the so-called "illicit gin" of official British colony usage), a product of the communities further south and nearer to the coast, and *burukutu*, locally produced from grains, and *gari*, a by-product of *cassava* which was introduced into the area in the 1920's and 1930's. *Emu ogoro* (*ogoro*), which is obtained from the rafia palm, became increasingly popular as demands for alcohol increased. Increasingly demands brought by the new op portunities also gave rise to the promotion of alcohol production to a full-time or semi-full-time profession. Immigrant palm wine tappers came from the adjacent Igbira division and parts of the mid-western state. Finally, local drinking houses for *otin*, *burukutu*, and *emu* [palm wine bars] made their appearance.

The emergence of an artisan class (*oluse owo*) as carpenters, brick layers, tailors, sawyers, mechanics, bicycle repairers, motor vehicle drivers, as well as others, even when some of these professions are supplemented by cash and food crop farming, has added to the occasions for celebrations. An apprentice carpenter, or tailor, upon successful completion of his training, is expected to provide a feast, usually financed by his relatives and sponsors, to celebrate his "freedom" when he receives his certificate. The opening of new school buildings, dispensaries, churches, or market stalls sometimes overlaps with visits of government officials, church dignitaries, etc., all of which create extra opportunities for the purchase of alcoholic drinks for consumption. To supplement the local products, European liquor, either imported or produced in factories on Nigerian soil, is becoming increasingly regular with the idea that it adds to the sophistication of parties and ceremonies. European liquor had been introduced by returning workers from centers like Lagos, Sapele, Burutu, and other Nigerian towns since the second and third decades of this century, but in general "European" liquor, either as beer, gin, or wine, was and still is too expensive for the quantity involved to be a viable alternative to locally produced drinks which still make up at least 90 percent of locally consumed alcohol drinks. This reveals the resilience of locally produced *u-un mumu*.

Of a different character is the situation of migrants who have moved from these "ritual" communities to urban areas, who are two or three generations removed from the pre-colonial traditional system. For these people, who still preserve their identity, make visits home, and retain contacts with the home to which they usually expect to return upon retirement, the discipline and the restricting influences of farm work and village life are gone. It is among these groups that alcoholics are to be found. While alcoholism is also apparent in present-day farming villages, the study of urban drinking is becoming increasingly important.

REFERENCES

BASCOM, W. R.
   1969   *The Yoruba of southwestern Nigeria.* New York: Holt, Rinehart and Winston.
FADIPE, N. A.
   1970   *The sociology of the Yoruba.* Ibadan: Ibadan University Press.
FORDE, C. D.
   1951   *The Yoruba speaking peoples of southwestern Nigeria.* London: International African Institute.
JOHNSON, S.
   1921   *The history of the Yoruba.* London.
OJO, G. J. A.
   1966   *The Yoruba culture: a geographical analysis.* London: University of London.

Summary of an Alcoholism Study in the Apurímac-Ayacucho River Valley, Peru

ALFREDO VELAPATIÑO ORTEGA

This report is a summary of more comprehensive work done in the Apurímac-Ayacucho River Valley, Peru, investigating the use of alcohol and the incidence of alcoholism. It is intended to be an anthropological study as well as a general view of the problems of alcohol use in this vast zone. This study was conducted for several important reasons. Because the characteristics of alcohol use in Peru are so alarming, they require study and discussion by many professionals — anthropologists, sociologists, doctors, and other authorities — to provide explanations and solutions to these problems which create discord and disequilibrium in society.

In order to get a better view of the problem of alcohol use, a brief physical description of the studied zone is necessary. The extensive valley of the wild and tropical Apurímac River reveals a cluster of towns inhabited by colonizing peasant farmers originally from the highlands and by aboriginal jungle natives, indigenous to the valley zone. Thus two cultures come together here: one is of the commercial or nontraditional type, while the other is of the noncommercial or traditional type where barter predominates among the inhabitants. There are nine villages and thirty-five hamlets (see Table 1). Two of the villages are comprised of people of native origin. The historical information on the remaining seven villages basically coincides with the intrusion of immigrant colonists.

Thirty percent of the immigrants came from the Ayacuchana Mountains and 60 percent came from the Huantina Mountains. Only 10 percent of them came from other zones of Peru. In 1940 commercial

Translated from the original Spanish by Gisela Jernigman.

agricultural colonists, who operate in this zone and within the small native hamlets, began to arrive in this region. A factor contributing to the growth of the area was the 1960 opening of the highway in the Apurímac River Valley. Thus we can see that the population of the zone has greatly increased. Although it is true that this increased communication brings some advantages for these intrusive peoples, this new impact is much more serious for the aboriginal natives.

Among the elements appearing at the beginning of this period was alcohol, introduced by the commercial colonists in an eagerness for economic gain. This intrusion into the native hamlets brought an array of conflicts within the indigenous social structure. Alcohol use has been and is a principal characteristic for the majority of these commercial colonists. Alcohol use was already known among them when they still lived in their zone of origin; among the natives, however, the use of alcohol was nonexistent, with the exception of the native *chicha* beverage which they had made since the days of their forefathers. *Chicha* is made from a base consisting of masticated *yucca* fermented by saliva, but it cannot be categorized as an alcoholic beverage because of its very low alcohol percentage. Thus in these native communities, alcoholism did not exist prior to the commercial penetration of the colonists.

On the other hand, among the colonists the use of alcohol has been and is common. Their intrusion into the native communities introduced a series of problems, among these the increasingly alarming problem of alcohol use among the natives. The problem in this rural zone can be better understood in figures for each of the villages, for the number of persons who use alcohol in a nonexcessive fashion and for those who could be called chronic or true alcoholics (see Table 1).

Table 1.   Village distribution of non-excessive and chronic drinkers

Community	Population	Percentage advanced	Percentage not advanced
San Francisco	11,950	15	45
Santa Rosa	9,800	14	34
Machente	7,360	14	38
Quimbiri	5,200	6	19
Pichari	4,900	8	15
Pasnato	4,540	3	8
Limonchayocc	1,120	1	3
Otari (native)	640	—	2
San Mateo (native)	256	—	3
Total	45,766	61	167

As we see in Table 1, the villages which are inhabited by the colonists are those which have a high percentage of advanced alcoholics, or a high percentage who are moving in the direction of chronic alcoholism but are not yet that advanced. In native communities such as Otari and San Mateo, called *campas* in Peru, true alcoholism does not exist among the inhabitants. But a trend toward alcoholism can be seen in most recent years due to the penetration of an alien culture with different customs and cultural patterns than those of the natives. Because this intrusive culture seeks self-benefit from the minimal commercial development of these natives, the latter are deceived with products that do not help them in any way in their development. One of the elements that hurts the native most and which offers no benefit to him is the alcohol which the colonists sell to these natives.

Among these natives sugar cane alcohol (*aguardiente*) is mixed indiscriminately with *chicha*, which is usually used to quench thirst and as nourishment. Only on very rare occasions do they use *chicha* to get drunk; before *aguardiente* was introduced into these communities there was no incentive, as there is today, to use alcohol excessively. Although one still does not see active or chronic alcoholics who use alcohol in an exaggerated way, it is likely that this *campa* culture will experience conflicts because of the introduction of alcohol. Its use is increasing and this increase is in proportion to the increase in culture contact between the two cultures.

Some anthropological studies conducted in Peru in the native communities reveal that these societies are facing new and increasingly more serious problems. One of these, if not the most important, is related to alcohol use. Among the agricultural colonists of the valley a majority of the population is gradually being afflicted by alcoholism. In Peru there are actually some 300,000 alcoholics among whom almost 70 percent belong to the agricultural masses living in the rural zone of Peru. This is reflected in the zone discussed here. Unlike the native communities, there is a higher percentage of persons in a state of alcohol addiction, either advanced or not advanced (see Table 1). There are occasional drinkers who, although they cannot be categorized as alcoholics, could become addictive drinkers at any moment, given the right circumstances.

An important factor that incites *campesinos* to drink is the total despair found in the entire population. Because of their very poorly developed agricultural technology, and because of the lack of aid by the state, conflict and disequilibrium are produced in the society and the family. Although it is true that economic failures and unemployment lead them to drink, there are also other factors such as psychoneurosis, sociocultural habituation, and sociopathic personality illnesses which occur among any people in their relation to society and the cultural environment. Besides this, with deeper study it can be seen that every one of the addicted drinkers has had a maladjustment in childhood: one can detect traits of neurotic adjustment and antisocial characteristics which probably developed out of deprivation, rejection, and parental indifference. Among those who show traits of neurotic maladjustment, it can be noted that some had been responsible workers in their homes in their childhood. But this latter type of case has very rarely been encountered in the zone studied. More often we find that the majority of the cases are types with antisocial characteristics who had maladjusted childhoods in their homes, who performed poorly in their work in the fields, and who had been undependable. All of these characteristics can be traced to their not having parents, to their having lived in broken homes, or their having to face other diverse problems of this kind.

The problem of the use of *coca* in regard to this problem of alcoholism cannot be ignored because the majority of the alcoholics use both *coca* and alcohol. In Peru and Bolivia they are intimately linked. Among women there are also signs that alcoholism can become a problem, though in a smaller proportion than among men. Among the native *campa* women, there are as yet no drinkers, but one cannot discount the possibility that this will change.

The alcoholics of this zone have had no help until now. Social and economic failures affect each of them increasingly. The economy of small, privately owned plots of land is gradually declining so that very few individuals are able to meet subsistence needs or to survive the social conflict. Health and psychiatric assistance or rehabilitation centers are nonexistent. Less than 1 percent of the drinkers go to the distant treatment centers; they are condemned to remain in their alcoholic state for the rest of their lives. Peru actually occupies first place in the use of alcohol, with 78 to 80 percent of its population consuming alcohol, while Poland, which is second, has only 61.2 percent drinkers. The consumption of *aguardiente* in the central and southern districts of Peru, in the Apurímac River Valley, is so high that of the 800 million *soles* that are spent in acquiring the *aguardiente* in the central country somewhat over 200 million are spent here.

In view of this discouraging information and the small amount of interest shown in finding solutions, the problem of alcohol use is going to persist and will increase. Nothing can be done unless more serious studies are conducted and attempts are made to resolve these problems.

PART FOUR

Physiological and Biomedical Aspects of Alcohol Consumption

Introduction

Alcohol, whatever else it is, is undeniably a powerful psychoactive substance. It directly affects major psychomotor functions through a set of complex physiochemical metabolic processes. Clinical and experimental research is now beginning to delineate the parameters and characteristics of these mechanisms. Yet virtually no attempts have been made to get at cross-cultural variation in the physiology of alcohol consumption. Population biology suggests that such variation is expectable; so does sociocultural research into behavioral variation in other domains. If there is a single critical issue in the area of alcohol studies, it is this: behavioral variation is linked to metabolic variation and both reflect cross-cultural differentiation.

The papers in this section are devoted to examining just this proposition. Madsen begins his brief but eloquent argument by pointing out the epistemological difficulties which have plagued the "nature-nurture" controversy in American scientific circles and how these have been responsible for the stalemate that exists in alcohol studies today. Behavioral science research on alcoholism is increasingly committed to a psychocultural analytic paradigm that is rapidly becoming obsolete in the face of mounting biomedical evidence of the importance of physiochemical and metabolic variables. This commitment, according to Madsen, is scientifically untenable and grounded in monotypic conceptualization which prevents (1) awareness of the usefulness of biomedical data and (2) perpetuates counterproductive psychocultural analytic approaches. Madsen does not call for the replacement of one model by the other; what he does call for is a synthesis of the two paradigms such that they cease to be viewed as contradictory, resulting in a synthetic theory of alcohol use and abuse.

The next paper (the only reprint in this volume), by Fenna and his colleagues, is a tentative effort to view alcohol metabolism in cross-cultural perspective. Because of the clinical possibility that Canadian Indian alcohol tolerance might be linked to subsequent problem drinking, Eskimo, Indian, and Anglo subjects were administered intravenous doses of ethanol. The rates of alcohol absorption were carefully measured and the result was significantly different metabolic profiles for the three groups. As Hanna notes in the next paper, there are difficulties with the interpretation of these differences in blood alcohol clearance. Beyond dispute, however, is the fundamental validity of using cross-cultural variation in physiological processes as a legitimate avenue of inquiry in alcohol research.

In the final paper in this section, Hanna argues persuasively in support of this proposition. Inter- and intra-population metabolic and morphological variation exists which could influence alcohol physiology. These differences are not only relevant to the basic question of how alcohol-affected psychomotor functions might vary from culture to culture, but also serve to indicate potentially important behavioral problems for investigation, such as sex-specific and age-specific drinking patterns. A great deal more research is needed before we can confidently talk of direct linkages between alcohol intolerance and problem drinking on a meaningful cross-cultural scale. Hanna's paper, as well as the preceding ones in this section, strongly supports the contention that (1) biocultural variables are an important but as yet untapped subject in alcohol research and (2) these variables may prove to be of paramount importance in the treatment of problem drinking and alcoholism. Only further interdisciplinary research efforts of the kind evident in this section's papers and in the volume as a whole will substantiate these propositions.

Body, Mind, and Booze

WILLIAM MADSEN

America has suddenly become conscious of the fact that alcoholism is a major health problem. With typical Yankee zeal we are rushing into a variety of crash programs to find the cause and the cure for this affliction. Throughout the country, specialists are engaged in research, innovative therapeutic approaches, and conferences in pursuit of "the answer." This new burst of energy and dedication is producing a flood of publications, a plethora of explanations and theories, and increasing the massive confusion on the nature of alcoholism, and perhaps slowing any meaningful approaches to relieve the problem. It is indeed indicative of our scientific inadequacies in this area that a system of folk psychotherapy called Alcoholics Anonymous has rehabilitated more problem drinkers than the combined facilities of medicine, psychology, and psychiatry (Maxwell 1967: 211). Most other therapies with any degree of success either incorporate AA principles into their programs or utilize Alcoholics Anonymous as an adjunct to their own approaches. When a folk approach so excels over so-called "scientific" approaches, it is time for us to re-examine our scientific assumptions about human behavior.

While the psychocultural dynamics of Alcoholics Anonymous are primarily responsible for the success of that organization (Madsen 1974), its basic assumptions about the nature of alcoholism are also vital to its recovery program. AA successfully uses a holistic approach and sees alcoholism as biological, psychological, and cultural (Alcoholics Anonymous 1955). While many alcohologists, scientific specialists in alcoholism, give lip service to multicausal factors, vast numbers rest all of their arguments on a dogmatic monocausality that is defended with all the fervor of a religious faith. As the literature on human behavior piles up in a massive outpouring of creativity, such dogmatists tend to form into tight little camps and read only the literature supporting their own stance while blithely ignoring or dismissing as irrelevant any work which contradicts their position. As a result, as Opler (1959: 125) has noted, the approaches in alcoholism "have consequently been marked by numerous confusions, by an air of the mystical."

This mystical-emotional attitude works against any objective approach to the problem. As noted by Linton (1964: 3) ". . . real understanding calls for an impersonal approach to problems and an open mind." Yet the cult-forming tendencies in the human sciences have always been present. In 1929 Lowie wrote: "But the individual scientist will go on spinning his cobwebs of fancy, weaker-willed fellows and disciples will make them into a holy of holies, and for the greater glory of the sect they will excommunicate the infidel, gloss over the patent facts, and even condone deliberate fraud. Science has made advances; the scientist is still a primitive man in his psychology" (Lowie 1929: 287).

The numerous minor skirmishes among the alcohologists actually constitute but small battles in the larger war of the biological determinists versus the psychocultural determinists. The nature-nurture controversy is as far from resolution today as it was in the mid-nineteenth century and the inability to resolve it will prevent us from coming to any valid understanding of human beings or of the alcoholics within their ranks.

A resolution of this conflict cannot begin until its reality is recognized. Social scientists are as deeply imbedded in cultural assumptions as are the subjects they study. "Nature" and "nurture" represent two "themes," to use Opler's terminology (1945), that have deep roots in Western thinking and that have confronted each other as either-or alternatives. This battle traces back to Zoroastrianism and into Christianity where one chooses sides with either Satan or God and no compromise is to be tolerated. In Hegel's terms, we play our game by creating a "thesis" and an "antithesis" and then fight for an unconditional victory. This is true in our sports, court procedures, and military backgrounds. We resist the "synthesis" postulated by Hegel and see attempts in this direction as unsavory compromises or peace with dishonor. Individual ego defense is all too often a stronger motive than a valid resolution of any problem.

The nature-nurture split probably had its genesis in the early Christian distinction between "soul" and "body." René Descartes, in his *Meditations on first philosophy* in the seventeenth century, translated the duality into one of "mind" and "body" and made the mind a valid subject for independent study. Locke laid the foundation for the psychocultural determinists in the same century when he defined man's mind as a *tabula rasa*, a "blank slate" to be filled in by cultural experiences. Watson early in this century created behaviorism, the dominant school in psychocultural determinism. His torch as the behaviorist leader has today passed to Skinner (1953, 1971).

Due to the historical ideology that went into the early social planning of America, this country was a fertile land for the blossoming of psychocultural determinism. The school was further strengthened by our war against a Nazi Germany which stood for everything evil including biological determinism. We have come to define as un-American any belief that biology may in any way affect behavior. Following our own historical orientations and our value system, this is entirely meaningful in the political arena. However, it may prove to be the primary block to any valid approaches to mental illness and behavioral problems. Our social scientists who see any significant biological factors in human behavior run the severe risk of being found politically unreliable; many are then attacked with an intense emotionalism that should really have no place in the arena of scientific debate. However, the biological determinists have not been silenced and, though a minority, have been loudly trying to explain everything from aggression and warfare to homosexuality and schizophrenia in terms of physiological causation. The engagement between the two camps has been described by Eysenck (1970: 340) as ". . . the futile battle between 'environmentalists' and 'hereditarians' with its undesirable political overtones."

In the area of mental illness, the psychocultural determinists have dominated the field and are reluctant to share any corner of it with the more biologically oriented disciplines. However, they have defended their territorial imperative over all emotional illness by beating off the competitors rather than by any notable success in curing their patients. Despite the many contributions of the psychological and psychiatric therapies, it has been repeatedly demonstrated that the recovery rate from mental illness is almost identical whether one is guided by a psychotherapist, a physician, or a faith healer (e.g. Asimov 1964; Berelson and Steiner 1964; Eysenck 1952; Watson 1972; Wechsler 1972). In fact, a recent study by Rosenhan (1973) has demonstrated the inability of psychiatric diagnostic skills to even separate "schizophrenics" and "normals." Likewise, orthodox psychotherapies have a difficult time defining and identifying "alcoholics" and have been almost totally inadequate in treating them.

The failure of psychotherapy in the treatment of all emotional ill-nesses, including alcoholism, may rest on the error in assuming that the mind is an autonomous thing that thinks, feels, and emotes without any reference to a physical body. Both Chapple (1970) and Chein (1972), among others, have pointed to the logical fallacy of this dogma. But the dogma continues.

Within the ranks of alcohologists, specialists are increasingly stating that alcoholism is so separated from a biological reality that it is a moral problem and not a disease. We are thus confronted with an argument to return alcoholism to the field of moral education. Among the leaders in this movement are Verden and Shatterly (1971) who see the disease concept as a fabrication by the alcoholics themselves in an attempt to hide their sinful natures from the general public. Steiner (1969, 1971) defines alcoholism as merely a "game."

Such psychocultural dogmatists totally ignore all of the valid research on the biological correlates of alcoholism. Yet, the evidence for a biological side of alcoholism is rapidly mounting. There is even con-vincing evidence that alcoholism may in part rest on an hereditary pre-disposition (e.g. Partanen, et al. 1966; Catanzaro 1967; Eysenck 1970; Schuckit, et al. 1972). As I write, a popular news magazine reports on the work of John Ewing which may indicate that Orientals have some genetic immunity to alcoholism because of an inherent low tolerance for ethanol (*Time* 1973). It is conceivable that alcoholics inherit a metab-olism which is so susceptible to alcohol-induced damage that drinking itself alters their biologies to produce the alcoholism. In any case, Myers (1963a, 1963b) has demonstrated that at the level of rats, intra-cranial injections of ethanol in "normal" rats produces "alcoholic" rats. Alcoholism is also probably a "stress-disease" (Selye 1956) and a deprived or oppressive childhood may weaken the individual's resis-tance to such alcohol-induced pathology.

The locus and full range of the alcohol biological pathologies are still not fully known. However, as in any stress disease, there is probably an inadequacy in the equilibrium-maintaining system, and a number of intertwined malfunctions have been indicated. Several studies have demonstrated a hypoglycemic correlate in alcoholism (Voegtlin, et al. 1943; Charaskin and Ringsdorf 1971; Lovell and Tintera 1951). This condition is probably related to malfunctions that have been identified in the hypothalmus (Williams 1971; Valles 1969), the pituitary (Smith 1951), the thyroid (Goldberg 1960), the adrenals (Lovell and Tintera 1951; Goldfarb and Berman 1949; Smith 1950), and the gonads (Gottesfeld and Yager 1950). As a product of these inadequacies, the alcoholic probably has high levels of epinephrine, lactate, adrenochrome (Hoffer and Osmond 1959), melatonin (Geller 1971), and serotonin (Myers and Veale 1968; Veale and Myers 1970; Myers and Cicero 1969; Myers and Tytell 1972; Davis and Walsh 1971). The pineal gland may also be of pivotal importance in the genesis of alcoholism (Geller 1971; *Science News* 1973). For years seen as a gland of little functional importance, the pineal has been shown by Axelrod (1972) to be a major regulator of neurochemical balance.

The evidence has mounted on all sides that alcoholism cannot be seen and understood from a single theoretical viewpoint. Each of the schools has presented us with some insight, for as Watts (1969: 2) has said: ". . . there is some truth in nearly all theories. . . ." What we need most urgently now is a synthesis of the valid contributions from each of the conflicting schools to present a valid, integrated, and meaningful model of alcoholism. No single discipline today is capable of undertaking this synthesis. A few decades ago, this approach would have been natural for anthropology, for in 1948 Kroeber repeated the dictum of his 1923 book and said: ". . . the specific subject matter of anthropology is the interrelation of what is biological in man and what is social and historical for him" (1948: 2). However, anthropology has drifted far from that position and comes increasingly under the domination of the psychocultural determinists. Some, like Goldschmidt (1966: viii), have questioned the validity of this trend. Others, like Chapple (1970), are openly seeking a synthesis of body, mind, and culture to explain the human animal. The ethologist Eibl-Eibesfeldt (1972) and the sociologists Mazur and Robertson (1972) have also written significant books seeking to resolve the nature-nurture conflict. They are returning to a basic truth realized by Plato over 2,000 years ago. Plato, as quoted by Dixon (1937: 43), said: "This is the greatest error in the treatment of illness, that there are physicians of the mind and physicians of the body and yet the two are indivisible." The alcohologist should listen.

REFERENCES

ALCOHOLICS ANONYMOUS
   1955   *Alcoholics anonymous* (revised edition). New York: Alcoholics Anonymous World Services.
ASIMOV, I.
   1964   *Guide to the biological sciences.* New York: Cardinal (Pocket Books).

AXELROD, J.

1972   "The pineal gland: a neurochemical transducer," in *5th International Congress of Pharmacology, abstracts of invited presentations*.

BERELSON, B., G. A. STEINER

1964   *Human behavior: an inventory of scientific findings*. New York: Harcourt, Brace and World.

CATANZARO, D. J.

1967   "Psychiatric aspects of alcoholism," in *Alcoholism*. Edited by David J. Pittman. New York: Harper and Row.

CHAPPLE, E. D.

1970   *Culture and biological man: explorations in behavioral anthropology*. New York: Holt, Rinehart and Winston.

CHARASKIN, E., W. M. RINGSDORF

1971   *New hope for incurable diseases*. New York: Exposition Press.

CHEIN, I.

1972   *The science of behavior and the image of man*. New York: Basic Books.

DAVIS, V. E., M. WALSH

1971   "Effect of ethanol on neuroamine metabolism," in *Biological basis of alcoholism*. Edited by Yedy Israel and Jorge Mardones. New York: Wiley-Interscience.

DESCARTES, R.

1960   *Meditations*. Translated by Laurence J. la Fleur. Indianapolis: Bobbs-Merrill.

DIXON, W. M.

1937   *The human situation: the Gifford lectures delivered in the University of Glasgow, 1935–1937*. London: Edward Arnold.

EIBL-EIBESFELDT, IRENÄUS

1972   *Love and hate: the natural history of behavior patterns*. New York: Holt, Rinehart and Winston.

EYSENCK, H. J.

1952   The effects of psychotherapy: an evaluation. *Journal of Consulting Psychology* 16:319–324.

1970   *The biological basis of personality*. Springfield, Ill.: Charles C. Thomas.

GELLER, I.

1971   Ethanol preference in the rat as a function of photoperiod. *Science* 173:456–459.

GOLDBERG, M.

1960   The occurrence and treatment of hypothyroidism among alcoholics. *Journal of Clinical Endocrinology* 20:609–621.

GOLDFARB, A. I., S. BERMAN

1949   Alcoholism as a psychosomatic disorder, 1: Endocrine pathology of animals and man excessively exposed to alcohol: its possible relation to behavioral pathology. *Quarterly Journal of Studies on Alcohol* 10:415–429.

GOLDSCHMIDT, WALTER
 1966 *Comparative functionalism.* Berkeley: University of California Press.

GOTTESFELD, B. H., H. L. YAGER
 1950 Psychotherapy of the problem drinker. *Quarterly Journal of Studies on Alcohol* 11:222–229.

HEGEL, G. W.
 1953 *Philosophy of Hegel.* Edited by Carl J. Friedrick. Westminister, Md.: Modern Library.

HOFFER, A., H. OSMOND
 1959 Concerning an etiological factor in alcoholism: the possible role of adrenochrome metabolism. *Quarterly Journal of Studies on Alcohol* 20:750–756.

KROEBER, A. L.
 1948 *Anthropology* (revised edition). New York: Harcourt, Brace.

LINTON, RALPH
 1964 *The study of man.* New York: Appleton-Century Crofts. (First published 1936).

LOCKE, JOHN
 1924 *Essay concerning human understanding.* New York: Oxford University Press.

LOVELL, H. W., J. W. TINTERA
 1951 Hypoadrenocorticism in alcoholism and drug addiction. *Geriatrics* 6(1):1–11.

LOWIE, R. H.
 1929 *Are we civilized? Human culture in perspective.* New York: Harcourt, Brace.

MADSEN, W.
 1974 *The American alcoholic: the nature-nurture controversy in alcoholic research.* Springfield, Ill.: Charles C. Thomas.

MAXWELL, M. A.
 1967 "Alcoholics anonymous: an interpretation," in *Alcoholism.* Edited by David J. Pittman, 211–222. New York: Harper and Row. (Reprinted in 1962 from *Society, culture and drinking patterns.* Edited by David J. Pittman and Charles R. Snyder, New York: John Wiley and Sons.)

MAZUR, ALAN, LEON S. ROBERTSON
 1972 *Biology and social behavior.* New York: The Free Press.

MYERS, R. D.
 1963a Alcohol consumption in rats: effects of intracranial injections of ethanol. *Science* 142:240–241.
 1963b "Modification of drinking patterns by chronic intracranial chemical infusion," in *Thirst: Proceedings of the First International Symposium on Thirst in the Regulation of Body Water.* Florida State University, Tallahassee, Florida, May, 1963.

MYERS, R. D., T. J. CICERO
 1969 Effects of serotonin depletion on the volitional alcohol intake of rats during a condition of psychological stress. *Psychopharmologia* 15:373–381. Berlin.

MYERS, R. D., M. TYTELL
  1972 Volitional consumption of flavored ethanol solution by rats: the effects of p-CPA and the absence of tolerance. *Physiology and Behavior* 8:403–408.

MYERS, R. D., W. L. VEALE
  1968 Alcohol preference in the rat: reduction following depletion of brain serotonin. *Science* 160:1469–1471.
  1971 "The determinants of alcohol preference in animals," in *The biology of alcoholism*, volume two. Edited by B. Bissin and H. Begleiter, 131–168. New York: Plenum.

OPLER, MARVIN K.
  1959 "Anthropological aspects of psychiatry," in *Progress in psychotherapy*, volume four: *Social psychotherapy*. Edited by J. Masserman and J. L. Moreno, 125–130. New York: Grune and Stratton.

OPLER, M. E.
  1945 Themes as dynamic forces in culture. *American Journal of Sociology* 51:198–206.

PARTANEN, J., K. BRUNN, T. MARKKANEN
  1966 *Inheritance of drinking behavior: a study of intelligence, personality and the use of alcohol in adult twins*. Helsinki: The Finnish Foundation for Alcohol Studies.

ROSENHAN, D. L.
  1973 On being sane in insane places. *Science* 180:365–369.

SCHUCKIT, M. A., D. A. GOODWIN, G. WINOKUR
  1972 A study of alcoholism in half-siblings. *American Journal of Psychiatry* 128:1132–1136.

Science News
  1973 *Alcoholism and a frisky pineal gland*. *Science News* 103(17):271.

SELYE, H.
  1956 *The stress of life*. New York: McGraw-Hill.

SKINNER, B. F.
  1953 *Science and human behavior*. New York: Macmillan.
  1971 *Beyond freedom and dignity*. New York: Alfred A. Knopf.

SMITH, J. J.
  1950 The endocrine basis for hormonal therapy of alcoholism. *New York State Journal of Medicine* 50:1704–1706, 1711–1715.
  1951 The blood eosinophol responses of the alcoholic to epinephrine and to ACTH, with a note on the treatment of chronic alcoholism with ACTH. *Proceedings of the Second Clinical ACTH Conference* 2:161–171.

STEINER, C. M.
  1969 The alcoholic game. *Quarterly Journal of Studies on Alcohol* 30:920–938.
  1971 *Games alcoholics play: the analysis of life scripts*. New York: Grove Press.

Time
  1973 Orientals and alcohol. *Time* 102(17):68.

VALLES, J.
  1969 *From social drinking to alcoholism*. Dallas: Tane Press.

VEALE, W. L., R. D. MYERS
1970   Decrease in ethanol intake in rats following administration of
p-chlorophenylalynine. *Neuropharmacology* 9(4):317–326.
VERDEN, P., D. SHATTERLY
1971   Alcoholism research and resistance to understanding the compul-
sive drinker. *Mental Hygiene* 55(3):331–336.
VOEGTLIN, W. L., P. O'HALLOREN, N. O'HALLOREN
1943   The glucose tolerance of alcohol addicts: a study of 303 cases.
Quarterly Journal of Studies on Alcohol 4:163–182.
WATSON, G.
1972   *Nutrition and your mind: the psychochemical response.* New
York: Harper and Row.
WATSON, JOHN BROADDUS
1970   *Behaviorism.* New York: Norton.
WATTS, A. W.
1969   *The two hands of God: the myths of polarity.* New York: Collier
Books. (First published 1963.)
WECHSLER, J. A.
1972   *In a darkness.* New York: Norton.
WILLIAMS, R. J.
1971   *Nutrition against disease: environmental prevention.* New York:
Pitman.

Ethanol Metabolism in Various Racial Groups

D. FENNA, L. MIX, O. SCHAEFER, and J. A. L. GILBERT

The effects of "firewater" on the native Americans have, since the days of the early explorers and traders, been described as unusually severe. More recently, accounts (Schaefer 1966; Schmitt, et al. 1966) have attested to its continuing and increasing importance as a cause of morbidity and mortality among the Indians and Eskimos of Canada.

There are unverified medical and law enforcement reports stating that Indians jailed while intoxicated take much longer to sober up than whites in similar conditions.

In view of the alleged differences in the rates of sobering up of native and white Canadians, and of the increasing importance of alcohol consumption and its effects in our native populations, we considered that an investigation into the rate of metabolism of alcohol in such populations was indicated and undertook comparative alcohol tolerance testing.

METHOD AND MATERIALS

Alcohol was administered to twenty-one Eskimo, twenty-six Indian, and seventeen white males. Nearly half of the Eskimos were volunteers

Originally published in *Canadian Medical Association Journal* 105: 472-475. Reprinted by permission of the authors and publisher.

We wish to acknowledge the help we have received in this project from: Dr. J. Donovan Ross, Minister of Health, for the grant to make this study possible; Dr. Gordon C. Butler, Director, Northern Regional Medical Services; Dr. A. G. Stewart, Department of Pediatrics, University of Alberta Hospital; also, Dr. G. C. Gray, Medical Director, Charles Camsell Hospital, the staff and students at Charles Camsell Hospital, and the two other medical students who assisted in this program, Elizabeth Cama and Noah Carpenter.

from the Inuvik district. The remaining subjects were chosen from among patients and staff of two Edmonton hospitals. Most of the patients were convalescing from fractures or acute infections and provided nearly all the remaining native subjects. The whites were predominantly staff members, including students. Persons having metabolic or gastrointestinal disease were excluded, as the rate of absorption and metabolism of alcohol could be affected by such disease processes.

Liver function tests, viz. BSP retention, SGOT, and alkaline phosphatase, were performed on all subjects before the alcohol tolerance tests. All had normal liver function.

The Eskimos ranged in age from 20 to 58 years with a mean of 38.5 years, were 157 to 178 cm. in height (mean 167.6 cm.), and weighed 60 to 104 kg. (mean 69.7 kg.). The Indians were from 22 to 63 years of age (mean 39.0 years), were 163 to 183 cm. in height (mean 172.5 cm.), and weighed 57 to 86 kg. (mean 68.3 kg.). The whites were from 20 to 69 years of age (mean 35.3 years), were 168 to 188 cm. in height (mean 177.3 cm.), and weighed 61 to 91 kg. (mean 75.7 kg.).

The tests were performed at 8:00 A.M. following an overnight fast. Alcohol was infused intravenously as 10 percent ethanol in normal saline at 10 ml. per minute, until blood levels of approximately 125 mg. percent were attained. This blood level was maintained for sixty minutes and the rate of disappearance of ethanol from the blood was observed for two hours after stopping the infusion.

The blood alcohol levels were determined by use of the Breathalyser. The Breathalyser was standardized before testing each subject by aerating a standard solution of alcohol in distilled water through the instrument. Readings were taken every five minutes during the induction period, every ten minutes during the maintenance period and every fifteen minutes during the post-infusion period.

CALCULATIONS

If C_t is the observed concentration of alcohol in the blood at time t, then the rate of decline of this concentration, β, can be obtained from successive values of C_t.

To calculate the rate of metabolism we must take into account the general concentration of alcohol in the body. Let p be body weight and r be the proportion of the body that attains alcohol concentrations equal to those of the blood. Then, since the amount of alcohol present in the body at any time plus the amount metabolized up to that time must equal the total administered, we have

$$A_0 = (C_t + \beta \cdot t)\ p \cdot r$$

where A_0 is the total amount administered.

Since A_0 and p are known, along with β and C_t for various t, we can determine r. The rate of metabolism can then be determined, being equal to $\beta \cdot t \cdot p \cdot r$.

RESULTS

The amounts of alcohol solution infused during the tests were measured as volume per kilogram of body weight and are shown in Table 1.

Table 1. Volume of alcohol required for induction and maintenance

	Induction	Maintenance	Total
Whites	9.47 ml./kg.	4.29 ml./kg.	13.76 ml./kg.
Indians	10.22 ml./kg.	3.75 ml./kg.	13.97 ml./kg.
Eskimos	10.49 ml./kg.	3.86 ml./kg.	14.35 ml./kg.

It can be seen from these figures that, while the volumes required for the separate stages of induction and maintenance were fairly varied, the total amounts were virtually the same for each group.

The rate of fall of blood alcohol levels is shown in Table 2.

Table 2. Rate of decline of blood alcohol levels

Whites	(17)	0.370 ± 0.127 mg. percent per minute
Indians	(26)	0.259 ± 0.024 mg. percent per minute
Eskimos	(21)	0.264 ± 0.011 mg. percent per minute

It is apparent from Table 2 that the decline of blood alcohol level was much higher in the whites than in the natives, the rate in the whites being 0.370 mg. percent per minute compared with 0.259 mg. percent per minute in the Indians and 0.264 mg. percent per minute in the Eskimos respectively. Statistical comparison of whites and Indians gives $t = 3.98$, $P < 0.001$; comparison of whites and Eskimos gives $t = 2.74$, $P < 0.01$.

The rate of metabolism of alcohol is shown in Table 3.

Again the Indians and Eskimos have similar figures but the whites have significantly elevated rates ($t = 4.235$, $P < 0.0005$ for whites compared to Indians; $t = 2.935$, $P < 0.0005$ for whites compared to Eskimos).

Table 3.   Rate of metabolism of alcohol (g. per kg. of bodyweight per hour)

Whites	(17)	0.1449 ± 0.0390
Indians	(26)	0.1013 ± 0.0207
Eskimos	(21)	0.1098 ± 0.0337

To assess the influence of previous alcohol intake, the subjects were classified according to the history each one gave, as light drinkers (consuming less than 10 bottles of beer or the equivalent in other forms of alcohol per week), moderate drinkers (10 to 20 bottles of beer per week), and heavy drinkers (more than 20 bottles of beer per week). The rate of decline of blood alcohol for each resulting subgroup is shown in Table 4.

Table 4.   Effect of previous alcoholic intake on the rate of decline of blood alcohol levels (mg. percent per minute)

	Whites	Indians	Eskimos
Light drinkers	(9) 0.357 ± 0.157	(4) 0.213 ± 0.027	(11) 0.229 ± 0.117
Moderate drinkers	(4) 0.377 ± 0.145	(11) 0.233 ± 0.027	(5) 0.254 ± 0.081
Heavy drinkers	(4) 0.384 ± 0.058	(11) 0.303 ± 0.027	(5) 0.351 ± 0.123

The whites showed little metabolic adaptation to alcohol ingestion. Thus, the difference in the rate of blood alcohol decline in the heavy and light white drinkers was 0.384 mg. percent per minute compared to 0.357 mg. percent per minute; in comparable groups of Indians and Eskimos the rates were 0.303 mg. percent per minute compared to 0.213 mg. percent per minute ($t = 900$, $P < 0.001$) and 0.351 mg. percent per minute compared to 0.229 mg. percent per minute (no significant difference) respectively. The associated rates of metabolism are shown in Table 5.

These rates of metabolism are somewhat more erratic than those for

Table 5.   Effect of previous alcoholic intake on the rates of metabolism of alcohol (g. per kg. of bodyweight per hour)

	Whites	Indians	Eskimos
Light drinkers	(9) 0.1377 ± 0.0459	(4) 0.0794 ± 0.0182	(11) 0.1045 ± 0.0336
Moderate drinkers	(4) 0.1588 ± 0.0449	(11) 0.1027 ± 0.0210	(5) 0.1041 ± 0.0280
Heavy drinkers	(4) 0.1472 ± 0.0131	(11) 0.1083 ± 0.0167	(5) 0.1272 ± 0.0398

decline of blood alcohol levels. There is again a discernible tendency to adaptation within each ethnic group but a statistically significant trend only for Indians ($t = 2.789$, $P < 0.01$ between light and heavy drinkers).

Comparing the ethnic categories it can be noted that the similarities of Indians and Eskimos and the elevation of white rates persist. Indeed, the rate of metabolism for each category of whites is higher than that for any group of Indians or Eskimos. The rate for whites is significantly greater than the rate for Indians in each of the three classes ($t +3.303$, $P < 0.005$ for light; $t = 2.402$, $P < 0.02$ for moderate; $t = 4.727$, $P < 0.0005$ for heavy). Other differences are of much lower significance.

Since the distinctive high protein diet of many natives was seen as a possible factor in alcohol metabolism, the native subjects were re-grouped, within drinker classifications, on the basis of high protein diet (50 percent or more of the calories were derived from fish and meat) versus high carbohydrate (CHO) diet (i.e. a diet similar to the average white Canadian diet with less than 50 percent fresh meat). Using these groupings, the decline in blood alcohol levels in the natives is shown in Table 6.

Table 6.   Effect of diet on the rate of decline of blood alcohol levels in the natives (mg. percent per minute)

	High protein diet	High CHO diet (average Canadian diet)
Light drinkers	(4) 0.147 ± 0.114	(10) 0.212 ± 0.024
Moderate drinkers	(5) 0.274 ± 0.024	(12) 0.210 ± 0.054
Heavy drinkers	(4) 0.298 ± 0.020	(12) 0.317 ± 0.030

According to these figures, dietetic differences do not produce a significant effect on the rate of decline of blood alcohol levels. For both light drinking and heavy drinking natives, a high carbohydrate diet correlates with higher rates of decline of blood alcohol levels (0.212 mg. percent per minute as compared to 0.147 and 0.317 mg. percent per minute as compared to 0.298, respectively). However, in the moderate drinking group of natives the situation is reversed; those on a high protein diet lower their blood alcohol more rapidly than those on a high CHO diet, the rates being 0.274 mg. percent per minute and 0.210 mg. percent per minute respectively. The rate of metabolism of alcohol in the natives when classified according to dietetic differences is shown in Table 7.

Table 7.   Effect of diet on the rate of metabolism of alcohol in the natives (g. per kg. of body weight per hour)

	High protein diet	High CHO diet (typical Canadian diet)
Light drinkers	(4) 0.0770 ± 0.0297	(11) 0.1053 ± 0.0301
Moderate drinkers	(5) 0.1016 ± 0.0127	(11) 0.1039 ± 0.0238
Heavy drinkers	(4) 0.1247 ± 0.0324	(12) 0.1107 ± 0.0245
All	(13) 0.1011 ± 0.0319	(34) 0.1067 ± 0.0256

Here again there is a suggestion that a high carbohydrate diet increases the rate of metabolism, but the indications are erratic and without significance.

DISCUSSION

Widmark (1932) found the slope of the disappearance curve of blood alcohol to be 0.015 percent per hour and the function to be linear. This average was substantiated by Gradwohl (1954), who found that the rate varies considerably among individuals. In 1943, Goldberg found that heavy drinkers metabolize alcohol up to 25 percent more rapidly than abstainers, but later (1950) he found that the rate of disappearance of alcohol was not significantly different in the two groups. Shumate, Crowther, and Zarafshan (1967: 83) found the disappearance curve to be linear in form and constant in that there is no relation between the amount of alcohol in the blood and its rate of disappearance. They also state that the rate of disappearance in the same individual at different times is constant, and suggest that people have a characteristic burning rate. They found that the average rate of metabolism of alcohol was 0.015 percent per hour in males and 0.0185 percent per hour in females.

There was no significant difference in the amount of alcohol infused into the members of our various groups to bring the blood alcohol levels up to desired height and to maintain them there (see Table 1).

In our series the rate of fall of blood alcohol among the whites is significantly greater than in either the Indians or Eskimos, viz. 0.370 mg. percent per minute as compared to 0.259 mg. percent per minute and 0.264 mg. percent per minute. The rate of fall within the various native population samples is not significantly different, and, in fact, may be considered equal (see Table 2).

Also, the rate of metabolism of alcohol amongst the whites is significantly greater than in either the Indians or Eskimos, viz. 0.1449 g. per kg. per hour as compared to 0.1013 g. per kg. per hour and 0.1098 g. per kg. per hour, and there is no significant difference between rates for the two native population samples (see Table 3).

Classification of the natives according to drinking habits revealed a preponderance of heavy and moderate drinkers among our Indian population when compared to the whites and Eskimos (see Table 4). The whites consisted largely of volunteers from the hospital staff and of medical students and was weighted with persons having little or no past experience with alcohol. This was also the case in the Eskimo population.

In each ethnic group a tendency to adaptation to alcohol was indicated, but only among the Indians was this significant. Expressed in terms of rate of decline of blood alcohol level (see Table 4) the rate for Indians increased from 0.213 mg. percent per minute for light drinkers to 0.303 mg. percent per minute for heavy drinkers; in terms of rate of metabolism (see Table 5) the increase was from 0.0794 to 0.1083 g. per kg. per hour. This greater adaptation among Indians may be due to greater alcohol intakes by their heavy drinkers than by the similarly classified whites.

Despite this general tendency for metabolic adaptation to higher alcoholic intakes, i.e. heavy drinkers metabolize alcohol faster than light drinkers or nondrinkers, even the subgroups of heavy drinkers among the natives had lower rates of metabolism than the subgroup of light-drinker whites.

The smallness of the ethnic/alcohol subgroups prompts caution in these interpretations of adaptation.

Vallee (1966: 72) suggested that racial differences in alcohol tolerance are related to variations of alcohol dehydrogenases in liver and other organs. Cammack (1969: 55) demonstrated elevated dehydrogenase activity in herbivores compared with carnivores. However, we were unable to demonstrate any significant difference in alcohol metabolism between the natives on high carbohydrate diets and those on high protein diets. Our grouping was based on dietary habits followed during the last ten to twenty years only and thus excluded any influence of genetically fixed variations in enzymatic activities that reflected the traditional protein-rich diet of the natives.

CONCLUSIONS

Indians, Eskimos, and whites require comparable amounts of alcohol per unit of body weight to achieve intoxicating blood levels, but the natives metabolize alcohol at a significantly slower rate than the whites.

The difference is not due to experience with alcohol or dietary protein/carbohydrate balance of the individuals concerned. It is probably due to differences in diet over many generations.

The finding of a lower rate of metabolism of alcohol in Indians and Eskimos may have important practical application in health education and preventive medicine in view of the fact that the effects of alcohol abuse have become a preeminent health problem in native Canadians.

REFERENCES

CAMMACK, R.
  1969   Assay, purification and properties of mammalian D-2-hydroxy acid dehydrogenase. *Biochemical Journal* 115:55–64.
GOLDBERG, L.
  1943   Quantitative studies in alcohol tolerance. *Acta Physiologica Scandinavica* 16:1–128.
  1950   "Tolerance to alcohol in moderate and heavy drinkers and its significance to alcohol," in *Proceedings of 1st International Conference on Alcohol and Road Traffic*, Stockholm.
GRADWOHL, R. B. N.
  1954   *Legal medicine,* chapter two. St. Louis: Mosby.
SCHAEFER, O.
  1966   Letter to editor referring to (5), in *Canadian Medical Association Journal* 94:684–685.
SCHMITT, N., L. W. HOLE, W. S. BARCLAY
  1966   Accidental deaths among British Columbia Indians. *Canadian Medical Association Journal* 94:228–234.
SHUMATE, R. P., R. F. CROWTHER, M. ZARAFSHAN
  1967   A study of the metabolism rates of alcohol in the human body. *Journal of Forensic Medicine* 14:83–100.
VALLEE, B. L.
  1966   Alcohol metabolism and metalloenzymes. *Therapeutic Notes* 14: 71–74.
WIDMARK, E. M. P.
  1932   *Die theoretischen Grundlagen und die praktische Verwendbarkeit der gerichtlich-medizinischen Alkoholbestimmung.* Berlin: Urban and Schwarzenberg.

Ethnic Groups, Human Variation, and Alcohol Use

JOEL M. HANNA

The problems surrounding alcohol use and alcoholism are complex in nature, involving both social and biological parameters. In practice, the study of alcohol use within the discipline of anthropology has emphasized the former to the exclusion of the latter. Thus we see elaborate social and psychological theories which have been derived to explain alcohol-related behavior with little recognition of the underlying biological differences which could modify that behavior. Few anthropologists would completely deny biological considerations, but fewer still could fully appreciate their implications. The purpose of this paper is to examine some aspects of human variation which might be expected to modify drinking behavior. It is assumed that physiological or morphological factors which could produce variation in brain alcohol concentration could also produce variation in the resulting behavior. The framework for their consideration will be between populations (ethnic groups in this case) and then within populations.

BIOLOGICAL DIFFERENCES BETWEEN MAJOR ETHNIC GROUPS WHICH COULD INFLUENCE ALCOHOL-RELATED BEHAVIOR

It has long been hypothesized that ethnic differences in alcohol tolerance exist. American Indians, for example, have a long-standing reputation for a weakness for alcohol and numerous epidemiological studies have tended to support this reputation (Kunitz, et al. 1971). Alcoholism and undesirable alcohol-produced behavior are extremely high in some groups (Schmitt, et al. 1966). Other ethnic groups, including Hawaiians, Samoans (Lemert 1964), and Irish (Knupfler and Room 1967) have similar problems. At the other extreme are Americans of Jewish ancestry and Chinese, who have low rates of alcohol use and alcoholism. In the case of the Chinese, the frequency of alcoholism is practically zero throughout the world; in Hawaii (Wedge and Abe 1949), San Francisco (Chu 1972) and Taiwan (Lin 1953) it has been less than 1 percent. Since Jewish and Chinese immigrants tend to maintain cultural identity, cultural factors must be involved, but since alcohol use also involves biological processes, some organic basis should also be considered.

It has only been recently that evidence relevant to a biological hypothesis of alcohol and cultural variation has become available. Specifically, a number of recent studies of alcohol metabolism or its consequences suggest that significant ethnic differences may exist in the physiology of alcohol use.

In the study by Fenna and his colleagues (1972), which appears in this volume, there is the clear suggestion of metabolic variation. They report systematic differences between Canadian Indians, Eskimos, and Canadians of European ancestry in their abilities to metabolize alcohol. The Europeans seem to show a propensity for more rapid metabolism than the native peoples. There were grave problems surrounding the selection of subjects for this study, but these notwithstanding, the group differences are considerable. It would be premature to propose that any differences in blood alcohol clearance are due to genetic differences, or even that the differences are real, but the specific parameter measured — rate of blood alcohol clearance — is known to involve some genetic component.

Vesell (1972) studied seven pairs of monozygotic twins and seven pairs of dizygotic twins. Their rates of blood alcohol clearance were measured after two weeks of abstinence from alcohol. The difference in clearance rates between identical twins was negligible, but the fraternal pairs showed differences equal to that expected between siblings. The correlations were 0.89 for monozygotic twins and 0.53 for dizygotic pairs. The calculated heritability — the ratio of genetic variability to environmentally produced variability — was 0.98. This value is so high as to be questioned, but it clearly implies that some genetic propensity exists and that it may be significant.

A second series of studies with similar implications has been reported by Wolff (1972, 1973). In an initial study, Japanese, Koreans, and Taiwanese were compared with Americans of European ancestry.

Rather than examine metabolism, Wolff was interested in some objective correlates of alcohol use, specifically face flushing, optical density, and changes in pulse pressure. Flushing was measured by direct observation, present or absent; optical density was measured directly; and pulse pressure was measured by changes in optic density corresponding to heart beat. The significance of any differences in these parameters is not clear but considerable differences in each were found. The Oriental subject showed a higher incidence of face flushing, greater changes in optical density, and greater increases in pulse pressure. In terms of onset response the Orientals were considerably faster than the Europeans, even though they had typically received about half the quantity of alcohol. In addition, the Orientals reported a variety of subjective sensations not reported by the Europeans. These included hot stomach, tachycardia, dizziness, and actually falling asleep. To ascertain if life experiences were important, Wolff also studied a group of Japanese, Taiwanese, and European infants. The overt responses of the infants paralleled those of the adult groups in most parameters.

In a second effort, Wolff (1973) studied several other groups including Cree Indians, American-born Chinese and Japanese, Oriental-European hybrids (with one parent of each race), and a small number of three-quarter European/one-quarter Oriental hybrids. All of these groups, including the hybrids, differed in response from a white control group in the same manner as did the original Oriental populations studied.

The significance of face flushing and changes in optical density is not clear and, until more data are reported, conclusions are difficult to interpret. Yet there are some implications. Since the Orientals required less alcohol to produce faster and more pronounced responses, a differential threshold in response to alcohol may be involved. This could be the result of Orientals flushing at lower levels of blood alcohol or alternatively experiencing a more rapid rate of absorption from the gastrointestinal tract. The magnitude of response differences is so great that the latter alternative is most unlikely. Alcohol uptake from the gastrointestinal tract is purely a physical process and it is difficult to imagine anything which could increase the rate of uptake so greatly. Alcohol diffusion is normally so fast that an active transport mechanism would not increase blood alcohol uptake to any appreciable degree. Hence the most likely alternative is that a differential in response is due to a differential in threshold. One group (Orientals) responds at a level of blood alcohol which is lower than that of the other (Europeans).

Since alcohol dehydrogenase is involved in the metabolism of ethanol, some differences in rate of metabolism may be related to its presence. Murry and Price (1972) report different frequencies of Types A and B — dehydrogenase in American Caucasians and Afro-Americans. The metabolic consequence of these differences was not determined, but if Types A and B have different rates of activity some difference in rates of clearance might follow.

In addition to physiological differences which might separate ethnic groups, there are also morphological and anatomical variants which could produce similar effects. One of the most obvious is simple differences in body mass. Ethanol is absorbed by the gastrointestinal tract and then diffuses throughout the body water space. Since the body is about 80 percent water, a larger individual will simply have more water to dilute the alcohol than the smaller one. This, in turn, means that the concentration of alcohol in the brain will be less in larger people and that less behavior modification would be anticipated. Thus a Negrito with a body weight of 40 kg. would experience a brain alcohol concentration about twice as high as a Hawaiian of body weight 80 kg., or in social context, the Hawaiian could drink twice as much to achieve the same concentration.

Size is not the only important factor in alcohol concentration; the specific components of the mass must also be considered. Some peoples, e.g. Polynesians and some southwestern Indians, are noted for their obesity. Since adipose tissue contains less water than muscle tissue, a fat and a lean man will receive a differential concentration of alcohol in the body water if they are of the same mass and they drink equivalent amounts. Obviously, the concentration of alcohol in the brain of the fatter man will be higher. Lean body mass or fat-free weight should thus be considered when intra-ethnic comparisons are to be made.

A final morphological phenomenon of interest is the possible difference between peoples in their internal architecture. Since alcohol diffuses through the lining of the stomach and the small intestine, any variation in the surface areas will lead to a potential for a more rapid rate of absorption. The greatest alcohol absorption takes place in the small intestine, which makes that area of great interest. The long-known differential in intestine length between Japanese, Chinese (Pan 1921), and American Indians (Wagner 1943), as compared to Europeans, might add some insight into the response differential between Caucasians and Orientals.

BIOLOGICAL VARIATION WITHIN POPULATIONS

While we are usually impressed by differences observed between ethnic groups, there is obviously a great amount of variation within those groups as well (Johnston 1966). Most of the parameters already discussed as differing between ethnic groups probably differ within them as well. For example, all human populations are polymorphic with respect to size and body fat. Less visible features — such as serological traits — also show polymorphisms.

It might be assumed that modern urban societies are the most variable because of their heterogeneous origins. But recent data show that even the most isolated groups who experienced little acculturation and minimal admixture also are polymorphic. Studies of isolated peoples of New Guinea (Giles, et al. 1966) and in Venezuela (Neel 1970) reveal that genetic differences between villages of the same population may be greater than those between villages and other more distant and nonrelated peoples. Biological variability is thus a basic characteristic of man, even in an isolated, nonurban environment. The biological factors influencing alcohol use should also be variable.

Considering alcohol metabolism, these observations of polymorphisms become important, for studies of alcohol dehydrogenase have indicated that it, too, is polymorphic. Murry and Price (1972) have found that there are at least two types of ADH and these types are variable within as well as between groups.

Differing rates of metabolism which may reflect ADH-type differences have been reported in a variety of studies (Wallgren 1970). Typical is Jokipii's 1951 research (cited in Wallgren 1970) which indicates that some Finns were able to metabolize alcohol twice as fast as others. This is somewhat greater variation than the 40 percent faster rate of Canadian whites as compared to Indians and Eskimos in the study of Fenna, et al. (1972). Such biochemical and metabolic variations are bound to exist in human populations and are largely undetectable at present, yet they are likely to influence drinking behavior.

While many of the factors producing variations in alcohol metabolism are presently undetected, there are several obvious population characteristics which could influence blood alcohol content. Sex and age, for example, are categories which are found in all ethnic groups and tend to correlate with biological realities as well.

Men and women differ in a number of biological parameters already discussed. Women are smaller and tend to be fatter, so that a given quantity of alcohol will be more concentrated in the body water of a woman than in a man. Women also have slightly lower metabolic rates (Guyton 1970: 828) which should reduce the rate of alcohol clearance. Social factors which limit access to alcohol may also differ between the sexes. If women have less access, they might be expected to show less adaptation, hence more pronounced alcohol mediated behavior. This could mistakenly be attributed to cultural phenomena alone.

Age is also a universal cultural category which has some consequence for alcohol metabolism. As men and women age, there is a general increase in body fat content. Muscles become less active and change in composition. There are also age related changes in the type of ADH present (Murry and Price 1972), such that youths have a different propensity to metabolize alcohol than do adults. These biological phenomena would have obvious behavioral correlates.

CONCLUSION

There is, then, ample evidence that people differ in physiological and morphological features which could influence brain alcohol content. Although variation within a given population is so high as to resist meaningful analysis, there are still major categories which might provide some insight. Age, sex, and size differences within the group are obvious examples. They reflect a biological substrate which could result in behavioral variants. Thus it would seem that a field anthropologist should at least note the behavior of members of these classes during research. Since they should be experiencing different blood alcohol levels, any differences in behavior are of interest. Of equal importance is that it might be possible to assess the relative importance of biological and social factors in the determination of drinking behavior.

Some of the biological parameters also follow major ethnic lines and may account for behavioral differences seen frequently in literature. Since American Indians are generally smaller than Afro-Americans or American whites, they should experience a proportionally greater increase in brain alcohol concentration per drink. These propensities may be enhanced by a slower rate of metabolism (Fenna, et al. 1972) and a lower response threshold (Wolff 1973). Presumably they should then show a greater behavioral response per drink. Given these predispositions, it might be expected that Indians and Europeans would have differing drinking habits and would behave differently while under the influence of alcohol, something the ethnographer should be aware of during his fieldwork on human alcohol use.

REFERENCES

CHU, G.
1972   Drinking patterns and attitudes of rooming house Chinese in San Francisco. *Quarterly Journal of Studies on Alcohol,* supplement 6:58–85.

FENNA, D., L. MIX, O. SCHAEFER, J. GILBERT
1972   Ethanol metabolism in various racial groups. *Canadian Medical Association Journal* 105:472–475. (Reprinted in this volume.)

GILES, E., R. WALSH, M. BRADLEY
1966   Micro-evolution in New Guinea: the role of genetic drift. *Annals of the New York Academy of Science* 134(2):655–665.

GUYTON, A.
1970   *Medical physiology.* Philadelphia: Saunders.

JOHNSTON, F.
1966   The population approach to human variation. *Annals of the New York Academy of Science* 134(2):507–515.

KNUPFLER, G., R. ROOM
1967   Drinking patterns and attitudes of Irish, Jewish, and white Protestant American men. *Quarterly Journal of Studies on Alcohol* 28(21):676–699.

KUNITZ, S. J., J. LEVY, C. ODOROFF, J. BOLLINGER
1971   The epidemiology of alcoholic cirrhosis in two southwestern Indian tribes. *Quarterly Journal of Studies on Alcohol* 32(3):706–720.

LEMERT, E. W.
1964   Forms and pathology of drinking in three Polynesian societies. *American Anthropologist* 66(2):361–374.

LIN, T.
1953   A study of the incidence of mental disorder in Chinese and other cultures. *Psychiatry* 16:313–316.

MURRY, R. F., P. H. PRICE
1972   Ontogenetic, polymorphic, and interethnic variation in the isoenzymes of human alcohol dehydrogenase. *Annals of the New York Academy of Science* 197:68–73.

NEEL, J. V.
1970   Lessons from a "primitive people." *Science* 170:815–822.

PAN, W.
1921   Further observations on the gastrointestinal tract of the Hindus. *Journal of Anatomy* 54:324–331.

SCHMITT, N., L. HOLE, W. BARCLAY
1966   Accidental deaths among British Columbia Indian tribes. *Canadian Medical Association Journal* 94:228–234.

VESELL, E. S.
1972   Ethanol metabolism: regulation by genetic factors in normal volunteers under a controlled environment and the effect of chronic ethanol administration. *Annals of the New York Academy of Science* 197:79–88.

WAGNER, F.
   1943   Racial differences in the colon in natives of Bolivia. *American Journal of Physical Anthropology* 1(4):313–323.
WALLGREN, H.
   1970   "Absorption, diffusion, distribution, and elimination of ethanol. Effect on biological membranes," in *International encyclopedia of pharmacology and therapeutics,* set twenty, volume one. Edited by J. Tremolieres, 161–188.
WEDGE, B., S. ABE
   1949   Racial incidence of mental disease in Hawaii. *Hawaiian Medical Journal* 8:337–338.
WOLFF, P.
   1972   Ethnic differences in alcohol sensitivity. *Science* 175:449.
   1973   Vasomotor sensitivity to alcohol in diverse Mongoloid populations. *American Journal of Human Genetics* 25:193–199.

PART FIVE

The Current Status of Cross-Cultural Theories

Introduction

There are theories and there are theories. It may seem to theoreticians as too simplistic to call a theory a word statement about certain relationships that seem to exist among words. But, in fact, whether we are describing a Neur theory of disease, a Ute theory of intoxication, or an anthropological theory of culture, we are making word statements about relationships among linguistic utterances or words that, in turn, have arbitrarily agreed upon references to certain empirically observable forms. Cross-cultural theories are exactly what the notion suggests: they are statements about relationships that seem to have some regularities across cultural boundaries. Different kinds of comparisons have characterized cross-cultural anthropology. Some are more restricted or controlled comparisons while others are more global. With respect to studies about alcohol and behavior, each kind of comparison generates its own kind of theoretical structure. All we need to do is see the different level of theorizing done in Bunzel's controlled comparison in contrast to Bacon's global comparison to realize this.

More recently it does seem, as noted in the Introduction to this volume, that the psychological theorists have tended to assert a dominant influence in cross-cultural theories. And, whether intended or not, the various theories proposed seem to be somewhat monotypic, something that anthropologists have considered both unfortunate and premature, in spite of the desirability of this ultimate concern in science.

Barry, in the first article in this section, provides what his studies consider important cross-cultural evidence in support of the global psychological reality of dependency conflicts that motivate drunkenness as a means of alleviating the dependency need. As an alternative global theory, again building on a psychological model, Boyatzis follows with cross-cultural evidence which validates the position that drinking and drunkenness are motivated by concerns about relative personal power and constitute means whereby individuals seek to compensate for its lack.

In his article on "Drunkenness and culture stress," Schaefer provides a cross-cultural or holocultural test to a number of the psychological stress theories by addressing himself to the problem of data quality and data reliability. For cross-cultural theories on drinking and drunkenness, this is an extremely valuable contribution. It does, however, end up supportive of psychological theories that utilize cross-cultural data, though it does not support those who wish to use cross-cultural comparisons to endorse monotypic theories. In fact, Schaefer provides good evidence to show the value, at least at our present state of development, of maintaining polytypic or competing theories at several levels of analysis.

De Lint, on the other hand, raises the question of multiple etiological or epidemiological sources of alcohol addiction and excessiveness, depending upon more specific sociocultural factors that cannot be readily accounted for in global psychological theories. His call seems to be for theories of the more middle range. Sargent, in the last article in Part 5, rather than posing a theory of alcohol and behavior, whether global or multicausal in character, addresses herself to a number of essential intellectual prerequisites for building any theory: namely, the theorist must be global in sampling the world's societies and cultures as well as the whole range of possible forms of drinking, including abstinence. In this respect, she would credit the global psychologizing theories as being on tactically solid ground. At the same time, she would likely argue that such global theories have not generally been able to consider the continuum of variation of behavior, for either by the theorist himself generalizing or by the ethnographer failing to account for the range of variation in his specific report, the total range of possible behaviors is not being sampled.

It is important, as one of the necessary characteristics in Sargent's guide to theory building, that cross-cultural theorists adopt a social problems orientation. This could be rejected as a requirement on a number of grounds, e.g. how to be sure that a term such as deviant behavior has conceptual equivalence cross-culturally, etc. Nonetheless, even if a global theory of social deviance is impossible, behavior has a normative dimension that should produce somewhat equivalent or comparable dimensions across societies. Especially with the convergence that modernization and technological advance have brought cross-nationally, it should be reasonably appropriate to develop a theory that has promise for solving cross-national if not cross-cultural problems produced by pandemic alcohol addiction. More specifically, such a theoretical perspective may do more to isolate what may be common to all varieties of alcoholism than it would to produce a theory of drinking.

Cross-Cultural Evidence That Dependency Conflict Motivates Drunkenness

HERBERT BARRY, III

Alcohol is used in a cultural context and the drinking becomes part of a larger pattern of social behavior. However, the cultural use of alcohol is adopted and persists because the drug gives pleasure or relief to the individual consumer. Therefore, it is necessary to explain the use of alcohol on the basis of the pharmacological actions of the drug, satisfying certain human needs.

Individuals who drink large amounts of alcohol compulsively over a prolonged period of time, to their social or physical detriment, are defined as alcoholics (Wallgren and Barry 1970; Chapter 11). The personality characteristics of alcoholics may indicate in an extreme and easily observable form the motivations for drinking which are obscured in the moderate, controlled user of alcohol. Lolli (1956) described the alcoholic as longing for the dependent state of infancy and at the same time desiring self-respect and independence. Therefore, conflict over dependency was identified as the primary motivation. Such a fundamental conflict may give rise to intense misery and anxiety which are relieved by intoxication. Blane (1968) contributed a more extensive discussion of dependency conflict as a prevalent personality characteristic of alcoholics distinguishing among dependent-independent, counter-dependent and overtly dependent personalities.

In a cross-cultural study, based on a sample of 139 preliterate societies, Bacon, et al. (1965) found that societies with high frequency of drunkenness tended to have several characteristics of child training and adult behavior which would be expected to give rise to conflict

Preparation of this paper was supported by Public Health Service Research Scientist Development Award K2-MH-5921 from the National Institute of Mental Health.

over dependency. Barry (1968) provided a summary of these data and further evidence that variations in conflict over dependency may account for cultural variations in alcohol use.

This paper gives a more general formulation of this concept of dependency conflict, relating it to general patterns of normal and abnormal personality development. This paper also summarizes new data on pharmacological actions of alcohol in the individual, and on the relationships between treatment of infants and frequency of drunkenness in a sample of preliterate societies.

Dependency conflict characterizes the earliest and most pervasive conditions in personality development. Therefore, it provides a broad base upon which specific predictions and explanations can be constructed. This general concept may encompass several more limited conditions which have been suggested as explanations for cultural variations in drinking, including evidence that alcohol alleviates anxiety (Horton 1943), arouses fantasies of power in men (McClelland, et al. 1972) and of femininity in women (Wilsnack i.p.), and evidence of cultural customs which restrain insobriety (Field 1962).

DEPENDENCY CONFLICT

The normal experiences of human development give rise to the opposing motivations of dependency and self-reliance. The infant is helpless and completely dependent on nurturance from the mother or other caretakers. This initial state is followed by gradual development of biological capabilities and cultural pressures toward self-reliance. The child can no longer depend on continuous protection and nurturance. The appropriate use of self-reliant behavior enables the individual to obtain various rewards and to avoid deprivations and dangers.

The opposing motivations of dependence and self-reliance necessarily conflict with each other. Much adult behavior constitutes methods of compromising or reconciling these motives. The normal, mature adult develops sociability, which expresses dependency, and self-control, which expresses self-reliance. The opposite behavior tendencies may be differentially expressed in appropriate situations, but both are present simultaneously and often give rise to incompatible behavior tendencies.

The conflict is aggravated if either dependency or self-reliance is not strongly and consistently rewarded during infancy and early childhood. If dependency is punished or inconsistently rewarded, the unreliability of the nurturant agent enhances the motivation for self-reliance which enables the individual to escape this unsatisfactory dependency. Conversely, if self-reliance is punished or inconsistently rewarded the motivation for dependency is increased.

Table 1 summarizes certain typical patterns of behavior which are outcomes of the designated combinations of reward, punishment, or both treatments for dependency and self-reliance. The combination of reward and punishment for both motivations gives rise to an intense conflict, identified as neurotic anxiety in the middle cell of Table 1. The conflict can be resolved by preponderant expression of dependency, such as submissiveness, or by preponderant expression of self-reliance, such as assertiveness. However, either trait results in a stereotyped behavior pattern which is maladaptive in some situations. If either dependency or self-reliance is predominantly punished, severe pathological behavior can be expected, as shown in the left-hand column and bottom row of Table 1.

Table 1. Behavior patterns resulting from three types of treatment for dependency (reward, punishment, both) in combination with the corresponding types of treatment for self-reliance

| | | Dependency | | |
		Punished	Both treatments	Rewarded
	Rewarded	alienation	assertiveness	flexible adjustment
Self-reliance	Both treatments	hostility	neurotic anxiety	sub-missiveness
	Punished	psychotic withdrawal from reality	depression	passivity

This combination of treatments, of course, oversimplifies the behavior patterns. Most people cannot be classified into a single one of the nine cells. Each individual is subjected in various degrees to all of the combinations of treatments and thus expresses all nine behavior patterns with various intensities and under different conditions.

The differential experiences are related to different stages of the life cycle. During early infancy, reward for dependency is necessarily predominant. If dependency is strongly punished at this stage, subsequent development is afflicted by the various forms of pathology shown in the left-hand and middle columns of Table 1. Rewards for self-reliance become more predominant during childhood and adulthood. However, punishment for self-reliance at any stage has adverse effects which persist even if this motivation is predominantly rewarded at a subsequent stage.

Cultural variations in reward and punishment for these motivations have been discussed by Barry (1969b). Reward and punishment for dependency result in a conflict between love and hate. Most societies give a high degree of nurturance to young infants and the few exceptions manifest severe pathology. However, there are great variations in reward for dependency in later childhood and adulthood. Rewards and punishments for self-reliance show large cultural variations which are related to other important cultural attributes (Barry 1969b). Subsistence economy appears to be an important factor. Barry, et al. (1959) found stronger training of children to be assertive in societies with low accumulation of food resources (food collecting economy) and stronger training of children to be compliant in societies with high accumulation of food resources (food producing societies). In most societies, girls are trained more strongly in compliance and boys more strongly in assertion (Barry, et al. 1957).

PHARMACOLOGICAL ACTIONS OF ALCOHOL

The cultural function of alcohol must be explained in terms of the effects of this drug on the motivations and behavior tendencies shown in Table 1. People or societies with differences in motivational pattern may be expected to differ correspondingly in their use of alcohol.

Effects of alcohol in humans and laboratory animals have been reviewed in detail by Wallgren and Barry (1970: Chapters 6, 7). A more recent summary (Barry 1973) focused on motivational and cognitive effects in humans. This drug is classified as a sedative, in common with barbiturates, ether, and other general anesthetics. Its principal action is depression of mental and physical activity, especially at high doses. However, the drug also has opposite stimulant effects which are attributable at least partly to a disinhibitory action. Normal behavior is largely controlled by inhibitory signals from the cortex; these inhibitory functions are highly susceptible to the depressant action of alcohol which thereby releases excitatory impulses. In addition, there is evidence for direct stimulant effects of low alcohol doses.

These effects of alcohol may be expected to relieve the conflict between dependency and self-reliance motivations. The disinhibitory actions of alcohol enable overt, satisfying expression of the motivations.

The sedative actions of the drug relieve the anxiety which normally prevents these expressions and also dull awareness of the logical incompatibility of these motivations. Therefore, behavior patterns which express both dependency and self-reliance can be expressed simultaneously when the person is intoxicated.

Since everybody suffers from the conflict between dependency and self-reliance motivations, drinking has a universal appeal which is indicated by its widespread popularity. Subjectively perceived effects of alcohol include both exhilarated and tranquil moods. Under the warm glow of intoxication, the drinker feels assertive and independent, while at the same time feeling affectionate and nurtured. The loosening of the bonds of reality is indicated by frequent reports that objectively measured performance is impaired while the drinker expresses a belief that the performance is normal or even improved.

Alcohol intoxication may sometimes appear to elicit only one of the conflicting motivational expressions. For example, McClelland, et al. (1972) have shown that drinking increases fantasies of power in men, measured by stories in response to pictures (Thematic Apperception Test). This expression of assertiveness appears to indicate a preponderance of self-reliance over dependency motivation. However, they also found that aggressive, individualistic fantasies ("personalized power") increased most after drinking a large amount of alcohol, whereas "socialized power" fantasies, expressing dependency motivations, increased only after a smaller amount of alcohol consumption. Wilsnack (i.p.) has found that drinking enhances feelings of femininity and nurturance in women. McClelland, et al. (1972) have emphasized their failure to find any increase in dependency fantasies after drinking. However, the general dependency motivation is expressed by sociability and affection, which are often increased by alcohol. People almost always prefer to drink in a social, convivial context which may be expected to encourage this response to alcohol. At an extreme level of intoxication, dependency is also expressed by stupor, amnesia, and loss of consciousness.

The most consistent effect of alcohol reported by McClelland, et al. (1972) is diminution of inhibition. This may be expected to release whichever behavior is dominant. In our society, men are encouraged to express self-reliance rather than dependency, so that their intoxicated behavior displays assertiveness more conspicuously than submissiveness.

In the cross-cultural study by Bacon, et al. (1965), drinking gave rise to boisterous rather than quiet behavior in almost all of the societies. Extreme expressions of assertiveness, reported in some societies, included exhibitionistic behavior, hostility, and rule breaking. However, the dependency behavior of extreme sociability (friendly, warm, outgoing) was reported in a substantial number of societies. The childlike dependent behavior of succorance was reported in several societies. Further evidence for expression of dependency in the drinking situation is the predominance of social rather than solitary drinking in this sample of preliterate societies. The alcohol consumption is often part of a religious ritual or ceremonial occasion.

INDIVIDUAL AND CULTURAL VARIATIONS

The simultaneous expression of both dependency and self-reliance, under the influence of alcohol, should be especially gratifying if these motivations have been punished or inconsistently treated. Therefore, variations among individuals and societies in frequency of alcohol intoxication should be associated with variations in the motivational characteristics and behavior patterns shown in Table 1.

Characteristics of alcoholics have been examined in a number of studies reviewed by Wallgren and Barry (1970: Chapter 11) and by Barry (1974, i.p.). All alcoholics are characterized by repeated drinking to intoxication and therefore provide evidence about the characteristics which are associated with strong craving for the pleasure and relief obtained from alcohol.

The stages of infancy and early childhood are crucially important for developing the motivations of dependency and self-reliance. Studies of alcoholics indicate a high incidence of disruptive events or pathological conditions in early life. Alcoholism, criminality, or other psychopathology is frequently reported in the parents of alcoholics. A broken home characterizes the childhood experiences of many alcoholics. These conditions may be expected to punish the dependency motivation and give rise to intensified self-reliance motivation. Concurrent punishment for self-reliance is indicated by reports of alcoholics that their mothers disapproved of assertive or independent behavior. Further evidence for conflict between dependency and self-reliance motivations has been inferred by Blane and Barry (1973) in a review of studies showing that alcoholics are frequently last born in large families. This birth position as "baby of the family," in combination with disruption of the family or other punishments for dependency, would be expected to intensify the conflict between dependency and self-reliance motivations.

The most valid evidence about personality traits associated with the development of alcoholism has been obtained from follow-up studies of boys and girls who subsequently became problem drinkers. Corroborative evidence is found in studies of youthful heavy drinkers, prior to the development of the adverse physical consequences of chronic, excessive drinking. These studies indicate a prevalence of assertive, uninhibited, sometimes hostile, and compulsively anti-social behavior among male alcoholics. McClelland, et al. (1972) have reported that men who consume large amounts of alcohol tend to indulge in fantasies of "personalized power." Sorenson (1973) has reported that themes of personalized power characterize the fantasies of alcoholic clergymen. These expressions of individualistic assertiveness might represent the attempt to resolve the basic conflict in a manner which is culturally encouraged for males. Studies of female alcoholics indicate intense conflict over feelings of femininity, which might represent an expression of conflict over dependency motivation. Wilsnack (1973) found that alcoholic women expressed overt femininity but covert masculinity.

Cultural variations in drinking have been studied in an extensive report on a sample of 139 preliterate societies (Bacon, et al. 1965). Further analysis of the data has been subsequently reported by McClelland, et al. (1972: Chapters 3, 4). However, these studies included few measures of infancy and early childhood, which may be crucial stages for the development of dependency and self-reliance motivations. Table 2 shows that several such measures were significantly correlated with frequency of drunkenness. The alcohol measure was an estimate of frequency of an extreme behavioral reaction, in conjunction with the drinking of large amounts of alcohol, if an unlimited supply of alcohol were available year around (Bacon, et al. 1965: 89). Most of the measures of infancy and early childhood were reported by Barry and Paxson (1971) for a worldwide sample of 186 societies, 70 of which were included in the sample studied by Bacon, et al. (1965).

Table 2 shows that several measures of low early indulgence are correlated with high frequency of drunkenness. High amount of crying by the infant reflects the prolonged crying which occurs if nurturance is slow or inadequate. Low anal socialization anxiety is an expression of a low degree of attentiveness on the part of the nurturant agent (Barry 1969b). These measures do not indicate extreme neglect or punishment, but they indicate that a low or inconsistent degree of reward for dependency characterizes infancy and early childhood in societies with high frequency of drunkenness.

The measures of low early indulgence shown in Table 2 are accom-

Table 2.   Infancy and early childhood characteristics associated with high frequency of drunkenness (Bacon, et al. 1965) in a sample of preliterate societies. Except when indicated otherwise, the childhood characteristics are from Barry and Paxson (1971)

Characteristics	High frequency of drunkenness	
	N	r
I. Low early indulgence		
Low general indulgence during infancy	26	0.40*
Low duration of bodily contact with caretaker during later stage of infancy	23	0.42*
High amount of crying during infancy	13	0.77**
Low ceremonialism centered around the child	38	0.42**
Low magical protectiveness of the child	39	0.37*
Low anal socialization anxiety (Whiting and Child 1953)	26	0.43*
II. Exclusive mother care		
Late introduction of new foods	23	0.59**
Low diffusion of nurturance (Barry, et al. 1967)	61	0.32*

  * $p < 0.05$
 ** $p < 0.01$

panied by a couple of measures of exclusive mother care which suggest a low degree of reward for self-reliance at this early stage of life in societies with high drunkenness. A severe conflict may be expected to arise from the combination of variables shown in Table 2.

Measures of later childhood and adulthood, correlated with high frequency of drunkenness, are shown in Table 3. In general, rewards for self-reliance or punishments for dependency seem to predominate

Table 3.   Characteristics in later childhood and adult life associated with high frequency of drunkenness in a sample of preliterate societies. Except when indicated otherwise, all the measures are from Bacon, et al. (1965)

Characteristics	High frequency of drunkenness	
	N	r
I. Later childhood traits		
High pressure toward achievement (Barry, et al. 1967)	56	0.28*
High anxiety over achievement (Barry, et al. 1967)	54	0.35**
High assertion (Barry, et al. 1959)	52	0.33*
II. Adult traits		
Low emotional dependence	45	0.38*
Low instrumental dependence	45	0.48**
III. Adult social behavior		
Low communal eating	51	0.30*
Low competition in acquisition of wealth	52	0.29*
High unreality of storing	48	0.34*

  * $p < 0.05$
 ** $p < 0.01$

at these later stages of life. Low competition in acquisition of wealth seems to be an exception, but this might express a tendency toward individualism and alienation. High unreality of storing might express avoidance of depending on other people for supplies.

The measure of high assertion represents the amount of pressure exerted on the child toward self-reliance and achievement in comparison with the amount of pressure toward obedience and responsibility. The relationship of the measure with frequency of drunkenness was further verified by Barry (1969a) in a comparison between pairs of closely related societies from the same culture clusters.

McClelland, et al. (1972) combined the Bacon, et al. (1965) ratings of frequency of drunkenness and amount of alcohol consumption to obtain a new measure of "drinking." This was positively correlated with the Barry, et al. (1967) childhood behavior measures of frequency of achievement ($r = 0.35$, $N = 40$, $p < 0.05$) and frequency of obedience ($r = 0.29$, $N = 52$, $p < 0.05$), although the two childhood measures were negatively correlated with each other. This finding gives further evidence that an intensified development of conflict between dependency and self-reliance is associated with drinking. Other measures reported by McClelland, et al. (1972), including key words in folktales, give evidence that fantasies expressing impulsive power are associated with drinking. This finding agrees with the correlations shown in Table 3.

Characteristics of the alcoholic or heavy drinker appear to agree well with characteristics of the society where drunkenness is frequent. The predominant behavior pattern is assertiveness, indicating greater reward for self-reliance than for dependency. The childhood experiences suggest severe punishments for dependency, so that the assertiveness expresses denial of the universal motivation for satisfaction of dependency needs. Even when drinking further enhances the expressions of assertiveness, an important source of the pleasure from intoxication appears to be the concurrent expression of dependency motivation.

RESTRAINTS AGAINST DRUNKENNESS

Intoxication provides a temporary escape from conflicts and anxieties without resolving the conflict or establishing new methods for relieving the anxieties. Therefore, the drinking behavior tends to be repeated regularly, to the exclusion of constructive efforts to change oneself or the environment. In this sense, drinking is a passive response pattern in spite of the expressions of assertion which typically accompany it. The pharmacological mechanisms of tolerance and physical dependence lead to a progressive increase in the quantity and frequency of alcohol consumption. In the single drinking episode, the disinhibitory effect of alcohol tends to induce the drinker to consume too much.

These conditions can lead to a vicious spiral in which the drinker receives progressively more punishments, and progressively less rewards, both for self-reliance and for dependency. The pathological behavior patterns shown in the left-hand column and bottom row of Table 1 all characterize many chronic alcoholics. These conditions motivate drunkenness, but the severe punishments also may be consequences of repeated, excessive drinking. Therefore, restraints against drinking are needed, both for the individual and for the society.

The simplest and most effective restraint is limitation of the availability of alcohol. In many of the societies studied by Bacon, et al. (1965), alcoholic beverages can be brewed or obtained only in small quantities or only at limited times of the year. This limitation may remove the necessity of imposing other controls. McClelland, et al. (1972) showed that a high drinking score tended to occur in societies which were located in cold, dry rather than warm, wet climates. The limited availability of alcohol in cold, dry climates may account for the absence of other controls on drinking. Barry (1968) commented on the rarity of reported chronic alcoholism or problem drinking, even in societies with high frequency of drunkenness.

Social controls of drinking may be needed in warm, wet climates, such as tropical jungles, where the raw materials are plentiful and fermentation is rapid. One form of control is the establishment of a religious or ceremonial context for drinking. In many societies with aboriginal use of alcohol, these are the principal or only settings for drinking. However, in some societies drinking is frequently a household routine, a mark of hospitality, or done at informal parties or in small drinking groups. In accordance with the predominantly social characteristic of alcohol consumption, solitary drinking is seldom reported. The ceremonial or religious context may be expected to limit the frequency of drinking and the range of people who may participate, although Bacon, et al. (1965) and Klausner (1964) have given evidence that it does not limit the amount of alcohol consumed.

Field (1962) has shown that a measure of insobriety (Horton 1943) was negatively correlated with several measures of highly organized, hierarchical or stratified social structure. McClelland, et al. (1972)

likewise found negative correlations between a drinking scale (Bacon, et al. 1965) and several similar measures of social structure which constituted strong male institutions. This relationship was partly attributable to the effect of a warm, wet climate, which was positively correlated with strong male institutions and also with the drinking scale. Strong male institutions continued to be negatively correlated with the drinking scale, but short of statistical significance, when the effect of climate was controlled.

Social disapproval of drunkenness may be an effective restraint. This probably tends to characterize societies with highly organized social structure. Barry (1968) has reviewed evidence for this method of control in certain ethnic groups, such as Jewish and Chinese. The tendency for women to drink less than men, reported in the cross-cultural study by Bacon, et al. (1965), might also be due to greater disapproval of drunkenness in women. However, this type of social control is generally accompanied by greater satisfaction of dependent motivation, as was pointed out by Barry (1968). Therefore, diminished motivation for the effects of alcohol might contribute to the effectiveness of this restraint on drinking.

An extreme form of restraint is abstinence, by the individual or by the entire society. This may be necessary if all other controls are absent or ineffective. Barry (1968) has pointed out that many North American Indian tribes had characteristics of child training and adult behavior which are related to high frequency of drunkenness. The absence of drinking aboriginally might have developed during their long history, or by selective survival of nondrinking societies, as the only effective means of restraint. This hypothesis is supported by the destructive effect of liquor when introduced to these people by the Western European intruders.

Even in societies with plentiful supply of alcohol and minimal social restraints, only a minority of the people become heavy drinkers or alcoholics. Most individuals maintain effective control over their drinking. Some people appear to be physically or emotionally sensitive to the effects of alcohol, so that intoxication is extremely unpleasant for them and therefore is avoided. However, the most prevalent method of restraint is probably a general trait of self-control or of strong inhibition. McClelland, et al. (1972) have given evidence that inhibitory themes, expressed in fantasy, characterize people who drink small amounts of alcohol. The general trait of self-control or inhibition may be expected to develop most strongly in people who have experienced consistent reward for both dependency and self-reliance, as shown in the upper-right cell of Table 1. Reward for dependency, in combination with punishment for self-reliance, would not develop self-control but might maintain the restraining influence of the nurturant agent. The uninhibited, impulsive behavior characteristic of the heavy drinker would be most likely to develop as a result of punishment for dependency in combination with reward for self-reliance.

The importance of inhibitory behavior as a restraint on drinking is further indicated by McClelland, et al. (1972) for the samples of societies studied by Bacon, et al. (1965). In folktales words which express inhibitions and conventionality were more frequent in societies with low drinking scores.

CULTURAL BENEFITS OF ALCOHOL

The widespread use of alcohol, in the sample of societies studied by Bacon, et al. (1965), gives evidence for the social usefulness of this drug. None of the societies was known to have renounced the use of alcohol. The widespread integration of drinking in cultural rituals and ceremonies is further evidence of an adaptive function of drinking. The festive drinking occasion, which provides the pleasurable satisfactions of dependency and self-reliance motivations, may be beneficial for the individual and for the society.

An indicative case is the Turkana which, unlike the other African societies studied by Bacon, et al. (1965), did not use alcohol. The people live in isolated family groups, but according to a personal communication from the ethnographer, P. H. Gulliver, when several families come together they often indulge in a feast and celebration at which exuberant, excited behavior is manifested without the aid of drugs. This response to the social occasions, without the influence of alcohol, suggests that the facilitation of this type of behavior constitutes an adaptive function of drinking.

Further evidence for a social value of alcohol is the fact that substitute drugs are used in most societies without alcohol. Several societies in Melanesia and Polynesia account for most of the societies in the sample of Bacon, et al. (1965) where alcohol was not used aboriginally or post-contact. These societies have a native beverage called *kava kava* which appears to have mild sedative and exhilirating effects. This is drunk with various rituals on ceremonial occasions, and for these societies it appears to be a satisfactory substitute for alcohol.

Tobacco was used aboriginally by North American Indian tribes, some of which did not use alcohol aboriginally. Tobacco was not indigenous to most of the societies in the sample studied by Bacon, et al. (1965), but post-contact its use has spread rapidly and was reported in almost all of these societies. The active constituent, nicotine, has a variety of stimulant and depressant effects. Therefore, it apparently can serve as a substitute for alcohol and may partly account for the failure of North American societies to adopt drinking aboriginally.

Gambling appears to be a nonpharmacological substitute for alcohol. McClelland, et al. (1972) reported that men who drink heavily tend also to be gamblers. Self-descriptions by alcoholics indicate a liking for gambling (Barry 1974). In a cross-cultural study, Barry and Roberts (1972) compared societies which had games of chance and physical skill with societies which had games of physical skill only. The presence of games of chance was related to low duration of bodily contact with the caretaker during infancy, which Table 2 shows was related to high frequency of drunkenness. The gambling was interpreted as an expression of dependency motivation which has been inconsistently satisfied during early development. The gambler also has an adventurous, assertive attitude which expresses self-reliance motivation. This simultaneous satisfaction of the conflicting motivations resembles the effects of alcohol described in this paper.

According to a study by Adler and Goleman (1969), the presence of drinking was negatively related to the presence of gambling in a sample of 129 societies. The authors suggested that drinking and gambling are equivalent but alternative expressions of the same motivations. Probably the classification of drinking was on the basis of aboriginal customs, because games of chance are present in most North American Indian tribes, where alcohol was generally absent aboriginally but introduced by the Western European intruders. The drinking measures of Bacon, et al. (1965) indicate that the two groups of societies studied by Barry and Roberts (1972) showed no consistent difference in proportion which used alcohol or in frequency of drunkenness. When two behavior patterns express similar motivations, other factors may determine which one is selected or whether both occur in the same society or individual.

Although various substitutes are available, alcohol appears to have some unique advantages. The dual sedative and disinhibitory effects of alcohol seem especially effective in relieving conflict and enabling the satisfying expression of dependency and self-reliance motivations. These effects constitute temporary relief from conflicts and anxieties. Excessive use is highly pathological. However, in combination with adequate restraints, alcohol can be beneficial for the individual and society.

REFERENCES

ADLER, N., D. GOLEMAN
  1969   Gambling and alcoholism: symptom substitution and functional equivalents. *Quarterly Journal of Studies on Alcohol* 30:733–736.
BACON, M. K., H. BARRY, III., C. BUCHWALD, I. L. CHILD, C. R. SNYDER
  1965   A cross-cultural study of drinking. *Quarterly Journal of Studies on Alcohol*, supplement 3.
BARRY, H., III
  1968   "Sociocultural aspects of alcohol addiction, "in *The addictive states*. Edited by W. Wikler. *Association for Research in Nervous and Mental Disease* 46:455–471.
  1969a Cross-cultural research with matched pairs of societies. *Journal of Social Psychology* 79:25–33.
  1969b "Cultural variations in the development of mental illness," in *Changing perspectives in mental illness*. Edited by S. C. Plog and R. B. Edgerton. New York: Holt, Rinehart and Winston.
  1973   Motivational and cognitive effects of alcohol. *Journal of Safety Research* 5:200–221.
  1974   "Pyschological factors in alcoholism," in *The biology of alcoholism*, volume three: *Clinical pathology*. Edited by B. Kissin and H. Begleiter. New York: Plenum.
  i.p.   "Personality of the individual who is vulnerable to alcoholism," in *Proceedings of the First International Medical Conference on Alcoholism*. London.
BARRY, H., III, M. K. BACON, I. L. CHILD
  1957   A cross-cultural survey of some sex differences in socialization. *Journal of Abnormal and Social Psychology* 55:327–332.
  1967   "Definitions, ratings, and bibliographic sources for child training practices of 110 cultures," in *Cross-cultural approaches*. Edited by C. S. Ford. New Haven: Human Relations Area Files Press.
BARRY, H., III, I. L. CHILD, M. K. BACON
  1959   Relation of child training to subsistence economy. *American Anthropologist* 61:51–63.
BARRY, H., III, L. M. PAXSON
  1971   Infancy and early childhood: cross cultural codes 2. *Ethnology* 10:466–508.
BARRY, H., III, J. M. ROBERTS
  1972   Infant socialization and games of chance. *Ethnology* 11:296–308.
BLANE, H. T.
  1968   *The personality of the alcoholic: guises of dependency*. New York: Harper and Row.
BLANE, H. T., H. BARRY, III
  1973   Birth order and alcoholism: a review. *Quarterly Journal of Studies on Alcohol* 34:837–852.

FIELD, P. B.
1962 "A new cross-cultural study of drunkenness," in *Society, culture, and drinking patterns*. Edited by D. J. Pittman and C. R. Snyder. New York: Wiley.

HORTON, D.
1943 The functions of alcohol in primitive societies: a cross-cultural study. *Quarterly Journal of Studies on Alcohol* 4:199–320.

KLAUSNER, S. Z.
1964 Sacred and profane meanings of blood and alcohol. *Journal of Social Psychology* 64:27–43.

LOLLI, G.
1956 Alcoholism as a disorder of the love disposition. *Quarterly Journal of Studies on Alcohol* 17:96–107.

MC CLELLAND, D. C., W. N. DAVIS, R. KALIN, E. WANNER
1972 *The drinking man*. New York: The Free Press.

SORENSON, A. A.
1973 Need for power among alcoholic and non-alcoholic clergy. *Journal for the Scientific Study of Religion* 12:101–108.

WALLGREN, H., H. BARRY, III
1970 *Actions of alcohol*, volume one: *Biochemical, physiological and psychological aspects*; volume two: *Chronic and clinical aspects*. Amsterdam: Elsevier.

WHITING, J. W. M., I. L. CHILD
1953 *Child training and personality*. New Haven: Yale University Press.

WILSNACK, S. C.
1973 Sex role identity in female alcoholism. *Journal of Abnormal Psychology* 82:253–261.
i.p. The effects of social drinking on women's fantasy. *Journal of Personality*.

Drinking as a Manifestation of Power Concerns

RICHARD E. BOYATZIS

The basic theoretical position of this paper is that men drink alcoholic beverages to attain, or regain, a feeling of strength. Thoughts about being big, strong, and important, about having more impact on others, dominating, or thinking about influence you have had to exert in a situation to fulfill your responsibility are all examples of a concern with "power." Drinking is only one manifestation of power concerns; that is, there are other behavioral means to attaining a similar satisfaction of power concerns, such as fighting or obtaining prestige or status in a social group.

A theory such as this must account for the situational and individual dispositions which lead to individual drinking behavior. It should also articulate the values and structural characteristics which lead to cultural drinking behavior. For example, if an individual man drinks as a result of concerns about power, then groups of men (cultures) should have high levels of drinking if their average individual concern about power is high. Thirdly, a theory must account for various levels of individual and cultural drinking, such as differentiating light, heavy, and abusive drinking patterns.

INDIVIDUAL DRINKING BEHAVIOR AND POWER

A first step in determining the factors which influence drinking behavior is to discover the impact of alcohol on the individual. Four experiments are reported in McClelland, et al. (1972) which examine the impact on fantasies of men of alcohol consumed. The research paradigm for all four studies was to have subjects complete a Thematic Apperception Test (TAT) before and after drinking in various settings and compare the stories which were written at these times.

The first two experiments examined the importance of setting on the effects of alcohol (Kalin, et al. 1965). No significant differences were found in the context of informal discussion groups of college age males in themes of physical sex or aggression, or sexual, fear, or aggressive restraints, in stories written by college age males after drinking during informal discussion groups. The second experiment reported by these authors revealed significant differences in the stories written before and after drinking in the context of cocktail parties with college age males. Subjects in drinking and nondrinking conditions showed increases in story themes of physical aggression and decreases in themes of aggressive retraints and fear restraints. The main point to be learned from these experiments is that the effects of alcohol on fantasy are more likely to appear in a relaxed social setting than a setting in which alcohol is not usually consumed.

The third experiment reported by these authors examined the effect of alcohol on the fantasies of college-age males in cocktail party settings with no faculty members or adult experimenters present. Story themes of physical sex increased and aggressive restraints decreased in the stories written. Also worthy of notation is that the average number of these themes found in the stories was higher for subjects who had consumed about five ounces of alcohol (86 proof) than for subjects who had consumed less than four or more than six ounces.

The fourth experiment studied the interaction of alcohol and setting (McClelland, et al. 1972). Several significant variations in fantasies written after drinking were found. Subjects in an apartment chose more alcohol to drink than subjects in the classroom. Physical sex themes increased in the alcohol conditions, in the apartment conditions, and in the apartment-alcohol condition when an attractive female folk singer was present. Themes of physical aggression were higher in the apartment-alcohol condition than in the apartment-dry condition (when the singer was not present). Themes of fear restraint were higher in the dry conditions than in the alcohol conditions.

Alcohol had an effect on certain types of fantasies of college-age males, but only in particular settings. When the setting is "relaxed," alcohol consumption leads to increased amounts of fantasies of physical sex and aggression and decreased amounts of fantasies of aggression restraints and fear. These themes can all be considered concerns about power: themes of physical sex and aggression are thoughts about the individual's ability to manipulate or have impact on others, while themes of aggression and fear restraints are thoughts about the impact of others, in the form of normative constraints of the behavior of the individual.

Research on the effects of alcohol on male behavior have demonstrated that persons become more talkative, less tense, and more "elated" in the presence of others following light to moderate consumption of alcohol (Wallgren and Barry 1970). Boyatzis (1973) reported that men (varying in age and socioeconomic status) demonstrated more interpersonal aggression following alcohol consumption than before in a somewhat stressful setting. Although aggressive interpersonal behavior can be seen as behavior emanating from concerns with power, the general increase in interpersonal activity reported in Wallgren and Barry (1970) must be examined carefully. This type of behavior can lead to a person gaining a focal position in an interaction, which possibly provides the feeling of importance which was sought. It is important to note that satisfaction of a person's power concerns DOES NOT require behavioral proof of an individual's impact but that the process of thinking he is powerful may provide the sensation of having risen above and become more powerful than his environment (or at least his internal representation of the environment).

If an individual's drinking behavior is caused by his power concerns, a person's level of power concerns should demonstrate a substantial correlation with his level of alcohol consumption. Winter (1973) reported the arousal studies and many experiments which demonstrated the reliability and validity of the power motive scoring system he developed. Because the meaning of the power motive score, as determined by coding TATs, appeared a more comprehensive and well validated score than measures of particular themes such as physical sex, and included many aspects of themes found to be relevant in the early studies, it was chosen as the main variable. Self-report of drinking levels did not correlate significantly with power motive scores for a sample of male college-age subjects (Winter 1967). Power motive scores did correlate with self-report liquor-drinking levels in a sample of working-class males ($R = 0.30, N = 50, p < 0.05$) but did not reach a significant level in another sample of 108 working-class males. Boyatzis (1973) reported that although it did not correlate significantly with alcohol consumed, or self-reports of drinking levels in males ranging in age and socioeconomic status, the need for power of subjects did predict level of intoxication in experimental drinking sessions when the person's prior drinking history was held constant.

There are three possible explanations for the ambiguous relationship found between the power motive score and drinking behavior. First, the theory may be incorrect. Second, drinking behavior may be related to a particular form of power concerns. A person might drink to satisfy uninhibited, impulsive, and egocentric power concerns, while a person with inhibited and less egocentric power concerns may seek other behavioral means of getting satisfaction. Third, drinking may only be the result of "aroused" power concerns. In this case, an individual's level of power concerns may correlate with his drinking only when such concerns have been stimulated by the particular setting (as when a female folk singer is present).

Returning to the second possibility, an attempt was made to determine the nature of impulsive versus other types of power concerns. Persons with a high level of power motive were split into two groups on the basis of the relative presence of activity inhibition themes in their TATs. It was found (McClelland, et al. 1972) that high power and low activity inhibition was present in 56 percent ($N = 20$) of the heavy drinkers in one bar study with working-class men and only 15 percent ($N = 16$) of the light drinkers. In the other similar bar study, high power and low activity inhibition was present in 61 percent ($N = 18$) of the heavy drinkers and only 31 percent ($N = 58$) of the light drinkers. A scoring system was developed on the basis of this difference which yielded an impulsive power score. This score correlated significantly with a self-report quantity frequency measure of liquor consumption in both bar studies ($r = 0.32, N = 50, p < 0.05$). Sorenson (1972) found that alcoholic priests ($N = 65$) had significantly higher levels of this impulsive power concern and significantly lower levels of other types of power concerns than nonalcoholic priests ($N = 56$). Although there are difficulties in obtaining this measure, the findings support the point that heavy drinking is primarily associated with impulsive power rather than controlled power concerns.

Another possibility is that the various forms of power concern may be similar in thought (themes evident in TATs) but may be expressed in behavior differently. For example, a person may have a high level of power concerns and seek influential positions in organization or social status as means of gratification rather than drinking. To test this possibility, several behaviors which could be considered alternative manifestations of power concerns were selected. These variables were standardized. The power motive score was then correlated with the maximum score on any of the variables for each person. Boyatzis (1973) chose four variables: number of organizational offices held, number of credit cards carried in one's wallet, frequency of being drunk in the recent past, and a sum of various aggressive actions, such as yelling at someone in traffic, throwing a book across a room, etc. The first two variables represent means of attaining power satisfaction in controlled, socially accepted ways and the last two represent more impulsive means of gaining power satisfaction. The correlation with the power motive score was highly significant ($r = 0.361$, $N = 139$, $p < 0.001$). Tests are presently being run to cross-validate this finding in earlier studies.

The third possible explanation of the ambiguous relationship between the power motive and drinking is that an individual's "aroused" power concerns lead to drinking. This means that a person who ordinarily has relatively low power concerns may be stimulated by responsibility or an argument into having power thoughts and then drink to satisfy these concerns. Davis (1969) conducted an experiment in which working-class men were assigned to be blindfolded or a guide for a blindfolded person. A guide and blindfolded person had to walk several blocks along busy city streets to a bar in which they removed the blindfolds and drank at their own pace. In one condition, the pairs were given "power-oriented" instructions, such as telling them that the blindfolded person was helpless and in the complete control of the guide. In another condition, the pairs were given "nurturance-oriented" instructions such as the blindfoldee will be taken care of by the guide and should feel secure. The pairs were matched on age, education, occupation, and prior drinking history. The guides ($N = 27$) drank significantly more in the bar following the game than did the blindfoldees ($N = 27$) overall, although the difference was greater in the power-oriented induction condition. The guides reported feeling significantly more powerful and less nurtured than the blindfoldees on a mood adjective checklist following the game for both conditions overall, although the differences in powerful feelings were significant within each condition as well. The correlation between feeling powerful after the game and alcohol consumed at the bar was significant ($r = 0.25$, $N = 54$, $p < 0.05$), while the correlation to feeling nurtured was not significant ($r = -0.03$, $N = 54$).

In a situation requiring responsible or influential behavior, subjects' power concerns were aroused and they drank more. Other aspects of life may arouse people's power concerns, such as stressful events. Boyatzis and Dailey (1973) found a significant correlation between recent stress-inducing life changes (such as changing jobs, getting a mortgage, etc.) and frequency of being drunk in two samples varying in age and socioeconomic status (sample A, $r = 0.277$, $N = 120$, $p < 0.01$; sample B, $r = 0.242$, $N = 136$, $p < 0.01$).

Although the association of power motives and drinking behavior appears somewhat complex in the sense that other variables modify it, some further studies will clarify the relationship.

CROSS-CULTURAL ANALYSIS OF FOLKTALES

Two cross-cultural studies were conducted to test the power theory of drinking (McClelland, et al. 1972). The results found in the studies will be combined here to test two hypotheses emanating from the theory: first, cultures with high levels of concern about power should have high levels of drinking behavior and *vice versa*; second, cultures high in drinking should have structural characteristics which arouse power concerns.

Folktales were chosen as the source of data about cultural concerns. It can be argued that they provide information as to the collective concerns of a culture and the relative intensity of these concerns. Folktales are potentially used to communicate norms and values, to establish adult behavioral and belief conformity, and to influence the formation of norms and values in youth. The presence of a thematic concern in a folktale reveals a specific awareness about an issue of a cultural group. They should, therefore, provide a more direct link to psychological processes than found in prior research.

Cultures were selected which differed in geographic location and/or language using Murdock's *Ethnographic atlas* (1960–1964). To be selected, each culture was required to have a folktale collection of at least 4,000 words and about ten separate tales. The reliability of the sources of folktales was important. If any source made reference to editing the original or difficulty in translation, it was dropped. Forty-four cultures were selected for analysis: nine African; seven Insular-Pacific; nine Eurasian; thirteen North American; and six South American. The average folktale collection consisted of 8,000 words and fourteen tales. When more than ten tales were available, ten were randomly chosen which were of approximately standard length. About two-thirds of the tales in the sample were collected by professional folklorists or anthropologists and the rest by amateurs who had clearly stated that no alterations were made in the original text. Tales which were originally myths or historical legends from the recent past and religious ritual or ceremonial tales were excluded fom the analysis.

The measure of drinking behavior was obtained from Bacon, Barry, and Child (1965) and Bacon, Barry, Child, and Snyder (1965). These authors provided four ratings obtained from factor analyses. Frequency of drunkenness and general consumption were both chosen because of their high intercoder reliability. Other variables were excluded because of low intercoder reliability and/or low frequency, such as amount consumed during ceremonies. The drinking measure used in this study was the sum of these two reliable variables. The interest was in obtaining a measure of level of drinking, not a measure of how people drank.

The method of analysis used was the Content General Inquirer developed by Stone, et al. (1966). The folktales are fed into a computer. A dictionary of verbal usages is constructed. The computer then determines the frequency of each tag for the folktale of each culture. The tags in the dictionary can be used either to test existing theories or to construct a new theory. For example, to test Horton's theory (1943) of causal factors relating to drinking, a dictionary of the following tags was used to get a substistence anxiety: fear, hunt, travel, and gather; deprivation or fear cues being in a sentence containing food cues. Reliability of the tag scores in a dictionary is then determined by correlating scores obtained from two halves of the text. A test of internal validity of the tag scores is accomplished by comparison of these scores to hand-coding of several folktales.

Table 1 presents the correlations of folktale themes and drinking for several theories. Tags that are significantly positively associated with drinking are: hunt, entering implements, change of state, eating, and oral body part ("sex" has a near significant association). Those that are significantly negatively associated with drinking are: fear, old and dead, activity inhibition, anger, and eating markers ("title" has a near significant association). A list of the most frequent words tagged under each concept in Table 1 appears in Appendix A.

Horton's hypothesis (1943) that anxiety over an insecure food supply leads to drinking does not appear supported. In fact, "fears" were less common in drinking societies. This suggests that heavy drinking societies are no more anxious than light drinking societies as he argued. Of course, if drinking did reduce this anxiety and the folktales were told when men were intoxicated, then the fewer "fears" found in drinking societies would support Horton. The most direct test of Horton's hypothesis (the "subsistence anxiety" tag) did not reveal any association. Finally, although "hunt" loaded in the direction Horton predicted, "travel and gather" did not. These findings suggest that Horton's hypothesis needs refinement.

Table 1. Correlations of folktale themes and drinking (N = 44). Abridged from McClelland, et al. (1972)

Tags relevant to:	Drinking
A. *Subsistence anxiety* (Horton 1943)	
Fear	—0.44***
Subsistence anxiety	0.09
Hunt	0.38***
Travel and gather	—0.18
B. *Formal organization* (Field 1962)	
Title	—0.30*
Vertical space	—0.12
Old and dead	—0.42***
Scheduling	—0.09
Activity inhibition	—0.35**
C. *Dependency* (Bacon, Barry, and Child 1965)	
Give	—0.06
Taking	0.21
Dependency	—0.09
Want	0.16
Capability	—0.04
Anal socialization anxiety	—0.06
D. *Social drinking affects* (Kalin, et al. 1965)	
Sex	0.27*
Aggression Tags	
Kill	0.21
Entering implements	0.35**
Violent physical manipulation	0.21
Anger	—0.30**
War	—0.17
Change of state	0.35**
E. *Orality themes* (Knight 1937)	
Eating	0.35**
Drinking	0.24
Cook	0.09
Oral body part	0.48***
Eating markers	—0.34**

$*\ p < 0.10$
$**\ p < 0.05$
$***\ p < 0.01$

Field's hypothesis (1962) was that highly organized societies with high levels of solidarity are less likely to drink than societies without these characteristics. The correlations strongly support this hypothesis. Three tags are negatively related to drinking indicating that sober societies think in terms of hierarchy ("title" and "old and dead") and social control ("activity inhibition").

Bacon, et al.'s hypothesis (1965) was that a desire for dependency leads to drinking. This hypothesis did not appear supported in any fashion by the content of the folktales. Thoughts about dependency are neither consistently present nor consistently absent (the latter could be a result of inhibitions caused by anxiety).

Kalin, et al.'s hypothesis (1965) was that themes found to increase after individual drinking (sex, aggression, and change of state[1]) should be associated with drinking at the societal level was partially supported. The tags "entering implements" and "change of state" are positively related to drinking as predicted by the hypothesis (as does the near significant association of "sex").

Knight's hypothesis (1937) is that drinking is related to a psychodynamic regression into an oral mode. This is supported by the significant positive association of "eating" and "oral body part." The negative association of "eating markers" refers to somewhat organized consumption of food (such as meals) and can be interpreted as opposite to the primitive egocentrism of the oral mode.

Several theories received direct support and others could be thought to have indirect support. For example, the Bacon, Barry, and Child dependency hypothesis could have received indirect support through the tags loading on the oral mode cluster. None of these perspectives appear to offer a clear answer to the question of why various cultures have differing levels of alcohol consumption.

Other tags were examined and tags found to be significantly related to drinking were re-categorized to use a more empirically based, inductive approach. The results are shown in Table 2. Regrouping the tags of "title," "fear," and "anger" as themes of organized respect reveals highly significant intercorrelations among these tags. The same phenomenon was revealed with the tags regrouped in the inhibition theme ("activity inhibition," "old and dead," "fish," and "eating markers"). Each of these clusters demonstrates substantial negative association to cultural levels of drinking. Regrouping the tags "hunt,"

---

[1] "Change of state" is a tag connotating a metamorphosis. McClelland, et al. (1972) report this to be similar to "Meaning contrast" which was a fantasy theme which increased in males after drinking but was not discussed earlier in this paper.

"entering implements," "eating," and "change of state," as sharing a theme of potency also reveals substantial positive intercorrelation of the items and a significant positive association to cultural levels of drinking. Potency refers to the means or indicators of an individual's impact on himself and his surroundings. Respect and inhibition themes can be interpreted as concerns about organized and socially controlled means to attaining impact on others.

Table 2.   Correlation of drinking and power-related folktale themes (N = 44). Abridged from McClelland, et al. (1972)

Variable	Drinking
A. Respect themes	
Title	—0.30**
Fear	0.44***
Anger	—0.30**
B. Inhibition themes	
Activity inhibition	—0.35**
Old and dead	—0.42***
Fish	—0.36**
Eating markers	—0.34**
C. Potency folktale themes	
Hunt	0.38**
Entering implements	0.35**
Eating	0.36**
Change of state	0.35**
D. Scales	
Power scale	0.06
Inhibition scale	—0.55***
Impulsive power scale	0.38**
Conventionality scale	—0.51***

  * $p < 0.10$
 ** $p < 0.05$
*** $p < 0.01$

A factor analysis of the tags was conducted. Two factors were extracted: a power factor, which loaded high on such tags as "hunt," "war," "having," and "vigorous activity"; and an inhibition factor which loaded high on such tags as "activity inhibition," "old and dead," and "fear." The two factors accounted for 44 percent of the total common variance, with no other factor accounting for more than 14 percent. To purify the loadings, the factors were rotated 20°. Two other factors were extracted. One was called IMPULSIVE POWER, which consisted of tags loaded high on the power factor and low on the inhibition factor ("violent physical manipulation," "eating," and "entering implements"). The other was called CONVENTIONALITY, which consisted of tags loading low on the power factor and high on the inhibition factor ("anger," "fish," "title," and "eating markers").

Table 2 presents the correlations of these scales and drinking. Although the power scale does not correlate significantly with drinking, the impulsive power scale does. This supports the hypothesis that a certain type of power concern is a critical determinant of cultural drinking levels. The significant negative correlations of drinking and the inhibition and conventionality scales indentify the folktale themes typical of societies which do not drink heavily. Of the twenty-two societies above the median on the power scale, eight out of ten of those low on the inhibition scale were heavy drinking societies, while only two out of twelve of those high on the inhibition scale were heavy drinking societies.[2]

The frequency of themes of impulsive power in the folktales of a culture appears positively related to its level of drinking behavior. The level of folktale themes relating to organized, controlled individual assertion of influence in a culture is negatively related to its drinking behavior.

CULTURAL CHARACTERISTICS, POWER, AND DRINKING

To help explain the findings from the folktale analysis, structural characteristics of cultures varying in power concerns and drinking levels may be examined. Table 3 presents correlations of a number of structural characteristics and drinking. Male solidarity was coded using Young's rating (1965) of presence or absence of ritualization of some male activity or separate male housing. Low male solidarity correlates significantly with drinking. Presence or absence of any unilineal descent groups was coded from Murdock (1960–1964). Nonlineal descent is significantly correlated with drinking. Structural differentiation at a local level was coded from Murdock. Low differentiation showed a near significant correlation with drinking, a near significant correlation with low male solidarity ($r = 0.26$, $N = 52$, $p < 0.10$), and a highly significant correlation with nonlineal descent ($r = 0.28$, $N = 173$, $p < 0.01$).

These three variables may interact in the following manner to encourage drinking. If indicators of structural differentiation are low within a

---

[2] Heavy drinking societies were identified by a median split on levels of drinking.

Table 3. Correlations of drinking and cultural characteristics. Abridged from McClelland, et al. (1972)

Variables	Drinking	
	r	n
A. Low male solidarity	0.41***	49
Nonlineal descent	0.23**	76
Low differentiation	0.20*	71
Small community size	0.27**	58
Egalitarian kin terms†		
Collateral terms	0.51***	44
Few first order generation terms	0.27*	44
Few "child" references	0.31**	44
B. Socioeconomic simplicity scale: Factor I		
Degree of dependence on hunting	0.29**	76
Open class system	0.21*	71
Low degree of jurisdictional hierarchy	0.19	70
Impermanence of settlement pattern	0.26**	71
Small size of local community	0.26**	58
Degree of dependence on agriculture	0.26**	76
C. Male institutions scale: Factor II		
Presence of male initiation	—0.30**	52
Clear initiation impact	—0.50***	46
Strong male solidarity	—0.34**	49
Long post-partum sex taboos	—0.36**	50
Exclusive mother-baby sleeping arrangements	—0.24*	48
Large sleeping distance of mother and father		
(monogamous position)	—0.31**	46
Warm winter temperature	—0.43***	54
Wet climate	—0.45***	46

  * $p < .10$
 ** $p < .05$
*** $p < .01$
  † obtained from folktales

social group, it can be expected that the individual will experience a persistent pressure to demonstrate his prowess and his right to claim a position of importance in the community. In a culture with few organized or structured means of attaining a sense of masculinity, such as a lack of a ritual connoting the male's membership in the social group as a warrior, the individual's attainment of a position of importance is at best temporary. His power is further weakened when lineal descent does not insure a position in the hierarchy. Therefore, the individual must face the conflict of self-assertion and achieving a position of importance with few organized supports or norms prescribing his right to retain that position. This interpretation suggests that it is this type of persistence ambiguity over his importance or power which is associated with drinking.

Community size was also coded from Murdock. Small community size shows a significant positive correlation to drinking. This further clarifies the above interpretation. When community size increases above a certain level, the means to attaining and/or maintaining influence often are institutionalized to maintain social order. Once this occurs, the male may experience more certainty over his status. Egalitarian kin terms were coded from the folktales and support the finding that low hierarchical differentiation is related to drinking.

To organize these findings, a factor analysis was conducted on these variables which correlated with drinking. Initially 168 variables were examined: 25 variables were found to correlate with drinking and had at least 100 observations on each. These variables were reexamined and recoded, when necessary, to provide clear ordinal scales. This left 18 variables. From Murdock, 76 societies were selected which had data on drinking variables and represented a geographic distribution. An orthogonal factor rotation was used revealing two factors which accounted for 51 percent of the total common variance with no other factor accounting for more than 12 percent of the variance. The 14 variables which had high, pure loadings on one of the two factors are presented in Table 3.

The socioeconomic simplicity scale consisted of items describing aspects of the social structure and economic dependence on various food sources. The degree of dependence on hunting, and lack of dependence on agriculture, open class system, low jurisdictional hierarchy, impermanence of settlement, and small community size describe a temporary and uncertain life style. The risks of obtaining meat as a result of hunting and securing a habitable physical settlement are great. The males are, therefore, under persistent pressure to assert themselves in situations of low probability of success. There are no stable mechanisms to maintain a position of importance without the male continually proving that he is worthy of it.

This cluster of variables, although suggesting support for Horton's hypothesis (1943) of "subsistence anxiety" being related to drinking, does not provide such support. Lee (1966) has shown that in these hunting societies the sources of food are highly dependable. For example, among the !Kung Bushmen approximately 75 percent of the food consumed is vegetable matter gathered by females and not the meat sought by males.

The second factor, termed the male institutions scale, mostly includes variables which indicate clear, stable mechanisms for attaining or maintaining a position in the male "group." Presence of male initiation, clear initiation impact, strong male solidarity, long post-partum sex taboos, exclusive mother-baby sleeping arrangements, and large sleeping distance between a monogamous mother and father are all stable structural aspects of the social group which reduce the pressure on the individual to continually assert himself.[3] Although warm winter climate and wet climate load significantly on this factor, it is not clear how they affect this structural dynamic. However, when societies in cold and warm climates are analyzed separately, low male solidarity is still consistently related to drinking.

Table 4 presents some of the intercorrelations of these two factor scales derived from folktale themes and drinking. The socioeconomic simplicity scale is positively correlated with drinking and negatively correlated with the male institutions scale (which is negatively correlated with drinking). These two scales appear to be describing two social syndromes which are oppositely related to drinking. The socioeconomic simplicity scale is positively correlated with the folktale power scale and impulsive power scale and negatively correlated with the conventionality scale. This supports the previously mentioned interpretation. The socioeconomic simplicity scale describes cultures in which the male is required to be continually assertive with few organized supports to maintain his position of influence or importance once attained. The male institutions scale correlates positively with the conventionality scale. This supports the link between clear, stable means to attaining membership in the male group and the organized, social control of means of attaining and/or maintaining prestige in such a society.

Combining all of the results presented, it can be seen that consumption of alcohol can be useful to males in certain cultures. If a person is continually faced with the tension of self-assertion in a situation containing few organized supports toward maintaining a position of prestige once acquired, then alcohol can help the individual by making him FEEL more powerful. He can fantasize encounters in which his prowess is great and undaunted. Alcohol also helps him by reducing inhibitions and releasing more aggressive behavior. Bolstered by alcohol, the individual can continue to face the day-to-day struggles of

---

[3] Post-partum sex taboos, exclusive mother-baby sleeping arrangements, and large sleeping distance between a monogamous mother and father are customs which emphasize the male's membership in the male group as a father. This position can be considered a stable indicator of status in the culture.

Table 4. Cultural characteristics, folktale themes, and drinking. Abridged from McClelland, et al. (1972)

A. Social syndromes							
Socioeconomic simplicity scale	0.31***	76	—		—		—
Male institutions scale	—0.52***	72	—0.30***	175	—		—
B. Folktale themes							
Power scale	0.06	44	0.41***	44	—0.17	40
Inhibition scale	—0.55***	44	—0.24	44	0.10	40
Impulsive power	0.38**	44	0.32**	44	—0.23	40
Conventionality	—0.51***	44	—0.37**	44	0.42***	40

$* \ p \geq .10$
$** \ p \leq .05$
$*** \ p \leq .01$

living in such a society. If the society contains mechanisms which decrease this pressure, then he has less need for alcohol and its "magical" effects.

THE SYNDROME OF POWERLESSNESS

To summarize up to this point, it appears that the arousal of power concerns in the individual either through culturewide concerns, his place in the social structure, or social demands for demonstrating his importance or prowess causes the person to seek outlets which make him feel more powerful. He can be described as feeling relatively powerless at these times. One interpretation is that this state of powerlessness evolves from the psychodynamic relationship between the self and the internal representation of the environment. As the discrepancy between the impact he has on himself and his environment and the impact his version of the environment has on him increases, tension builds. In the situation where the individual experiences the environment as more powerful than himself, he will probably attempt to redress this imbalance by asserting his supremacy over the environment as proof that he is NOT WEAKER, BUT STRONGER than his surroundings. This objective can be attained by aggrandizing the self, minimizing the threat of the environment, or both.

Two types of interactions between the individual and his image of his environment can cause this dynamic tension to build. One tension-causing interaction is characterized by the individual with moderate to high power needs living in a situation which allows him few opportunities to satisfy these needs and feel powerful. The second type of interaction has not been discussed in previous work, but has become clear through clinical work. This tension-building interaction is characterized by the individual with moderate to low power needs living in a situation which demands that he exert much influence in the form of responsibility, decision making, or controlling others. In either type of interaction, the type of tension is created which makes the individual feel powerless.

As a result of clinical work, clues have been found as to how this syndrome operates in several types of situations in which men are involved that lead to drinking. For example, an experience of failing to meet the behavioral standards of others in demonstrating competence, especially when someone else does meet this standard or surpasses it, can create the feeling of being "weaker'" than others and incapable of competing with the standard. An experience of rejection from a person or relationship which is important to the individual can also create the sensation of being at the mercy of the environment (which includes other people). Either of these experiences establishes the possibility that mere anticipation of such events will create a sensation of powerlessness.

Alcohol can relieve this tension by releasing compensatory fantasies of the individual's sexual potency and aggressive strength, while reducing awareness of the restraints to such activity present in the environment. These fantasies may be enough; if not, the individual may seek behavioral proof of his supremacy through aggressive acts.

The experience of boredom can arouse the tension created by feeling powerless. This occurs through a process of perceiving a lack of opportunities for need-satisfaction (having nothing to do) and accepting this as evidence of one's relative weakness with respect to his surroundings. The search for an outlet may lead to alcohol which physiologically and psychologically replaces the boredom with excitement, more specifically excitement which increases the individual's sense of being able to influence himself and others.

This tension may also emanate from a situation in which powerful or influential behavior is "demanded" of the person. A job which entails responsibility for others, such as a therapist, teacher, or executive, can create the sensation that the individual is FORCED to influence others. The burden of responsibility can result in the person feeling weaker than his surroundings. Alcohol can relieve this tension by releasing impulsive, irresponsible fantasies or behavior in which the sole objective is the egocentric satisfaction of the person's needs.[4]

Alcohol as a solution to the dilemma of feeling powerless offers, at best, temporary relief. When these pressures are present in a person's life, as they must be in cultures requiring male assertiveness with a lack of organized supports for prestige or importance, the individual will seek proof of his supremacy over the environment, either through alcohol, aggression, or some other impulsive power-enhancing acts. If these demands are consistently present, a consistent behavioral pattern seeking self-aggrandizement or derogation of the potency of the environment will be observable.

ALCOHOL, AGGRESSION, AND POWERLESSNESS

This theoretical perspective predicts that men, in a stressful setting which would stimulate concerns about power, will seek proof of their impact on others. According to the theory, if given the opportunity one alternative would be to consume alcohol and act aggressively as behavioral proof of their impact.

There is some cross-cultural evidence to support the findings that alcohol consumption is related to aggressive behavior while drinking. Ratings of the following behaviors exhibited during drinking "bouts," coded by Bacon, et al. (1965) for various cultures, were found to correlate significantly with cultural levels of drinking behavior (McClelland, et al. 1972): intensity of exhibitionistic behavior ($r = 0.52$, $N = 24$, $p < 0.05$), change in exhibitionistic behavior ($r = 0.57$, $N = 20$, $p < 0.05$), occurrence of extreme hostility ($r = 0.42$, $N = 41$, $p < 0.05$), and boisterousness ($r = 0.60$, $N = 57$, $p < .01$). These behaviors appear related to aggression and impulsive concerns about one's impact on others.

Boyatzis (1973) reported an experiment intended to test this hypothesis. Male subjects ranging in age from twenty-five to fifty years old from all levels of socioeconomic status completed a battery of personality and behavioral activities questionnaires. In groups of six to eight, they participated in four-hour parties which occurred in a "bar room" atmosphere. Alcohol was served for the first two and a half hours (liquor in one condition and beer in the other). Subjects were encouraged to play competitive games, such as darts, cards, and liars dice as

---

[4] The Davis study (1969) provided direct support for this hypothesis. The subjects who were guides (responsible for the safety of blindfolded subjects) drank more in the bar following the game than did the blindfoldees.

the experimenters attempted to stimulate competitive stress. Alcoholic beverages were available to subjects to consume at their own discretion. Subjects were videotaped early, middle, and late during the sessions. Coding systems for aggressive behavior and social behavior were used to determine each subject's behavior during each videotaped period.[5]

Subjects were assigned to one of four groups on the basis of behavior during the evening session: (a) decreasing in aggressive and social behavior; (b) increasing in social behavior but decreasing in aggressive behavior; (c) increasing in aggressive behavior but decreasing in social behavior; and (d) increasing in aggressive and social behavior. The aggressives (subjects increasing in aggressive behavior and decreasing in social behavior) had significantly higher blood alcohol concentrations early, middle, and late in the evening in the alcohol conditions than did subjects in the other classifications.[6] In self-report measures of alcohol consumption, aggressives of both conditions distinguished themselves as heavier drinkers than subjects in other classifications, specifically in quantity of beer usually consumed, quantity/frequency of liquor usually consumed, and frequency of being drunk (this last variable demonstrated near significance, $p < 0.10$). Aggressives reported significantly higher frequencies of committing various aggressive acts, like throwing a book in anger or yelling at someone in traffic, and participation in physical fights with a near significant higher number of violent arguments than subjects in other classifications. To summarize, subjects who drank heavily and acted aggressively in a laboratory setting were people who drank heavily and acted aggressively outside of the laboratory when compared with other subjects in the same setting.

Furthermore, on a self-description adjective checklist completed during the testing session (sober), aggressives of all three conditions felt more powerless than subjects in the other classifications (near significant relationship, $p < 0.09$). Power motive scores (obtained through a TAT early in the "bar room" session) were significantly higher for aggressives in the alcohol conditions than subjects in other classifications. This confirms the hypothesis presented earlier that when the discrepancy between need for power and perceived demands or opportunities for power satisfaction from the environment becomes great, the individual seeks proof of his potency. In this case, the proof took

[5]   Intercoder reliability among four independent scorers of these coding systems was above 0.89 for aggressive behavior and social behavior.

[6]   Sixteen of 49 subjects in the liquor condition and 25 of 59 subjects in the beer condition were classified as aggressive.

the form of alcohol consumption and subsequent aggressive interpersonal behavior.

A study of alcohol-related automobile accidents supported these conclusions. Pelz and Schuman (1973) studied the alcohol-related driving problem of eighteen to twenty-four-year-old male drivers. They claimed that "hostility" was an indicator of wanting influence while "alienation" was a measure of powerlessness. They found that for males who felt hostile toward others, or alienated from their educational system, drinking was related to reckless driving. For males not in this group, drinking appeared to have little relationship to reckless driving. They interpreted alcohol-related reckless driving as characteristic of young males who felt powerless with respect to their surroundings.

When this evidence is combined with other findings about alcoholics, it becomes increasingly more difficult to conceptualize people who drink heavily, or drink and engage in aggressive activities as seeking nurturance, or dependency. On the other hand, it is easier to conceptualize the aggressive, power-seeking behavior demonstrated following alcohol consumption as evidence of the needs which drinking is intended to satisfy.

PRESSURE IN ADVANCED SOCIETIES

Recently in northern Greece and northern Italy, relatively low levels of alcohol consumption (other than at meals) as compared to the United States and other cultures have been noted. Much higher levels of alcohol consumption (not associated with meals) by men in northern Italy as compared to northern Greece were observed. Closer examination of living conditions relating to work for men in these areas revealed an interesting observation. Northern Italy has attained a more advanced stage of industrial growth than has northern Greece. Along with this advancement has come a greater requirement for the individual to assert himself in choosing a career, getting a job, keeping a job, and seeking a better job. Many aspects of these pressures are suggestive of the demands hunting and gathering societies placed on males. Northern Greece and northern Italy have strong hierarchical societies with high male solidarity, and both have low levels of excessive drinking and drinking other than with meals as compared to many other cultures. The higher level of concern about power observed in northern Italy could be associated with the nature of work and work relationships characteristic of an advanced industrial state. It is an intriguing observation which bears testing with systematic methods.

WOMEN AND ALCOHOL

Before concluding, a statement as to the relationship of power concerns and female drinking behavior should be made. Wilsnack (1972) has attempted the only study of the effects of alcohol on fantasies of women known to this author. She concluded that moderate social drinking does not affect female fantasies of nurturance or dependency. Alcohol consumption at this level appeared to increase fantasies of "womanly feelings" and to decrease fantasies of "masculine assertiveness" and similar forms of power concerns. Wilsnack's examination of female problem drinkers (1972) revealed a characteristic conflict between unconscious orientations toward masculinity and conscious wishes to be feminine and womanly.

If the physiological effects of alcohol consumption are similar for men and women (which they may not be), it can be concluded from this single study that the psychological effects and determinants of drinking behavior are linked to cultural sex roles. Of course, more evidence is required before we can articulate the impact of alcohol on women and the secondary effects of alcohol consumption by women on their families, immediate social environment, and occupation environment.

APPENDIX: Dictionary of Words Used to Measure Frequency of Various Concept Tags (abridged from Mc Clelland, et al. 1972)

Concept (and Words)

Activity inhibition (not, catch, stop)
Anal socialization anxiety (dung, excrement + fear or negation)
Anger (anger, rage, fury)
Capability (make, could, can)
Change of state (become, feel, change, awake)
Child (child[ren], baby, grandchild)
Collateral (uncle, nephew, aunt, niece, cousin)
Cook (cook, roast, pan)
Dependency (ask, carry, help)
Drinking (drink, milk, beer thirst[y])
Eating (eat, meal, fat, fruit, hunger)

Eating markers (food, feast, meal)
Entering implements (arrow, knife, spear)
Fear (afraid, fear, fright)
First order generation (mother, father, son, daughter)
Give (give, let, help)
Hunt (hunt, hunter)
Kill (kill, slaughter, stab, slay)
Negation (not, no, never)
Old and dead (old, dead, death)
Oral body parts (mouth, stomach, tongue)
Scheduling (time, after, before, next)
Subsistence anxiety (eating, eating markers, or cook + negation, fear or
    hunger)
Taking (take, seize, collect)
Title (king, priest, queen, prince)
Travel and gather (went, go, find, gather)
Vertical space (under, above, below)
Violent physical manipulation (throw, cut, hit)
Want (want, wish, need)
War (shoot, fight, war)

REFERENCES

BACON, M. K., BARRY, H., I. L. CHILD
  1965   A cross-cultural study of drinking, II: Relation to other features
         of culture. *Quarterly Journal of Studies on Alcohol* 3:29–48.
BACON, M. K., H. BARRY, I. L. CHILD, C. R. SNYDER
  1965   A cross-cultural study of drinking, IV: Detailed definitions and
         data. *Quarterly Journal of Studies on Alcohol,* supplement 3:78–
         111.
BOYATZIS, R. E.
  1973   "Alcohol and aggression: a study of the interaction." Paper pre-
         sented to the National Institute on Alcohol Abuse and Alcoholism.
BOYATZIS, R. E., C. DAILEY
  1973   "Alcohol consumption and aggression in relation to life stress."
         Unpublished manuscript.
DAVIS, W. N.
  1969   "Drinking: a search for power or for nurturance?" Unpublished
         Ph.D. dissertation, Harvard University.
FIELD, P. B.
  1962   "A new coss-cultural study of drunkenness." in *Society, culture,
         and drinking patterns.* Edited by D. J. Pittman and C. R. Snyder,
         48–74. New York: Wiley.
HORTON, D.
  1943   The functions of alcohol in primitive societies: a cross-cultural
         study. *Quarterly Journal of Studies on Alcohol* 4:199–320.

KALIN, R., D. C. MC CLELLAND, M. KAHN
  1965   The effects of male social drinking on fantasy. *Journal of Personality and Social Psychology* 1:441–452.
KNIGHT, R. P.
  1937   The psychodynamics of chronic alcoholism. *Journal of Nervous and Mental Diseases* 86:538–543.
LEE, R. B.
  1966   "What 'hunters' do for a living: or, how to make out on scarce resources." Paper presented to the "Man the Hunter" Symposium, Chicago, April 6–9.
MC CLELLAND, D., W. DAVIS, R. KALIN, E. WANNER
  1972   *The drinking man.* New York: Free Press.
MURDOCK, G. P.
  1960–1964   Ethnographic atlas. *Ethnology* 1:4.
PELZ, D. C., S. H. SCHUMAN
  1973   "Drinking, hostility and alienation in driving of young men." Paper presented at the Third Annual Alcoholism Conference of the National Institute on Alcohol Abuse and Alcoholism, June.
SORENSON, A. A.
  1972   Need for power among alcoholic and non-alcoholic clergy. *Journal for the Scientific Study of Religion.*
STONE, P. S., D. C. DUNPHY, M. S. SMITH, D. M. OGLIVIE
  1966   *The general inquirer: a computer approach to content analysis.* Cambridge Mass.: M.I.T. Press.
WALLGREN, H., H. BARRY, III
  1970   *Actions of alcohol:* volumes one and two. New York: Elsevier.
WILSNACK, S. C.
  1972   "Psychological factors in female drinking." Unpublished Ph.D. dissertation, Harvard University.
WINTER, D. G.
  1967   Power motivation in thought and action." Unpublished Ph.D. dissertation, Harvard University.
  1973   *The power motive.* New York: The Free Press.
YOUNG, F.
  1965   *Initiation ceremonies.* Indianapolis: Bobbs-Merrill.

Drunkenness and Culture Stress:
A Holocultural Test

THEORETICAL FRAMEWORK

The leading ideas about drunkenness during the last three decades have emerged from three major holocultural (cross-cultural) surveys. The hypotheses are: (1) that as levels of anxiety increase in a society, drunkenness increases (Horton 1943); (2) that frustration during the socialization process among the young leads to heavy alcohol consumption among adults (Bacon, et al. 1965); and (3) that as need for personal power increases, drinking increases (McClelland, et al. 1972). Other holocultural surveys on drunkenness have attempted to clarify and expand on these basic hypotheses (Field 1962; Klausner 1964; Davis 1964). For a detailed theoretical review of these studies see Schaefer (1973: 1–26).

This study was designed to bring new evidence to bear on these hypotheses on drunkenness, and to provide vigorous control tests to ascertain the adequacy of the hologeistic method.

New codings on family structure and sentiment were made following suggestions from the recent work of Hsu and others (Hsu 1959, 1965, 1969a, 1969b, 1972). Space restrictions do not allow a discussion of how these codes were derived, but essentially an attempt was made to find which set of nuclear dyadic interactions in the family were predominant in kin-related behavior. An effort was also made to determine which sentiments characterized the context of the dominant dyadic networks. The primary goal was to see if father-son dyadic dominance correlated with sobriety, and if husband-wife dyadic dom-

This work was supported by University of Montana Foundation grant No. 841-0/L.

inance correlated with insobriety. Related sentiments with the former were to include continuity, inclusiveness, dominance/subdominance, asexuality, and dependency. Related sentiments with the latter were to include discontinuity, exclusiveness, egalitarianism, sexuality, and independence. These attributes of family organization and sentiment were thought to be sensitive indicators of moral, normative guidelines of contrastive social situations. These situations were thought to be basic to the ongoing process of adapting to differing levels of tension in society. No previous study on drunkenness had attempted to measure the "tightness" or "looseness" of society as directly, although several studies have strongly suggested that these structures and sentiments are core features of sober and drunken societies (Field 1962; McClelland, et al. 1966, 1972).

Another facet of the study was a reconsideration of the place of supernatural beliefs in the body of theory on drunkenness and culture stress. In general, it is known that belief structure is an important component of the cultural system. Most theoreticians suggest that beliefs are reflective of ongoing behavior (Lowie 1924; Malinowski 1948; Swanson 1960; Banton 1966; Tatje and Hsu 1969). Few would deny the importance of feedback relationships between behavior (action) and beliefs (ideas). While these functional assertions have intuitive appeal, demonstrations of how these interactions take place are few and far between (cf. Spiro 1961, 1965a; Lévi-Strauss 1965; McKinley 1971).

In this study supernatural beliefs were codes with respect to peoples' connections of what happened to dead persons, following suggestions by Tatje and Hsu (1969). We were primarily interested in correlations between respectful, authoritative, supernatural spirits and gods, and sobriety, and between unpredictable, malicious, and capricious supernatural spirits, and extreme drunkenness. Previous holocultural studies on drunkenness had indicated a lack of support for such contentions (Field 1962; McClelland, et al. 1966, 1972); however, the indicators used were suspect (Schaefer 1973: 27ff, and see below).

In addition to the new variables, many of the precoded variables in Murdock's *Ethnographic atlas* (1967) were used to re-study key social and political conditions previously established in the drunkenness literature.

METHODOLOGY

The most recently developed control tests and vigorous procedures in holocultural, or cross-cultural, survey methods were followed in this study. Holocultural studies are one of a class of hologeistic or global-based survey studies. In holocultural studies, theoretical propositions are statistically tested in random probability samples of tribal societies around the world. In such studies, many problems arise which must be addressed (see Naroll 1970a and Sipes 1972 for summary statements). The major problems are: sampling (what is the proper sample size, sample universe, sampling technique?), units of study (what is being counted in computing tests of association and significance?), Galton's Problem (was diffusion a plausible factor in explaining theoretical results?), statistics (what statistical tests are appropriate for the data in the study?), data quality controls (how can trustworthy data be obtained from untrustworthy sources like some ethnographic monographs?), coding reliability, validity and documentation (how can the critic be assured that the data used for evidence is reliable, valid and replicable?), categorization (how do indicators used relate to theories, or how were theories operationalized?), and deviant cases (why were there exceptions to the general theory?).

Each of these issues was squarely faced in the study. A sample of fifty-seven tribal societies was chosen from the bibliographically controlled HRAF quality-controlled sample universe (Human Relations Area Files 1967). A stratified random probability sample was taken from that universe.

Each tribal group was defined in terms of a cultural focus (Murdock and White 1969), cult unit (Naroll 1964, 1970b), and double language boundary (Naroll 1971). Together with the sampling technique, these procedures assured the independence of each tribal unit, thereby reducing the plausibility of historical connection and duplication.

Control tests for Galton's Problem were performed using four different linked-pair alignments. No theoretically damning evidence was found in support of the rival diffusionary hypothesis (Schaefer 1972).

The statistical tests used for tests of association and tests of insignificance were phi and Fischer's Exact Test (Siegel 1956: 114; Naroll 1972). These tests were appropriate for the nominal scale data that were collected.

Data quality control tests were run in order to determine whether systematic informant bias, ethnographer bias, or comparative bias were present (Naroll 1962; Schaefer 1973: 103–108). None of the tests for systematic bias were supported.

Each newly coded trait was tested for reliability and cross-study validity. Three independent codes were made (two coders were ignorant with respect to the hypotheses under study, the writer was the third coder). Correlational tests confirmed that theoretically important variables were reliably coded and cross-study tests suggested that independent research on drunkenness and spirit belief traits were generally in agreement (Schaefer 1973: 184–200). (A complete listing of codings, references, and page citations are included for documentation purposes in Schaefer 1973: 361–389.)

Theoretical indicators were all operationally defined and discussed prior to undertaking the study. Several pilot studies at the beginning of the coding work allowed for refinement of several problematic variables (i.e. family structure and sentiment). And finally, deviant cases, those societies which did not fall into predicted portions of the theoretical presentation, were examined. In several instances, deviant patterns were explained in terms of a more generalized theoretical argument. For example, it was noted that several unilocal (i.e. matrilocal versus patrilocal) post-marital residence typed societies failed to conform to the predicted model. A high correlation between drunken brawling and patrilocality was expected (cf. van Velsen and van Wetering 1960). It was found that matrilocal societies tended to brawl more than patrilocal societies (Schaefer 1973: 174–176). However, upon further examination it was found that nearly all the matrilocal brawlers had simple political organizations (i.e. decision making at the local level only), while nearly all the nonbrawling patrilocal groups had complex political organizations. This finding is further supported by a substantial correlation between drunkenness and drunken aggressiveness, and political organization (see Table 1 L/A. L/B0). Political organization turned out to be the most predictable culture trait in explaining drunken behavior.

General tests for group significance also suggested that the large number of correlations reported in the study could not have occurred by chance alone (cf. Naroll 1970a: 1237–1238).

To sum up, methodological control procedures briefly reviewed here lend credibility to the theoretical findings to be discussed below. In contrast to previous holocultural studies on drunkenness, the study has disproved many of the classic rivaling hypotheses due to questions about method (Kobben 1952, 1967; Schapera 1953; Lewis 1956). The success achieved in disproving these rival hypotheses raises the presumption that the theories studied here for the first time, as well as theories on drunkenness supported by this study, stand on firm methodological ground.

DISCUSSION

Extreme Drunkenness

GENERAL FINDINGS   In the present study, many important theoretical linkages were found between extreme and aggressive drunkenness and other sociocultural traits (see Table 1). Strong correlates of drunkenness were fear of supernatural spirits, weak family structure, hunting and gathering technoeconomy, simple division of labor, simple political system, absence of social-class distinction, and low societal complexity. Each of these linkages was predicted before the study was undertaken. One predicted linkage, a new theoretical variable concerning family sentiment (attitude) patterns, did not correlate to the degree expected. The general correlation pattern fits nicely into the general explanation offered for extreme and aggressive drunkenness by Horton some thirty years ago. In fact, the new linkage found between fearful supernatural spirit beliefs and drunkenness adds further support to his general argument (treated in detail below). The other linkages in the study closely parallel the findings of previous hologeistic studies in drunkenness (Horton 1943: 276–278; Field 1962: 53–61; Davis 1964; Barry, et al. 1965: 71–74; McClelland, et al. 1966: 326, 1972: 65; Wanner 1972: 90). Not all these studies have agreed on an interpretation of the correlation patterns discovered. Davis (1964) and Barry, et al. (1965) have shown supplementary linkages between drunkenness and aspects of dependency conflict in childhood training and drunkenness in later life. These findings led Davis and Barry and his colleagues to suggest that Horton's anxiety reduction hypothesis for drunkenness was not sufficiently general. In another study, McClelland, et al. (1972) have shown new linkages between personalized power themes in folktales and drunkenness. While McClelland claims to have disproved Horton's anxiety reduction hypothesis for drunkenness, he proposes a "new" hypothesis concerning NEED FOR POWER that is very reminiscent of Horton's earlier idea (1943) about anxiety and drunkenness. McClelland suggests that drinking alcoholic beverages can give a person a momentary feeling of power. His claim is that, where men are under certain pressures from a highly unpredictable sociocultural environment, they tend to feel anxious or powerless. Drinking helps make people in such circumstances feel stronger. Therefore, drinking provides a source of imaginary superhuman control over many anxiety-producing situations encountered in daily life.

Table 1. Statistical summary of correlations on drunkenness (from Naroll 1972)

Key		A	B	C	D	E
Drunken brawling	A		<0.011	<0.10	<0.95	<0.95
Extreme male insobriety	B	0.55		<0.05	<0.75	<0.25
Malicious, capricious spirits	C	0.27	0.27		<0.05	(<0.20)
Rewarding, punishing spirits	D	−0.00	−0.07	−0.29		<0.50
Family structure husband–wife	E	0.02	0.17	0.21	0.11	
Family structure father–son	F	−0.19	−0.24	−0.17	−0.00	−0.38
Hunting and gathering	G	0.40	0.06	0.14	−0.06	0.09
Fixed settlement pattern	H	−0.47	−0.03	−0.11	0.00	−0.15
Complex division of labor	I	−0.61	−0.13	−0.09	0.20	−0.03
Permanent post-marital residence	J	−0.03	0.05	0.20	−0.10	0.15
Bilateral kin-grouping	K	0.03	0.10	0.26	−0.42	0.20
Simple political system	L	0.84	0.36	0.37	−0.32	0.10
Social class distinctions absent	M	0.56	0.56	−0.06	−0.08	−0.11
Low social complexity	N	0.63	0.63	0.24	−0.27	0.00

Legend: Lower half of table are all phi coefficients.
Upper half of table consists of probability statements. A through N squared to F are a

F	G	H	I	J	K	L	M	N
0.20	<0.05	<0.025	<0.005	<0.95	<0.95	<0.001	<0.005	<0.005
0.10	<0.75	<0.90	<0.50	<0.95	<0.70	<0.05	<0.005	<0.005
0.70	<0.50	<0.50	<0.70	<0.25	(<0.10)	<0.03	<0.75	(<0.20)
0.90	<0.75	<0.95	<0.25	<0.70	<0.01	<0.05	<0.70	(<0.20)
0.005	<0.70	<0.50	<0.90	<0.50	<0.25	<0.70	<0.70	<0.98
	<0.70	<0.80	(<0.10)	<0.80	<0.95	(<0.20)	<0.80	<0.50
-0.06		<0.002	0.009	0.78	(0.12)	0.004	0.0004	—
0.06	-0.48		(0.14)	0.75	0.21	0.006	(0.11)	—
0.31	-0.42	-0.22		0.28	0.49	0.001	<0.0005	—
-0.05	-0.06	-0.05	0.15		0.03	0.33	0.69	—
-0.00	0.24	-0.18	0.06	0.36		<0.05	0.45	—
-0.27	0.48	-0.44	-0.53	0.13	0.33		0.001	—
-0.04	0.49	-0.24	-0.56	<0.02	0.07	0.64		—
-0.15	—	—	—	—	—	—	—	—

ased on Chi Square (Siegel 1956:114). G through N squared are all based on Fisher's Exact Test One ailed. N ranges from 22 to 57.

There is little that distinguishes McClelland's theory about need for power from Horton's original thesis of the anxiety reduction function of drinking in preliterate society. It is true that Horton's "subsistence anxiety" evidence was indirect and limited in scope; but, as will be argued subsequently, McClelland's "powerlessness" evidence can be questioned on very similar grounds. The fact remains that Horton's general theory still rings true now, even after thirty years of challenging research, the benefit of hindsight, new conceptual breakthroughs, and more sophisticated methodology.

Back in 1943, Horton proposed a theory that drunkenness increased as anxiety increased. He presented as evidence a series of correlations between aspects of simple hunting and gathering economy and extreme aggressive drunkenness. He interpreted his empirical findings as evidence that the specified technoeconomic base provided an insecure subsistance base — an anxiety source — which was regularly overcome by excessive drinking.

Wanner (1972: 90–94) recently has re-focused attention on Horton's suppositions about hunting and gathering technoeconomy. He suggests that the subsistence insecurity of the hunting and gathering technology, or other small-scale adaptations, is still relatively unknown. He points to Lee's recent nutritional studies (1968) on the !Kung Bushmen suggesting that dietary needs are well met. The question of hunting and gathering subsistence security is not new. Holmberg (1950) argued that the Siriono were forever hungry; but Needham (1954) argued that the Penan, another hunting and gathering group, were rarely concerned about food. While this hunger issue remains unsolved, few would question the insecure nature of the sociocultural setting in hunting and gathering or similar small-scale societies. This is the point Wanner wishes to make clear. He suggests that the linkage Horton found so long ago between hunting and gathering technoeconomy and extreme drunkenness might have been better interpreted as evidence of "status insecurity" rather than "subsistence insecurity." In fact, the general notion that hunting and gathering societies tend to have many other sources of anxiety than those concerning food have been made clear from many studies besides those connected with the study of drunkenness.

Diverse sources of anxiety, or "feelings of powerlessness" (following McClelland), have been suggested for small-scale societies with simple technoeconomic bases: adults are pressured to be individualistic, assertive, and adventuresome (Barry, et al. 1965: 247–248); hunting tasks tend to be high risk and low net gain activities (Lee 1968: 30); inter-

and intra-political community conflicts are frequent (Otterbein and Otterbein 1965: 1470–1482; Otterbein 1970, 1972); social etiquette is characterized mainly by egalitarianism (Denton 1968); long post-partum sex taboos, high infanticide, prevalent sorcery, and general polygyny link up with patterns of violence, ritualism, and magical practices (B. Whiting 1965; J. Whiting 1964; Whiting, et al. 1960; magical thinking prevails (J. Whiting 1959, 1967: 155; Wanner 1972: 90); social class system is open (Textor 1967: FC68/100; Wanner 1972: 90–93); political system is weak (Textor 1967: FC88/100; Wanner 1972: 90); guidance is often acquired through dreaming (D'Andrade 1961; Bourguignon 1972; Wallace 1972); low indulgence of dependency and high achievement pressures exist (Bacon, et al. 1965); and pressure towards continence in situations of cross-generational marriage is present (Thomas 1965: 89). These observations attest to the prevalence of many DIFFERENT sources of anxiety in simple small-scale societies. That these societies tend to drink to excess and have frequent aggressive episodes while drinking stands to reason. All this evidence points to the importance of the anxiety reduction function of alcohol in primitive societies.

Major refutations of the general anxiety reduction theory have come from Field (1962), who challenged Horton's interpretations about anxiety using supernatural belief evidence and David McClelland's group, who challenged many previous interpretations of drunkenness findings using folktale evidence. These positions may, in turn, be challenged in light of the present study.

ANXIETY, POWERLESSNESS, AND EXTREME DRUNKENNESS: CONFLICTING EVIDENCE   Our findings on fear of supernatural spirits and extreme drunkenness are important because they lend support to the general notion of anxiety reduction as a functional explanation for extreme drunkenness and contradict directly the findings of Field (1962) and indirectly those of McClelland, et al. (1966, 1972).

The first test of the hypothesis that fear of supernatural beings was associated with extreme drunkenness was performed by Field (1962). He suggested that fear of supernatural beings was a better indicator of relative anxiety in a society than was Horton's more indirect subsistence anxiety measure (1943). Field used codings on fear, various spirits from Whiting and Child (1953), and fear of ghosts at funerals from Friendly (1956). His codings on drunkenness came from Horton (1943).

Field (1962: 51) found no relationships between fear of supernatural beings and drunkenness that were of statistical interest. His findings raised the presumption that fear and anxiety were unrelated to extreme, aggressive or mild, passive drunkenness.

This conclusion may have been apparent from the empirical evidence, but it is one that does not agree with other studies on the function of feared supernatural beings in society. Moreover, using the exact same test of the anxiety reduction hypothesis for drunkenness, we found strong correlations between fearful supernatural beliefs and extreme, aggressive drunkenness ($\emptyset + 0.27$; $X^2 = 3.87$; $p < 0.05$; $N = 56$). These correlations emerged from new and highly reliable codings on fear of supernatural spirits and extreme drunkenness (Schaefer 1973: 158, 192–197). Field's borrowed codings on supernatural beliefs were not highly reliable (J. Whiting 1967: 154; also see Guthrie 1971: 322). Findings parallel to ours have been published but have gone unnoticed in Textor (1967: 476/437).

Field's failure to find linkages between fear of supernatural spirits and extreme drunkenness allowed him to ignore Horton's anxiety hypothesis while focusing on his own provocative hypothesis about SOBRIETY. But his findings, with regard to Horton's anxiety reduction hypothesis for drunkenness, provided stimulus for several other hologeistic studies. An intriguing one has been McClelland's study of folktales and drunkenness. Of special interest here is McClelland's support of Field's contention that fear of supernatural beings is unrelated to drunkenness (Kalin, et al. 1966: 584–586; McClelland, et al. 1966: 320, 1972: 59, 86).

McClelland's group found "fear themes" from folktales consistently correlated with indicators of MILD DRUNKENNESS. They maintained that people in societies with extreme drunkenness "worry less, or at least refer to fear of being afraid less in their folk tales" (McClelland, et al. 1972: 59). McClelland, et al. contend that their negative findings in regard to fear and extreme drunkenness are even more conclusive than Field's. The present study suggests that both Field and McClelland may be mistaken in their arguments against Horton. Our findings directly contradict Field's supernatural belief evidence and indirectly contradict McClelland's folktale evidence. These differences require a further discussion.

Supernatural Spirit Belief Evidence

The central problem here is to explain the empirical finding of an association between fear of supernatural spirits and extreme and aggressive drunkenness.

SPIRIT

The spirit beliefs that correlated so well with measures of drunkenness were beliefs that the spirits of the dead ancestors of living people were malicious and capricious. It is presumed that spirits of the malicious and capricious sort are perceived by the members of a culture as realistic entities. The spirits are thought to enter forcefully into the peoples' daily lives. People tend to fear arbitrary harm from them (Tatje and Hsu 1969: 157). Other spirits, to be sure, may also be perceived as harmful to the living by some peoples, i.e. punishing spirits; but they tend to be more predictable. In short, the arbitrariness and unpredictive nature of malicious and capricious spirit types are probably quite indicative of the worldview of societies that drink excessively. Malicious and capricious spirits appear to be an important source of anxiety due to their unpredictability. Their threat of arbitrary harm probably has quite a psychological impact, especially to those persons who take their threats seriously. To such people, the belief is strong, the threat is real, and the anxiety felt needs to be relieved.

The emphasis on beliefs and what people think and treat as real is important. Much time has been spent discussing the differences between fear and neurotic anxiety. Freud (1936) and Mowrer (1939) and their followers sought to distinguish instinct based fear — what they called "neurotic anxiety" — from what they called empirically verifiable fear (Hallowell 1941: 869–871; 1967: 250–265). In this discussion no light can be shed on the instinct based or biogenic variety of anxiety. We have no way of controlling for the relative influence that that particular condition may have had on specific adult drinking patterns. This is not to say that some stressful cultural traditions can be discounted as plausible selective factors in societies that drink excessively and behave aggressively. It only means that they are specifically unaccounted for in the present discussion. The focus, instead, is on the sociocultural functions of "objective anxiety" or fear.

The argument offered is that when the supernatural belief structure is predominated by ancestral spirit beliefs which involve active, malicious, and capricious spirits, that by their very nature are unpredictable, people will tend to be anxious. There is, of course, a rival explanation: if people are anxious, they imagine capricious spirits and then drink excessively. In either case, they will tend to drink to relieve these and other anxieties. They will drink frequently to excess, primarily because alcohol gives them a momentary feeling of power and strength (McClelland, et al. 1972: 334). The momentary feeling of power may well be taken seriously, adding to the potential danger in the drinking setting. Some drinkers may even be physically more powerful in their drunken

stupor. Such a physical and momentary, even fleeting, feeling of prowess may give rise to a drunken brawl and other aggressive acts.

What evidence is there for this interpretation? First, there is evidence
from the writer's own study regarding spirit beliefs and drunkenness.
Second, there is a body of theory on the function of beliefs in society.
Let us turn briefly to each of these.

Consider the spirit beliefs of some of the societies in the present
study that had extreme drunkenness and drunken brawling. The Korean
spirit world is "dictated by dread that ancestral spirits may do harm
to their descendants" (Bishop 1898: 61). The Mataco of South America
have a "death spirit [that] is generally the object of fear . . . smaller
spirits cause curable illnesses, others cause mortal diseases" (Karsten
1932: 115, 118). The Aweikoma of South America say "we are afraid
of the ghost-souls" (Henry 1941), while a belief spread widely among
the Chukchee is that the "deceased become, after death, a kind of kelet
(evil spirit) hostile to man, and inclined to do harm" (Bogoras 1904–
1909). The Aleut have a belief "that spirits of the dead influence to
some extent the lives of the living . . . [similar] spirits who annoy people
are also there" (Shade 1948: 97–98). And the Tarahumara of Mexico
believe that a "dead man can harm his family . . . they implore their
departed to leave them alone . . . [the] dead do no damage outside their
family" (Bennett and Zingg 1935: 249–251).

Ethnographic discussions of supernatural beliefs suggest that the impact of these malicious and capricious spirits is continuous throughout
the lives of the members of the cultures that believe in them. That is,
the knowledge of arbitrary, unpredictable harm from dead ancestors
is imparted early in life and continuous through life. Indeed, Lambert,
et al. (1959: 162–163) suggest that in cultures where people practice
painful, rough, physically punishing child training, people tend to believe in aggressive, malevolent spirits. Lester (1966: 741–742) has cor-
roborated their basic findings. J. Whiting (1967: 154) further suggests
that societies with strong fear of spirits are generally more concerned
with moral behavior than other societies. These behavior patterns are
constant factors throughout these peoples' lives.

How belief systems function in society has been a general subject of
inquiry for many years. Spiro suggests that belief systems play an
intricate role in one of the functional necessities for any society's
existence, namely, the displacement of ingroup hostilities (1965b).
Much of the research on supernatural beliefs has been predicated on
similar assumptions. For example, Kluckhohn (1944) and Tatje and
Hsu (1969) suggest that belief structures derive from the working

models that people create to cope with their everyday problems. Such general models, regarding various role-playing behavior, have had a special place in the major work of several psychological anthropologists (Whiting and Child 1953; J. Whiting 1959; Lambert, et al. 1959; Opler 1965; Spiro and D'Andrade 1958). But Spiro's study of ingroup hostility displacement functions has special importance to the present interpretation of the linkage found between fear of spirits and extreme drunkenness (Spiro 1961, 1965a, 1965b).

Spiro (1961: 820–824) argues that a belief in fearful spirits is an efficient way to cope with ingroup hostilities. His argument is general. He suggests that there are innumerable structural arrangements that function primarily to displace overt or covert ingroup hostilities. Other cultural arrangements that have similar functions are witchcraft, sorcery, and gossip. The present research suggests that drunkenness is another alternative.

Spiro's contention that fearful, evil spirit beliefs are efficient in the displacement of ingroup hostilities is based on the idea that the individual takes out his frustrations and anxious feelings on a supernatural being, thereby avoiding overt conflict. Such an adaptation is less likely to cause physical harm or even destruction of reputation for the individual and his group. In this sense, the other practices (i.e. witchcraft, sorcery, gossip, extreme drunkenness, and aggressive drunkenness) are less efficient.

Projecting anxieties onto non-empirical entities such as supernatural spirits can temporarily alleviate perceived anxieties. This is an especially effective practice if the spirit beings do not actively enter into the daily lives of the members of a society. If evil, unpredictable spirits are viable entities in a society, then it is conceivable that spirit beliefs may help alleviate some felt hostility. But, if these same spirits are believed to be active in the affairs of the living, they may feed back into the society as sources of anxiety. Indeed, the adaptations a group has for dealing with various anxieties may be quite complex. Some practices may alleviate certain frustrations, while other beliefs or action patterns may exacerbate anxiety or powerlessness situations.

The spiral of anxiety or powerlessness may be temporarily, or even permanently, alleviated by a counter-spiral of cultural practices. In line with Spiro, it is thought that these adaptations to felt anxiety may be judged more or less efficient in terms of their ability to displace hostile feelings within a group.

Drunkenness may be added to such a list of displacement activities. Drinking can provide a great release from various sources of anxiety;

but it also can lead to physical violence. Therefore, drinking may be an efficient displacement activity only under certain circumstances.

Spiro's theory adds a new perspective to the anxiety reduction hypothesis for drunkenness, especially with respect to the linkage between a belief in fearful supernatural spirits and extreme and aggressive drunkenness.

In light of this interpretation, neither our positive findings, nor Field's failure (1962) to find a relationship between feared supernatural spirits and extreme drunkenness is surprising. It is plausible that the societies in this study sample were NOT effectively handling their ingroup hostilities or anxieties. On the other hand, the societies in Field's sample may well have been EFFECTIVELY handling the ingroup hostilities or anxiety, perhaps in nonalcoholic ways. However, as already indicated, Field's study of spirits is of questionable worth because of the unreliable codings used in his study (J. Whiting 1959: 154; Guthrie 1971: 322). But even if his codes were reliable, it may be that SOME societies in his sample displaced their feelings of anxiety into fearful spirits RATHER THAN into excessive drinking, while other societies in his sample feared spirits AND drank excessively. In either case, the ingroup hostilities or anxiety could have been dealt with. Coincidence in sampling cannot explain away our contradictory evidence. To speculate further, a reconstruction of Field's correlation matrices, his sample, and other codings would be required. That is beyond the scope of the present discussion.

Additional evidence for the argument offered comes from Horton (1943: 273–275). Earlier, he studied the relationship between sorcery and extreme drunkenness and found low correlations. However, he found strong correlations between sorcery and drunken aggression (1943: 286). From the arguments raised above, it would seem that both Field's and Horton's evidence add to our contention that drunkenness is a relatively inefficient displacement activity. Note that Field found fear of supernatural spirits unassociated with excessive drunkenness and moderate drunkenness. Horton found sorcery unassociated with extreme drunkenness, but strongly associated with aggressive drunkenness. We found fear of supernatural spirits associated with extreme drunkenness, but found an even stronger association when fear of supernatural spirits was correlated with drunken aggressiveness (brawling).

To sum up, if anxieties are present in societies, several responses may be expected. Some responses may be sufficient to cope with or temporarily allay manifest or latent anxieties. Additional responses may emerge as needs arise or change in emphasis. It is suggested, in line with Spiro, that the most adaptive response to stress is one not harmful to oneself, to other people, or to reputations. One apparently adaptive response to stress is a belief system emphasizing evil, malevolent, or feared spirits. Other functionally less efficient means for coping with hostilities may be practiced (cf. B. Whiting 1950). These functional alternatives may be witchcraft, sorcery, extreme drunkenness, or aggressive drunkenness. These are tentatively listed in terms of decreasing order of functional efficiency. The least efficient forms are those that do not displace anxiety or ingroup hostility at all. A key point is the suggestion that fear of supernatural spirits may be meaningfully (functionally) intertwined with sorcery and extreme aggressive drunkenness. They have been shown to be intercorrelated by Horton (1943: 276) and by this study. They may become manifest cumulative — covarying with increasing loads of anxiety. As anxiety becomes more intense, the likelihood of real harm to humans becomes less easy to avoid. Fear of supernatural spirits diminishes some anxiety in and of itself, especially when overt hostility in social patterns is tabooed (Spiro 1961). But, however efficient fear of supernatural spirits may be in relieving anxiety in some cultures, these projective techniques may well lead to more anxiousness in other cultures. Where this is the case, sorcery and/or drunkenness may also increase. The two may function as tension reducers, but they hold the potential for overt hostility. Sorcery and/or drunkenness momentarily provide escapes from reality; but in the long run, they are less efficient functional alternatives to the simple projective techniques of supernatural beliefs.

In this way, fear of supernatural spirits, sorcery, and extreme aggressive drunkenness are thought to be closely intertwined in simple, small-scale societies where anxiety levels tend to be high. Current research is under way concerning these contentions, and several discriminating statistical tests will be applied to determine the relative influence of these factors on culture stress.

Folktale Evidence

McClelland, et al. (1972: 76–78) have provided thematic evidence from folktales that they claim disprove Horton's anxiety reduction hypothesis for extreme drunkenness. McClelland indicated that themes of fear in folktales correlated negatively and significantly with extreme drunkenness. He also indicated that the presence of themes of fear had no relationship to ratings on hunting and gathering economy. He claimed that this clearly discredited Horton's hypothesis about subsistence insecurity (via hunting and gathering) and extreme drunkenness. Moreover, he claimed to have supported Field's contention (1962) that fears fail to characterize situations where extreme drunkenness is present (Kalin, et al. 1966: 585–586; McClelland, et al. 1966: 320, 1972: 59).

However, this study revealed evidence that SUPPORTS the general anxiety reduction hypothesis using the exact same test used by Field (1962). The reasons why feared supernatural spirit beliefs function in societies with extreme drunkenness have already been disclosed. Moreover, McClelland's "new" theory of need for power, which seems to be a restatement of Horton's anxiety reduction hypothesis, was used to embellish the interpretation for the "new" finding of this study.

What are the sources of the discrepancies? It is suggested that McClelland's folktale indicators are of questionable worth.

McClelland suggests that people drink primarily to feel stronger. His argument is that, for the powerless or anxiety ridden person, drinking gives the feeling of momentary power — a sort of magical control over events. Because such feelings of magical control are short lived, the person tends to drink frequently. McClelland claims that for individuals whose power drives are worked out in more rewarding activities, drinking poses no serious problem. These people tend to drink in moderation and act passively while drunk because their needs for power are diffuse rather than alcohol centered (McClelland, et al. 1972: 332–336).

What evidence does McClelland cite to support these provocative arguments? "Impulsiveness" and the "need for power" do not lend themselves into readily operational terms. But McClelland attempted to test his theory by measuring these states of mind through Thematic Apperception Tests (TATs) and thematic analysis of folktale content.

In controlled psychological tests, he indicated that impulsiveness and power imagery increased as alcohol intake increased (McClelland, et al. 1972: 3–47, 99–213). In his cross-cultural surveys he indicated that "impulsive power" themes in folktales correlated strongly with measures of extreme drunkenness (McClelland, et al. 1966: 320; 1972: 38–98).

McClelland's work (1972: 293–315) with TATs, before and after controlled drinking settings, is rather persuasive evidence for his interpretation of drinking motives. His conclusions are limited to his sample populations of American college men and working-class men, and he has argued his theory convincingly for scattered populations in other cultures (i.e. Spanish Americans, Anglo-Americans, Indian Americans, Jews, Irish, Finns, and Chinese).

His cross-cultural folktale work, however, is not convincing. In his 1972 book, *The drinking man*, McClelland (1972: 52) devotes only one paragraph to the description of the folktale selection process. He fails to discuss the shortcomings of his sample with respect to folktales. Moreover, he fails to discuss the internal consistency or lack of consistency as to folktale representativeness. He does not sample randomly from folktale collections, nor does he assure us that the collections are anything like complete.

While McClelland's group has been cautious in their folktale work, perhaps they have not been cautious enough. They themselves have paid some attention to the weakness of their interpretations (McClelland, et al. 1972: 46, 73–84). Even so, their interpretations based on content analysis of folktales must be met with healthy skepticism. Briefly, let us summarize their procedure, some problems with it, and some critical observations on it.

The "General Inquirer" computer technique for folktale text analysis is rather straightforward (Colby, et al. 1963). The computer has folktale texts in English read into it through cards, tapes, or discs. A program tells the computer to search the texts for similar words. It collects them, keeping track of the frequency of occurrence of each word. Word frequencies are tabulated, making a "dictionary," organized by "tags" of conceptually similar words and their frequencies. This last task is mediated by the researchers, since the computer cannot recognize the necessary conceptual transformations (Stone, et al. 1966). "Themes" are created by combining various meaningful sets of "tags" or associated words. McClelland (1972: 53–59) provides some description of the "theming" process. For example, the "fear theme" consisted of the following "tagged" words: afraid, fear, fright, dread, flinch, and scare(d), scaring (McClelland, et al. 1972: 54, 58). Other thematic concepts were created in a similar manner.

Several "reliability coefficients" created by comparison of frequencies of key word combinations in different halves of the texts were reported (McClelland, et al. 1972: 54–55). But what do they reveal about reliability? Is there any reason why words appearing often in one portion of a folktale collection should match the frequency of the same words in other proportions? Masumura (1972), in a critique of McClelland's work, suggests that these questions become important when considering the sorts of tale collections with which McClelland and his computer were faced. Consider Lessa's collection of *Tales from Ulithi Atoll* (1961) which includes "Tales of animals." Masumura (1972: 18) suggests that word tags occurring often in "tales of beginnings" need not be found frequently in "tales of ogres." Yet thematic analysis demands consistency of this very sort.

The issue of congruence among folktale words, computer frequency tags, and thematic content is very important for McClelland's study of drunkenness. He claims (McClelland, et al. 1966, 1972: 59–71, 78–88) to have retested by folktale themes the drinking theories offered by Horton (1943), Field (1962), Bacon, et al. (1965), Kalin, et al. (1966), Knight (1937), Davis (1964), and MacAndrew and Edgerton (1969). However, he accomplished this by making up key themes for crucial aspects of each of the above mentioned studies. For example, Horton was concerned with "subsistence anxiety" in his theory of drunkenness, so McClelland constructed a "subsistence anxiety theme." Bacon, et al. (1965) were concerned with "dependency" in their theory, so McClelland constructed a "dependency theme." The "dependency theme" subsumed folktale words of "ask," "carry," and "help." But as Masumura (1972) points out, if a folktale had the following phrases — "he asked a question," "he carried wood," and "he helped himself," would the researchers claim that "asked," "carried," and "helped" denoted dependency? Perhaps not; but even if they DID, how would the computer know? What about "subsistence anxiety" that was tagged by words indicating food (e.g. bread, fruit, breakfast), accompanied by words of negation (e.g. no, not, never)? These examples point to questionably constructed themes and possible invalid taggings.

For McClelland's interpretations to be correct, one must be convinced that the computer analysis of folktale words means what he suggests that it means, and that it collectively measures the themes he suggests it collectively measures. Abrahams (1971), Bauman (1969) and Ben-Amos (1971) recently have reviewed the debate current among folklorists on these very same problems.

In somewhat smaller hologeistic studies involving thematic analysis of folktales, more control over meaning has been evident (Wright 1954; Child, et al. 1957; McClelland and Friedman 1952). In Wright's study, for example, he read tales for aggressiveness, coding each society's collections separately. Then he made comparisons between aggressiveness in myth and in real life (Wright 1954: 523). Clearly, his careful subjective and objective analysis of the relationships between aggressive themes and aggressive acts surpasses the aforementioned computer content analysis technique. His control over meaning was more direct.

Surely, in the computer style analysis of McClelland's group, the meaningful connections of words to "themes" is less clear.

The issue of meaning and function of folktales in society is a central problem to cross-cultural studies that use them. But the problem of meaning in folktales is not new. Boas (1897, 1916, 1940) devoted much effort to show that folktale materials are ethnographically rich but difficult to interpret. In his classic "Tsimshian mythology" (Boas 1916: 880), he reminds us that "It is true enough that these tales are not directly taken from everyday experience: that they are rather contradictory to it." He also stated that "mythological narratives and mythological concepts should not be equalized; for social, psychological, and historical conditions affect both in different ways" (Boas 1948: 450). Boas, of course, must be credited with the important discovery that, for the Northwest Coast peoples in America, folktales do reflect SOME aspects of real life (Lévi-Strauss 1967: 20).

Fischer's (1963: 236, 239, 244–245, 256–257) masterful review of social and psychological functions of folktales in culture repeatedly warns that the function, structure, content, and context of folktales is highly variable. He points out, for example, that tales are full of disguised symbolism. There are good reasons for disguising moral guidelines behind a façade of symbolic rhetoric. For example, Fischer (1963: 244) suggests that social conditions often warrant the use of metaphor (as in folktales) rather than direct public sanction. Direct sanction could aggravate social or individual psychological conflict, whereas folktale telling might not. One wonders about folktales told during drinking bouts.

Claude Lévi-Strauss (1967: 20), a leading interpreter of myth, also cautions against simplistic one-to-one correlations between folktales and ongoing behavior. He sees myths as somewhat related to observed behavior, but argues that myths are not mere "representations" of behavior. He argues that myths can present the very opposite of reality, especially when the myth expresses a negative truth. For example, he (1967: 29) points out the disjunction between mythical post-marital residence (patrilocal) versus real post-marital residence (matrilocal) in the Asdiwal myth. He (1967: 30ff) further suggests that such oppositions in myths impart important messages to kin-based groupings who may be in reciprocal alliances.

Along similar lines, Douglas (1967: 63) and Fischer (1963: 287) point out that poetry and myths that are famous obtain their reputation because they can be enjoyed in many ways. What makes them so enjoyable is the inclusion of words that are richly polysemic. In other words, the best words (thoughts) are AMBIGUOUS. On this point, Lévi-Strauss would probably concur. He advocates the position that inverted imagery is transformed not only variably but easily in mythological context, but that such transformations are key processes in a culture's worldview.

The point of this discussion is that McClelland's high dependence on word occurrence in folktales is risky. There is little assurance that the folktales analyzed by computer in his study were the most frequently told tales, were representative of the tales told, were or were not told in drinking settings. More importantly, the validity of "themes" from folktales, purporting to characterize mental sets in culture, is questionable. The meanings of words used to generate "themes" may have even had opposite meanings. The functions of folktales, while plausible in terms of the purposes McClelland claims for them in general, are not convincingly demonstrated.

If the above arguments are reasonably correct, then what light do they shed about the correlations McClelland reports? Do they support or discredit any of the theories on drunkenness offered so far?

The current study on drunkenness gives us reason to be skeptical about some of McClelland's interpretations. The problem is not with his theory, but with his use of folktale evidence. He has not been convincing on folktale indicators concerning "subsistence anxiety," "dependency," or "fear." His "dung" or "excrement," plus "fear" or "negation" tags for the "anal socialization anxiety theme" stretch the imagination to the extreme (McClelland, et al. 1972: 58–59).

It follows that his contentions about the inadequacies of Horton's subsistence anxiety hypothesis, Bacon, Barry and Child's dependency conflict hypothesis, and his support of Field's restatement of Horton's anxiety "fear" hypothesis are all questionable.

This study can only indirectly challenge the arguments of McClelland, et al. (1972: 58–59) about Bacon, Barry and Child's dependency conflict hypothesis since the relationships between variables in this study and child-training variables in Bacon, et al. (1965) were not directly studied. However, this study did have an indirect measure of dependency conflict, as discussed by Davis (1964) and Bacon, et al. (1965). They suggested that matrilocal family settings influence maladjusted adult life leading to alcoholism. Matrilocality was, in part, measured by the mother-daughter dyad type in our family structure codings. Three of the four societies so coded had drunken brawling absent, while two of these societies were rated as rarely drunk. The third society did not have brawls, and men tended to drink in moderation. The fourth society that was coded as a mother-daughter type did brawl and drink excessively (Schaefer 1973: 200). These indirect indicators and associations with measures of drunkenness are encouraging to dependency conflict theorists such as Bacon, Barry, and Child, and Davis. Thus the findings of this study do indirectly challenge McClelland's folktale findings on dependency conflict theory.

To sum up, the current study provides strong support for the anxiety, or powerlessness reduction hypothesis for extreme drunkenness: (1) in the form of numerous correlations between key social, political, and extreme and aggressive measures of drunkenness, and (2) in the form of correlations between fear of supernatural spirits and extreme and aggressive measures of drunkenness. The latter relationship directly reverses the presumption raised by Field (1962) that fear and drunkenness are in no way related. The presumption raised by McClelland, et al. (1966, 1972) that "thematic fear" from folktales and extreme drunkenness are negatively related is also disproved. It is argued that "thematic fear" from folktales may be questionably derived. But even if it is accurately derived and indicative of themes important in the culture, fear in folktales may be therapeutic rather than anxiety provoking (in line with Spiro). Moreover, folktales with fear themes may not provide impact of the sort that fear of real or imagined harm brings to the minds of those who drink. In fact, this study suggests that fear of supernatural spirits is functionally linked with extreme and aggressive forms of drunkenness because men tend to drink to feel stronger.

It is further suggested that political organization is one of the best predictors of aggressive drunkenness. Where men drink and the political organization is not ramified above the local level, political leaders have difficult times maintaining law and order. It is suggested that there tends to be no regular control maintained over instances of drunken brawling in such cases. The political organization and the degree of authority maintained by the political leader(s) are minimal among small-scale societies where drinking and brawling are associated. It is suggested that these political factors increase men's anxieties or need for personalized power. These findings (Schaefer 1973: 147–162, 174–182) are in contrast to McClelland (1972: 68) and Wanner (1972: 90), although our conclusions draw heavily from their power-related restatement of Horton's anxiety reduction hypothesis.

MILD DRUNKENNESS

People who are in anxious or powerless sociocultural conditions drink excessively. Conversely, people in other sociocultural conditions, where feelings of anxieties or power drives are satisfied, do not drink excessively. This is the argument behind Field's "solidarity and respect" theory of sobriety (1962). More specifically, Field (1962: 53–72) suggested that people in tightly knit societies, that are maintained in a spirit of respect for authority, tend to drink moderately and behave passively when drunk.

Up to now, no one had directly tested Field's solidarity and respect notion for sobriety. Field had generalized from numerous correlates of social structure and drunkenness. He himself had made no direct tests of his hypothesis. This study looked for evidence of a relationship between respectful intrafamilial structure, sentiment, and mild drunkenness, and a relationship between respectful ancestral spirit beliefs and mild drunkenness. In addition, a search for other correlates of mild drunkenness was conducted using previously coded materials.

FAMILY STRUCTURE, SENTIMENT, AND SOBRIETY   Hsu (1965, 1966, 1969a, 1969b, 1972) provided an intriguing hypothesis about the influence of family structure and sentiment on cultural patterns. He suggested that elementary dyadic relationship within the family, conditioned by predominant behavioral interactions, strongly influenced nonfamily behavior. Early in this study of drunkenness, it was found that Hsu's ideas lent themselves conveniently to an elaboration of Field's hypothesis about respect and sobriety. Even Hsu (1969a: 95) suggested, for example, that the husband-wife dyad (structure), conditioned by various qualitative interactions (content-sentiment), might be interconnected with some social patterns like drunkenness. It was suggested that qualitative attributes of discontinuity, exclusiveness, sexuality, egalitarianism, and independence that characterized husband-wife dyads would likely be found in association with high rates of alcoholism. Many other similar associations were made relating other behavior patterns with other family structure(s) and sentiment (Hsu 1969a; Tatje and Hsu 1969).

In the previous discussion of extreme drunkenness, it was noted that the study of the linkage between the husband-wife dyad, its purported qualitative attributes, and extreme drunkenness did not correlate as expected. Intercoder reliability on many of these traits was high but none of the correlations was statistically significant. That the key correlation patterns were in the predicted direction and insignificance levels relatively low ($p < 0.25$) does not suggest conclusively that something of interest was demonstrated. The most damning evidence was the total lack of adherence between qualitative attributes and the husband-wife dyad (see below). It was initially thought that dyad dominance patterns would be determined in part by the qualitative conditions specified as typifying the behavioral interactions in the family. If the intrafamilial behavior was characterized by exclusive, independent, sexual, volitional, and egalitarian person-to-person interaction, it was thought that the typical dominant dyad would be the husband-wife dyad. Independent codings of the dyads and the specified qualitative attributes did not verify the expectation. There were some coding difficulties. Dyad attribute codes were not highly reliable, but dyad dominance codes were highly reliable. Neither linked well with drunkenness.

In line with Hsu (1969a: 90–95), it was argued that the father-son dyad and associated qualitative interactions were the reverse of the husband-wife dyad. This point led to the suggestion that the father-son dyad would probably provide social conditions typical of sober societies in line with Field.

Sober societies are thought to minimize lengthy feelings of anxiety or powerlessness, thereby reducing the need to drink. The father-son dyad type, as characterized by Hsu, was quite reminiscent of the picture Field (1962) and McClelland, et al. (1966, 1972) presented of sober societies. They had suggested that tightly knit societies, tempered by traditions of continuity and respect, would use alcohol moderately.

The use of Hsu's dyad hypothesis made the theoretical interconnections with drunkenness seem quite plausible. The matter of evidence, as with husband-wife dyads, however, raised several problems. What is father-son dyad dominance? How does one measure it? How reliable are the indicators used?

In order to adequately answer these questions, considerable time was spent constructing coding schedules for ethnographic analysis by independent coders. The task was not merely to code husband-wife or father-son dyad dominance patterns, but to search out intrafamily structural dominance patterns present in the family in each of the sample societies coded. In the end, the coders carefully read ethnographic passages on family behavior, characterizing briefly the diversity of interactions for the typical family. After exhausting the ethnographies for this material, a judgment was made on which dyad or dyads were most important in family affairs. The coders used their reduced behavioral characterizations in judging stipulated qualitative behavioral attributes. The reduced passages were read and a recording was made as to whether the qualitative relationships focused upon more inclusive rather than exclusive, sexual or asexual, dominant or egalitarian, continous or discontinuous, dependent or independent.

For coding dyad and attribute types, dependence had to be placed upon the ethnographer's descriptions of family life. Judgments were highly influenced by the ethnographer's emphasis on family matters. Any errors on his part magnified our coding errors; however, the three independent coders (the writer was one) agreed substantially on the two theoretically interesting dyad types (husband-wife and father-son), and data quality checks failed to support rival hypotheses concerning systematic bias among ethnographers.

Systematic bias among the coders was controlled for by using two independent coders that did not know the hypothesis. Although I attempted to remain objective there is a possibility that my codes systematically favored the variables of interest to my theory. That is, when doubt arose concerning a dyad dominance pattern, it was probably called a husband-wife dyad dominance or a father-son dominance type rather than some other theoretically unlinked dyad type. Evidence of this bias shows up in the intracoder correlation matrices (Schaefer 1973: 148–153, Tables 16, 17, and 18). Correlations between the writer's husband-wife dyad dominance type and extreme drunkenness are relatively high compared to the unbiased coders (0.35 contrasted to -0.08 and 0.087 for coders B and F, respectively). But in the father-son dyad dominance type and mild drunkenness correlations all coders did not diverge much from each other (-0.12 and -0.35, -0.12 and -0.08, and -0.19 and -0.24). This might suggest that while the writer might have been favoring certain societies with father-son types — and with mild drunkenness types — the independent coders were too. And they did not know that this pattern WAS favorable to the general theory.

It must be noted that systematically using societies "known" to be extreme or mild drinkers in terms of particular dyad dominance patterns was highly unlikely. In the first place, the coding on drunkenness was done quite apart from the dyad, attribute, and spirit belief coding process. Secondly, fifty-seven societies were so carefully studied in the coding process that, without deliberately looking ahead of time to see what codings were present on the key variables, one could not recall what drinking pattern, what dyad pattern, what attribute pattern, or what spirit belief pattern was present. The procedure of not looking at coding that was completed was strictly followed. Data reduction began after all coding work was done.

Codings for dyad types were reliable in four instances (father-son, husband-wife, brother-sister, and parent-child). But the codings for dyad attributes were unreliable. The only dyad linked qualitative attribute that was consistent across independent coders was "dominance" and the father-son dyad type.

The encouraging results of the husband-wife and extreme drunkenness test have already been noted. The father-son and extreme drunkenness linkage was negative and statistically significant. While the supporting qualitative evidence, save "dominance," is not too encouraging, it suggested that the linkage found between the father-son dyad dominance type and extreme drunkenness is theoretically interesting.

It may be inferred that family patterns dominated by the father-son dyad engender respect and continuity of tradition and tend to deter drunkenness. In line with Hsu (1972: 516–524) it may be suggested that father-son dyad systems facilitate general respect for and adherence to extra familiar authority. And, in line with Field (1962), Young (1965), and McClelland, et al. (1972), it may be suggested that father-son dyad type systems are characteristic of those situations that presumably engender the loyalty and cooperation essential for managing complex agricultural societies. Loyalty, obedience, cooperation, respect for authority, continuity of tradition, all of these and probably others, too, make demands on agricultural peoples to have tightly knit social structures.

From Field and McClelland, it follows that these societies are more likely to encourage less drinking. Indeed, it was found that other correlates of mild drunkenness were agricultural technology, fixed settlement patterns, complex division of labor, complex political systems, social class distinction, and high social complexity. Correlates of the father-son dyad were not as numerous or as dramatic in statistical significance. Only mild drunkenness, complex division of labor, and unilineal descent were linked to any significant degree. So, while the numerous other culture traits correlated well with the new codings on drunkenness, they did not do as well with the new coding on intrafamilial structure and sentiment.

The findings on agricultural societies, their social structure, political and economic systems, and absence of extreme drunkenness, closely parallel the findings of others in hologeistic studies on drunkenness: Field (1962: 53, 55, 61), Davis (1964), Barry, et al. (1965, 71–74), McClelland, et al. (1966: 326, 1972: 65), Wanner (1972: 90), and Textor 1967: FC 476/44, 51, 188, 437).

SUPERNATURAL RESPECT AND SOBRIETY   Another aspect of the respect and solidarity hypothesis for mild drunkenness proposed by Field

(1962) was examined in this study, namely, the belief in rewarding and punishing ancestral spirits.

It was expected that this aspect of "respect" would parallel closely the notion of respect and inhibition that McClelland, et al. (1966, 1972) suggested characterized the world view of sober societies. McClelland's primary evidence again was from thematic analysis of folktales. He indicated (McClelland, et al. 1972: 71) that folktale themes of "respect" and "inhibition" correlated well with measures of mild drunkenness. His "respect" theme consisted of the tags: "title," "fear(!)," and "anger." His "inhibition" theme consisted of the tags: "activity inhibition," "old and dead," "fish," and "eating" markers. The numerous objections that might be raised concerning the meaningful connections between the word tags and the cultural themes need not be reiterated. Suffice it to say that the evidence is questionable.

As an indicator of respect, the current study used the belief in rewarding and punishing spirits. It was thought that where people believed that their dead ancestors remained active in the affairs of the living, and where such activity focused upon proper moral behavior, people would not drink excessively. In line with Horton, Field, and Spiro, it was thought that if people drank to relieve anxiety, and if they lived in a tightly knit social structure, then their need to drink to gain personalized power would be lessened by the influence of a protective yet exacting supernatural spirit. Beliefs in spirits that were rewarding and punishing them would help people to overthrow their momentary feelings of anxiety and powerlessness. Overcoming these feelings is the key to sobriety according to Field and McClelland.

The findings were disappointing. No support was found for the expected relationship between beliefs in respectful ancestral spirits and mild drunkenness. The correlations were in the predicted directions but statistically insignificant.

These findings could be interpreted as disproving the solidarity and respect model for sobriety as proposed by Field (1962) and as supported by McClelland, et al. (1966, 1972). However, the indicator of "respect" — for supernatural beings in this case — may not have been general enough.

Agricultural societies have complex religions. Many studies have shown the diverse nature of religion where permanent towns and cities are supported by agricultural technology, and where tightly knit social, economic, and political institutions are present. Such societies include beliefs in inactive (otiose) gods, active yet unapproachable gods, and varieties of ancestral spirits as well as lesser spirits (Tylor 1871;

Swanson 1960; Textor 1967; Tatje and Hsu 1969; Otterbein 1972).

Singling out a specific belief in ancestral spirits as indicative of a general trend of respect in agricultural worldview was probably inadequate.

This short-sighted approach to worldview in agricultural societies might have been misleading. To check on a more appropriate interpretation of the findings for spirit beliefs, cross checks were run with precoded data on high gods (Swanson 1960; Murdock 1967). Averaged codings for belief in rewarding and punishing ancestral spirits and in active high gods were negatively correlated ($\emptyset = -0.34$, $X^2 = 3,93$, $p < 0.05$, $N = 34$, $Df = 1$). So, where people construed their ancestral spirits as rewarding and punishing, they failed to have active high gods as supplementary beliefs. But those societies having a belief in high gods that were active in moral affairs of the people tended to drink and brawl to a lesser extent than those societies with inactive (otiose) gods ($\emptyset = 0.30$, $X^2 = 3.12$, $p < 0.10$, $N = 34$, $Df = 1$).

To sum up, a new test for Field's solidarity and respect hypothesis for sobriety was attempted using what was presumed to be an indicator of "supernatural respect." A low correlation was found between rewarding and punishing ancestral spirit beliefs and measures of mild drunkenness. At the surface, this finding appeared to disprove Field's hypothesis. However, upon further consideration, it was thought that the study of ancestral spirit beliefs alone was inadequate to test the general sobriety hypothesis. It is apparent that in complex agricultural societies world view is diverse. In fact, when rewarding and punishing ancestral spirit codes were correlated with codes of active high gods, a significant negative finding emerged. Moreover, when codes for high gods that were believed to be active in the moral affairs of the living were correlated with codes for mild drunkenness, a finding just short of the 5 percent significance level emerged.

The ancestral-spirits/high-god comparison suggests that among agricultural peoples supernatural beliefs need not be parallel. Spirits may be used for some purposes, high gods for others. It may also be tentatively suggested that among agricultural peoples active spirits have less influence with regard to drunkenness than active high gods do.

On balance, Field's solidarity and respect hypothesis appears to be tentatively supported by the tests concerning "respectful" world view.

SUMMARY

The most striking findings of this study were new correlations established between supernatural beliefs and drunkenness, and between family structure and drunkenness. In addition, strong support was found for several previously suggested hypotheses by correlating newly coded variables with previously coded data.

The correlations between fearful and capricious supernatural spirits and extreme and aggressive drunkenness strongly support the theory that people who are anxious drink excessively (Horton) or that people who are in unpredictable situations that leave them feeling powerless drink excessively (McClelland). On the other hand, the finding regarding father-son family structure dominance and absence of extreme drunkenness strongly supports the theory that people who have their needs for power socialized through a network of relations modeled on the father-son authority structure of the family tend to control their alcohol consumption to moderate or rare episodes (Field).

Other supportive evidence generated by this study included strong correlations between simple political systems and extreme aggressive drunkenness, and complex political systems and peaceful sobriety. Other technological, social, and religious factors also aligned with the general anxiety or powerlessness reduction hypothesis for explaining alcohol behavior.

With the new evidence on fearful, unpredictable supernatural spirits and excessive drunkenness in hand, an attempt was made to see connections between the body of theory on drunkenness and the body of theory on culture stress (cf. Naroll 1962). Spiro (1961: 820–824) suggested that a belief in fearful spirits could be an efficient way to cope with ingroup hostilities. He noted that there could be many structural arrangements whose function is to displace overt or covert ingroup hostility. He suggested that witchcraft, sorcery, and gossip have similar functions in this regard. Likewise, this study suggests that drunkenness may be an alternative displacement activity. Drunkenness, like other safety valve mechanisms, is not fail-safe. This is clear since it has been shown that fearful supernatural beliefs are linked with drunkenness. In terms of adaptation to stress, it may be that societies with projective systems such as fearful supernatural beliefs have an effective means for diffusing rising anxieties among their members. In other societies, it may be that the fearful and unpredictable supernatural spirits exacerbate the spiraling levels of anxiety, and so, the members of the society might turn to sorcery, witchcraft, gossip, or drunkenness. Each of these practices has its social costs. Some adaptations are less likely to cause physical harm or destruction of reputations of individuals or groups within the society. The spiral of anxiety or feeling of powerlessness may be temporarily, or even permanently, alleviated by a counter-spiral of cultural practices.

Drunkenness can provide a great release from various sources of anxiety; but it can also lead to physical violence. It has been suggested that where the political system is simple, where political leaders may have a poor following, and where such leaders have little control over information that might be useful in regulating political action, anxiety, or a feeling of powerlessness is great and extreme, aggressive drunkenness is highly likely. Under these circumstances, aggressive activities among drunkards cannot be controlled. On the other hand, where political leaders have their political organization well attuned to the needs of people, and where the social structure provides a variety of achievable statuses and roles, anxiety will tend to be low, and feelings about personal power will tend to be reinforced, and extreme, aggressive drunkenness will be highly unlikely. Under these circumstances, aggressive acts among all peoples, drunk or not, will tend to be controlled.

REFERENCES

ABRAHAMS, R. D.
  1971   Personal power and social restraint. *Journal of American Folklore* 84:16–30.
BACON, M., H. BARRY, III., I. CHILD
  1965   A cross-cultural study of drinking. *Quarterly Journal of Studies on Alcohol*, supplement 3:29–48.
BANTON, M., *editor*
  1966   *Anthropological approaches to the study of religion*. London: Tavistock.
BARRY, H., III, M. K. BACON, I. CHILD
  1965   A cross-cultural study of drinking. *Quarterly Journal of Studies on Alcohol*, supplement 3.
BAUMAN, R.
  1969   Towards a behavioral theory of folklore. *Journal of American Folklore* 84:3–15.
BEN-AMOS, D.
  1971   Toward a definition of folklore in context. *Journal of American Folklore* 82:167–170.
BENNETT, W. C., R. M. ZINGG
  1935   *The Tarahumara: an Indian tribe of northern Mexico*. Chicago: University of Chicago Press.
BISHOP, D. L.
  1898   *Korea and her neighbors*. New York: F. H. Revell.

BOAS, F.
1897   "The social organization and secret societies of the Kwakiutl In-
       dians, in *Report of the United States National Museum for 1895*,
       311–378. Washington: United States Printing Office.
1916   "Tsimshian mythology," in *United States Bureau of American
       Ethnology. Thirty-first annual report*, 43–881. Washington: Uni-
       ted States Printing Office.
1948   *Race, language and culure*. New York: Macmillan.

BOGORAS, W.
1904–1909   *The Chukchee*. Leiden: E. J. Brill.

BOURGUIGNON, E.
1972   "Dreams and altered states of consciousness in anthropological
       research," in *Psychological anthropology* (second edition). Edited
       by F. L. K. Hsu. Cambridge: Schenkman.

CHILD, I. L., T. STORM, J. VEROFF
1957   "Achievement themes in folktales related to socialization prac-
       tices." Unpublished manuscript, Yale University, New Haven.

COLBY, B. N., G. A. COLLIER, S. K. POSTAL
1963   Comparison of themes in folktales by the general inquirer system.
       Journal of American Folklore 76:318–323.

D'ANDRADE, R.
1961   "Anthropological studies of dreams," in *Psychological anthropol-
       ogy*. Edited by F. L. K. Hsu. Hometown: Dorsey Press.

DAVIS, W. N.
1964   "A cross-cultural study of drunkenness." Unpublished A.B. thesis,
       Harvard University, Cambridge.

DENTON, R. K.
1968   *The Semai: a non-violent people*. New York: Holt, Rinehart and
       Winston.

DOUGLAS, M.
1967   "The meaning of myth with special reference to La Geste d'As-
       diwal," in *The structural study of myth and totemism*. Edited by
       E. Leach. London: Tavistock.

FIELD, PETER B.
1962   "A new cross-cultural study of drunkenness," in *Society, culture,
       and drinking patterns*. Edited by D. J. Pittman and C. R. Snyder.
       New York: J. Wiley and Sons.

FISCHER, J. L.
1963   The sociopsychological analysis of folktales. *Current Anthropol-
       ogy* 4:234–296.

FREUD, S.
1936   *The problem of anxiety*. Translated by H. A. Bunker. New York.

FRIENDLY, J.
1956   "A cross-cultural study of ascetic mourning behavior." Unpublished
       manuscript, Department of Social Relations, Radcliffe College,
       Cambridge.

GUTHRIE, G. M.
1971   Unexpected correlations and the cross cultural method. *Journal
       of Cross-Cultural Psychology* 2:315–323.

HALLOWELL, A. I.
1941 The social function of anxiety in a primitive society. *American Sociological Review* 6:869–880.
1967 *Culture and experience.* New York: Schocken.

HENRY, J.
1941 *Jungle people.* New York: Vintage Books.

HOLMBERG, A. R.
1950 *Nomads of the long bow: the Siriono of eastern Bolivia.* Smithsonian Institutions, Institute of Social Anthropology Publication 10. Washington: Government Printing Office.

HORTON, D.
1943 The functions of alcohol in primitive societies: a cross-cultural study. *Quarterly Journal of Studies on Alcohol* 4:199–320.

HUMAN RELATIONS AREA FILES
1967 The Human Relations Area Files quality control sample universe. *Behavior Science Notes* 2:81–88.

HSU, F. L. K.
1959 Structure, function, content and process. *American Anthropologist* 61:790–805.
1965 The effect of dominant kinship relationships on kin and non-kin behavior: a hypothesis. *American Anthropologist* 67:638–661.
1966 Rejoinder: a link between kinship structure and psychological anthropology. *American Anthropologist* 68:999–1004.
1969a *The study of literate civilization.* New York: Holt, Rinehart and Winston.
1969b *Japanese kinship and iemoto.* Tokyo: Baifufan.
1972 "Kinship and ways of life: an exploration," in *Psychological Anthropology* (second edition). Edited by F. L. K. Hsu. Cambridge: Schenkman.

HSU, F. L. K., *editor*
1971 *Kinship and culture.* Chicago: Aldine.

KALIN, R., W. N. DAVIS, D. C. MC CLELLAND
1966 "The relationship between use of alcohol and thematic content of folktales in primitive societies," in *The general inquirer: a computer approach to content analysis.* Edited by P. J. Stone, et al., 568–688. Cambridge: M.I.T. Press.

KARSTEN, R.
1932 *Indian tribes of the Argentine and Bolivia Chaco.* Helsingfors: Akademische Buchhandlung.

KLAUSNER, S. Z.
1964 Sacred and profane meanings of blood and alcohol. *Journal of Social Psychology* 64:27–43.

KLUCKHOHN, C.
1944 *Navaho witchcraft.* Papers of the Peabody Museum 22. Cambridge: Harvard University.

KNIGHT, R. P.
1937 The dynamics and treatment of chronic alcohol addiction. *Bulletin of the Menninger Clinic* 1:233.

KOBBEN, A.
1952   New ways of presenting an old idea: the statistical method in social anthropology. *Journal of the Royal Anthropological Institute of Great Britain and Ireland* 82:129–146.

1967   Why exceptions? The logic of cross-cultural comparison. *Current Anthropology* 8:3–34.

LAMBERT, W. W., L. M. TRIANDIS, M. WOLF
1959   Some correlates of beliefs in the malevolence and benevolence of supernatural beings: a cross-societal study. *Journal of Abnormal Social Psychology* 58:162–169.

LEE, R. B.
1968   "What hunters do for a living: or, how to make out on scarce resources," in *Man the hunter*. Edited by R. B. Lee and I. Devore. Chicago: Aldine.

LESSA, W. A.
1961   *Tales from Ulithi Atoll*. Folklore Studies 13. Berkeley and Los Angeles: University of California Press.

LESTER, D.
1966   Antecedents of the fear of the dead. *Psychological Reports* 119: 741–742.

LÉVI-STRAUSS, C.
1963   "The structural study of myth," in *Structural anthropology*. Edited by C. Lévi-Stauss. New York: Basic Books.

1965   "The future of kinship studies," in *Proceedings of the Royal Anthropological Institute*, 13–22.

1967   "The story of the Asdiwal," in *The structural study of myth and totemism*. Edited by E. Leach. London: Tavistock.

LEWIS, O.
1956   Comparisons in cultural anthropology, in *Readings in cross-cultural methodology*. Edited by F. Moore. New Haven: Human Relations Area Files Press.

LOWIE, R. H.
1924   *Primitive religion*. New York: Boni and Liveright.

MAC ANDREW, C., R. B. EDGERTON
1969   *Drunken comportment: a social explanation*. Chicago: Aldine.

MALINOWSKI, B.
1948   *Magic, science and religion and other essays*. Glencoe: Free Press.

MASUMURA, W. T.
1972   *Folktales and drunkenness: a critique of McClelland's The drinking man*. Missoula: University of Montana.

MC CLELLAND, D. C., W. N. DAVIS, R. KALIN, E. WANNER, *editors*
1972   *The drinking man*. New York: Free Press.

MC CLELLAND, D. C., W. N. DAVIS, E. WANNER, R. KALIN
1966   A cross-cultural study of folktale content and drinking. *Sociometry* 29:308–333.

MC CLELLAND, D. C., G. A. FRIEDMAN
1952 "A cross-cultural study of the relationship between child training practices and achievement motivation appearing in folktales," in *Readings in social psychology*. Edited by G. E. Swanson, et al., 243–249. New York: Holt.

MC KINLEY, R.
1971 A critique of the reflectionist theory of kinship terminology. *Man*, new series 6:228–247.

MOWRER, O. H.
1939 *A stimulus response analysis of anxiety and its role as a reinforcing agent*. Psychological Review 46.

MURDOCK, G. P., *editor*
1967 *Ethnographic atlas*. Pittsburgh: University of Pittsburgh Press.

MURDOCK, G. P., D. R. WHITE
1969 Standard cross-cultural sample. *Ethnology* 8:329–369.

NAROLL, R.
1962 *Data quality control*. New York: Free Press.
1964 On ethnic unit classification. *Current Anthropology* 5:283–312.
1970a What have we learned from cross-cultural surveys? *American Anthropologist* 72:1227–1288.
1970b "The culture bearing unit in cross-cultural surveys," in *A handbook of method in cultural anthropology*, 721–765. Edited by R. Naroll and R. Cohen. New York: The Natural History Press.
1971 The double language boundary. *Behavior Science Notes* 6:95–102.
1972 *Program phi. Tapes, decks for CDC 6400*. New York: SUNY/Buffalo.

NEEDHAM, R.
1954 Siriono and Penan: a test of some hypotheses. *Southwestern Journal of Anthropology* 10:228–236.

OPLER, M. K., *editor*
1965 *Culture and mental health*. New York: Whiting.

OTTERBEIN, K. F.
1970 *The evolution of war: a cross-cultural study*. New Haven: Human Relations Area Files Press.
1972 *Comparative cultural analysis*. New York: Holt, Rinehart and Winston.

OTTERBEIN, K. F., C. S. OTTERBEIN
1965 An eye for an eye, a tooth for a tooth: a cross-cultural study of feuding. *American Anthropology* 67:1470–1482.

ROHNER, R., R. PELTO
1970 Sampling methods: Chaney and Ruiz Revilla comment, No. 2. *American Anthropologist* 72:1453–1456.

SCHAEFER, J. M.
1972 "Galton's problem in a holocultural study on drunkenness." Paper presented at the 71st Annual Meeting of the American Anthropological Association, Toronto.
1973 "A hologeistic study of family structure and sentiment, supernatural beliefs and drunkenness." Unpublished manuscript. SUNY/Buffalo.

SCHAPERA, I.
1953   Some comments on comparative method in social anthropology. *American Anthropologist* 55:353–361.

SHADE, C. I.
1948   *The outside man and his relation to Aleut culture.* Cambridge: Harvard University Press.

SIEGEL, S.
1956   *Non-parametric statistics for the behavioral sciences.* New York: McGraw-Hill.

SIPES, R. G.
1972   Rating hologeistic method. *Behavior Science Notes* 7:157–198.

SPIRO, M. E.
1953   Ghosts: an anthropological inquiry into learning and perception. *Journal of Abnormal and Social Psychology* 48:376–382.

1959   "Culture heritage, personal tensions, and mental illness in a South Sea culture," in *Culture and mental health.* Edited by Marvin K. Opler. New York: Macmillan.

1961   Sorcery, evil spirits, and functional analysis: a rejoinder. *American Anthropologist* 63:820–824.

1965a   "Ghosts, Ifaluk, and teleological functionalism," in *Reader in comparative religion.* Edited by W. A. Lessa and E. Z. Vogt, 432–436. New York: Harper and Row.

1965b   "Mental illness in a South Sea culture: Ifaluk," in *Culture and mental health.* Edited by M. K. Opler. New York: Macmillan.

1972   An overview and a suggested reorientation," in *Psychological anthropology.* Edited by F. L. K. Hsu, 573–607. Cambridge: Schenkman.

SPIRO, M. E., R. G. D'ANDRADE
1958   A cross-cultural study of some supernatural beliefs. *American Anthropologist* 60:456–466.

STONE, P. S., O. C. DUNPHY, M. S. SMITH, D. M. OGILVIE, *editors*
1966   *The general inquirer: a computer approach to content analysis.* Cambridge: M.I.T. Press.

SWANSON, G. E.
1960   *Birth of the gods: the origin of primitive beliefs.* Ann Arbor: University of Michigan Press.

TATJE, T. A., F. L. K. HSU
1969   Variations in ancestor worship beliefs and their relation to kinship. *Southwestern Journal of Anthropology* 25:153–172.

TEXTOR, R. B.
1967   *A cross-cultural summary.* New Haven: Human Relations Area Files Press.

THOMAS, L. M.
1965   *The harmless people.* New York: Random House.

TYLOR, E. B.
1871   *Primitive culture: researches into the development of mythology, philosophy, religion, language, art, and custom.* New York: Holt.

VAN VELSEN, T., W. VAN WETERING
  1960 Residence, power groups, and intrasocietal aggression. *International Archives of Ethnography* 49:169–200.
WALLACE, A. F. C.
  1972 *The death and rebirth of the Seneca.* New York: Random House.
WANNER, E.
  1972 "Power and inhibition: a revision of the magical potency theory," in *The drinking man.* Edited by D. C. McClelland, et al. New York: Free Press.
WHITING, B. B.
  1950 *Paiute sorcery.* Viking Fund Publications in Anthropology 15.
  1965 Sex identity conflict and physical violence: a comparative study. *American Anthropologist* 57:123–140.
WHITING, J. W. M.
  1959 "Sorcery, sin and the superego: a cross-cultural study of some mechanisms of social control," in *Nebraska Symposium on Motivation.* Edited by M. R. Jones. Lincoln: University of Nebraska Press.
  1964 "Effects of climate on certain cultural practices," in *Explorations in cultural anthropology.* Edited by W. Goodenough, 511–544. New York: McGraw-Hill.
  1967 "Sorcery, sin, and the superego: a cross-cultural study of some mechanisms of social control," in *Cross-cultural approaches.* Edited by C. S. Ford. New Haven: Human Relations Area Files Press.
WHITING, J. W. M., I. CHILD
  1953 *Child training and personality: a cross-cultural study.* New Haven: Yale University Press.
WHITING, J. W. M., R. KLUCKHOHN, A. A. ANTHONY
  1960 "The function of male initiation ceremonies at puberty," in *Readings in social psychology.* Edited by E. E. Macoby, F. M. Newcomb and E. L. Hartley. New York: Wiley.
WRIGHT, G. O.
  1954 Projection and displacement: a cross-cultural study of folktale aggression. *Journal of Abnormal and Social Psychology* 49:523–528.
YOUNG, F. W.
  1965 *Initiation ceremonies: a cross-cultural study of status dramatization.* New York: Bobbs-Merrill.

The Epidemiology of Alcoholism with Specific Reference to Sociocultural Factors

JAN DE LINT

THE PROBLEM OF DEFINING ALCOHOLISM

One of the most difficult tasks in the epidemiology of alcoholism is to try to establish the magnitude of this problem. Various attempts to define alcoholism in a useful and meaningful way, surely a prerequisite to prevalence estimation, have not been too successful. Indeed, the manifestations and consequences of this behavioral disorder, such as the craving for alcohol, the inability to stop drinking at some or at many of the drinking occasions, the repetitive intake of alcohol usually in large quantities, the damage done to health or to society, are all too ambivalent to allow us to identify each and every alcoholic in any given population. How much craving, loss of control under what kind of circumstances, what quantity of alcohol consumed and in what frequency, what kind of damages to health or to society, should define alcoholism? Perhaps the elusive nature of this problem can best be illustrated by the alcohol consumption distribution curve which shows the frequency distribution of all the alcohol consumers in a population according to the quantity of alcohol each of them consumes.

Expressed as a daily average, these individual consumptions range from very small quantities, consumed by many, to near lethal amounts consumed by only a few (see Figure 1; also de Lint 1973).

Within this range each individual consumption level occurs with a certain frequency (see Figure 2).

Thus several drinkers may typically consume up to 1 cl. of absolute alcohol as a daily average. Others may drink between 1 and 2 cl. of absolute alcohol daily, and, again, others, 2 to 3 cl. and so forth.

0   10   20   30   40

Centilitres of absolute alcohol daily

Figure 1.   The range of alcohol consumption

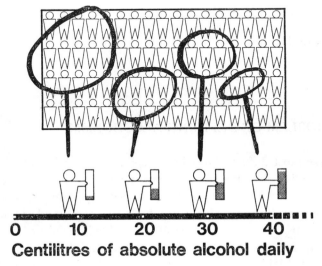

0   10   20   30   40

Centilitres of absolute alcohol daily

Figure 2.

It has been demonstrated for a wide variety of populations that the distribution of these different frequencies tends to be log normal in character and to approximate a rather smooth, skewed curve (Ledermann 1956; de Lint and Schmidt 1968; Mäkelä 1971; de Lint 1973). For example, in a population with an average yearly consumption of 15 liters of absolute alcohol, the distribution curve would be as follows (see Figure 3).

It can be presumed that alcoholics, by almost any definition, are located somewhere in the upper ranges of the alcohol consumption distribution curve. But how can the alcoholics be separated from the nonalcoholics on the basis of average daily alcohol consumption quantities? For example, is a person consuming in excess of a daily average of 15 cl. of absolute alcohol an alcoholic, or must he drink at least 20 cl. to qualify? (See Figure 4.)

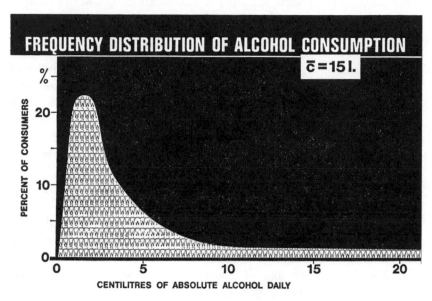

Figure 3.

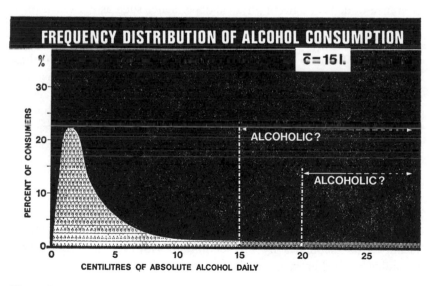

Figure 4.

The results of some investigations of self-reported alcohol consumption behaviors of patients admitted to alcoholism clinics would seem to offer a solution to our dilemma. These findings do suggest that the condition of such patients tends to be associated with a range of alcohol consumption in excess of a daily average of about 15 cl. of absolute alcohol (Lereboullet and Biraben 1964; Lelbach 1966; Schmidt and Popham 1968; Wilkinson, et al. 1969; Lundquist 1972). It follows that a drinker of such quantity is similar in his consumption behavior to a person admitted to an alcoholism clinic. However, the question remains whether such a drinker should be labelled an alcoholic for purposes of prevalence estimation. In my view such a definition would not do sufficient justice to the complexity of the "alcoholism" problem. Specifically, it would not take into account the extent to which other behaviors and conditions, which form part of or are associated with the "alcoholism" problem, are also present. Thus many of the drinkers in the tail-end of the alcohol consumption distribution curve probably have sustained some damage to health as a consequence of their alcohol use; they may exhibit loss of control during some or many of their drinking occasions, may experience family or job problems, may have a tendency to neglect their health and proper nutrition, probably smoke heavily, and may have severe emotional difficulties. In addition, their chronic excessive alcohol consumption very likely resulted in the appearance of certain signs of physical dependence such as increased tolerance to the effects of alcohol and withdrawal symptoms.

The problem of defining drinkers in the tail-end of the distribution curve as alcoholics is further complicated by the fact that many of these behaviors and conditions are present to varying degrees. For instance, at what point can one speak of alcohol-related physical damage, or of loss of control? What is needed before it can be argued that job performance is impaired? When is a person really negligent with respect to this personal health care and nutrition? How are emotional problems defined? Evidently, at lower levels of consumption, drinkers do exhibit fewer of the alcohol-related behaviors and conditions and to a lesser degree than at higher levels of consumption. Indeed, drinkers of very large amounts of alcohol probably exhibit, quite noticeably, many alcohol-related behaviors and conditions and would undoubtedly be identified as alcoholics by any definition. However, at lower levels, as indicated earlier, a great deal of ambiguity exists.

INDIRECT MEASURES OF ALCOHOLISM PREVALENCE

Because of the elusive nature of the "alcoholism" problems, illustrated using the distribution of alcohol consumption model, epidemiologists working in the alcoholism field have found it more useful and meaningful to try to establish rates of excessive alcohol use and rates of alcohol-related mortality rather than rates of "alcoholism." Indeed, for many years, alcohol consumption and alcohol-related mortality statistics have frequently been used as rough indices of the magnitude of the problem of "alcoholism." In Table 1, estimated rates of alcohol consumption in excess of a daily average of 15 cl. of absolute alcohol are shown for a number of countries (de Lint 1973).

Table 1. Rates of excessive alcohol use in a number of countries, 1970

Country	15 cl.*	Country	15 cl.
France	9,050	East Germany	2,760
Italy	7,390	U.S.A.	2,690
Spain	5,350	Yugoslavia	2,680
Luxembourg	5,000	Denmark	2,470
West Germany	4,820	Canada	2,460
Portugal	4,690	Great Britain	2,130
Switzerland	4,420	Sweden	1,990
Czechoslovakia	4,290	Netherlands	1,870
Austria	3,690	Poland	1,870
Belgium	3,650	Republic of Ireland	1,830
Hungary	3,630	Finland	1,500
Australia	3,290	Norway	1,150
New Zealand	3,040		

* Rates of alcohol use in excess of a daily average of 15 cl. of absolute alcohol per 100,000 persons 15 years and older.

With reference to the use of these rates as indices of the magnitude of the "alcoholism" problem, it has been well documented that they do reflect, more or less, the prevalence of many of the behaviors and conditions typically referred to in definitions of "alcoholism," such as certain forms of organic damage and signs of physical dependence (Ledermann 1964a; Lelbach i.p.; de Lint 1973).

However, it should be recognized that relative to the total volume of consumption, there may be noticeable differences in the proportionate occurrence of at least some of the alcohol-related behaviors and conditions, such as loss of control, social damage, and emotional disturbance. Thus the consumption-distribution curve of a low-consumption population (e.g. a population with a daily average of 15 cl. of absolute alcohol) represents a relatively small, and what is more important, an isolated segment of the drinking population (see Figure 5).

In such a population, it would indeed not be surprising that the heavy drinkers are deviant in many other ways as well. In contrast, in a high consumption population (e.g. a population with an average yearly consumption of 25 liters), drinking in excess of a daily average of 15 cl. of absolute alcohol is a much more common behavior, and one would expect many such drinkers to show severe emotional problems or other manifestations of deviance.

In short, whereas rates of excessive alcohol use do tend to reflect rates of alcohol-related health damage and the frequency of signs of physical dependence, the situation is a bit more complicated in the case of conditions such as loss of control, social damage, or emotional disturbance. Relative to the overall volume of alcohol consumption, these conditions may well occur more frequently in populations with low rates of excessive alcohol use as compared to those with high rates.

DRINKING CUSTOMS

In the history of alcoholism research, considerable variation in customary drinking practices has been documented (Popham and Yawney 1967; Heath, this volume). Thus, wines, beers, and distilled spirits may be consumed at meal times, festivals, social gatherings, religious observances, business meetings, and many other occasions. Or they may

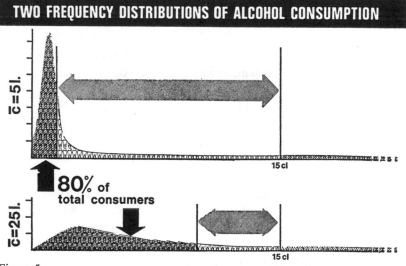

Figure 5.

be taken primarily for their medicinal properties, e.g. to promote sleep, to relax.

Much attention has also focused on the relationship between alcoholism and drinking customs (Bales 1946; Lolli, et al. 1958; Snyder 1958; Popham 1959; Pittman and Snyder 1962). For example, the low prevalence of alcoholism among Jews in North America has been attributed to their strong disapproval of drunkenness and their use of alcoholic beverages in their religious observances (Snyder 1958).

In contrast, the drinking practices of the Irish have been characterized as predominantly utilitarian; for example, the use of liquor to alleviate physical and emotional discomfort (Bales 1946). The allegedly high rates of alcoholism among them have been attributed to this attitude. The Italian custom of drinking with meals (Lolli, et al. 1958) is said to be conducive to a low prevalence of alcoholism, whereas the high rate of alcoholism in France has been attributed to the custom of drinking on many occasions throughout the day.

On the basis of these and similar cross-cultural studies, it has been proposed that certain drinking customs, e.g. drinking wine with meals, are typically associated with LOW rates of alcoholism and are therefore DESIRABLE modes of drinking, and that other drinking customs, e.g. drinking to relieve anxiety, are typically associated with HIGH rates of alcoholism and are therefore UNDESIRABLE modes of drinking (Wilkinson 1970).

However, such a conclusion is not justified for the following reasons: first, the assumed rates of alcoholism for these cultural groups are not always supported by estimates based on alcohol consumption and liver cirrhosis mortality data (see Table 1). In the case of Italy, both of these measures indicate a very extensive alcoholism problem. Conversely, these same measures show that the Irish in Ireland have relatively low rates of alcoholism despite their customary preference for so-called utilitarian drinking.

Second, and most importantly, a description of the relationship between drinking habits on the one hand, and alcoholism on the other, should not ignore an important and consistent epidemiological observation, namely, that alcoholism prevalence rises and falls with the overall level of alcohol consumption in a population (Ledermann 1956; Seeley 1960; de Lint and Schmidt 1971; Popham 1970). Thus, rate variation in alcoholism and alcohol use reflects the extent to which different use patterns are integrated in the lifestyles. Where alcohol use is a rather common and incidental part of everyday life, as in France, rates of alcoholism are high.

Ironically, Ullman (1958: 50) came to a rather different conclusion:

... in any group or society in which the drinking customs, values and sanctions — together with the attitudes of all segments of the group or society — are well established, known to and agreed upon by all, and are consistent with the rest of the culture, the rate of alcoholism will be low.

He goes on to state that:

... under conditions in which the individual drinker does not know what is expected or when the expectation in one situation differs from that in another, it can be assumed that he will have ambivalent feelings about drinking. Thus, ambivalence is the psychological product of unintegrated customs (Ullman 1958: 50).

Evidently, he concluded that it did not matter how often and at how many occasions alcohol is consumed as long as it was customary to do so. In the writer's view, this conclusion is difficult to reconcile with the numerous cross-cultural observations that do exist and particularly those pertaining to the high rates of alcoholism in France, Italy, Portugal, Spain, Chile, etc.

ACCESSIBILITY

An important factor to be considered in addition to the degree of traditional acceptance of various alcohol use patterns in society is the accessibility of beverage alcohol. Again, in countries ranking highest in overall level of alcohol consumption and in rates of alcoholism-related mortality, alcoholic beverages are readily available and quite inexpensive. Indeed, it would be difficult to envisage alcoholic beverages as an incidental part of everyday living if they were expensive and difficult to obtain.

The etiological significance of the accessibility of beverage alcohol in alcoholism is also evident from studies of occupational mortality (Bertillon 1889; Guralnick 1962; Febvay and Aubenque 1957). Rates of death from liver cirrhosis have always been quite high among publicans, waiters, brewery workers, and persons in other occupations where they are much exposed to beverage alcohol.

Finally, access to alcoholic beverages is affected by their cost. As they can be produced and distributed quite inexpensively, variation in price among countries and from period to period depends largely on differences in taxation policies. These policies have a long history. Originally they reflected the concern of legislators over the allegedly high incidence of drunkenness among the working classes during the nineteenth century and early twentieth century (Sariola 1951; Reuss

1959; Coffey 1966). At present, the relatively high taxes on alcoholic beverages in many countries still tend to be considered an important method to control alcoholism and other alcohol problems.

It has been observed that temporal variations in the price of alcohol relative to average disposable income correlate inversely with level of consumption (Sariola 1951; Seeley 1960; Nyberg 1967; Mikolaj 1969; Nielson and Stromgren-Risskov 1969; Walsh and Walsh 1970; Lau 1972). Unfortunately, these investigations usually covered periods during which price relative to income has decreased and consumption has increased. One would like to know whether this relationship would also hold as consistently in a reverse situation, i.e. under a gradual increase of prices. Another difficulty may be that the amount of alcohol taxation, and thus the cost of beverage alcohol, tends to reflect the degree of acceptance of alcohol use. Accordingly, variation in consumption cannot be attributed to differences in the cost factor alone.

URBANISM

In North America, the incidence of liver cirrhosis mortality and therefore of alcoholism rises and falls with the extent of urbanism (Jellinek 1947). This variation may to a certain degree be attributable to reporting artifacts. For example, the quality of diagnostic facilities, rates of autopsy, and the nature of the relationship between the diagnostician and the family of the deceased have been singled out as factors influencing the accuracy of reporting deaths from this cause. However, the observed rural-urban differences in rates of alcoholism are too large to be fully explained by such factors. Rather, they seem to reflect the presence of strong temperance sentiments in many parts of rural North America. In fact, a relatively large proportion of the population in these areas voted against the repeal of Prohibition (Seeley 1962).

A more speculative interpretation refers to the "input-overload" in modern cities. Specifically, it proposes that high population density implies a mutual overstimulation which results in various collective pathologies such as alcoholism (Seeley 1962).

With reference to the latter suggestion, it is important to note that urban-rural differences in alcoholism rates are by no means universal. For example, in France, liver cirrhosis rates and consumption averages do not vary with urbanism (Ledermann 1956). This would suggest that the urban environment *per se* does not necessarily bring about higher rates of alcoholism.

SEX

All available indices of alcohol abuse — liver cirrhosis, mortality, consumption data, drunkenness arrests, and hospital admissions — show a difference between men and women in the prevalence of alcoholism. In Canada and the United States, the ratio is about six males to one female alcoholic (Snyder 1959). Although international differences have been observed in the size of this ratio (Jellinek 1945), the higher rate among males appears to be a general phenomenon. It has been suggested that the difference is a reflection of the double moral standard in Western societies. Thus it is generally less acceptable for a woman to drink heavily than for a man. Particularly, drunkenness among women is regarded with great disapproval.

In view of the apparently fixed relationship between the total volume of alcohol typically commanded in a population and the prevalence of alcoholism, it can be assumed that similar sex differences should be found in per capita consumption. Indeed the results of a number of drinking surveys seem to support this contention (Kuusi 1957; Gadourek 1963; Cahalan, et al. 1969; de Lint, et al. 1970).

STRESS-INDUCING EVENTS

Numerous retrospective studies have documented the apparent etiological significance of parental attention in early childhood, loss of job, and marital difficulties, in alcoholism. Undoubtedly, some sociocultural environments are more conducive to the occurrence of such unfortunate events in one's life, or at least tend to worsen their impact on the individual, than are others. However, one must be careful with the interpretation of life history data. Admission to alcoholism clinics comes at a late stage in a continuous process of selection or drift towards this condition. Certain events taken from a case history may well have no relevance to the inception of alcoholism but may merely represent early phases in the process of becoming an alcoholic. In any event, it would seem rather difficult at the population level to try to explain some of the rate variation in alcoholism on the basis of rate variation in the occurrence of these childhood and adulthood events. It certainly cannot be assumed that such factors as parental deprivation, job loss, or changes in marital status are more common in France, Italy, and Spain than in Norway or Finland (see Table 1). On the other hand, there is no doubt that within a population these factors do affect one's probability of becoming an alcoholic.

THE ISSUE OF PREVENTION

In recent years, rates of excessive alcohol use and alcohol-related mortality have risen sharply in many countries. During the same period, the relaxation of alcohol control measures and increased affluence have made it easier and easier to obtain alcoholic beverages. Figure 6 shows the increase in beer, wine, and distilled spirits consumption from 1960 to 1970 for a number of countries.

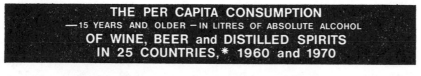

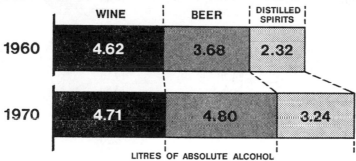

* Italy • Spain • Portugal • W. Germany • E. Germany • Czechoslovakia • Poland Austria • Switzerland • Yugoslavia • Hungary • Denmark • Finland • Norway Sweden • Belgium • Netherlands • Luxembourg • Gt. Britain • Rep. Ireland Canada • USA • Australia • N. Zealand • France

Figure 6.

Increases in the consumption of absolute alcohol per capita, 15 years and older, is illustrated in Table 2.

With the sole exception of France, levels of alcohol use have all risen considerably during this period. As can be expected, this progressive integration of alcohol-use patterns in current lifestyles has significantly increased rates of alcoholism, as indicated by the liver cirrhosis mortality figures in Table 3.

From a public health point of view, it is quite evident that ways must be found to halt or reverse these trends.

In the past, programs of prevention have included prohibition of the sales of alcoholic beverages, control of the number and type of outlets, control of advertising, the taxation of beverage alcohol, and alcohol education.

On the question of prohibition, the late Sully Ledermann (1964b: 1) remarked:

If the quasi-mathematical connection between consumption averages and alcoholism rates cannot be broken, and if one considers as an absolute priority the elimination of alcoholism, there remains no apparent solution other than the suppression of alcohol in all forms in which it is consumed.

Table 2. Total alcoholic beverage consumption per capita 15 years and older in 1950, 1960, and 1970 for a number of countries in liters of absolute alcohol

Country	1950	1960	1970
Australia	7.90	9.50	11.70
Austria	6.30	10.90	13.30
Belgium	10.40	11.70	13.20
Canada	6.60	7.90	9.60
Czechoslovakia	8.70	10.40	14.60
Denmark	5.50	6.10	9.70
East Germany	2.00	7.30	10.50
Finland	3.70	3.90	6.30
France	25.40	27.30	24.00
Hungary	6.80	9.20	13.00
Italy	14.70	19.10	20.70
Luxembourg	N.A.*	13.80	16.20
Netherlands	3.00	3.80	7.80
New Zealand	N.A.*	9.50	11.00
Norway	3.00	3.60	4.40
Poland	4.40	6.20	7.50
Portugal	N.A.*	15.30	13.80
Ireland	4.60	4.90	7.30
Spain	10.50	11.90	16.90
Sweden	6.10	5.90	7.90
Switzerland	10.70	12.60	14.50
Great Britain	6.30	6.80	8.30
U.S.A.	7.70	7.80	9.70
West Germany	4.60	10.20	16.00
Yugoslavia	N.A.*	6.80	10.40

* Not available.

But, a public health program in the field of alcohol problems cannot ignore many of the benefits associated with alcohol consumption. Indeed, many drinking habits, such as the OCCASIONAL use of beverage alcohol to enhance a festive event, as part of a religious observance, or to promote sleep and relaxation, are quite pleasurable and relatively harmless. Where such customs prevail, consumption averages and rates of excessive use tend to be low. Moreover, in populations with low consumption averages, the few who drink excessively deviate considerably from the drinking norm. Effective prohibition would eliminate their alcoholism but certainly not the socio- or psychopathology manifested by such deviance (see Figure 5).

Table 3. Rates of deaths from liver cirrhosis per 100,000 persons 15–75 years in a number of countries, 1960 and 1968

Country	1960	1968
Australia	6.3	7.7
Austria	25.6	35.6
Belgium	10.4	12.2
Canada	7.9	9.9
Czechoslovakia	10.5	13.8
Denmark	8.4	7.4
Finland	3.8	4.3
France	38.7	44.9
Hungary	10.6	13.0
Ireland	4.5	4.1
Italy	20.0	31.4
Netherlands	4.0	4.2
New Zealand	2.8	3.9
Norway	4.5	4.3
Poland	4.7	8.9
Portugal	25.0	36.8
Sweden	5.4	8.0
Switzerland	13.6	17.8
Great Britain	3.3	3.6
U.S.A.	15.6	20.1
Yugoslavia	8.5	13.2
West Germany	19.0	26.9

The most widely used and perhaps the oldest method to control alcohol abuse has been taxation of alcoholic beverages. Indeed, during an eighteenth-century debate in the Irish Parliament, it was said that, "It is the duty of the Legislature to make the means of intoxication as difficult to come by as they possibly can, this can only be done by laying duties as high as the article will bear" (Lynch and Vaizey 1960: 63). The effect of taxation has been examined for many countries and regions (Popham, et al. 1971; de Lint 1973). It has been found to be quite closely related to the overall consumption and prevalence of alcoholism.

In recent years the relative price of beverage alcohol (the price of beverage alcohol relative to personal disposable income) has decreased in many countries. Undoubtedly, this decrease in the effective cost of beverage alcohol has greatly facilitated the current trends towards higher levels of alcohol consumption.

Alcohol education programs have largely ignored the sociocultural aspects of the alcoholism problem. Instead, they seem to adhere to the notion that the real cause of alcoholism lies in the person of the alcoholic, that he is somehow unique in his physical or mental make-up, that his drinking is symptomatic, and that the prevalence of his alcoholism can be reduced or prevented if such a person is detected early in his drinking career and persuaded not to drink.

The evidence to date, however, suggests that alcohol education programs must widen their scope considerably. There seems to be little doubt that the magnitude of alcoholism is largely determined by the extent to which a wide variety of alcohol-use patterns have become integrated into everyday social life. Thus the alcohol educator should try to disseminate all current knowledge pertaining to the health hazards and other costs associated with high levels of alcohol consumption in a population and to the contagious aspects of alcohol use in society (see Figure 3).

REFERENCES

BALES, R. F.
   1946   Cultural differences in rates of alcoholism. *Quarterly Journal of Studies on Alcohol* 6:480–489.
BERTILLON, J.
   1889   De la morbidité et de la mortalité professionalle. *Annuaire statistique de la ville de Paris*, 186–236.
CAHALAN, D., I. H. CISIN, H. CROSSLEY
   1969   *American drinking practices: a national study of drinking behavior and attitudes.* Monograph 6, Rutgers Center of Alcohol Studies. New Haven: College and University Press.
COFFEY, T. G.
   1966   Beer Street; Gin Lane; some views of the 18th century drinking. *Quarterly Journal of Studies on Alcohol* 27(4):669–692.
DE LINT, J.
   1973   "The epidemiology of alcoholism: the elusive nature of the problem, estimating the prevalence of alcohol use and alcohol related mortality, current trends and the issue of prevention," in *Proceedings of the First International Medical Conference on Alcoholism.* London.
DE LINT, J., W. SCHMIDT
   1968   The distribution of alcohol consumption in Ontario. *Quarterly Journal of Studies on Alcohol* 29:968–973.
   1971   Consumption averages and alcoholism prevalence: a brief review of epidemiological investigations. *British Journal of Addiction* 66:97–107.
DE LINT, J., W. SCHMIDT, K. PERNANEN
   1970   *The Ontario drinking survey: a preliminary report.* Toronto: Addiction Research Foundation.
FEBVAY; AUBENQUE
   1957   La mortalité par catégorie professionelle. *Etudes statistiques* 33: 39–44. Institut National de Statistique et des Etudes Economiques.

GADOUREK, I.
1963 *Riskante gewoonten en zorg voor eigen welzijn* [Hazardous habits and human well-being]. Groningen: Wolters.

GURALNICK, L.
1962 "Mortality by occupation and industry among men 20 to 64 years of age, United States 1950," in *Vital statistics, special reports,* volume fifty-three, 49–92.

JELLINEK, E. M.
1945 "The problems of alcohol," in *Alcohol, science and society,* Lecture 2, 13–29. New Haven: Journal of Studies on Alcohol.
1947 Recent trends in alcohol consumption. *Quarterly Journal of Studies on Alcohol* 8:1–42.

KUUSI, P.
1957 *Sales experiment in rural Finland.* Helsinki: Finnish Foundation for Alcohol Studies.

LAU, H.
1972 *Time series regression analysis of per adult Canadian consumption of alcoholic beverages, 1949–1969.* Toronto: Addiction Research Foundation.

LEDERMANN, SULLY
1956 *Alcool, alcoolisme, alcoolisation: données scientifiques de caractère physiologique, économique et social.* Institut National d'Etudes Démographiques, Travaux et Documents, Cahier 29. Paris: Presses Universitaires de France.
1964a *Alcool, alcoolisme, alcoolisation: mortalité, morbidité, accidents du travail.* Institut National d'Etudes Démographiques, Cahier 41. Paris: Presses Universitaires de France.
1964b "Can one reduce alcoholism without changing total alcohol consumption in a population?" in *Proceedings of the 27th International Congress on Alcohol and Alcoholism,* 1–9. Frankfurt.

LELBACH, W. K.
1966 Leberschaden bei chronischem Alkoholismus. *Acta hepat.-splenol.* 13:321–349.
i.p. "Organic pathology related to volume and patterns of alcohol use," in *Research advances in alcohol and drug problems.* Edited by R. J. Gibbins, Y. Israel, H. Kalant, R. E. Popham, W. Schmidt, and R. G. Smart. New York: John Wiley and Sons.

LEREBOULLET, J., J. N. BIRABEN
1964 Bilan de l'alcoolisme en France. *Rev. Prat.,* supplement 14:I–XII.

LOLLI, G., E. SERIANNI, G. M. GOLDER, P. LUZZATTO-FEGIZ
1958 *Alcohol in Italian culture.* Yale Center of Alcohol Studies, Monograph 3. Glencoe: The Free Press.

LUNDQUIST, G. A. R.
1972 Alkoholberoendets Yttringar Och Forlopp [Alcohol dependence — its symptoms and development]. *Alkoholfragan* 66:3–13.

LYNCH, P., J. VAIZEY
1960 *Guinness' brewery in the Irish economy, 1797–1876.* Cambridge. Cambridge University Press.

MÄKELÄ, K.
   1971   Alkoholikulutuksen jakautama [The distribution of alcohol con-
          sumption]. *Alkoholiksysymys* 39:3–13.

MIKOLAJ, T.
   1969   The policy of pricing versus rising consumption of alcohol. *Alko-
          holizmu* 4:7–10.

NIELSEN, J., E. STROMGREN-RISSKOV
   1969   Über die Abhängigkeit des Alkoholkonsums und der Alkohol-
          krankheiten vom Preis alkoholischer Getränke. *Akt. Fragen
          Psychiat. Neurol* 9:165–170.

NYBERG, A.
   1967   *Alkoholjouminen kulutus ja hinnat* [Consumption and prices of
          alcoholic beverages]. The Finnish Foundation for Alcohol Studies,
          Monograph 15. Helsinki: The Finnish Foundation for Alcohol
          Studies.

PITTMAN, D. J., C. R. SNYDER, *editors*
   1962   *Society, culture, and drinking patterns.* New York: John Wiley
          and Sons.

POPHAM, R. E.
   1959   Some social and cultural aspects of alcoholism. *Canadian Psychi-
          atric Association Journal* 4(4):222–229.
   1970   "Indirect methods of alcoholism prevalence estimation: a critical
          evaluation," in *Alcohol and alcoholism,* 294–306. Edited by R. E.
          Popham. Toronto: University of Toronto Press.

POPHAM, R. E., W. SCHMIDT, J. DE LINT
   1971   *The prevention of alcoholism: epidemiological studies of the
          effects of government control measures.* Toronto: Addiction Re-
          search Foundation.

POPHAM, R. E., C. D. YAWNEY
   1967   *Culture and alcohol use: a bibliography of anthropological studies*
          (second edition). Bibliographic Series 1. Torcnto: Addiction Re-
          search Foundation.

REUSS, C.
   1959   *History of beer consumption in Belgium 1900–1957.* Institut de
          Recherches Economiques et Sociales de l'Université de Louvain,
          Louvain.

SARIOLA, S.
   1951   *Prohibition in Finland 1919–1932: its background and consequen-
          ces.* Helsinki: The Finnish Foundation for Alcohol Studies.

SCHMIDT, W., R. E. POPHAM
   1968   *Alcohol consumption of alcoholics in Ontario.* Toronto: Addic-
          tion Research Foundation.

SEELEY, J. R.
   1960   Death by liver cirrhosis and the price of beverage alcohol. *Cana-
          dian Medical Association Journal* 83:1361–1366.
   1962   "The ecology of alcoholism: a beginning," in *Society, culture and
          drinking patterns.* Edited by D. J. Pittman and C. R. Snyder. New
          York: John Wiley and Sons.

SNYDER, C. R.

1958 *Alcohol and the Jews: a cultural study of drinking and sobriety.* Yale Center for Alcohol Studies. Glencoe: The Free Press.

1959 "A sociological view of the etiology of alcoholism," in *Alcoholism: an interdisciplinary approach,* chapter three. Edited by D. J. Pittman. Springfield, Ill.: Charles C. Thomas.

ULLMAN, A. D.

1958 Sociocultural backgrounds of alcoholism. *Annals of the American Academy of Political Science* 315:48–54.

WALSH, B. M., D. WALSH

1970 Economic aspects of alcohol consumption in the Republic of Ireland. *Economic and Social Review* 2:115–138.

WILKINSON, P., J. N. SANTAMARIA, J. G. RANKIN, D. MARTIN

1969 Epidemiology of alcoholism: social data and drinking patterns of a sample of Australian alcoholics. *Medical Journal of Australia* 1:1020–1025.

WILKINSON, R.

1970 *The prevention of drinking problems — alcohol control and cultural influences.* New York: Oxford University Press.

Theory in Alcohol Studies

MARGARET SARGENT

Alcohol studies seem to have reached a stage where a theoretical framework as a basis for future thinking and research is essential. Many theories have been proposed in the past, some of which incorporated concepts still useful and relevant, but there are few with the breadth desirable for an adequate theory (Myerson 1940; Horton 1943; Ullman 1956; Jellinek 1960; Field 1962). The objective of this paper is twofold: first, to list all the characteristics ideally needed by a theory of drinking and, second, to present very tentatively a sketch of a theoretical framework which includes some of these characteristics.

CHARACTERISTICS NEEDED FOR A THEORY OF DRINKING

The first essential is that the theory should be applicable to all societies, whether simple or complex. It also needs to be universal in the sense of covering the whole range of drinking on a continuum of behavior extending from abstinence to alcoholism.

It is important for a theory of drinking to be compatible with broad sociological and anthropological theories embracing wider areas of behavior. One way of achieving this is to regard alcoholism as deviance or as an aspect of social disorganization. The theoretical framework for drinking would then be applicable to other forms of deviant be-

This paper is a modified form of material presented in full in Sargent (1973).

havior — for example, drug dependence, some forms of mental illness, homosexuality, gambling, or delinquency — and would incorporate the notion that behavior deviant in one society is not necessarily deviant in another.

A useful concept to include at this juncture could be functional equivalence: different forms of deviance would thus be regarded as alternatives — as substitutable for each other in certain circumstances — for bringing about social change. Transitional states of drinking patterns such as those now seen in Japan would then be covered by the theory (Sargent 1967).

For the theory to be useful scientifically, it must be testable. It should be possible to formulate relevant hypotheses which can be investigated empirically. The theory can then be refined and gradually built up, or, alternatively, rejected. At the same time, the theory must be broad enough to cover adequately the apparently multicausal nature of drinking and alcoholism. It would therefore allow for a combination of social, psychological, physiological, economic, environmental, political, and other factors. It should preferably not be confined to any one explanatory feature such as dependency, power, social integration, anomie, or ambivalence, for these seem all to be related to drinking even within a single complex society. Since so many diverse etiological factors are to be allowed for, the theory cannot be confined to any one level or discipline of the social sciences. This means that all the techniques available will probably be needed for testing hypotheses, and workers will have opportunities to refine and develop a variety of methods and approaches. In alcohol studies, the problem of the validity of results has not been solved — it is not known if our current techniques really measure what they purport to measure — and the use of a variety of methods within the same context can give a certain amount of information concerning validity.

For research purposes, investigators need the kind of theory which will make it possible to coordinate research in different countries. Such a theory would promote the comparability of results in different investigations.

Lastly, and perhaps most important of all, the theory should be relevant to practical policy needs. This would mean that social scientists could gradually organize information so that it could be applied to the prevention of alcoholism through educational programs or by programs of treatment, thus aiding in the containment of alcohol problems. It would then become easier to accept the idea that one of the prime tasks of researchers in alcohol studies is to change public attitudes towards the social problem of alcoholism in such ways that official policy could then be appropriately modified. No doubt there are other characteristics desirable in an alcohol theory which could be added to those which have been mentioned.

It is not very difficult to make a list of principles to which a theory should conform. It is much harder to formulate a theory which abides by these principles; what follows is only a preliminary attempt at drawing up a theoretical framework.

A THEORETICAL FRAMEWORK

The focus is on alcoholism as a social problem (Sargent 1973). Alcoholism, drinking, and abstinence are regarded as behaviors which not only differ from society to society but are also perceived and interpreted differently by the members of each society. To demonstrate this, illustrations of variations in Australian drinking will be drawn.

In order to avoid a culture-bound conception of alcoholism it is necessary to attempt an answer to the following question: what are the distinguishing characteristics, found in all societies, of people known as "alcoholics"? The answer cannot constitute a DEFINITION of "alcoholism," but rather a DESCRIPTION of how, why, and to what sorts of people the word "alcoholism" is generally applied. Many definitions have been attempted, but they have lacked a common basis for agreement. The formulation of definitions, apart from operational definitions for the purpose of research, is inappropriate in the case of alcoholism. It is rather a matter for research to discover how and in what circumstances the word is commonly used, and then to describe in detail what characterizes the persons known as alcoholics. The same applies to any other term in society which is used in a similar way to "alcoholism."

A first characteristic of alcoholism is HIGH CONSUMPTION of alcohol. Although all alcoholics drink quantities in excess of the average range of consumption for their society, this is true not only of alcoholics but also of heavy drinkers, many of whom will never be regarded as alcoholics.

DEVIANT BEHAVIOR is a second characteristic of alcoholics that distinguishes them from heavy drinkers. Behavior which lies outside the range of socially acceptable behavior in a given group or society may be said to be deviant. Such behavior may be regarded as breaking the unwritten rules, that is, not conforming to the social norms. In Western society and in Australia, these norms include the maintenance of self-control, the fulfillment of expected roles (including the roles of bread-winner, nurturant parent, work performed in return for wages, citizen abiding by the laws of public order) and the conformance to accepted rules of social drinking, such as "holding one's liquor."

A third characteristic of alcoholism is LABELLING (Becker 1963). Certain types of deviant behavior, including some which result from drinking, are regarded in some societies as SOCIAL PROBLEMS. It is their perception of certain behavior which determines that people will label or define that behavior as constituting a problem; for example, drug dependence, delinquency, or alcoholism. When a certain type of behavior is regarded as a social problem the implication is present of a need for SOCIAL CONTROL, that is, action or intervention of some kind. The role of the perceiver determines, in part, the nature of the problem he perceives and the kind of action he considers appropriate. For example, if the perceiver is a member of the branch of the police force concerned with maintaining public order he will tend to emphasize the threat of alcoholism to public order as the social problem, and inter-vention by the police as the kind of action needed. An employer or a family welfare worker would define differently both the problem and the kind of intervention appropriate.

For a variety of reasons, there is often delay before a person is labelled as an alcoholic. For instance, many drinkers get drunk at times and fail to conform to social norms, and these occasional lapses are not generally judged as indicative of alcoholism. Again, in some popu-lation subgroups and societies, heavy drinking and occasional drunken-ness are normative behavior, for example, in miners, salesmen, seamen, and Australian aborigines, and early alcoholic behavior is not very far beyond this norm. Covering up by friends and relatives means that for a period it is not apparent to others that there are deficiencies in role performance. In higher social status groups, there is security of employ-ment, well-established family life, and financial position. People assign high prestige to these groups and hesitate to define their members as alcoholic, so covering up is more feasible than in lower status groups. There is little delay, however, in labelling the most socially visible deviants, usually the methylated spirits drinker stereotype. Labelling tends to occur in certain circumstances, for example, by doctors and by other patients during hospitalization for an acute alcoholic state, or by a fellow alcoholic who recognizes the behavior as similar to his own or to that of members of Alcoholics Anonymous. Or a person may be labelled alcoholic when the diagnosis is made of "physical complica-tions of alcoholism," such as peripheral neuritis or cerebellar ataxia, by general practitioners and other doctors. Or the labelling may be done by employers, relatives, friends, police, and magistrates who point out the person's failure to perform his social roles.

At the same point in time at which a person is defined as a deviant and an alcoholic, in most Western societies he is segregated by hospitalization, punished by imprisonment, dismissed by employers, and divorced by his wife — measures which signify to him his rejection by society. He may be simultaneously accepted as a member of a nonconforming group such as A.A. or a drinking group consisting entirely of practicing alcoholics. He is thus confirmed in the deviant role which he may have hitherto played half-heartedly or subconsciously and is now generally accepted to behave as the habitual drunkard who no longer accepts responsibility for others' welfare or for his own. The way back to acceptance again in the larger society is possible for only a few alcoholics and may lie in the acceptance of a sick role. Most present forms of treatment for alcoholism offer the opportunity for the alcoholic, regarded as suffering from a disease, to assume temporarily a sick role. Although this role must also be considered deviant, it has the advantages of reducing self-blame in the patient, of offering hope of treatment and resultant rehabilitation, and of being temporarily rather than permanently deviant.

Unfortunately, the proportion of alcoholics thus rehabilitated is small. Repeated experiences of "treatment" at a variety of institutions, with intermittent periods in jail for drunkenness, perpetuate the alcoholic way of life by offering a "revolving door." The alcoholic finds that the community appears to assume responsibility for caring for and rehabilitating him as it would if he had appendicitis. This encourages a passive acceptance in the patient while, rather illogically, persons treating him seek evidence of his motivation towards recovery. When signs of motivation are lacking, or when the patient, by getting drunk, seems to stop wanting to recover, he is often discharged reproachfully and barred from readmission for six months. Back on the road again without shelter or employment, the only solution may appear to be a new start in a different environment. To Australian "alkies," the result is cynically known as the "geographical cure" and consists of hitchhiking interstate where usually further episodes of revolving door treatment and imprisonment occur. In most less complex societies, there is great protectiveness towards alcoholics, usually based on close family relationships, so social rejection is more rare though even more devastating for the individual when it does occur.

One of the earliest statements of ways in which social organization and attitudes[1] could influence rates of alcoholism was made by Bales (1959: 263):

The first [way] is the degree to which the culture operates to bring about acute needs for adjustment, or inner tensions, in its members. There are many of these: culturally induced anxiety, guilt, conflict, suppressed aggression, and sexual tension of various sorts may be taken as examples.

The second way is the sort of attitudes toward drinking which the culture produces in its members.

The third general way is the degree to which the culture provides suitable substitution means of satisfaction.

A corollary which can be derived from this general statement is that in a society where some members have acute needs for adjustment, if drinking as a means of adjustment is available, then a high rate of tension-relieving drinking will occur. The kind of drinking which can relieve tension includes the heavy consumption of alcohol and, occasionally at least, drunkenness. Even where needs for adjustment exist in the individual, it seems likely that, for deviant drinking to develop, cultural attitudes which offer little counter-anxiety (anxiety over the effects of drinking) are necessary. The attitudes provide "a setting," a context in which deviant drinking may or may not be appropriate behavior. Each cultural pattern can be regarded as having a given range of behavior, including deviant behavior, which is integral to the culture (Benedict 1935). In attempting to define the sort of social organization which would offer a range of behavior inclusive of heavy drinking and alcoholism, Bales cited various attitudes to drinking which might help to determine this range. His description of attitudes can be regarded as a useful tool rather than a typology.

ABSTINENCE. For one reason or another, usually religious in nature, the use of alcohol as a beverage is not permitted for any purpose ... a RITUAL attitude is also religious in nature, but it requires that alcoholic beverages ... should be used in the performance of religious ceremonies. Typically ... the partaking ... is a ritual act of communion with the sacred. ... With a convivial attitude ... drinking is a "social" rather than a religious ritual, performed both because it symbolizes social unity or solidarity and because it actually loosens up emotions which make for social ease and good will. ... A utilitarian attitude ... includes medicinal drinking and other types calculated to further self-interest or exclusively personal satisfaction. It is often "solitary" drinking, but is is possible to drink for utilitarian purposes in a group and with group approval ... (Bales 1959: 263).

An example of the utilitarian attitude, which of the four is probably

[1] This attitude or "orienting factor" was described as a "nuclear structure of more or less fixed ideas and sentiments beyond the immediate control of the individual" (Bales 1944).

the most conducive to problem drinking, is Australian society (including aborigines) where there is certainly a social problem of alcoholism. There are also elements of the convivial in "mateship" drinking among men and of abstinence in certain conservative Protestant groups.

In general cultural attitudes, predominantly ritual or abstinent, seem to be associated with a form of drinking highly integrated with other cultural characteristics and consistent throughout a given culture. Utilitarian attitudes, on the other hand, seem to be found mainly in modern, complex societies in which both attitudes and drinking behavior are pluralistic and at times inconsistent. Convivial attitudes manifest themselves in a wide range of forms. In some cases, they seem to be predominantly integrative and associated with a low rate of alcoholism (Lemert 1954; Mangin 1957; Lolli 1958). But where convivial attitudes also have utilitarian aspects, as in Japan, there is generally a higher rate of alcoholism together with a diversity of drinking behavior which is not wholly integrated. Probably it is not simply the case that pluralism of attitude and drinking behavior is linked with a high rate of alcoholism, but rather that the ambivalence, the uncertainty generated in the individual about what is permitted behavior, allows more deviant behavior to occur. In Australia, the wide variety of drinking norms among different social groups no doubt contributes to the ambivalence in attitudes.

The way in which the term "cultural attitude" is used needs clarifying, particularly as the writer's usage differs from Bales', who considered that the cultural attitude influences an individual's drinking pattern because the individual holds that attitude himself. My point of view is that a cultural attitude is an attitude which is held by many members of the cultural group and therefore influences the behavioral norms of the group; thus the individual member's drinking patterns are determined, in part at least, by the social expectations for drinking behavior which constitute the group norms. For example, some Australians with an abstinence orientation due to their religious training may nevertheless consume alcohol when under social pressure to do so, for this pressure conveys the norms of Australian society as a whole. For instance, probably about half the Methodists in Australia are "social drinkers."

The view has been expressed that, even in the absence of any form of predisposition, exposure to heavy drinking may lead to alcoholism. An alternative, but not compatible, hypothesis is that the same causal factors operate to produce both heavy drinking and alcoholism. For some people, it is the psychological and social rewards of drinking groups which help to channel them into heavy drinking and fix the use of alcohol as an adjustment technique. However, in Australia, at least, neither habitual heavy drinking nor frequent participation in drinking groups seems to be sufficient to account for the adoption of the alcoholic way of life; either some form of predisposition or a precipitating factor is probable in all cases of alcoholism. Nevertheless, drinking groups do play an important role in relation to alcoholism in that they conceal the developing alcoholic. There are many drinkers who will never be regarded as alcoholic, yet their drinking patterns may be superficially similar to those of early alcoholics in that they drink large amounts of alcohol and have occasional episodes of drunkenness. They differ from alcoholics in that they are able to change their pattern of drinking if it begins to affect their role performance. But within a drinking group, differences between the behavior of normal drinkers and that of early alcoholics are often not apparent to the members. Typically, alcoholics develop high tolerance and are able to consume large quantities of alcohol without undue behavior affects; even when they become drunk, there may be no obvious release of aggressive or sexual impulses. So few sanctions such as disapproval or rejection from the group are exercised; the alcoholic continues to drink heavily and to become more disturbed in his social roles. He may sometimes progress gradually to more deviant drinking groups; there again he experiences little or no disapproval within the drinking group. Therefore, the alcoholic, through the experience of rewards but few negative sanctions in the drinking group, may progress to a chronic stage of alcoholism without being labelled as an alcoholic; by this time sanctions do not have the effect of forcing the drinker to conform, for his dependence on alcohol is already too great.

It would appear extremely probable that psychological predisposition to alcoholism exists in some people. In any case, by positing social factors alone, it seems impossible to account for the "channelling" of some persons into alcoholism while others with similar social backgrounds become delinquent or suffer from anxiety neurosis or psychosomatic complaints. The nature of predisposing factors needs to be determined by research, but it is taken here to include such influences as conflict over drinking in the childhood home, an alcoholic relative or family friend whose behavior might constitute a model, early parental deprivation or other childhood trauma, and emotional maladjustment. Some of these factors might be sufficient to cause predisposition specific to alcoholism. Others might result in a more general psychological vulnerability which is channelled into alcoholism by exposure to certain kinds of drinking.

We need to know how these factors operate in other societies. By combining them, one may derive patterns of the development of alcoholism in Australia and use them as a basis for comparison with different cultures. A development pattern which seems often to occur is the result of a combination of psychological vulnerability with exposure to the experience of drinking-group rewards. The rewards of drinking groups, together with the operation of social pressures to increase consumption, encourage heavy drinking. The pattern may be formulated as follows:

a. Vulnerability — drinking-group rewards — heavy drinking — alcoholism. In clinical practice, it is possible to distinguish a few alcoholics in whom initial vulnerability appears to have been negligible and this has led to the supposition that exposure to heavy drinking and the rewards of drinking-group participation alone bring about the development of alcoholism in some persons. However, it seems likely that "loss of control" of drinking is precipitated in these cases by events such as migration or a wife's death. Generally, the nonvulnerable or "reactive" alcoholic seems, before the precipitating event, to have been a heavy drinker but without loss of control or any effect of drinking on his role performance. This pattern may be described thus:

b. Drinking-group rewards — heavy drinking — precipitating factor — alcoholism. There are also alcoholic patients, generally very vulnerable personalities, whose experience has never included drinking in groups. These persons are probably incapable of deriving the rewards of drinking groups owing to difficulties in interpersonal relationships. Such cases seem to occur commonly among female alcoholics who rarely enjoy satisfactory drinking-group relationships, partly because of social disapproval of female heavy drinking. A third pattern is then as follows:

c. Vulnerability — solitary drinking — heavy drinking — alcoholism. These patterns probably vary from society to society according to the kind of particular drinking patterns and attitudes which predominate.

For this theory to reach the social problem level, it is necessary to examine how the concepts of deviance, labelling, and social control can be usefully combined. The theoretical framework includes many steps between social organization and alcoholism, some of which are predisposing factors and precipitating events which help to channel the individual into alcoholic behavior. Other connecting and interacting factors are those which instigate different types of behavior thought deviant in a given society. A theory of deviance compatible with this theoretical approach could offer an explanation of the psychological aspects of deviance in terms of "anomia" — or possibly, alternatively, of anxiety, dependency, power, or a combination of these. Anomia is a psychological state in the individual which is not necessarily related to externally existing circumstances (Srole 1956). The subjective state is related to the individual's own expectations for his achievement, and how far he experiences a feeling of frustration, alienation, or other negative psychological state, in response to the blocking of legitimate means of achieving his goals. This response could be to actual blocking or to expected or imagined blocking. For example, a person with congenital hip disease might be mistakenly convinced that his condition prevents him from achieving his goal, but his mental state might still be characterized by anomia. There are almost certainly other relevant frustrating factors in addition to the blocking of legitimate means and these are a matter for research.

It would be possible to incorporate the concept of social control in a definition of deviance. For example, Jessor defined deviance as behavior which "must depart substantially from normative standards; the departure must be of sufficient magnitude to mobilize social control responses" (Jessor, et al. 1968: 44). It seems preferable, however, to define behavior not within the socially acceptable range as deviance, whether or not it mobilizes social control. The social control response to a given behavioral act varies considerably with the age, sex, social status, and other characteristics of the actor. For example, a group of young boys seen smoking together triggers social disapproval and sometimes actual intervention, while the same behavior in a group of men provokes little response. It seems more useful, therefore, to attach the concept of mobilization of social control to the situation where labelling takes place. Labelling, in fact, seldom occurs except where a need for social control is also implied.

The subjective state of anomia may consist primarily in a feeling of alienation, despair, or of personal disorganization, but whatever this feeling, it creates psychological tensions within the individual. Thus, the many different types of deviant behavior, and also some normal behavior, can be viewed as responses to the inner tensions in the individual and in society. There are various types of behavior which have the function of providing relief from the tension which would otherwise accumulate, cause stress and strain, and eventually produce some form of breakdown. Insofar as all these kinds of behavior have a similar antecedent (tensions) and a similar result (tension relief), they are all functional equivalents. If this is so, then if one type of deviance is reduced in a given society by some sort of social control, it is probable that, if other conditions remain the same, another type of deviance will be substituted. It becomes apparent that to treat the social problem of alcoholism it is necessary to investigate and reduce overall the sources of tension and factors instigating deviance. These efforts need to be concentrated on the societies and population groups in which alcoholism is most prevalent.

CONCLUSION

If some theoretical basis such as that described is adopted, the method of cross-cultural investigation is seen to be essential for furthering knowledge in alcohol studies. By this technique it is possible, for example, to explore both the attitudes which seemingly encourage a high rate of alcoholism in a society and also those which are associated with a low rate. Certain attitudes can perhaps be discovered which, if generally adopted, could be expected to reduce the rate of alcoholism and other alcohol-related problems. The goal of promoting such attitudes could provide the starting point of a rational education program on drinking.

Needless to say, the present theory does not embrace all the factors involved in the etiology of alcoholism. Social, economic, political, and environmental factors which probably play a part include availability of alcoholic liquor, viticulture, the degree of development of a country, the power and nature of authority of government, educational and religious institutions, and the situation of the society in relation to others. For the formulation of theories which are not culture bound, which is of some importance at this stage of alcohol studies, the adoption of a broad anthropological perspective is necessary. We need also to be personally committed to finding ways of remedying social problems, for the time of "value free" social sciences is like the days of wine and roses. . . .

REFERENCES

BALES, R. F.
1944 "The fixation factor in alcohol addiction: an hypothesis derived from a comparative study of Irish and Jewish social norms." Ph.D. dissertation, Harvard University, Cambridge, Mass.

1959 "Cultural differences in rates of alcoholism," in *Drinking and intoxication: readings in social attitudes and controls*, p. 263. Edited by R. G. McCarthy. Glencoe: Free Press.

BECKER, H. S.
1963 *The outsiders: studies in the sociology of deviance*. Glencoe: Free Press.

BENEDICT, R.
1935 *Patterns of culture*. London: Methuen.

FIELD, P. B.
1962 "A new cross-cultural study of drunkenness," in *Society, culture and drinking patterns*, 48–74. Edited by D. J. Pittman and C. R. Snyder. New York: J. Wiley and Sons.

HORTON, D.
1943 The functions of alcohol in primitive societies; a cross-cultural study. *Quarterly Journal of Studies on Alcohol* 4:199–320.

JELLINEK, E. M.
1960 *The disease concept of alcoholism*. New Haven: Hillhouse Press.

JESSOR, R., T. D. GRAVES, R. C. HANSON, S. JESSOR
1968 *Society, personality and deviant behavior: a study of a tri-ethnic community*. New York: Holt, Rinehart and Winston.

LEMERT, E. M.
1954 *Alcohol and the Northwest Coast Indians*, 303–406. Berkeley: University of California Press.

LOLLI, G.
1958 *Alcohol in Italian culture: food and wine in relation to sobriety among Italians and Italian Americans*. New York: Free Press.

MANGIN, W.
1957 Drinking among Andean Indians. *Quarterly Journal of Studies on Alcohol* 18:55–66.

MYERSON, A.
1940 Alcohol: a study in social ambivalence. *Quarterly Journal of Studies on Alcohol* 1:12–20.

SARGENT, M. J.
1967 Changes in drinking patterns in Japan. *Quarterly Journal of Studies on Alcohol* 28:709–722.
1973 *Alcoholism as a social problem*. London: Angus and Robertson.

SROLE, L.
1956 Social integration and certain corollaries: an exploratory study. *American Sociological Review* 21:709–716.

ULLMAN, A. D.
1958 Sociocultural backgrounds on alcoholism. *Annals of the American Academy of Political and Social Sciences* 315:48–54.

PART SIX

Methodological Considerations and Data Collection

Introduction

Methodologizing is a perplexing process. Quantitative techniques have produced superbly elegant results in various disciplines and there now exist several sophisticated analytic strategies for the alcohol researcher. But which one to use and where? Is a statistical test of significance appropriate for data derived from observations both in a fieldwork setting and in a clinical setting? What relationship is there between a decision table and an intravenous dose of ethanol? Are careful cross-cultural comparisons as reliable as variation framed in intracultural terms? In the area of alcohol studies, as in other scientific arenas, the answers to these and related queries must be couched in a combined perspective of theory building and pragmatics. As Sargent pointed out in the previous section, theory without application is like explanation devoid of understanding. A methodological strategy is judged appropriate if it contributes meaningfully to the exposition of the theoretical proposition in question. At the same time, the analytic approach must produce solutions to the practical problems which gave rise to the theoretical formulation.

This seems a moot point in areas of investigation like alcohol studies, where intellectual and pragmatic concerns are intimately linked in the pursuits of socially relevant problem solving. Yet a trend toward monotypic method and data collection is clearly evident in the voluminous literature on human alcohol use and abuse. The papers in this section (and those in Parts 4 and 5) suggest that such a tendency can only be counterproductive to explanation and understanding. From the antiseptic tools of the clinician to the cross-national survey questionnaires, cross-disciplinary, polytypic methodological strategies appear to hold the greatest promise for analytic usefulness in alcohol studies.

This section begins appropriately with Westermeyer's comprehensive review of cross-cultural alcohol research in clinical settings. As the author points out so succinctly, cross-cultural clinical research has been unsystematic and often unmindful of just those behavioral variables which have preoccupied social scientists. After summarizing the types of clinical strategies used in cross-cultural alcohol studies, Westermeyer goes on to provide a much-needed assessment of the contributions of clinical methods to our understanding of the major issues in alcohol research. His insightful conclusions echo the theme of this volume: no single analytic strategy can function autonomously; clinical research paradigms must be coupled with behavioral ones to provide the most effective approach to explanation and understanding.

This notion is carefully developed in Topper's paper dealing with cognitive models in alcohol research. The author has combined linguistic, ethnographic, psychological, communications, and computer science techniques to produce a promising approach to critical problems in alcohol studies. Topper's "verbal action plans" and decision models are significant because they provide a direct link from cognition to behavior in a fashion which can be quantitatively measured and tested. Moreover, as he goes on to point out, data generated from this model, because of their ethnographic qualities, can be utilized profitably in therapeutic and clinical settings. The cross-cultural usefulness of cognitive approaches to alcohol use and problem drinking is clearly evident in Topper's Navajo Indian research and in his attempts to develop comparable paradigms for Anglo-American culture.

Cahalan, in the following paper, argues persuasively that the search for cross-cultural methodology should not ignore the wealth of data contained in national and cross-national surveys conducted in this and other countries. Ahlström-Laakso's paper in Part 2 strongly supports Cahalan's position, and the papers of Bacon (Part 1), Barry (Part 5), and Schaefer (Part 5) provide models for the utilization of cross-national survey data. As the author so clearly demonstrates, these surveys can serve to indicate important areas of research along other methodological avenues. At the same time, they can provide significant checks on the pressing issue of intracultural variation in drinking behavior.

In the final paper in this section, Keller briefly describes the bibliographic research facilities at the Rutgers University Center of Alcohol Studies. Because of the unsystematic character of cross-cultural alcohol studies in the past, it is imperative that future research strategies be developed on firm problem-solving ground. The repository at Rutgers is an important documentation resource in this kind of undertaking. Methodological strategies come and go, but there can be no substitute for adequate resource documentation. Without this control, our goal of systematic, interdisciplinary, cross-cultural alcohol research will remain on the drawing board.

Cross-Cultural Studies of Alcoholism in the Clinical Setting: Review and Evaluation

JOSEPH WESTERMEYER

Clinical studies have contributed much of what is known about alcoholism. Until recently, most of these studies have focused on the "medical syndrome" and "epidemiologic" models of alcoholism. Study methods have emphasized physiological and biochemical factors underlying alcohol addiction or have utilized questionnaires to elicit drinking histories and to isolate demographic variables. Despite the fact that psycho-behavioral correlates are fundamental to alcoholics, clinical studies in this area have appeared only in the last several years.

Unfortunately, the cultural aspects of alcoholism have been ignored by most clinical investigators until recently. Field investigators (epidemiologists, anthropologists, sociologists) have led the way in pointing out important cross-cultural differences in alcohol usage and alcohol-related problems. Only in the last few years have several clinicians with behavioral science training undertaken cross-cultural studies of alcoholism in the clinical setting; a few behavioral scientists have also begun to make observations in the same settings.

1. STRATEGIES

STUDIES BY INVESTIGATORS FROM DIFFERENT ETHNIC GROUPS Cross-cultural "armchair" analysis can be done using studies performed by different investigators, each in his own society. Their results can be compared to assess in what ways alcohol-related problems resemble or differ across cultural boundaries.

The problem with this method is comparability of data. The degree of success from this approach may be related to the clarity and specificity of the parameters being studied. Thus, for example, cross-cultural studies bear out the relationships of child abuse and birth order to alcoholism. In these cases, the parameters have been fairly simply and explicitly defined by different clinicians around the world. In other cases, however, the studies — while appearing to address the same problem — are not comparable at all: follow-up studies to evaluate anatabuse (disulfiram), vocational counseling, and group therapies have been done in different cultures but the criteria for "improvement" vary so greatly as to defy comparison.

STUDIES BY THE SAME INVESTIGATOR   This more "activist" method requires the collaboration of clinicians and anthropologists, or the combination of the two in one person; neither condition occurs commonly. The method further requires that the investigator(s) have access to two or more separate clinical settings which serve culturally different people or to a single clinical facility which serves two or more culturally distinct groups; again, neither situation occurs frequently.

Once these personnel and logistical problems are resolved, all of the usual problems of cross-cultural investigation emerge. Emic-etic (intracultural/cross-cultural) issues involving diagnosis, non-random selection factors, communication barriers, transference and counter-transference problems (both to the individual and to his cultural group) must be taken into account.

2. TYPES OF CLINICAL STUDIES

In-Patient Alcoholics

People with alcohol-related problems come to detoxification centers, general hospitals, state hospitals, halfway houses, and long-term residential facilities. Admission to a treatment facility for alcoholism is a social event which can be clearly demarked. It further requires that (1) the individual (or his relatives) and (2) the admitting officer at the facility concur that an alcohol-related problem is indeed present. At least for general hospital admission, certain minimal criteria obtain to warrant hospital admission. Various research methods have been employed as follows:

1.   Questionnaire   In-patient alcoholics have been questioned on a multitude of topics thought to be significant in the genesis of alcoholism. These have included birth order and parental loss, drinking history, black-outs, demographic characteristics, sexual activity, and family history.

Cross-cultural example Studies conducted by indigenous clinical investigators in the United States, Austria, Australia, and England indicate that alcoholics are more apt to be "later born" in families rather than "early born" and to have experienced parental loss or parental absence in childhood. Careful reading of this literature suggests that the birth order phenomenon might be due to parental deprivation in early childhood, since parents are more apt to die or leave the family when the later born are still quite young than when the first born are young (de Lint 1964; Sampson 1965; Dennehy 1966; Ackerman 1968; Koller and Castaños 1969).

Many such surveys have been done in the United States and England which also suggest certain other demographic and clinical consistencies (Glatt 1967; Skopkova 1967; Kinsey 1968; Stein, et al. 1968; Horn and Wanberg 1969; Goodwin, et al. 1969; Wanberg and Horn 1970). However, the data are often not comparable, though they might be so if patient samples were more fully described and if more uniform questionnaires were utilized.

2. *Withdrawal Signs* Patients admitted to alcohol treatment facilities have been examined and rated for types and severity of withdrawal signs (e.g. pulse, temperature, tremulousness). This has afforded a more objective standard for comparison than the questionnaire method.

Cross-cultural example Chippewa Indians and majority alcoholics in the Twin Cities have been compared for demographic variables and severity of withdrawal. Both groups were noted not to differ greatly for age, sex ratio, hepatomegaly, liver function tests, and associated psychopathology. Similar proportions of both groups showed no objective signs of withdrawal upon admission. Indian alcoholics were statistically more likely to be unemployed and to have no spouse. Among those having withdrawal signs, the Indian group had significantly more toxicity (Westermeyer 1972). Using more sensitive scales for withdrawal, black and white alcoholics have been compared in Brooklyn. White patients were older, had more medical complications, and were more likely to be discharged to a state hospital. Black patients had a higher percentage of hallucinations (Gross, et al. 1972).

3. *Psychometrics* Various learning and personality tests have been used to study alcoholic populations (Kinsey and Phillips 1968; Hoffman 1972; Piskin and Frikken 1972). Since most such tests are strongly affected by educational and ethnic differences, it is often difficult to know what factors might be adjudged to account for testing differences.

Perhaps when such tests have been standardized to other "normal" populations besides that in which they have evolved, they might become more useful in the cross-cultural study of alcoholism.

4. Genetics   A consistent finding in the field has been the high incidence of alcoholism among parents and siblings of alcoholics. Genetic studies have been undertaken to assess whether this high correlation might be due to "environmental child-raising" factors or to "genetic-constitutional" factors. Such studies consist of noting the incidence of the condition in the following: (1) dizygotic twins and (2) offspring of parents who have the condition where the offspring have been raised apart from their parents (Rosenthal 1970).

Cross-cultural example   Incidence of alcoholism in children who had an alcoholic biologic parent (identified through treatment facilities) but who were raised by other parents has been studied by different investigators in the United States and Denmark. In both studies a "genetic-constitution" factor was significantly indicated (Schuckit, et al. 1972; Goodwin 1973).

5. Follow-up   Studies of discharged alcoholics have been of two kinds: mortality and clinical improvement (Gillis 1969; Schmidt and De Lint 1969; Gillis and Keet 1969; Gallant, et al. 1973). Though some of these studies come from different cultures, varying methods and criteria (as well as inadequate description of the patient sample) have limited their comparability.

Postmortem

Examination of human remains offers certain advantages in the study of alcoholism. For one, death is a distinct identifiable event that can often be accurately compared across cultural boundaries. For another, there is the opportunity to examine the body more thoroughly than can be done in premortem.

1. Cirrhosis of the Liver   Since Jellinek's early work in the 1940's (Jolliffe and Jellinek 1941), such studies have been popular despite more recent methodological arguments (Seeley 1959; Jellinek 1959). Though differences in diagnostic criteria, nutritional factors, and non-alcoholic cirrhosis becloud the method, it nonetheless continues to be employed with reasonably productive results.

Cross-cultural example   A comparative study of two Southwestern Indian tribes showed that one had a cirrhosis rate four times higher than the other;

contrasting drinking patterns were felt to account for this difference (Kunitz, et al. 1971). Liver deaths in the United States in 1890 recorded the same ethnic differences as have been observed more recently by other methods: high rate among Irish, intermediate rates among Germans and American-born, and low rates among Italians and Russian Jews (Room 1968). Liver cirrhosis mortality rates in the United States, Wales, Canada, and Paris all fell during World War I and then arose again afterwards except in the United States during Prohibition (Terris 1967).

2. Blood and Tissue Levels of Ethanol Routine blood ethanol determinations in all cases of violent deaths are becoming more frequent. Brain and liver concentrations of ethanol have also been employed as a research procedure in the United States (Haddon and Bradess 1959). Of course, precise percentages of alcohol-related violent death are not possible with postmortem studies alone since much of the alcohol has been metabolized several hours after the accident. Where the individual lives some hours or days following the accident, studies may be falsely negative.

Cross-cultural example Violent deaths among Indian and non-Indian people were analyzed for the years 1964–1969. Mean concentrations of blood alcohol between the two groups were found to be about equal in positive cases, though the Indian group had a significantly higher rate of positive blood alcohol. The Indian group was younger and had more homicide and less suicide than the non-Indian group (Westermeyer and Brantner 1972).

3. Alcohol-Related Death Death from various causes has been related to alcohol using two methods: liver cirrhosis found at autopsy and patient records. Alcoholism in the United States has been found to be associated with death from cancer of the larynx, cancer of the esophagus, peptic ulcer, pneumonia, accidental death of all kinds (vehicular, falling, drowning, overdosage), homicide, suicide, cirrhosis, pancreatitis, and beriberi (Jellinek 1943; Derrick 1967; Chomet and Guch 1967; Rushing 1969)

Monitored Alcohol Administration

Over the last several years, alcohol has been administered within clinical settings in which behavioral observations have been made.

1. Administration to Patients Several investigators have done excellent studies with oral administration of alcohol to American and British alcoholics (Marconi, et al. 1967; McNamee, et al. 1968; Tamerin and Mendelson 1969; Tamerin, et al. 1970; Ryback 1970; Nathan, et al.

1970; Allman, et al. 1972); one group has employed the intravenous route of administration (Mayfield and Allen 1967; Mayfield 1968). While these studies have contributed significantly to an understanding of the behavioral, emotional, and social concomitants of alcoholism, they have not yet been applied to cross-cultural questions. The one cross-cultural study done so far only examined biochemical variables and the groups which were "compared" were not in the least composed of similar samples (Fenna, et al. 1971).

2.   *Administration to "Normals"*   The behavioral and psychological effects of alcohol on American college-age men have been carefully studied under laboratory conditions much like those used in the hospital setting (Bennet, et al. 1969; Kastl 1969). Unfortunately, the one cross-cultural study done in this manner compared only physiological responses (Wolff 1972).

3.   *Alcohol as Therapy*   Beer and wine have been given to American geriatric nursing-home patients and to hospitalized patients for therapeutic effect (Funk and Prescott 1967; Black 1969; Chien, et al. 1973). No cross-cultural studies have been done to date.

In-Patients Not Admitted for Alcoholism

As the high correlation between alcoholism and a variety of medical and surgical conditions has become evident, a variety of such studies has been undertaken by clinicians over the last decade.

1.   *Medical In-Patients*   Clinical studies have replicated the post-mortem studies of diagnosed alcoholics indicating that certain cancers, pneumonia, ulcer, trauma, pancreatitis, certain neuropathies, and certain myocardiopathies are highly correlated with alcoholism. While such studies come from a variety of ethnic groups, much of the work cannot be statistically compared because of inadequate sample description and different methods. However, the general trends reinforce rather than contradict each other (Pincock 1964; Barcha, et al. 1968; Sievers 1968; Martínez 1969).

2.   *Psychiatric In-Patients*   Among American patients with self-inflicted wounds, both a high rate of intoxication and of chronic alcoholism was observed (Mayfield and Montgomery 1972). Geriatric men-

tally ill patients in the United States were found to have a high alcoholism rate, especially among the first generation Irish-Americans (Simon, et al. 1968).

Out-Patient Alcoholics

In general, out-patients are not so available for research activities as are in-patients. Also, the characteristics of the sample population are apt to vary more among out-patients since socioeconomic factors are generally more influential and biomedical factors are often less so. On the other hand, out-patients can usually be followed over a long time period and they may comprise a sample somewhat different from, but overlapping with, in-patients.

1. "Improvement" Studies Studies of out-patient treatment have been carried out in different cultures (Pattison, et al. 1968; Goldfried 1969; Shore and Von Fumetti 1972). However, the variations in treatment and inadequate sample description render the studies incomparable. Another major difficulty is inconsistency and (sometimes) vagueness regarding what constitutes "improvement."

2. Disulfiram Studies The few studies available in this area have controlled at least one variable to some extent by specifying a treatment modality that can be more readily replicated across cultural boundaries. While patient description and "improvement" variables do not permit adequate statistical comparison, contrasting psychosocial aspects of the drug and its usage in different cultures can be inferred (Savard 1968; Gerrein, et al. 1973).

Out-Patients Not Seen for Alcoholism

Following the in-patient and postmortem studies indicating high correlations between alcoholism and certain disorders, out-patient studies were undertaken. They have the advantage that some kinds of problems can be examined that are not so likely to be encountered in an in-patient setting.

1. Pediatric Studies For certain pediatric problems, the families of the child patient have often been seen in evaluation. Some American clinicians have observed high rates of alcoholism among the parents of certain children such as those with burns or hyper-activity syndrome (Crikelair, et al. 1968; Cantwell 1972).

Cross-cultural example   Studies from Germany, France, Australia, and the United States have documented the high correlation between child abuse and parental alcoholism (Nau 1967; Niemann 1968; Grislain, et al. 1968; Birrell and Birrell 1968; Swanson 1968; Chase and Martin 1970).

2.   *Emergency-Room Studies*   Alcohol-related problems commonly surface to medical recognizance in the emergency room (Schwary and Fjeld 1969). This provides an opportunity to study certain kinds of alcohol-related events. In an American study of 5,622 home accidents treated in an emergency service, a breathalyzer was employed (Wechsler, et al. 1969). No cross-cultural studies are available as yet.

"Soft" Methods

Certain kinds of "soft" studies are extremely difficult to replicate between cultures. However, studies can be helpful in generating hypotheses which might then be tested with more definitive methods.

1.   *Case-Study Method*   Intensive study of one of more alcoholic individuals may provide important clues to cross-cultural similarities and differences (La Barre 1941; Devereaux and McCormick 1972).

2.   *Psychodynamic Interpretation*   Virtually any data can be used for this approach, from psychotherapy experiences (Sands, et al. 1967) to alcoholic hallucinations (Boyer 1964). The main difficulty in this area is the generation of useful hypotheses (not just *a posteriori* "explanations") that can be operationalized and tested with other methods.

3.   ASSESSMENT OF THE CLINICAL METHOD

Definitions

1.   *Definition of Alcoholism*   Various clinical investigators do not always apply the term "alcoholic" in the same ways; or, depending upon socioeconomic factors (so important in alcoholism), one clinician's "alcoholic" sample often bears only tenuous resemblance to another's sample. Attempts have recently begun to place the "alcoholism" diag-

nosis on a more firm, replicable basis (Criteria Committee, National Council on Alcoholism 1972). Of course, where clinicians and field investigators use the same terms — such as addiction — they often mean quite different things, and the communication gap grows even wider (Westermeyer 1971).

2. *Definition of Improvement* Follow-up studies commonly refer to percentage of patients improved in treatment programs. Unfortunately, criteria for "improvement" are often so vague as to defy replication or comparison. Since "improvement" appears strongly related to socioeconomic factors, it seems important to describe the sample demographically, as well as those who improve and those who do not.

3. *Definition of Therapy* Treatment studies generally refer to "counseling" or "vocational guidance" without specifically stating the activities, frequency or duration of contact, or qualifications of the therapists. Again, replication and comparison become virtually impossible.

Sampling

1. *Description of Subjects* No clinic population can be considered a random sample since so many factors influence who comes to them and who does not. However, the sample which does come can be accurately described in both demographic and clinical terms. These descriptions do allow certain kinds of cross-cultural comparisons to be made despite the sampling bias inherent in the clinical method. Certain admission criteria, such as those for admission of alcohol-dependent patients to general hospitals (Committee on Alcoholism 1969) help to validate further the use of in-patients as an alcohol sample.

2. *Ethnic Differences in Access to Medical Care* Where ethnic groups use the same clinical facility, one can usually presume the existence of factors which result in differential access to the facilities (Kosa, et al. 1969). Perhaps some of these ethnic factors might theoretically be ameliorated by attending carefully to the composition of the staff and to community attitudes towards the facility. Multiple non-ethnic factors, such as distance from home to the facility, also play a role in access to medical care (Mellsop 1969).

3. Migration Factors Where two ethnic groups inhabit the same geographic area, cross-cultural studies can often be carried out conveniently. In such circumstances, however, one group has often migrated into the area in more recent times. Since differences secondary to migration itself may persist for at least two or three generations (and often longer) the investigator may unearth spurious correlations. Generally also, the more recent immigration has lower socioeconomic status (Warner 1937; Malzburg and Lee 1956).

Research Strategies

1. Native versus Foreign Investigator Most desirable appears to be the situation in which several clinical investigators, each in his own society, use similar criteria and research tools to study the same phenomenon. Such cooperation does not ordinarily occur voluntarily, however, and this approach often occurs only by chance. It appears most apt to occur where the criteria and phenomena under consideration are simple and explicit. Of course, some cultural groups do not have investigators trained to do this kind of research work.

Where criteria, tools, or phenomena become more vague or complex, or where trained people are not available, the "multiple negative investigators" method breaks down. The single investigator approach (or single group of investigators) then appears most likely to give results. But such investigators can usually be "native" to only one culture. One's very foreignness can lead to particular problems in the field like alcoholism; for example, social definitions regarding what comprises problematic behavior or questions regarding what social problems are alcohol related become issues. Communication and transference problems also combine with culture-bound definitions and attitudes to make this area a quagmire for the uninitiated (Hall 1959; Caudill 1959–1962; Wedge 1959–1962; Useem 1959–1962; Langer and Michaels 1963; Cooper, et al. 1969; Del Castillo 1970; Mackinnon and Michels 1971; Hsu and Tseng 1972; Lurie and Lawrence 1972; Carter and Harzlip 1972; Marcos, et al. 1973).

2. Advantages of the Clinical Setting Certain kinds of alcohol-related problems can be most efficiently studied in clinical settings: alcohol addiction; the medical, psychiatric, and surgical sequelae of problematic alcohol usage; controlled drinking studies. Other genera of problems are best focused upon elsewhere (e.g. alcohol-related driving offenses, bankruptcy). Of course, cross-cultural questions can and should be broached in various settings in order to appreciate the multi-faceted nature of alcoholism in various cultures.

In-patient studies allow the researcher to have access to the subject for days or weeks, thus permitting collection of considerable amounts of data. Out-patient studies permit prolonged, repetitive contact with the patient over months or years. A variety of biological, psychological, and sociocultural data can be correlated with one another in order to discern ways in which these factors do or do not vary together. Collection and examination of biological and some psychological data require elaborate equipment which are generally present only at larger clinical facilities.

Clinical facilities often elicit reasonably good cooperation from subjects who — in their role as patients — are ordinarily motivated to involve themselves in collaboration with clinicians for their own betterment. Large numbers of alcohol subjects can be obtained at clinical facilities, since so many medical problems are alcohol related and some facilities treat only alcoholics.

3. Complementary Studies Clearly, clinical investigations alone cannot provide the breadth of studies so crucial to a comprehensive understanding of alcoholism. But they can contribute a great deal to the cross-cultural study of alcoholism, especially when the possible sources of bias are explicitly recognized and controlled for insofar as possible. Comparison of "alcoholics" encountered at separate institutional loci — only infrequently undertaken (Selzer 1969) — may assist in this effort.

Research Tools

1. Culture-Bound Research Tools Questionnaires and psychological tests are especially prone to inherent cross-cultural bias unless they have been standardized to the population in which they have been used. The same may be true even of some "hard" biological tests which tap nutritional and genetic-constitutional differences. Indeed, it would seem that any and all research instruments should be expected to contain such bias until it has been demonstrated on "normal" random samples of all reference groups that they do not contain such bias.

2. Observation of Drinking Behavior A multitude of moral and other beliefs becloud the entire issue of alcohol usage, both among "normals" and "alcoholics." Actual observation of drinking, and replication of these studies, have begun to place the entire study of alcohol problems on a more solid foundation. Many assumptions, long held in the field, have now begun to come under scrutiny. Hopefully, this method will soon be applied to cross-cultural aspects of alcoholism.

3.   Demographic, Historical, and Clinical Variables   Even such simple demographic variables as age may not be strictly comparable between cultures, since some people do not record their age, while others tend to overstate or understate their age. Social factors, such as marital status or employment, may be even more difficult to compare.

Historical questionnaires are also subject to cultural bias. For example, where a society values drunkenness as a social excuse for breaking ideal norms, one might expect a high rate of amnesia for social behavior (alcoholic "blackout") as compared to a society in which drunkenness does not provide a similar excuse.

Clinical variables may provide more objective measures. Withdrawal toxicity, rate of metabolism of alcohol, breathalyzer and serological tests, postmortem studies should be employed in cross-cultural studies. They can also be correlated with demographic and historical factors. However, even these more "objective" observations can be related to observer variation or to ethnic-environmental factors, such as nutrition and access to medical care, so that one must be wary of invoking genetic-constitutional factors in explaining differences.

4.   SUMMARY

Thus far, cross-cultural alcohol studies in the clinical setting have been few. This setting does lend itself to certain investigations which cannot readily be done elsewhere, such as the testing of linkage theory between biological, behavioral, and social parameters. However, one must always beware of generalizing from data observed only in the clinical setting since numerous confounding problems are inherent in the method.

REFERENCES

ACKERMAN, J. M.
1968 "Clinical events attending father loss in the histories of V. A. schizophrenic and alcoholic patients." Ph.D. dissertation, University of Colorado, Denver.

ALLMAN, L. R., H. A. TAYLOR, P. E. NATHAN
1972 Group drinking during stress: effects on drinking behavior, affect and psychopathology. *American Journal of Psychiatry* 129:669–678.

BARCHA, R., M. A. STEWART, S. B. GUZE
1968 The prevalence of alcoholism among general hospital ward patients. *American Journal of Psychiatry* 125:681–684.

BENNET, R., A. BUSS, J. CARPENTER
1969 Alcohol and human physical aggression. *Quarterly Journal of Studies on Alcohol* 30:870–876.

BIRRELL, R. G., J. H. BIRRELL
1968 The maltreatment syndrome in children: a hospital survey. *Medical Journal of Australia* 2:1023–1029.

BLACK, A. L.
1969 Altering behavior of geriatric patients with beer. *Northwest Medicine* 68:453–456.

BOYER, L. B.
1964 "Psychological problems of a group of Apaches: alcoholic hallucinations and latent homosexuality among typical men," in *The Psychoanalytic study of society*. Edited by W. Muensterberger and S. Axelrod. New York: International Universities Press.

CANTWELL, D. P.
1972 Psychiatric illness in the families of hyperactive children. *Archives of General Psychiatry* 27:414–417.

CARTER, J. II., T. M. HARZLIP
1972 Race and its relevance to transference. *American Journal of Orthopsychiatry* 42:865–871.

CAUDILL, W.
1959–1962 *Some problems in transcultural communication*. Group for the Advancement of Psychiatry, Symposium 7. New York: Group for the Advancement of Psychiatry.

CHASE, H. P., H. P. MARTIN
1970 Undernutrition and child development. *New England Journal of Medicine* 282:933–938.

CHIEN, C. P., B. A. STOTSKY, J. O. COLE
1973 Psychiatric treatment for nursing home patients: drug, alcohol, milieu. *American Journal of Psychiatry* 130:543–548.

CHOMET, B., B. GACH
1967 Lobar pneumonia and alcoholism: an analysis of thirty-seven cases. *American Journal of the Medical Sciences* 253:300–304.

COMMITTEE ON ALCOHOLISM
1969 Guidelines for admission of alcohol-dependent patients to general hospitals. *Journal of the American Medical Association* 210:121.

COOPER, J. E., R. E. KENDALL, B. J. GURLAND
  1969   Cross-national study of diagnoses of the mental disorders: some results from the first comparative investigation. *American Journal of Psychiatry*, supplement 125:21–29.
CRIKELAIR, G. F., F. C. SYMONDS, R. N. OLLSTEIN
  1968   Burn causation: its many sides. *Journal of Trauma* 8:572–582.
CRITERIA COMMITTEE, NATIONAL COUNCIL ON ALCOHOLISM
  1972   Criteria for the diagnosis of alcoholism. *American Journal of Psychiatry* 129:127–135.
DEL CASTILLO, J. C.
  1970   The influence of language upon sympatomatology in foreign-born patients. *American Journal of Psychiatry* 127:242–244.
DE LINT, J. E. E.
  1964   Alcoholism, birth rank and parental deprivation. *American Journal of Psychiatry* 120:1062–1065.
DENNEHY, C. M.
  1966   Childhood bereavement and psychiatric illness. *British Journal of Psychiatry* 112:1049–1069.
DERRICK, E. H.
  1967   A survey of mortality caused by alcohol. *Medical Journal of Australia* 2:914–919.
DEVEREAUX, M. W., R. A. MC CORMICK
  1972   Psychogenic water intoxication: a case report. *American Journal of Psychiatry* 129:628–630.
FENNA, D., L. MIX, O. SCHAEFER, J. A. L. GILBERT
  1971   Ethanol metabolism in various racial groups. *Canadian Medical Association Journal* 105:475–475. (Reprinted in this volume.)
FUNK, L. P., J. H. PRESCOTT
  1967   Study shows wine aids patient attitudes. *Modern Hospital* 108:182–184.
GALLANT, D. M., M. P. BISHOP, A. MOULEDOUZ, M. A. FAULKNER, A. BRISOLARA, W. A. SWANSON
  1973   The revolving door alcoholic. *Archives of General Psychiatry* 28:633–635.
GERREIN, J. R., C. M. ROSENBERG, V. MANOHAR
  1973   Disulfiram in outpatient treatment of alcoholism. *Archives of General Psychiatry* 28:798–802.
GILLIS, L. S.
  1969   The mortality rate and causes of death of treated chronic alcoholics. *South African Medical Journal* 43:230–232.
GILLIS, L. S., M. KEET
  1969   Prognostic factors and treatment results in hospitalized alcoholics. *Quarterly Journal of Studies on Alcohol* 30:426–437.
GLATT, M. M.
  1967   Complications in the social sphere. *British Journal of Addiction* 62:35–44.
GOLDFRIED, M. R.
  1969   Prediction of improvement in an alcoholism outpatient clinic. *Quarterly Journal of Studies on Alcohol* 30:129–139.

GOODWIN, D. W.
  1973 "Is alcoholism inherited?" Paper presented at the Annual Alcoholism Conference of the National Institute of Alcohol Abuse and Alcoholism, Washington, D.C.
GOODWIN, D. W., J. B. CRANE, S. R. GUZE
  1969 Alcoholic "blackouts": review and clinical study of 100 alcoholics. *American Journal of Psychiatry* 126:191–198.
GRISLAIN, J. R., R. MAINARD, P. DE BERRANGER
  1968 Child abuse: social and legal problems. *Annals of Pediatrics* 15: 440–448.
GROSS, M. M., S. M. ROSENBLATT, E. LEWIS, S. CHARTOFF, B. MALENOWSKI
  1972 Acute alcoholic psychoses and related syndromes: psychosocial and clinical characteristics and their implications. *British Journal of Addiction* 67:15–31.
HADDON, W., V. BRADESS
  1959 Alcohol in the single vehicle fatal accident: experience of Westchester County, New York. *Journal of the American Medical Association* 169:1587–1593.
HALL, E. T.
  1959 *The silent language.* Greenwich: Fawcett Publications.
HOFFMAN, H.
  1972 "Hospitalized Minnesota Indians: their psychiatric history, psychopathology and motivation." Paper presented at the International Congress on Alcoholism and Drug Dependence, Amsterdam.
HORN, J. L., K. W. WANBERG
  1969 Symptom patterns related to excessive use of alcohol. *Quarterly Journal of Studies on Alcohol* 30:35–38.
HSU, J., W. TSENG
  1972 Intercultural psychotherapy. *Archives of General Psychiatry* 27: 700–704.
JELLINEK, E. M.
  1943 "Death from alcoholism" in the United States in 1940. *Quarterly Journal of Studies on Alcohol* 3:465–494.
  1959 Estimating the prevalence of alcoholism: modified values in the Jellinek formula and an alternative approach. *Quarterly Journal of Studies on Alcohol* 20:261–296.
JOLLIFFE, N., E. M. JELLINEK
  1941 Cirrhosis of the liver. *Quarterly Journal of Studies on Alcohol* 2:544–583.
KASTL, A. J.
  1969 Changes in ego functioning under alcohol. *Quarterly Journal of Studies on Alcohol* 30:371–383.
KINSEY, B. A.
  1968 Psychological factors in alcoholic women from a state hospital sample. *American Journal of Psychiatry* 124:1436–1466.
KINSEY, B. A., L. PHILLIPS
  1968 Evaluation of anomy as a predisposing or developmental factor in alcohol addiction. *Quarterly Journal of Studies on Alcohol* 28: 892–898.

KOLLER, K. M., J. N. CASTAÑOS
  1969 Family background and life situation: a comparative study of parental deprivation and other features in Australians. *Archives of General Psychiatry* 21:602–610.

KOSA, J., A. ANTONOVSKY, I. K. ZOLA
  1969 Poverty and health. Cambridge, Mass: Harvard University Press.

KUNITZ, S. J., J. E. LEVY, C. J. ODOROFF, J. BOLLINGER
  1971 The epidemiology of alcoholism in two Southwestern Indian tribes. *Quarterly Journal of Studies on Alcohol* 32:706–720.

LA BARRE, W.
  1941 A cultist drug addiction in an Indian alcoholic. *The Bulletin of the Meninger Clinic* 5:40–56.

LANGER, T. S., S. T. MICHAELS
  1963 *Life stress and mental health.* New York. Free Press of Glencoe.

LURIE, H. J., G. L. LAWRENCE
  1972 Communication problems between rural Mexican-American patients and their physicians: description of a solution. *American Journal of Orthopsychiatry* 42:777–783.

MACKINNON, R. A., R. MICHELS
  1971 "Interviewing through an interpreter," in *The psychiatric interview in clinical practice.* Philadelphia: Saunders.

MALZBURG, B., E. S. LEE
  1956 *Migration and mental disease.* New York: Social Science Research Council.

MARCONI, J., K. FINK, L. MOYA
  1967 Experimental study on alcoholics with an "inability to stop." *British Journal of Psychiatry* 113:543–545.

MARCOS, L. R., M. ALPERT, L. URCUYO, M. KESSELMAN
  1973 The effect of interview language on the evaluation of psychopathology in Spanish-American schizophrenic patients. *American Journal of Psychiatry* 130:549–553.

MARTÍNEZ, I.
  1969 Factors associated with cancer of the esophagus, mouth and pharynx in Puerto Rico. *Journal of the National Cancer Institute* 42:1069–1094.

MAYFIELD, D. G.
  1968 Psychopharmacology of alcohol, I: Affective change with intoxication, drinking behavior, and affective state. *Journal of Nervous and Mental Diseases* 146:314–321.

MAYFIELD, D., D. ALLEN
  1967 Alcohol and affect: a psychopharmacological study. *American Journal of Psychiatry* 123:1346–1351.

MAYFIELD, D., A. MONTGOMERY
  1972 Alcoholism, alcohol intoxication, and suicide attempts. *Archives of General Psychiatry* 27:349–353.

MC NAMEE, H. B., N. K. MELLO, J. H. MENDELSON
  1968 Experimental analysis of drinking patterns of alcoholics. Concurrent psychiatric observations. *American Journal of Psychiatry* 124:1063–1069.

MELLSOP, G. W.
  1969   The effect of distance in determining hospital admission rates. *Medical Journal of Australia* 2:814–817.

NATHAN, P. E., N. A. TITHER, L. M. LOWENSTEIN, P. SOLOMEN, A. M. ROSSI
  1970   Behavioral analysis of chronic alcoholism. *Archives of General Psychiatry* 22:419–430.

NAU, E.
  1967   Kindermisshandlung [Child abuse]. *Monatsschrift Kinderheilkunde* 115:192–194.

NIEMANN, N.
  1968   Child abuse. *Semaine des hospitaux de Paris* 44:1523–1525.

PATTISON, E. M., E. B. HEADLEY, G. C. GLESER, L. A. GOTTSCHALK
  1968   Abstinence and normal drinking: an assessment of changes in drinking patterns in alcoholics after treatment. *Quarterly Journal of Studies on Alcohol* 29:610–633.

PINCOCK, T. A.
  1964   Alcoholism in tuberculosis patients. *Canadian Medical Association Journal* 91:851–854.

PISKIN, V., S. FRIKKEN
  1972   Concept learning in chronic alcoholics: psychophysiological and sex functioning. *Journal of Clinical Psychology* 28:328–334.

ROOM, R.
  1968   Cultural contingencies of alcoholism: variations between and within nineteenth century urban ethnic groups in alcohol-related death rates. *Journal of Health and Social Behavior* 9:99–113.

ROSENTHAL, D.
  1970   *Genetic theory and abnormal behavior.* New York: McGraw-Hill.

RUSHING, W. A.
  1969   Suicide and the interaction of alcoholism (liver cirrhosis) with the social situation. *Quarterly Journal of Studies on Alcohol* 30:93–103.

RYBACK, R. S.
  1970   Alcohol amnesia. *Quarterly Journal of Studies on Alcohol* 31:616–632.

SAMPSON, E. E.
  1965   The study of ordinal position: antecedants and outcomes. *Progress in Experimental Personality Research* 2:175–228.

SANDS, P. M., P. G. HANSON, R. B. SHELDON
  1967   Recurring themes in group psychotherapy with alcoholics. *Psychiatric Quarterly* 41:474–482.

SAVARD, R. J.
  1968   Effects of disulfiram therapy in relationships within the Navajo drinking group. *Quarterly Journal of Studies on Alcohol* 29:909–916.

SCHMIDT, W., J. DE LINT
  1969   Mortality experiences of male and female alcoholic patients. *Quarterly Journal of Studies on Alcohol* 30:112–118.

SCHUCKIT, M. A., D. A. GOODWIN, G. WINOKUR
  1972   A study of alcoholism in half siblings. *American Journal of Psychiatry* 128:1132–1136.

SCHWARY, L., S. P. FJELD
  1969   The alcoholic patient in the psychiatric emergency room. *Quarterly Journal of Studies on Alcohol* 30:104–111.

SEELEY, J. R.
  1959   Estimating the prevalence of alcoholism: modified values in the Jellinek formula and an alternative approach. *Quarterly Journal of Studies on Alcohol* 20:245–253.

SELZER, M.
  1969   Alcoholics at fault in fatal accidents and hospitalized alcoholics: a comparison. *Quarterly Journal of Studies on Alcohol* 30:883–887.

SHORE, J. H., B. VON FUMETTI
  1972   Three alcohol programs for American Indians. *American Journal of Psychiatry* 128:1450–1454.

SIEVERS, M. L.
  1968   Cigarette and alcohol usage by southwestern American Indians. *American Journal of Public Health* 58:71–82.

SIMON, A., L. EPSTEIN, L. REYNOLDS
  1968   Alcoholism in the geriatric mentally ill. *Geriatrics* 23:125–131.

SKOPKOVA, H.
  1967   Catamnestic study of 366 voluntary and constrained patients admitted to the anti-alcoholic ward. *British Journal of Addiction* 62:275–280.

STEIN, L. I., D. NILES, A. M. LUDWIG
  1968   The loss of control phenomenon in alcoholics. *Quarterly Journal of Studies on Alcohol* 29:598–602.

SWANSON, D. W.
  1968   Adult sexual abuse of children. *Diseases of the Nervous System* 29:677–683.

TAMERIN, J. S., J. H. MENDELSON
  1969   Psychodynamics of chronic inebriation: observations of alcoholics during the process of drinking in an experimental group setting. *American Journal of Psychiatry* 125:886–889.

TAMERIN, J. S., S. WEINER, J. H. MENDELSON
  1970   Alcoholics' expectancies and recall of experiences during intoxication. *American Journal of Psychiatry* 126:1697–1704.

TERRIS, M.
  1967   Epidemiology of cirrhosis of the liver: national mortality data. *American Journal of Public Health* 57:2076–2088.

USEEM, R.
  1959–1962   *Interpersonal relationships between Indians and Americans in India.* Group for the Advancement of Psychiatry, Symposium 7. New York: Group for the Advancement of Psychiatry.

WANBERG, K., J. HORN
  1970   Alcoholism symptom patterns of men and women, a comparative study. *Quarterly Journal of Studies on Alcohol* 31:40–61.

WARNER, W. L.
  1937   The society, the individual, and his mental disorders. *American Journal of Psychiatry* 94:275–284.
WECHSLER, H., E. H. KASEY, D. THUM, H. W. DEMONE
  1969   Alcohol level and home accidents. *Public Health Report* 84:1043–1050.
WEDGE, B.
  1959–1962   *Towards a science of transnational communication.* Group for the Advancement of Psychiatry, Symposium 7. New York: Group for the Advancement of Psychiatry.
WESTERMEYER, J.
  1971   Uses of alcohol and opium by the Meo of Laos. *American Journal of Psychiatry* 127:1019–1023.
  1972   Chippewa and majority alcoholism in the Twin Cities, a comparison. *Journal of Nervous and Mental Diseases.* 155:322–327.
WESTERMEYER, J., J. BRANTNER
  1972   Violent death and alcohol use among the Chippewa in Minnesota. *Minnesota Medicine* 55:749–752.
WOLFF, P. H.
  1972   Ethnic differences in alcohol sensitivity. *Science* 175:449–450.

The Cultural Approach, Verbal Plans, and Alcohol Research

MARTIN D. TOPPER

The cultural approach to alcohol studies was demonstrated by Bunzel over thirty years ago. Recently, other anthropologists such as Mandelbaum (1965), Lomnitz (1969), Heath (1962, 1964), Hage (1971), Spradley (1970, 1971), Everett (1972a, 1972b, 1973), Everett, et al. (1973), Topper (1973, i.p.), and Waddell (1973) have shown an interest in the further development around the use of an ethnoscience methodology. Those using ethnoscience to study drinking see alcohol use within any particular culture as being related to a much larger set of cultural beliefs, rules, and plans which govern more than just drinking behavior. To quote Everett (1972a: 1):

... Superficial cross-cultural surveys and the unsystematic ethnographies upon which these are based exhibit a severe shortcoming .... They have been primarily behavioristic, i.e. focused on empirical observations of drinking activities as perceived and conceptualized by a presumably objective observer. The problem, of course, is that even though the perceptions of the observer and participant may be similar, these may take on conceptual or cognitive dimensions of quite a different order and magnitude. One possible solution to this problem is to construct theories of drinking in specific cultures and a general theory of drinking in terms of both behavior and meaning.

The cultural approach has been criticized from several perspectives. Many of these criticisms were discussed at the recent "Conference on Alcohol Studies and Anthropology," where many of the papers in this

I thank the Smithsonian Institution, the National Institute of Health, and the National Institute of Alcohol Abuse and Alcoholism for inviting me to this conference held at the University of Chicago, August 27–30, 1973.

volume were presented (see the Introduction to this volume). A question was raised about the difficulty which the cultural approach presents for the study of alcohol use in large, culturally plural nation states which may not have easily identifiable subcultures. Others commented on the difficulty of getting lost in the data and never abstracting hypotheses which can be tested cross-culturally. Finally, there is one public health viewpoint. It is quite possible that normative drinking patterns may have serious long-term consequences for the physical and mental health of the people being studied; for example, the fact that French workers drink moderate amounts of wine throughout the day leads to a high incidence of cirrhosis of the liver in the population. The cultural or "ethnoscientific" approach was further criticized with regard to the study of alcohol and mental health problems; it was noted that cultural descriptions were valid only when accompanied by data derived from observation. Thus, it is important to know what informants were "actually" doing as well as what they and others thought was going on. In this way, the clinician can understand normative and deviant behavior from both a cultural and a clinical perspective.

This paper presents a research strategy designed to help resolve some of the questions raised about the use of the cultural perspective in alcohol studies. The strategy has been recently developed during several years of fieldwork on the Navajo Indian Reservation in northern Arizona. It involves the elicitation of verbal plans for both drinking behavior and for the daily activities of the informant. The domain of drinking activity, both normative and deviant, as seen by the informant is investigated first. Then verbal activity plans are elicited for the daily life of the informant. The two sets of plans are compared to develop a picture of how drinking activities are coordinated with other culturally patterned behavior. Third, the events at which drinking occurs are observed as much as possible by the investigator. In this way some measurement can be made as to the coincidence of "real" and "ideal" behavior patterns. Finally, the investigator uses his participant-observations of the culture of the informants to develop an overall theory of drinking.

THE CULTURAL INVESTIGATION OF DRINKING

The methodology which I employed to study the cultural perspective of Navajo Indian drinking is described elsewhere in considerable detail (Topper i.p.). However, the general procedure can be briefly reviewed.

The Taxomonic Investigation of the Domain of "Drinkers"

The first step in the cultural investigation of drinking behavior is the elicitation, in the native language of the informants, of a taxonomy of drinking types (see Spradley 1970: Chapter 3). Such a taxonomy for Navajo drinkers is presented in detail in Figure 1. The use of such a taxonomy tells the investigator several things about the culture which he is studying. First, it tells him who may drink. It provides the investigator with a cultural definition of normative and deviant drinking behavior. And finally, the breakdown of the drinking categories by distinctive attributes gives him an indication of the salient features of the native definition of drinking types. For example, the Navajo taxonomy of drinking types employs the semantic dimensions of age and sex to form the first set of categories, the native definition of normative versus deviant behavior to form the second, and the type of liquor to form the third.

Verbal Plans

Once a taxonomy of drinking types has been elicited, it is possible to elicit verbal plans for the drinking behaviors of the various categories of drinkers. At this point, an interesting phenomenon has been found to occur in previous studies. Verbal plans cannot be elicited for all levels of the taxonomy. The Navajo have no general plan which covers the entire domain of drinkers. However, when one gets to the second level of the taxonomy, it is possible to elicit verbal plans. But then one must add one additional piece of information. It was found that it was very important to know which drinking environment the informant was describing. With Navajos, and with Anglo-Americans as well, drinking behaviors are patterned to closely coincide with their environments. This should not be construed to be a statement for environmental determination because the drinking environments, like the drinking patterns, are cultural artifacts. Simply stated, people alter the natural environment to create environments for culturally patterned behaviors. For example, we have built universities for the conduct of specific cultural behaviors which we refer to as "higher education." And even when university buildings are not being used specifically for instructional purposes, the behaviors which occur in these buildings coincide with the structure of the artificial environment, but they are in no way "determined by it."

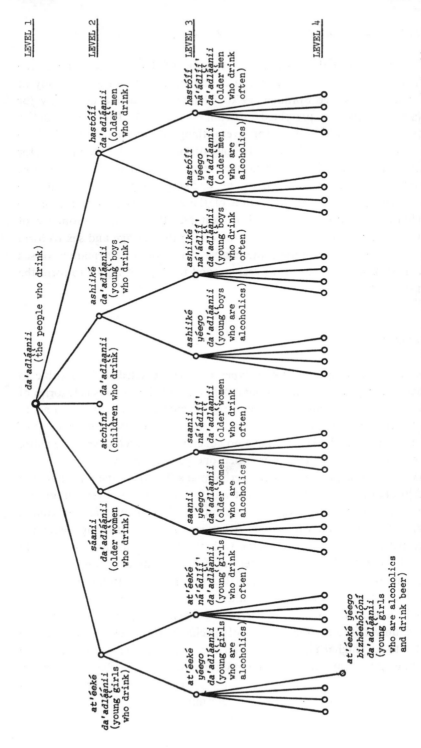

Figure 1.   Composite taxonomy of Navajo drinking types. The distinctive attribute at Level 4 is type of beverage: beer, whiskey, wine, and home-made wine. For example, "the young girls who are alcoholics and drink **beer**" (from Topper 1973)

Verbal Plans: History

Before the actual elicitation of the verbal plans is discussed, it is necessary to provide the reader with a short description of the history and theoretical basis of the verbal plan. The verbal plan as presented here was first developed by Oswald Werner in 1965, who used it to describe the daily activities of one of his Navajo informants. Werner's basic idea was to have his informant give a native language in-sequence description of the activities which he performed during the course of his daily life. The data were elicited in a strict framework based on theoretical constructs proposed by Chomsky (1965) and Miller, et al. (1960). After Werner's initial work, the plans were revised and subsequently retested by Werner and myself. During this period of testing, several improvements were made. New methods of drawing the plans were attempted. The theoretical bases of the plans were made clearer. A vastly improved decision model was added.

Verbal Plan: Theory

The end result was a data-eliciting technique which can be used to develop structural native descriptions of planned activities in the language of the informant. This means that the anthropologist is no longer bound to use his own participant-observation as his major method of describing his informant's behavior. He can now use his informant's structured descriptions as a means of checking the "accuracy" of his observations. By eliciting the informant's plans for an activity sequence before observing it, the anthropologist can clearly see which segments the informant considers to be the most "important." The fieldworker can then compare his observations to theirs. In short, the verbal plan provides the anthropologist with a much desired means of establishing a native "control" by which to judge his observations and to study the relationship of "ideal" to "real" behavior.

Although a descriptive device like the verbal plan has been sought in anthropology for a long time (see Sturtevant 1964: 130–131), it has only been recently that our knowledge of language and cognitive psychology has become sufficient to allow its development. Much of the theory upon which the plans are based has been developed by the earlier work of the linguistic anthropologists (for a review, see Sturtevant 1964). Other aspects have come from the work of linguists, cognitive psychologists, and computer-programming experts.

The linguistic anthropologists have contributed a great deal with their studies of semantic structure as exhibited in the language of peoples of non-Western cultures. Three recent works which have been very important to the development of the verbal plan have been Casagrande and Hale (1967), Werner (1969, 1972), and Werner, et al. (1969). These papers deal with the development of a typology of semantic relationships. Included among these relationships is that of sequencing (Werner's queuing) which is the crucial element of the verbal plan. It is this relationship of queuing which allows the informant to string phrases together to provide a step-by-step description of an activity. The partial demonstration of the cross-cultural applicability of the queuing relationship and its proposal as a semantic universal by Werner (1969) is extremely important. One of the major goals of good ethnography is good ethnology. If the verbal plan is derived by methods based on semantic universals, then the structures of the plan can theoretically be compared across languages and cultures. The importance of this proposed comparability for the development of a cross-cultural theory of alcohol use is clear.

The development of the theory behind verbal plans was also aided by cognitive psychologists. They provided a working model for the plan. This is the TOTE model proposed by Miller, et al. (1960), a model based on a proposed four-part interaction between an organism and its environment. The four parts fit together in the sequence: Test, Operate, Test, Exit. Miller, et al. (1960) also stated that TOTE units are hierarchical in nature. Therefore, one large unit can contain many levels composed of smaller units. This indicates that a person performing a task can operate on many levels simultaneously. For example, a woman can be "pushing a needle through a piece of cloth" and at the same time be performing the task called, "sewing a dress."

Finally, there are the contributions which have been made from the fields of computer programming and logic. Miller, et al. (1960: 36) provided a working model for the plan, but their method of diagramming left much to be desired. Their flow charts were difficult to read, and they consumed a considerable amount of space. Furthermore, the charts used required a considerable amount of footnoting. To meet these problems, Werner and I experimented with several different methods of drawing the flow charts. Two major improvements came with Werner's use of an inverse of Bierman's associational model for the construction of the flow chart and the introduction of decision logic tables to describe the interaction between the individual and his drinking environment (see McDaniel 1968; Pollack, et al. 1971). The decision tables were a major improvement since they provided a model for the alteration of planned behavior as well as a model for the mediation of environmental inputs in the mind of the informant.

Verbal Plan: Structure

The basic structure of the verbal plan is quite simple. There are four main elements: the lines, the nodes (or circles), the decision tables, and the verbal descriptions for each step which are listed at the bottom of each page (see the Appendix).

The lines represent lexical phrases. They are the steps in the plan. Each line corresponds to a numbered verbal description at the bottom of the page. For example, the line marked IV in the diagram corresponds to the verbal statement marked IV below the diagram. It states that "people volunteer their contributions." The lines and phrases also represent TOTE units. In this case, the TOTE unit is one involving group action. The reader will notice that this TOTE unit is composed of two smaller ones labelled A and B.

The nodes or circles which connect the lines represent the queuing relationship. The relationship has a specific lexical label. In English that label is "and then," in Navajo it is *aadoo*. One of the primary tasks of the investigator is to discover the phrases which his informants use for sequencing in their native language. This then becomes one of the basic elements of the eliciting frame (see Spradley 1971: 241) used to elicit plans. If more than one phrase may be used, it is important to discover which one has the broadest possible usage. In this way, the plans will be as context free as possible.

Finally, there are the decision tables. Each decision table represents a special kind of step in the plan. It is a step in which the actor takes account of the environment[1] and chooses one of several potential action sequences.[2] These sequences are then performed (barring unexpected interruption) until another decision table is reached or until the informant ends his daily activities by going to sleep.

The decision table is composed of four basic parts: the condition stub, the action stub, the condition entry, and the action entry (for a fuller explanation, see Pollack, et al. 1971). The condition stub contains all of the possible environmental influences (both "internal and "external")

[1]   It is important to note that the environments referred to here involve both internal inputs from the informant's mind (such as desires, moods, and states of mind) as well as the inputs from the social and physical environment outside of the informant.
[2]   With group decisions, the decision tables represent one informant's view of the group decision-making process. A complete view of the process would require the elicitation of decision tables from all participants in the group.

which the informant feels impinge upon the decision situation. The action stub contains all of the possible actions which the informant may take in a particular decision situation. The condition entry contains those conditions which occur in any given decision situation. And the action entry contains those actions which are appropriate for any given set of conditions in the condition entry. When a condition entry and its appropriate action entry are combined, a decision rule is formed. The rule represents one possible pathway through a decision table (see Figure 2).

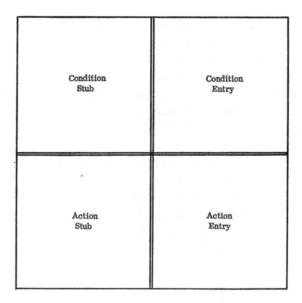

Figure 2.   The basic structure of decision table

Verbal Plans: Reading

Since the verbal plan has been designed along the principles of a flow chart, it is relatively easy to read. One simply begins at the left and reads toward the right. However, a few complexities do appear as one goes through the plan. The first arises from the hierarchical nature of the plan. The examples in the Appendix to this paper indicate that any step in a plan may also have substeps. Up to the present, it has been possible to elicit as many as four levels of substeps for any single step in a plan. Given the hierarchical nature of Miller's TOTE unit, the reader of a plan should expect to frequently find steps which have substeps.

A second area of potential difficulty lies in the reading of the repeat sequences. These are special kinds of TOTE units. They are symbolized by a capital "R" placed on top of the sequencing node. When this symbol is encountered (see the Appendix), the reader is told that the informant must follow the arrow back several steps and repeat the immediately preceding sequence of operations until a final test is satisfied. Once this happens, the informant continues on with the plan.

Finally, there may be some difficulty in reading the decision tables. Although there is a decision table symbol on the flow chart where a decision table would normally be found, the tables themselves are drawn on a separate sheet of paper. This has been done to reduce the size of the flow charts. Actually, this was one of the major breakthroughs in getting the plans down to a size which could be published. Some of the decision tables which have been encountered have had up to thirty-eight separate conditions and actions. A decision table this large takes several pages to diagram. If such tables were inserted into the flow charts, one would lose all sense of continuity in the plan. Therefore, a simple box with a numbered rule leading out of it has been put into the flow chart to indicate that a decision has been made and that a specific rule is in operation.

Verbal Plan: Eliciting

The verbal plan is a rather complex model of cognition. Many readers of this paper may wonder if it is possible to elicit a structured description of this complexity in the field among non-Western peoples. The answer to this appears to be yes. In fact, both Werner and the writer have found that our informants readily used this eliciting structure once they had some practice. The key to eliciting the plans rests in developing a step by step strategy (i.e. a plan), for explaining our procedure to informants. The first and most crucial step in the procedure is the search for the proper translation label for the sequencing relationship. Without this, it would be impossible to elicit plans in the native language of the informant.

Once this has been accomplished, the topic for elicitation is chosen. With drinking studies, a category of drinkers is chosen. Usually the informant is asked to categorize himself according to his own taxonomy of drinkers. A list of drinking environments in which the informant participates is then elicited. Then a verbal plan is elicited for the informant's behavior in each of these environments.[3] In the next step, the

---

[3] If a study of total vs. shared vs. individual cultural knowledge is desired, the in-

plans are drawn by the investigator, and after a few days rest, the informant is asked to go through the plan and fill in as many substeps as possible. On occasion, the informant may indicate that he had forgotten a step and that he wants to add it to the plan. To be sure that the plans are as complete as possible, it is best to have each informant go through each plan three times.

Finally, the decision tables are elicited. These are placed at points in the plan where the informant claims that a decision must be made. Usually during the initial eliciting session, only rudimentary decision table structures will be elicited. The informant is asked what he usually does in the decision situation and what the alternatives are. He is then asked to choose the course of action which he feels is most representative and continue with the plan. This de-emphasis on decision making is done so that the flow of the plan can be preserved in the informant's mind.

Those aspects of decision table elicitation occurring at later eliciting sessions are done in five steps. First, the informant is again asked to list all of the actions which he could take when he arrives at a decision point in the plan. This provides the action stub. Then he is asked what could lead to his taking each of these potential actions. This provides at least part of the condition stub. At this point, the decision tables are drawn, adding those conditions which are needed in order to make the logical structure of the tables work (see Pollack, et al. 1971; McDaniel 1968). At a later session, the added conditions and the decision rules are tested against the informant's knowledge. As a fourth step, various algorithms for reducing the number of decision rules are developed. It might also be possible to determine dependencies among conditions or actions. This would further reduce the complexity of the decision table structure. The fifth step is to check these changes in the tables against the informant's knowledge.

The Observation of Drinking Behavior

At this point, a fairly thorough description of the drinking behavior as seen by the informant has been developed. The next step in the methodology involves the observation of informants in the environments where they drink.

The first step in this procedure is to study the various drinking environments. In the past, it has been found convenient to draw a map of each environment. In doing so, close attention is paid to those features of the

---

formants can all be asked to generate verbal plans about the drinking behaviors of other categories of drinkers in the environments where they drink. Then the cultural knowledge of informants from various categories of drinkers can be compared.

environment which the informants mentioned in their plans. For example, teenage drinkers at Navajo western stomp dances show considerable concern about the whereabouts of the tribal police in their drinking plans. Therefore a map should include a description of the police patrol patterns, and observations of the police should include an estimate of their frequency in covering various areas of their "beats."

In addition to features which are specifically mentioned by informants, the map should also contain those features which the observer considers important. For example, the snack bar at a stomp dance was a place where a significant amount of social interaction occurred, but relatively little drinking. Therefore, it was generally omitted by the informants in their plans. Finally, features should be included in the map which were generally prominent in the environment, but where little or no drinking or socializing occurred. An example is the stage area of the gymnasiums where the western stomp dances were held. These were reserved for the country and western bands, and very limited social interaction occurred there.

Once the environments are mapped, the behavior of informants is then observed (as much as that is possible in large crowded dance halls or other places). They are observed as they move through various sub-environments (those defined for drinking and those for nondrinking). Their interactions with various individuals of all ages, sexes, and authority ranks are observed. In addition, the events in the general environment are noted. The number of people present, the kinds of activities which they were performing, and the general chronology of major group events (if any) during the observation period are measured. Observations are kept on small pieces of paper; when this is not possible, an account is written later.

During the early part of our Navajo research, an attempt was made to employ Barker's methodology (Barker and Wright 1951; Barker 1968) for the study of the environment of behavior. However, when it was employed in traditional Navajo settings, some difficulties arose which suggested that it was not applicable to non-Western societies. An attempt was made to rate traditional Navajo environments on the criteria Barker (1968: Chapter 4) established for a K-21 behavior setting. However, the necessary "action pattern ratings" could not be established because they were based on value judgments peculiar to Western civilizations such as "Aesthetics, Business, Education, Government, Nutrition, Personal Appearance, Physical Health, Professionalism, Recreation, Religion, and Social Contrast" (Barker 1968: 52). Most of these are almost totally inapplicable to the more traditional of today's Navajos.

Putting It All Together

Once the initial verbal plans for drinking behavior have been elicited from several informants, the observation is begun. The observation data and the data from elicitation are combined with several purposes in mind. The first is to check on the "accuracy" of the informants' statements. When the observations do not fit the informants' statements, it then becomes necessary to elicit some form of explanation. During our Navajo research, this only happened once on a scale of major importance. Informants were observed taking a risk they had earlier denounced as "foolish." The explanation was that, "When you get too worn down, you'll do anything." This points out an interesting correlation between intoxication and planned behavior. As one becomes more and more intoxicated, his plans seem to be more and more unstructured and temporary until he passes out and becomes essentially planless. This is, of course, a second argument for the use of observation as well as elicitation in drinking record.

A third and final reason for the integration of elicitation and observation comes from the use of a second type of observation. This is general participant-observation of the culture of the informant and the community in which he resides. This is very important for later use in attempting to develop an overall statement on the "functions" of drinking behavior (see Topper 1972, i.p.). It is also important for developing a rationale for understanding certain aspects of the verbal action plans. For example, the use of alcoholic beverages is prohibited for Navajos by tribal law. Under the law, however, persons under eighteen cannot be prosecuted. They are merely detained. It is also true that detaining every minor who has had a drink would interfere terribly with the main purpose of policing drinking events, namely, the prevention of violence. When the risk taking activities of Navajo minors in the drinking environment is considered in light of these observed and elicited police behaviors and attitudes, a partial "explanation" can be developed for its high incidence. This can then be used as a means of questioning the informants about the verbal plans and about the "meaning" and the "reasons" for both normal and "deviant" drinking as they define them.

SUMMARY: THE CULTURAL PERSPECTIVE AND ALCOHOL STUDIES

At the beginning of this paper, a number of questions raised about the usefulness of the cultural perspective for the study of drinking and "alcoholism" were presented. It is my belief that the methodology outlined in this paper provides at least a partial answer to these questions. Furthermore, the development of the verbal plan has provided a method of eliciting statements which is a great improvement over the traditionally unstructured (or nearly so) oral history. But let us consider each of those early questions in light of the present paper.

First, the point concerning subcultures is well taken. However, the cultural approach offers a more accurate means of subculture selection than many other techniques currently being employed to study pluralistic societies. One needs only to think about the difficulties encountered in urban surveying by census tract. Even a random sampling of census tracts can allow for a potential error when studying urban populations. In such a case, the cultural approach would argue for the study of various subcultures as they are defined by themselves and by the members of other subcultures in the urban area. The development of a definition of the subcultures in an urban population may prove to be a difficult task, but Spradley (1970, 1971) has already shown that it is quite feasible. A picture of the drinking patterns of an urban population could then be compiled as a combination of the various patterns of its subcultures. One could then compare the drinking patterns and cultural knowledge of various subcultures and arrive at a theoretical statement concerning similarities and differences in drinking behavior, knowledge, and "function" in a specific urban area.

One important aspect of the cultural approach is that it can be used as a complementary methodology to a statistical study of drinking patterns (sociological model of Spradley 1971: 240). For example, our study of Navajo drinking patterns in semi-urban environments (Topper i.p.) complements Graves' research (1970, 1971) on Navajo drinking in Denver. Graves does a good job of describing who is most likely to get arrested among urban Navajos and of defining the correlation of high arrest rate with underlying economic, social, educational, and "psychological" factors. But his research cannot tell us why Navajo arrest rates are so high to begin with. To do this, one must take a cultural approach and see how the informant defines normative and deviant drinking and how he defines his drinking environment. One must also study the environment in which the drinker has learned to drink. When one does this for the Navajo the higher rate of arrest in urban areas becomes quite understandable. Many Navajos are simply not capable of adapting their reservation-learned drinking patterns to the crowded, intense environment of the Anglo-American bar room (see Topper 1973b). In short, the cultural approach to drinking studies adds the necessary detail or flesh to the bare bones of demographic patterns.

The cultural approach also provides us with data on culturally defined normative drinking patterns which the "social problems" orientation of the sociological model ignores (Spradley 1971: 240). This definition of what is culturally "normal" by the informants is a necessary first step in the description of the drinking patterns of a specific population. From that point, sociological, legal, and medical (public health) models can be applied if one wants to know if that population's "normative" patterns are "deviant" from the point of view of another larger and "dominant" cultural group. Such a combined approach could be very valuable in applied anthropology.

The second problem, of not being able to abstract theory from the data, is not so serious as it might appear at first glance. This methodology does indeed produce a wealth of data. But those data are gathered from a viewpoint which is very theoretical from the start. The entire concept of culture as an integrated (structured) system of cultural knowledge is currently one of the major theoretical "paradigms" of anthropology. It goes under the various labels of "ethnoscience," "ethnoepistemology," "cognitive anthropology," and "linguistic anthropology." Furthermore, taking such an approach when studying drinking initially gives one a theoretical position to test. That position, stated simply, says that drinking is a cultural "artifact" and that within any particular cultural group, drinking behavior will be related to a shared set of knowledge which will define the various categories of drinkers, the places in which they may drink, and the behaviors which they may exhibit while drinking.

Once the data have been gathered and the structure of the informants' cultural knowledge about drinking has been defined, it should then be possible to compare these structures cross-culturally. This is because the semantic relationships upon which the structures are based have been proposed as semantic universals (see Werner 1969, 1972). From this point, one may then compare the entire sets of cultural knowledge and then develop cross-culturally testable hypotheses about the nature of alcohol use and abuse. Bunzel's (1940) early comparative work in Mexico and Guatemala established the potential for such cross-cultural research, but, as of yet, there has been no test of this approach from the standpoint of present-day cognitive anthropology. The methodology of cognitive anthropology is yet in its infancy. But with methods such as the ones presented here and those others like Spradley (1970, 1971), Everett (1972a, 1972b), Waddell (1973), and Hage (1971) have presented, it is hoped that a test may soon be possible. Even so, at the present time it can be said with some certainty that drinking behavior does appear to be regulated to a very great degree by the cultural knowledge which the drinker possesses. This in itself is a major theoretical advancement.

Finally, there is the position that studies of "ideal" behavior may have limited relevance for the clinician. This point is made even stronger by the notion that even if ideal behavior correlated strongly to behavior which was observed, it still may be very difficult to correlate an ideal cultural model with actual cases of "deviant" drinking behavior (Westermeyer, personal communication). The point is well taken, but it is often more difficult to use data gathered using the sociological model to help understand actual clinical cases. Part of the problem arises from the fact that the clinician rarely treats a patient whose mental difficulties manifest themselves as "simple alcohol problems." Psychologists and psychiatrists spend the greatest portion of their time treating patients whose behavior and psychological problems are more socially disruptive and complex than those of the "problem drinker" however he or she is defined. The treatment of the "alcoholic" (unless he is wealthy) is usually left to the mental health worker or some other form of "counsellor."

It is precisely these people who are not seen to be in need of extensive psychotherapy who can be at least partially understood by the data gathered by the cultural model of alcohol use. This understanding comes on several levels. First, many of the psychiatric social workers, family therapists, and other psychiatric counsellors often come from a subculture different from that of many of their clients. Their cultural knowledge of drinking is based on their own experience. Their knowledge of deviant drinking behavior is often based on psychological theories which have been proposed as universals, but never tested in the cauldron of cross-cultural research. If the subcultural differences are not too great, then communication between counsellor and client may be successful. However, when cultural differences on the level of a Navajo or Mexican-American client or an Anglo-American counsellor are confronted, then communication may be nearly impossible, even if they speak the same language.

It is at this point that an ethnographic description of drinking behavior from the informant's (client's) culture and point of view can be very valuable. Such a description can give the counsellor the kind of information which he or she might not gain even by years of work in a community. Many clients and friends in the community may act as subcultural interpreters (Spradley 1971: 237). They will try to explain their "problems" and the "problems" of the community in the counsellor's terms. This can give the counsellor the mistaken belief that his conception of deviant drinking is that held by the people he is serving. Secondly, the counsellor may never get to see the culturally defined normative drinking patterns of his client's culture. There is the possibility that the behavior patterns which the counsellor defines as deviant and attempts to alter in his client may be defined as "normative" by the client's peers. In these cases, the enthographic description can help the counsellor properly interpret what his clients are trying to tell him. It can also help the counsellor avoid the pitfalls of the subcultural interpreter. Finally, it may aid him in altering his treatment design to better conform with the needs of his client. The sociological model does not have the power to do this.

There is one additional aspect of the cultural approach to drinking which may be useful for the counsellor and therapist beyond general education and overall treatment design. It is still very early to tell, but the verbal plans might prove to be useful in behavior-modification therapy. The verbal plans provide a detailed description of the informant's perception of a decision situation. It might, therefore, be possible to use behavior-modification techniques to inhibit the selection of decision rules which lead to types of drinking behavior which the therapist considers "undesirable." At the present, this "plan therapy" is an untested concept. But as our knowledge of verbal planning becomes better and our methods of drawing plans more efficient and quick, it may be worth seriously investigating.

This paper has argued for more than just a new research methodology. It has presented a case for the re-development of the cultural approach through the methods and theories of ethnoscience. The end result is a research design which is relatively free of the cultural biases of the investigator. This is not true of the sociological, legal, and medical models described by Spradley (1971: 240–241). The cultural approach also uses participant observation, but in an unusual manner. It pits the biases of the anthropologist against the biases of the informant. In this way, it tries to develop a balanced view of drinking behavior. It is this union of elicitation and observation which may ultimately allow the integration of sociological, legal, and medical models with the cultural approach.

At present, the cultural approach is still under development. It has not yet produced a unified and cross-cultural theory of drinking behavior. But works like those of Spradley (1970, 1971), Hage (1971), Everett (1972a, 1972b, 1973), Everett, et al. (1973), Waddell (1973), and Topper (1973, i.p.) indicate that the cultural approach may have a bright future in both theoretical and applied research.

APPENDIX

Verbal Plan for an Impromptu Party Elicited from an Anthropology Graduate Student of Anglo-American Origin

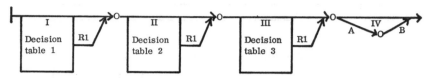

I. I think about getting together with my friends.
    R1: Spend the evening with the anthro friends.
II. I think about calling my other close friends in the anthropology department.
    R1: I do not call anyone.
III. We decide where to have dinner.
    R1: Eat at an anthro friend's home.
IV. People volunteer their contributions (of food).
    A. Someone suggests the main course.
    B. Others volunteer side dishes and beverages including wine or beer.

Decision table 1. I think about getting together with my friends

	1	2	3	4	5	6	7	8	9
Do you want to get together with friends?	y	y	y	y	y	n	y	y	y
Do you want to drink?	y	y	y	y	y	–	y	y	y
Are your anthropology friends around?	y	n	–	y	–	–	y	y	n
Are your non-anthro friends around?	n	y	–	n	–	–	–	–	n
Do you want to be with the anthros?	y	n	–	–	n	–	y	y	–
Do you want to date a girl alone?	n	n	–	n	y	–	n	n	y
Is there a girl available?	–	–	–	–	y	–	–	–	y
Do you have enough money?	y	y	n	y	y	–	y	y	y
Is there a movie that you want to see?	n	n	–	y	y	–	n	n	n
Is it dinner time?	y	y	–	y	y	–	y	y	y
Can you spend the whole evening?	y	y	–	y	y	–	n	n	y
Do you only have time for dinner?	–	–	–	–	–	–	n	y	
Must you study after dinner?	–	–	–	–	–	–	y	y	–
Must you study all evening after dinner?	–	–	–	–	–	–	n	y	–
Do you have any other plans?	n	n	–	n	n	–	n	n	n
Meet the anthros for dinner only.	–	–	–	–	–	–	–	x	–
Meet the anthros for dinner and after study.	–	–	–	–	–	–	–	–	–
Meet the anthros after study.	–	–	–	–	–	–	x	–	–
Spend the evening with the anthro friends.	x	–	–	x	–	–	–	–	–
Spend the evening with non-anthro friends.	–	x	–	–	–	–	–	–	–
Spend the evening with a girl.	–	–	–	–	x	–	–	–	x
Go to the movies.	–	–	–	x	x	–	–	–	–
Other.	–	–	x	–	–	x	–	–	–

Decision table 2.   I think about calling my other close friends in the anthropology department

	1	2
Are there some close anthro friends not present?	n	y
Call these friends.	–	x
Do not call them.	x	–

Decision table 3.   Decide where to have dinner

	1	2	3	4	5	6	7	8	9
Do you volunteer to be the host?	n	y	n	n	n	y	n	n	n
Does a friend volunteer to be the host?	y	n	n	n	n	n	n	y	n
Does someone suggest eating out?	–	–	y	y	y	y	y	y	y
Do you all agree?	–	–	y	y	y	y	y	y	y
Does someone suggest Mexican food?	–	–	y	y	–	y	y	–	y
Do you all agree?	–	–	y	n	–	y	n	–	y
Does someone suggest Chinese food?	–	–	–	y	–	–	–	y	–
Do you all agree?	–	–	–	y	–	–	–	y	–
Does someone suggest American food?	–	–	–	–	y	–	y	–	y
Do you all agree?	–	–	–	–	y	–	y	–	n
Host the dinner.	–	x	–	–	–	–	–	–	–
Eat at your friend's house.	x	–	–	–	–	–	–	–	–
Decide on a Mexican restaurant.	–	–	x	–	–	x	–	–	x
Decide on a Chinese restaurant.	–	–	–	x	–	–	–	x	–
Decide on an American restaurant.	–	–	–	–	x	–	x	–	–
Other.	–	–	–	–	–	–	–	–	–

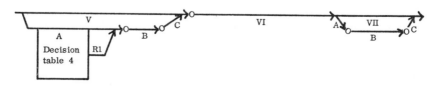

V.   They go get them (their contributions of food or beverage).
   A. They think about getting food, drinks, and extra cars.
      R1: Go together in one car.
   B. They get in the car.
   C. They go to the stores.

VI.   They arrive at the house.

VII. They begin preparing dinner.
   A. The host (person who lives in the house) does the main dish.
   B. Some (members of the group) volunteer to help with the side dishes.
   C. Others (members of the group) are asked to do the remaining jobs (set table, etc.).

Decision table 4.   They think about getting food, liquor, and extra cars

	1	2	3	4
Is the group small?	y	y	n	n
Is only one car available?	y	n	n	n
Is it more convenient to split up?	–	y	y	y
Are some people left without a task?	–	n	y	n
Will additional cars be needed?	–	n	n	y
Go together.	x	–	–	–
Split up: some get food, some get liquor.	–	x	–	–
Split up: some get food, some get liquor, some go to house.	–	–	x	–
Go and get other cars first; then split up: some get liquor and some get food.	–	–	–	x
Go and get other cars first; then split up: some get liquor, some get food, some go to house.	–	–	–	–
Other.	–	–	–	–

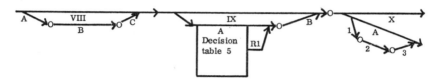

VIII. They also begin drinking.
    A. Someone offers beer or wine.
    B. He or she distributes it.
    C. They drink while they prepare dinner.

IX.   Dinner is served.
    A. Decide how to do it.
      R1: Put the food on the table in big dishes.
    B. The cook and some volunteers carry the food from the kitchen to the table.

X.   We eat.
    A. We pass the food around.
      1. We load our plates.
      2. We have a moment of silence.
      3. We begin eating.

Decision table 5.   Decide how to do it

	1	2
Are there hamburgers or sandwiches?	n	y
Is the food easier to serve in big dishes?	y	n
Load the plates in the kitchen.	–	x
Put the food on the table in big dishes.	x	–

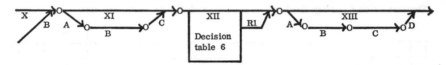

X.   Continued.
    B. Continue talking while eating.

XI.   Clean up.
    A. Some pick up the plates and carry them to the kitchen while others put the food away.
    B. Some wash the dishes while others clean up the table.
    C. The dishes are left to dry.

XII. Reconsider what to do for the rest of the evening.
    R1: Go to the Greenville Grill.

XIII. Buy a pitcher of beer.
    A. One of us goes to the bar.
    B. He orders a pitcher (of beer) and enough glasses (for the group).
    C. He brings it to the table where we are sitting.
    D. He pours everyone a glass (of beer).

Decision table 6.   Reconsider what to do for the rest of the evening

	1	2	3	4	5	6	7	8
Is there a movie that you all want to see?	n	y	n	n	y	n	n	n
Can you get to the movie on time?	–	n	–	–	y	–	–	–
Do you all want to go to the Greenville Grill?	y	n	n	n	n	n	n	n
Would you rather go to a different bar?	n	n	y	n	n	n	n	n
Is there a party at another friend's house?	–	y	–	–	–	n	n	n
Is there something you all want to see on TV?	n	n	n	y	n	n	n	y
Is there a game you all want to play?	n	n	n	n	n	n	y	y
Do you all want to sit around and talk?	n	n	n	y	n	y	y	y
Go to the movie.	–	–	–	–	x	–	–	–
Go to the Greenville Grill.	x	–	–	–	–	–	–	–
Decide on another bar.	–	–	x	–	–	–	–	–
Go to the other party.	–	x	–	–	–	–	–	–
Stay and watch TV.	–	–	–	x	–	–	–	x
Stay and play a game.	–	–	–	–	–	–	x	x
Stay and talk.	–	–	–	x	–	x	x	x
Other.	–	–	–	–	–	–	–	–

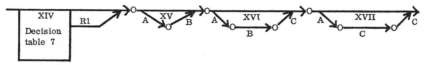

XIV. We decide which game to play.
   R1: Play shuffleboard.
XV. We choose sides.
   A. We think about who the best players are.
   B. We put the good players on opposite sides (teams).
XVI. Clean the table and put down sawdust.
   A. One person gets a towel.
   B. He walks the length of the board and wipes off the sawdust.
   C. Someone follows him and puts new sawdust down.
XVII. Practice.
   A. Stand up to the board.
   B. Shoot a few pucks.
   C. When you have the feel back off and let your friends do it.

Decision table 7.   We decide which game to play

	1	2	3	4	5	6	7	8
Is the shuffleboard game free?	y	n	n	n	y	n	n	n
Do you all want to wait for it?	–	y	y	n	–	y	n	n
Do two of you want to challenge?	–	n	y	y	–	n	n	n
Would two of you rather play pinball?	n	n	y	n	y	y	y	n
Do any of you want to play the jukebox?	n	y	n	y	y	y	n	n
Play shuffleboard.	x	–	–	–	x	–	–	–
Wait for the shuffle board to be free.	–	x	x	–	–	x	–	–
Challenge the table (the current winners).	–	–	x	x	–	–	–	–
Play the pinball machines.		–	x	–	x	x	x	–
Play the jukebox.	–	x	–	x	–	x	–	–
Other.	–	–	–	–	–	–	–	x

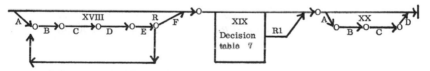

XVIII. Start to play (shuffleboard).
   A. One end of the board starts first.
   B. They shoot.
   C. Their score is counted.
   D. The others shoot.
   E. The score is counted.
   F. Repeat until the game is finished.
XIX. Decide what to do next.
   R1: Go home in your own car.
XX. I drive home in my car.
   A. I get in the car.
   B. I start it.
   C. I back it into the street.
   D. I head off toward home.

Decision table 8.   Decide what to do next

	1	2	3	4	5	6	7
Are you challenged (if you have won)?	–	y	n	n	n	n	–
Do others in your group want to play?	–	n	y	n	n	n	–
Do you all want to go to a friend's home?	n	n	n	y	n	n	n
Is it late?	y	n	n	n	n	y	y
Is the bar closing?	y	n	n	n	n	n	y
Do you (personally) want to go home?	y	n	n	n	n	y	n
Do you (personally) want to play another game?	–	y	n	n	y	n	–
Do you have your own car there?	y	–	–	–	–	y	–
Continue playing shuffleboard.	–	x	–	–	x	–	–
Accept the challenge.	–	x	–	–	–	–	–
Let your other friends play.	–	–	x	–	–	–	–
Sit down and watch the others play.	–	–	–	–	–	–	–
Go back to a friend's home.	–	–	–	x	–	–	–
Ask a friend to take you home.	–	–	–	–	–	–	–
Go home in your own car.	x	–	–	–	–	x	–
Other.	–	–	–	–	–	–	x

REFERENCES

BARKER, R. G.
  1968   *Ecological psychology: concepts and methods for studying the environment of human behavior.* Stanford: Stanford University Press.
BARKER, R. G., H. E. WRIGHT
  1951   *One boy's day.* New York: Harper and Row.
BUNZEL, RUTH
  1940   The role of alcoholism in two Central American cultures. *Psychiatry: Journal of the Biology and Pathology of Interpersonal Relations* 3(3): 361–386.
CASAGRANDE, J., K. HALE
  1967   "Papago folk definitions," in *Studies in Southwestern ethnolinguistics.* Edited by Dell Hymes. The Hague: Mouton.
CHOMSKY, N.
  1965   *Aspects of the theory of syntax.* Cambridge: M.I.T. Press.
EVERETT, M. W.
  1972a   "Drinking and trouble: the Apachean experience." Unpublished manuscript, Department of Anthropology, University of Kentucky.
  1972b   "White Mountain intergenerational problem drinking." Paper presented at the 1972 American Anthropological Association Meeting, Toronto.
  1973   "Verbal conflict and physical violence: the role of alcohol in Apache problem solving strategies." Unpublished manuscript, Department of Anthropology, University of Kentucky.

EVERETT, M. W., C. J. BAHA, E. DECLAY, M. R. ENDFIELD, K. SELBY
1973 "Anthropological expertise and the 'realities' of White Mountain Apache adolescent problem drinking." Paper presented at the 1973 Society for Applied Anthropology Meeting, Tucson, Arizona.

GRAVES, T. D.
1970 The personal adjustment of Navajo Indian migrants to Denver, Colorado. *American Anthropologist* 72:35–54.
1971 "Drinking and Drunkenness Among Urban Indians," in *The American Indian in urban society*. Edited by J. O. Waddell and O. M. Watson. Boston: Little, Brown.

HAGE, P.
1971 "Munchner beer categories." in *Culture and cognition: rules, maps, and plans*. Edited by J. P. Spradley, 263–278. San Francisco: Chandler Publishing.

HEATH, D. B.
1962 "Drinking patterns of the Bolivian Camba," in *Society, culture, and drinking patterns*. Edited by D. J. Pittman and C. R. Snyder, 22–36. New York: John Wiley and Sons.
1964 Prohibition and post-repeal drinking among the Navajo. *Quarterly Journal of Studies on Alcohol* 25:119–135.

LOMNITZ, L.
1969 Patterns of alcohol consumption among the Mapuche. *Human Organization* 28:287–297.

MANDELBAUM, D. G.
1965 Alcohol and culture. *Current Anthropology* 6:281–288.

MC DANIEL, H.
1968 *An introduction to decision logic tables*. New York: John Wiley and Sons.

MILLER, G. A., E. GALANTER, K. H. PRIBRAM
1960 *Plans and the structure of behavior*. New York: Holt, Rinehart and Winston.

POLLACK, S., H. T. HICKS, W. J. HARRISON
1971 *Decision tables: theory and practice*. New York: John Wiley and Sons.

SPRADLEY, J. P.
1970 *You owe yourself a drunk*. Boston: Little, Brown.
1971 "Adaptive strategies of urban nomads" in *Culture and cognition: rules, maps, and plans*. Edited by J. P. Spradley. San Francisco: Chandler Publishing.

STURTEVANT, W. C.
1964 Studies in ethnoscience. *American Anthropologist* 66:99–131.

TOPPER, M. D.
1972 "The daily life of a traditional Navajo household: a study in the ethnography of human daily activities." Ph. D. dissertation, Northwestern University, Evanston, Illinois.
1973 "Navajo culture, social pathology, and alcohol abuse: a broad interpretation." Paper presented at the 1973 Society for Applied Anthropology Meeting, Tuscon, Arizona.
i.p. "Drinking and adolescence: the Navajo experience," in *Indian*

drinking in the Southwest: an anthropological perspective. Edited by M. W. Everett and J. O. Waddell.

WADDELL, J. O.

1973   "For individual power and social credit: the use of alcohol among Tucson Papagos." Paper presented at the 1973 Society for Applied Anthropology Meeting, Tucson, Arizona.

WERNER, O.

1969   "On the universality of lexical/semantic relationships." Paper presented at the 1969 American Anthropological Association Meeting, New Orleans.

1972   "Ethnoscience 1972." in *Annual review of anthropology*. Palo Alto: Annual Reviews.

WERNER, O., G. ROTH, W. HAGGEDORN, L. URIARTE

1969   "Some new developments in ethnoscience." Unpublished manuscript. Northwestern University, Evanston, Illinois.

Observations on Methodological Considerations for Cross-Cultural Alcohol Studies

DON CAHALAN

These observations are directed at the field of anthropology from the perspective of a non-anthropologist. Although the focus is on how they might do more effective research on drinking practices, anthropologists are not singled out for special criticism because most of these observations will apply also to the other behavioral sciences.

First, there is great urgency for the behavioral sciences (especially including anthropology) to get together for some direct discussion and action to bring about some agreement on policies for priorities in alcohol research goals. We can no longer afford, in these days of emphasis upon cost/benefit evaluations, to have every scientist continue to do his or her own thing without having any sense of common priorities. If we do not come to some consensus as to the priorities in alcohol studies, and work together to carry out the priorities we agree upon, we will find ourselves eaten up by the King Storks or Casper Weingbergers brought in by the federal budget authorities to set our priorities for us, by default. While vigorous disagreement on priorities is healthy if based upon direct discussion of research issues, in the past many of us have continued merely to ignore the relevant work of others in doing our own research planning, or to talk past each other in professional meetings, each continuing happily in C. P. Snow's "euphoria of isolation and ignorance."

Heath (this volume) has made a plea for more intensive research on alcohol by anthropologists, saying they have studied alcohol only incidentally. This is quite significant, particularly since any anthropologist who looks about him will see that alcohol is so deeply embedded in the folkways of almost every culture on either a positive or negative basis, or both; and thus a study of alcohol behavior will reveal much about other aspects of any culture. It is also surprising that most of the anthropologists who have studied alcohol have overlooked one of the richest sources of research data in quantitative surveys of drinking practices that have been conducted in most Western urbanized societies. The United States itself is particularly an area worthy of intensive study, because it has so many ethnocultural groups interacting in a changing society that offers such a fertile field for the development of stresses in which alcohol can play a constructive or destructive part. Let us look at some illustrations, from American surveys of drinking practices and problems, of phenomena which anthropologists should find profitable to study in detail.

AREAS FOR ANTHROPOLOGICAL RESEARCH

Sex Variations in Drinking

In comparing drinking by the two sexes, in the United States a much higher proportion of men (about three-fourths) drink than is the case for women (about 60 percent), a difference that might be accounted for in part by the relatively lower power status of the women (Cahalan, et al. 1969: 2). However, in America the woman who does drink heavily is more likely than others to have psychological and interpersonal problems (Cahalan, et al. 1969: 6). There is much less difference between men and women in the proportion of drinkers among those of upper socioeconomic status than among those of lower status, which also fits in with anthropologically useful observations of other behavior to the effect that when those of lower power (such as women in America) gain more autonomy, they are freer to adopt a wider range of behaviors previously dominated by males. If anthropologists were to study such quantitative survey findings closely, they should be able to make material contributions to understanding why the rate of consumption of alcohol has been growing rapidly in affluent post-war America, particularly among women. The drinking behavior and problems of women in America have been sadly neglected in much of our research.

Age Variation in Drinking

Age is another anthropologically interesting variable. We have found that among American men aged twenty-one to fifty-nine, the rate of problem drinking in the aggregate is double for those in the youthful group aged twenty-one to twenty-four over those in any older group (Cahalan and Room 1974), despite the common assumption among traditional alcohologists that drinking problems must be most prevalent in the early forties because this is the age of the average "alcoholic" who is treated in clinics. This national finding is consistent with the findings of Pelz and Schuman (1971) that young men aged sixteen to twenty-four show a very high rate of drinking-related accidents, as well as other types of accidents, and also of various types of friction with other people. This is indicative that the process of growing up in America is very stressful; but how many anthropologists have studied the process of coming of age in America, in relation to the number of studies of coming of age in Samoa or other nonindustrialized areas? If anthropologists study urban American youth at all intensively, they will come up with some material contributions to provide viable alternatives to excessive use of alcohol or other drugs.

Ethnocultural Variation in Drinking

Ethnocultural groups have been of traditionally high interest to anthropologists. Our national probability sampling studies yield results that are highly consistent with past ethnographic and anecdotal reports in that we actuallly do find that the Irish Catholics in America drink more often to excess (and have more problems over drinking) than is the case with the Jews and Italians and WASPS in America (Cahalan, et al. 1969: Chapter 2; Cahalan 1970: Chapter 4). The richness and complexity of such ethnocultural data available to anthropologists in these quantitative surveys of drinking practices are also illustrated by the finding, in our most recent San Francisco survey, that if a man from a heavier-drinking group (such as the Irish Catholics or Scandinavians) associated primarily with men from traditionally more moderate-drinking groups (such as the Italians or Jews), then the man from the heavier-drinking group is found on the average to be not really more moderate than those who associate with men from their own heavy-drinking ethnocultural groups. An ironical twist is that while those from the more moderate groups who associated with men from their own groups tended to be moderate in their drinking, men from moderate-drinking groups who associated with men from heavier-drinking groups tended to be fairly heavy drinkers (Cahalan and Room 1974: Chapter 8). The contributions of anthropologists would be welcome in helping us to understand the processes involved in the development and evolution of subcultural differences in drinking practices and problems in complex industrial societies like the United States; and anthropologists would have much to gain by a more intensive study of such quantitative survey findings.

METHODOLOGICAL CONSIDERATIONS

There is a crying need for us to do a better job of specifying the units of analysis in alcohol studies; there is still too much confusion, even among alcohol specialists, concerning such concepts as "alcoholism" and "alcoholics," "problem drinking" and "problem drinkers," and the various models of the etiology of "alcoholism" and "alcohol problems." In addition, alcohol studies are based too heavily on medical and pathological models rather than upon environmental/cultural models. In our studies, we find that we can explain far more of the variance in drinking problems on environmental/cultural grounds than we can on medical or psychological grounds, again indicating the potential importance of environmentally oriented anthropology in the future study of drinking behavior.

A related point is that anthropology can make an important contribution in the study of the role of institutions, laws, and federal authorities' treatment funding patterns in determining how institutional behavior tends to have subcultural rules of its own which often defeat the very purposes for which the institutions were presumably established. Organizational behavior in the alcohol treatment field is a grievously underdeveloped field which should be of keen interest to anthropologists, particularly if they adopt a "systems" model. In such a model one studies how it is that the various participants in a socially unhealthy interaction (such as the alcoholic derelicts in skid row areas who make the rounds of missions, hospitals, and correctional establishments as well as the other players in the "loop" — the police and the treatment and correctional people) all remain prisoners of the system because all players continue to "get something" out of the continuance of the system (Wiseman 1970).

There is a real need for more cross-cultural analyses, whether based upon general population surveys or upon other quantitative data of adequate reliability. The concept of "dependence" in cross-cultural studies, for example, is too broad by itself and needs to be operationally defined in greater detail; one of the ways in which we can stumble forward into better operational definitions of what we are measuring in cross-cultural studies is to make better use of already available survey data on complex societies in multivariate analyses, which should lead to specifying the contingencies under which certain kinds of dependencies (for example) tend to be associated with certain kinds of roles and statuses and events among different subcultures.

Finally, I wish to make a plea for an amicable and cooperative division and sharing of labor between the various schools of anthropologists and other behavioral scientists. In this cooperation, anthropological approaches would be more widely utilized in studies of complex societies such as the United States in developmental hypothesis-formulation and preliminary testing, followed by further conceptual contributions by sociologists and social psychologists. This would be followed by large-scale quantitative surveys to test hypotheses on differences among subcultures. Then a re-analysis of the data would be conducted by anthropologists to revise their concepts, followed by additional quantitative studies. There is hardly any danger that we will run out of interesting work within the forseeable future, provided we all work together to resist sectarian and reductionistic temptations to justify our own favorite methods (whether they be qualitative or quantitative) as being the only valid ones, when experience should tell us that, appropriately used, our various methods should be complementary, rather than competitive, in solving problems of methodology or of policy.

REFERENCES

CAHALAN, D.
  1970   *Problem drinkers*. San Francisco: Jossey-Bass.
CAHALAN, D., R. ROOM
  1974   *Problem drinking among American men*. New Brunswick: Rutgers Center of Alcohol Studies.
CAHALAN, D., I. H. CISIN, H. M. CROSSLEY
  1969   *American drinking practices: a national survey of drinking behavior and attitudes*. New Brunswick: Rutgers Center of Alcohol Studies.
PELZ, D. C., S. H. SCHUMAN
  1971   "Motivational factors in crashes and violations of young drivers." Paper presented at the Annual Meeting of the American Public Health Association, Minneapolis.
WISEMAN, J. P.
  1970   *Stations of the lost*. Englewood Cliffs, N. J.: Prentice-Hall.

A Documentation Resource for Cross-Cultural Studies on Alcohol

MARK KELLER

There are some excellent sources of information (such as the Human Relations Area Files), but many anthropologists are unaware of one source that can be very helpful in studies relevant to drinking and alcohol. This is the documentation system maintained at the Rutgers University Center of Alcohol Studies.

The staff of the Center's Documentation Division fine-combs all possible reference sources of scientific-scholarly publications related to alcohol in all languages, worldwide. A bibliography of newly acquired titles is published in each alternate (documentation) issue of the *Journal of Studies on Alcohol* (formerly quarterly, now a monthly). Each documentation issue also features more than 300 abstracts and reviews of new publications, with a very detailed subject index which allows immediate location of antropological as well as all other topics. The abstracts are detailed and informative (rather than merely indicative).

A series of volumes, *The International Bibliography of Studies on Alcohol*, cumulates the bibliographic acquisitions; these too are provided with subject indexes.

A selection (consisting of a large majority) of the current abstracts is published in a second form: the *Classified Abstract Archive of the Alcohol Literature* (CAAAL). This form consists of edge-notched cards, the notches representing (a) the subject index and (b) other accession features, such as year of publication. By means of a needle the cards, or special groups of cards, can be hand-sorted to extract quickly the bibliography and abstracts on any desired topic. The number of cards now in the system is near 15,000 but it is usually necessary to sort only a small portion (main-topic groups) for a particular topic.

One of the main-topic groups in CAAAL of particular interest to anthropologists is Code Letter P, encompassing sociology, anthropology, culture, customs, history. There are up to ninety-two sortable subdivisions on the cards coded in the P category, examples of which are: 1, women; 12, preliterates; 15, age; 20, family; 28, biological aspects; 30, sex behavior; 39, ceremonial, ritual drinking; 58, statistics; 63, historical; 68, folklore, mythology. The literature on highly specific topics can be located by sorting for such combinations as, for example, in Code Letter P cards, the numerals 1, 12, and 39, which would yield ceremonial or ritual drinking by women in preliterate societies; one could add 4 if the interest were in the kinds of beverages so used. Another especially relevant main-topic group is Code Letter Q, geographical-ethnological divisions, in which it is possible to locate the literature on religions and people.

The CAAAL system is a particularly valuable resource for study, as groups of cards can be separated, recombined, and resorted to yield answers to different aspects of researchable questions. The system is fully described in the *CAAAL Manual* (1965). The *Manual* includes the entire Code Dictionary (twenty-four letter-identified main topics, including, for example, A, metabolism of alcohol; J, psychology, experimental; L, alcohol addiction or alcoholism; O, genetics; S, statistics, socioeconomic; W, education and propaganda; each with up to ninety-two possible subtopics) and an Index Key to Sorting.

CAAAL headquarters, at the Center of Alcohol Studies (Rutgers University, New Brunswick, New Jersey, 08903), responds to questions and provides bibliographies as well as photocopies of abstracts at nominal cost. A brochure, *Documentation and information services of the Rutgers Center of Alcohol Studies*, is available on request. Also available is a reprint describing the entire documentation-publications system and its ideology: *Documentation of an interdisciplinary field of study: alcohol problems.*

Library space at the Rutgers Center is made available to scholars and students for direct use of a set of the CAAAL cards. The Center Library also houses a collection of the full-text documents abstracted in CAAAL, which are immediately accessible by serial number to users of CAAAL at this library.

Sets of CAAAL are also available for direct consultation at depositories in over ninety locations in eighteen countries. The address of the nearest depository may be obtained on inquiry from the Rutgers Center of Alcohol of Studies.

Biographical Notes

JOAN ABLON (1934–) is Associate Professor of Medical Anthropology in Residence, Department of Psychiatry, University of California at San Francisco. She received her B.A. (1955) from the University of Texas and her M.A. (1958) and Ph.D. (1963) from the University of Chicago in Social Anthropology. Her current research interests include family behavior and alcoholism, urban middle-class lifestyle, and therapeutic self-help groups. Her previous research activities and publications have focused on the urban adaptations of American Indians and Samoans.

SALME AHLSTRÖM-LAAKSO (1945–) took her M.A. in Sociology in 1968 and a licentiate's degree in 1969 at the University of Helsinki. Her thesis was a comparative study of drunkenness arrests as a method of formal social control in Helsinki and Copenhagen. During her studies she worked at the Social Research Institute of Alcohol Studies in Helsinki and has been a Research Fellow there since 1969. At present she is engaged in an investigation of the consumption of alcohol by young people with special emphasis on a comparison of drinking habits among Finnish youth in the 1960's and the 1970's. Her publications include research reports and articles on deviant behavior and social control, as well as alcohol studies.

MARAGARET K. BACON (1909–) is a Professor of Anthropology at Rutgers University. She received her Ph.D. from Brown University in

Participants in the Conference on Alcohol Studies and Anthropology who are not contributors to this volume are indicated by an asterisk.

1940 and was employed at Yale University as an Instructor (1943–1944), Assistant Professor (1944–1946), and Research Associate (1950–1962). Her research interests have included cross-cultural studies of socialization, cross-cultural studies of drinking customs, and parental cognitive structuring of child behavior.

SELDEN D. BACON (1909–   )* received his Ph.D. from Yale University in 1939. He is Professor of Sociology and Director of the Center of Alcohol Studies, Rutgers University, the State University of New Jersey — the Center having moved from Yale to Rutgers in 1962. His particular interest is the social phenomena of the use of alcoholic beverages with particular attention to what are called "problems and the programs arising to meet those problems related to alcohol." Numerous publications include titles dealing with alcohol and law, education, the Temperance Movement, religion, highway problems, minority groups, and industry.

HERBERT BARRY, III (1930–   ) was born in New York City. He majored in Social Relations at Harvard College (B.A., 1952) and in Experimental Psychology at Yale University (M.S., 1953; Ph.D., 1957). He did psychopharmacology research and taught psychology at Yale (1957–1961) and at the University of Connecticut (1961–1963). Since 1963 he has been at the University of Pittsburgh where he is Professor of Pharmacology and also of Pharmaceutics in the School of Pharmacy, and where he is also Professor of Anthropology. Since 1967 he has been a recipient of a U.S. Public Health Service Research Scientist Development Award from the National Institute of Mental Health. He is also a Managing Editor of *Psychopharmacologia* and a consultant for the National Institute on Alcohol Abuse and Alcoholism.

RICHARD E. BOYATZIS (1946–   ) is Director of Research at McBer and Company. He received his B.S. from Massachusetts Institute of Technology, M.A. and Ph.D. in Social Psychology from Harvard University. His early research publications focused on problems of behavior change, helping relationships and human motivation. His more recent work has focused on the treatment of alcohol abuse and research on causes of alcohol abuse, the effect of alcohol on human aggression, and evaluation of rehabilitation programs. His publications include several articles in these areas of alcohol research and development of instructional material for the training of alcohol counselors.

RUTH BUNZEL is a Research Associate at Columbia University, New York.

DON CAHALAN (1912–) is Professor of Behavioral Sciences in Residence and Director of the Social Research Group, School of Public Health, University of California, Berkeley. He received his B.A. and M.A. from the State University of Iowa and his Ph.D. in Psychology from George Washington University. A social psychologist, his primary publications are in the field of survey research methodology and, more recently, on alcohol-related social behavior and problems. His writings include *American drinking practices* (with Ira Cisin and Helen M. Crossley; Rutgers Center of Alcohol Studies, New Brunswick, N.J.), *Problem drinkers* (Jossey-Bass, San Francisco, 1970), and *Problem drinking among American men* (with Robin Room; Rutgers Center on Alcoholic Problems, 1974). He is a member of the American Psychological Association, the American Sociological Association, and the American Public Health Association.

JAN E. E. DE LINT (1929–) was born in Breda, the Netherlands. He received his B.A. in Anthropology in 1959 and an M.A. in sociology in 1962, both from the University of Toronto. From 1964 to 1969 he held the position of Assistant Professor and later Associate Professor with the Department of Anthropology and Faculty of Medicine, University of Toronto, teaching courses in social and medical anthropology. Since 1960 he has been associated with the Addiction Research Foundation of Ontario, Canada, where he has done extensive work on the development of the distribution of alcohol consumption theory. He is also engaged in a long-term follow-up study of the mortality experiences of clinically treated alcoholics and has authored or co-authored a large number of research reports on the epidemiology of alcoholism and alcohol-related health damage as well as other aspects of the alcoholism problem.

MICHAEL W. EVERETT (1943–) received his doctorate in anthropology from the University of Arizona in 1970. He taught at the University of Kentucky before joining the faculty at Northern Arizona University. His past research among several Southwestern American Indian groups has been concerned with health and illness, suicide, homicide, alcoholism, and interpersonal conflict. He is currently active in American Indian health/manpower-training development, serving as Director, Tribal Health Authority, White Mountain Apache Tribe, White River, Arizona.

D. FENNA.   No biographical data available.

FRANCES NORTHEND FERGUSON (1925–   ) was born in Hartford, Connecticut. She received the M.A. degree (1959) and the Ph.D. (1972) in Cultural Anthropology from the University of North Carolina at Chapel Hill. Study in India (1961–1962) was undertaken with an NIMH predoctoral fellowship, followed by work with Navajo Indians (1964–1968) in northwestern New Mexico. During the summer of 1975 she taught at the University of Kentucky. Her current area of interest is in modes of personal adaptation to modernization.

ORVOELL ROGER GALLAGHER (1916–1975)* was Professor of Anthropology at Skidmore College in New York. He received his B.A. at the University of California, his M.A. from the London School of Economics, and his Ph.D. from Columbia University. His interests were in the general area of social-cultural change (peasant France and tribal India). At the time of his death he was also studying the use of alcohol in India.

J. ALAN L. GILBERT graduated from the University of Edinburgh. In 1947 he was "highly commended" for his thesis on "The metabolic effects of partial gastrectomy." He is Professor of Medicine at the University of Alberta. His research has been in the field of alcohol metabolism, diabetes mellitus, and medical education. He is a life member of the Canadian Diabetic Association and President of the International Society for Research in Medical Education.

JOEL MICHAEL HANNA (1938–   ) is Associate Professor of Physiology and Anthropology at the University of Hawaii. He received his B.S. and M.A. from Pennsylvania State University and his Ph.D. in Physical Anthropology from the University of Arizona in 1968. His professional interests include human variation, the social biology of drugs, and human ecology.

DWIGHT B. HEATH (1930–   ) is Professor of Anthropology at Brown University and a Consultant in Mental Health to the World Health Organization. He earned his B.A. at Harvard College and his Ph.D. (in Anthropology) at Yale University. Apart from cross-cultural studies in general and anthropological studies of alcohol, his special interests include interethnic relations (*Contemporary cultures and societies of Latin America*, 1974), ethnohistory (*A journal of the Pilgrims at Plymouth: Mourt's relation*, 1963), social organization (*Land reform and social revolution in Bolivia*, 1969), cultural change (*Historical dictionary of Bolivia*, 1972), and applications of anthropology to contemporary problems in many fields.

VLADIMIR HUDOLIN (1922–)* studied medicine at Zagreb University and specialized in Neurology and Psychiatry. He received his Ph.D. in 1961 ("Pneumoencephalographic patterns of the brain in chronic alcoholism"). He was elected Head of the University Department of Neurology and Psychiatry of Dr. M. Stojanović" University Hospital, Zagreb, in 1959. He is Professor of Neurology and Psychiatry on the Faculty of Dentistry, Zagreb University, as well as at the Music Academy, Zagreb, where he lectures on music therapy. He is Editor-in-Chief of two medical journals (*Journal on Alcoholism and Related Addictions* and *Anali Kliničke bolnice "Dr. M. Stojanović"*) and is also President of the International Association of Social Psychiatry. His special interests include studies of neurological changes due to alcoholism, treatment of alcoholism, social psychiatry, cross-cultural studies of alcoholism in Yugoslavia, studies in the working ability of alcoholics, etc. He has also founded clubs for treated alcoholics all over Yugoslavia. He has published more than 250 scientific papers and books, including: "Alcohology," "Evaluation of invalidity and working ability of alcoholics," "Alcoholism in Croatia," "Alcoholism in Yugoslavia," "A contribution to the diagnosis of tuberous sclerosis." "Brain changes due to alcoholism," "Experiences of treating alcoholics in clubs," *Little encyclopedia of alcoholism*, and *Lexicon of psychiatry and psychology*.

RICHARD JESSOR (1924–)* was born in Brooklyn, New York. He received his B.A. from Yale, an M.A. from Columbia, and his Ph.D. from Ohio State University (1951). He is Professor in the Department of Psychology and Director of the Research Program on Problem Behavior of the University of Colorado Institute of Behavioral Science. With his associates, he authored *Society, personality, and deviant behavior: a study of a tri-ethnic community*. In 1965–1966, he was an NIMH Special Research Fellow at the Harvard-Florence Research Project in Florence, Italy, and conducted cross-cultural research on Italian youth and on urban migrants in Tunisia. From 1972 to 1974 he was Chairman of the Research Review Committee of the National Institute on Alcohol Abuse and Alcoholism. He and his wife are preparing a book on their current longitudinal study of the socialization of problem behavior in youth.

MARK KELLER (1907–   ) is a Research Specialist in Documentation (Professor) at the Rutgers University Center of Alcohol Studies, and Editor of the *Journal of Studies on Alcohol*. He was privately educated. His special interest is the systematization of knowledge with an interdiscipliinary perspective, and his field of work is alcohol problems. His publications include *The alcohol language* (1958), *A dictionary of words about alcohol* (1968), *CAAAL manual, a guide to the use of the classified abstract archive of the alcohol literature* (1965), and numerous theoretical articles on addiction, alcohol problems, and information science. He serves on the Faculty of the Rutgers University International Center for the Soviet Union, Eastern Europe, and China, and on the Faculty for the New Jersey Centralized Residency Training Program, and is a member of the World Health Organization Steering Group on Standardization of Criteria for Classifying Disabilities Related to Alcohol Consumption.

A. EUGENE LEBLANC (1940–   )* was born in Timmins, Ontario, Canada. He graduated from Queen's University at Kingston, Ontario, with a B.A. in Biochemistry. His studies were continued at the University of Toronto, where he received his Ph.D. in Behavioral Pharmacology (1972) with a dissertation on behavioral and pharmacological variables in the development of ethanol tolerance. His research interests have continued in the field of drug tolerance and dependence, including drug interactions and behavioral toxicity. He has been author and co-author of numerous publications in these fields in recent years. Currently he holds the posts of Assistant Head of the Research Division of the Addiction Research Foundation of Ontario and Assistant Professor in the Department of Pharmacology, University of Toronto.

LARISSA LOMNITZ is a social anthropologist specializing in urban problems. A graduate of Berkeley and of the Universidad Iberoamericana, she lives in Mexico, where she is a staff member of CIMAS, the Center for Applied Mathematics and Computer Sciences at the University of Mexico. Her current interests include models of social interaction, networks of reciprocity and mutual assistance, and the influence of the power structure on human creativity. She is teaching at the School of Urban Planning and at the Graduate School of Anthropology, both at the University of Mexico. Her recent publications include "Reciprocity of assistance among the urban middle class of Chile," "The social and economic organization of a Mexican shanty town," and "Power structure and scientific productivity in a research institute."

WILLIAM MADSEN (1920–   ) was born in Shanghai, China. He received his B.A. from Stanford University and a Ph.D. in Anthropology from the University of California at Berkeley in 1955. He has taught at the University of Texas, the University of California at Berkeley, Purdue University, the University of Puerto Rico, and is currently a Professor of Anthropology at the University of California at Santa Barbara. He has published on Mexican religious syncretism and on the culture of the Mexican Americans of South Texas. In 1974 he published *The American alcoholic* (Thomas Publishers) and "Alcoholics Anonymous as a crisis cult" (Proceedings of the 1973 NIAAA Conference, Washington, D.C.).

DAVID G. MANDELBAUM (1911–   )* has been Professor of Anthropology at the University of California, Berkeley, since 1948. He received the B.A. (1932) at Northwestern, and the Ph.D. (1936) at Yale. His first field research was among San Carlos Apache (1933), Plains Cree (1934, 1935), and in a small town in Connecticut (1935–1936). In 1937–1938, he began his fieldwork in South Asia and since then has often returned for more field research there, especially in South India. His interests include general theory ("Variations on a theme by Ruth Benedict," in *Psychological anthropology*. Edited by T. Williams, World Anthropology, 1975), psychological anthropology ("The study of life history: Gandhi," 1973), social organization (*Society in India*, two volumes, 1970), applied anthropology (*Human fertility in India: social components and policy perspectives*, 1974). His current work includes the writing of a book on the Todas of the Nilgiri Hills and a general work on religion.

MAC MARSHALL (1943–   ) was born in San Francisco. He received his B.A. from Grinnell College in 1965, an M.A. from the University of Washington in 1967, and a Ph.D. in Anthropology from the University of Washington in 1972. He conducted anthropological fieldwork on Namoluk Atoll, Eastern Caroline Islands, Micronesia, from 1969 to 1971, and since 1972 he has served as Assistant Professor of Anthropology at the University of Iowa. His current major research interest is alcohol use and abuse in Oceania.

ADE M. U. OBAYEMI is with the Centre for Nigerian Cultural Studies at the Ahmadu Bello University, Zaria, Nigeria.

MARGARET SARGENT is a Lecturer in Sociology in the Social Work Department of the University of Sydney, Australia. After obtaining qualifications in psychology from the Universities of Birmingham and Cambridge she practiced as a clinical psychologist in England, Japan, and Australia. Her interest in the causation of alcoholism carried her from psychological into sociological research in the subject and to a doctorate in sociology taken at the University of New South Wales. She has also worked in the sociology of the arts. She is currently Editor of the *Australian Journal of Social Issues.*

JAMES M. SCHAEFER attended the University of Montana and received his Ph.D. in Anthropology from the State University of New York at Buffalo in 1973. The cross-cultural method and alcohol usage have comprised his major interests to date. He is now in the Department of Anthropology at the University of Montana. His paper here reviews the current status of multi-cultural studies, a method which has undergone considerable modification and sophistication over the last several years.

OZZIE G. SIMMONS (1919–   )* is Program Officer, Population and the Social Sciences, The Ford Foundation, presently stationed in Bangkok, Thailand. He received his B.S. from Northwestern University in 1941 and his M.A. (1948) and Ph.D. (1952) in Sociology from Harvard. Positions held include: Director in Peru, Institute of Social Anthropology, Smithsonian Institution, and Visiting Professor, University of San Marcos, Lima, 1949–1952; Consulting Anthropologist, Institute of Inter-American Affairs, Santiago, Chile, 1953; Associate Professor of Social Anthropology, School of Public Health, Harvard University, 1953–1961; Professor of Sociology and Director, Institute of Behavioral Science, University of Colorado, 1961–1968. He joined the Ford Foundation in 1968. He is the author of many research articles and a number of books and monographs, including, as co-author, *The mental patient comes home,* which was awarded the Hofheimer Prize of the American Psychiatric Association for "outstanding creative research in human behavior."

MARTIN D. TOPPER (1946–   ) is Assistant Professor of Cultural Anthropology at Southern Methodist University in Dallas, Texas. He received his B.A. from the University of Illinois at Urbana and his M.A. and Ph.D. from Northwestern University. In addition, he has done postdoctoral study at the University of Chicago. He has conducted a wide variety of research projects among American Indians and Americans of European ancestry. His current interests include studies of alcoholism, cognitive anthropology, and the anthropology of mass communications. He has published articles which concern all three of these research areas.

ALFREDO VELAPATIÑO ORTEGA (1949–) graduated in Anthropology in 1972 from the Universidad Nacional de San Cristóbal, Huamanga, Peru, where he did research on alcoholism among the native tribes of the plains in the tropical region of Peru. He later studied the rural communities in the Andes region (Ayacucho) and is presently doing research on alcoholism in fishing ports on the north coast of Peru.

JACK O. WADDELL (1933–) is Associate Professor of Anthropology and Chairman, Anthropology Section, in the Department of Sociology and Anthropology, Purdue University, Lafayette, Indiana. He received his B.A. from the University of Kansas in 1955, an M.A. from the University of Texas, Austin in 1962, and his Ph.D. in Anthropology from the University of Arizona in 1966. His research has focused on contemporary adaptations of Papago Indians to Anglo-American institutions and values. Most recently, he has been investigating the role of drinking and intoxication in Papago adaptations to contemporary life. Recent publications include: *The American Indian in urban society* (1971), *American Indian urbanization* (1973), "Drink, friend! Social context of convivial drinking and drunkenness among Papago Indians in an urban setting" (1973), and *Papago Indians at work* (1969).

JOSEPH WESTERMEYER is a Professor in the Department of Psychiatry, University of Minnesota.

Index of Names

Index of Subjects